Ius Comparatum - Global Studies in Comparative Law

Volume 21

More information about this series at http://www.springer.com/series/11943

Académie Internationale de Droit Comparé
International Academy of Comparative Law

Karen B. Brown

Editor

Taxation and Development - A Comparative Study

 Springer

Editor
Karen B. Brown
George Washington University Law School
Washington, DC, USA

ISSN 2214-6881   ISSN 2214-689X   (electronic)
Ius Comparatum - Global Studies in Comparative Law
ISBN 978-3-319-42155-1   ISBN 978-3-319-42157-5   (eBook)
DOI 10.1007/978-3-319-42157-5

Library of Congress Control Number: 2016962635

Printed on acid-free paper

This Springer imprint is published by Springer Nature
The registered company is Springer International Publishing AG
The registered company address is: Gewerbestrasse 11, 6330 Cham, Switzerland

Preface

No worthwhile writing project can be completed without the support and encouragement of others. This book is no exception. I, therefore, would like to thank the following individuals: Neil Olivier and Diana Nijenhuijzen of Springer Publishers for their unfailing support and encouragement; Professor Dr. Bea Verschraegen and Professor Dr. Martin Schauer, who chaired the Steering Committee for the impressive 19th World Congress of the International Academy of Comparative Law (IACL) held in Vienna, Austria, in 2014, for their invaluable assistance and patience; the IACL National Reporters for the Taxation and Development topic for their superb work; the officers of the IACL for their fine leadership; and my very talented research assistants, Emily Wheatley and Melissa Seyhun, 2016 graduates of the George Washington University Law School, for outstanding research support. Finally, this volume is dedicated to my parents, Marion J. Brown and the late Kenneth A. Brown, Sr., with much appreciation for their constant love and support.

Washington, DC, USA   Karen B. Brown

Contents

Contributors

Serviliano Abache Carvajal Central University of Venezuela, Catholic University "Andrés Bello", Caracas, Venezuela

Karen B. Brown George Washington University, Law School, Washington, DC, USA

Rita Cunha University of London, London, UK

Fernando Daniel de Moura Fonseca LL.M. Degree in Economic and Financial Law from the University of São Paulo (USP). LL.M. Degree in International Taxation from the New York University (NYU). Lawyer and Accountant Taxation, New York University, Sacha Calmon, Misabel, Derzi, Brazil

Misabel Abreu Machado Derzi Full Professor of Tax Law at the Federal University of Minas Gerais (UFMG). Ph.D. in Public Law from the Federal University of Minas Gerais (UFMG). Lawyer Tax Law, Federal University of Minas Gerais, Minas Gerais, Brazil

Thomas Dubut University of Paris-Dauphine, Paris, France

Andrew Halkyard Law Faculty, Hong Kong University, Pok Fu Lam, Hong Kong

University of New South Wales, Sydney, New South Wales, Australia

Taxation Law and Policy Research Group, Monash University, Clayton, Australia

Moran Harari College of Management, The Tax Justice Network, Rishon LeZion, Israel

Kevin Holmes International Tax Consultant, Wellington, New Zealand

Jalia Kangave International Centre for Tax and Development (ICTD) at the Institute of Development Studies, UK

Tracy Kaye Seton Hall University Law School, Newark, NJ, USA

Nataša Žunić Kovačević Faculty of Law, University of Rijeka, Rijeka, Croatia

Sagit Leviner Ono Academic College Faculty of Law and Ono Academic College Faculty of Business Administration, Kiryat Ono, Israel

Raymond H.C. Luja Maastricht University, Maastricht, The Netherlands

Yoshihiro Masui University of Tokyo, Tokyo, Japan

André Mendes Moreira Associate Professor of Tax Law at the Federal University of Minas Gerais (UFMG). LL.M. Degree in Tax Law from the Federal University of Minas Gerais (UFMG). Ph.D. in Economic and Financial Law from the University of São Paulo (USP), Lawyer

Wlodzimierz Nykiel University of Lodz, Lodz, Poland

Michal Radvan Department of Financial Law and Economics, Faculty of Law, Masaryk University, Brno, Czech Republic

Fernando Rocha Andrade University of Coimbra, Coimbra, Portugal

Jennifer Roeleveld University of Cape Town, Cape Town, South Africa

Claudio Sacchetto University of Turin, Turin, Italy

Tamir Shanan College of Management, Haim Striks School of Law, Rishon LeZion, Israel

Dana Šramková Department of Financial Law and Economics, Faculty of Law, Masaryk University, Brno, Czech Republic

Miranda Stewart Tax and Transfer Policy Institute, Crawford School of Public Policy, The Australian National University, Canberra, Australia

Edoardo Traversa Catholic University of Louvain, Brussels, Belgium

Craig West University of Cape Town, Cape Town, South Africa

Michał Wilk University of Łódź, Łódź, Poland

Gaëtan Zeyen University of Liège, Brussels, Belgium

About the Contributors

Serviliano Abache Carvajal is Tax Law Professor at the Central University of Venezuela and the Catholic University "Andrés Bello". He is also a Professor of Legal Theory at the Central University of Venezuela and of Legal Reasoning at the Catholic University "Andrés Bello". He holds an LL.M. degree in Taxation Law from the Central University of Venezuela and an LL.M. degree in Legal Reasoning from the University of Alicante, Spain. He is a member of the Board of Directors of the Venezuelan Association of Tax Law, where he also coordinates the Tax Law Journal.

Karen B. Brown is the Donald Phillip Rothschild Research Professor of Law at the George Washington University Law School in Washington, D.C.

Rita Cunha is a Ph.D. candidate at the Institute of Advanced Legal Studies (IALS), University of London. Her research is being funded by Fundação para a Ciência e para a Tecnologia. She holds an LL.M. from New York University and a law degree from Universidade Católica Portuguesa (Lisbon). Her main research areas include general anti-avoidance rules and tax avoidance-related issues in developing countries. She is currently writing her doctoral dissertation on tax avoidance in India.

Fernando Daniel de Moura Fonseca holds an LL.M. in Taxation from New York University School of Law.

Misabel Abreu Machado Derzi is Full Professor of Tax Law at the Federal University of Mina Gerais, Brazil.

Thomas Dubut is Associate Lecturer, University of Paris-Dauphine, France, and International Tax Advisor.

Andrew Halkyard is Adjunct Professor, Hong Kong University and Atax, ASB, University of New South Wales, and Senior Research Fellow, Taxation Law and Policy Research Group, Monash University.

Moran Harari, Adv., is Director of Tax Justice Network Israel and Research Analyst Consultant, Tax Justice Network, Israel.

Dr. Kevin Holmes is an International Tax Consultant, Wellington, New Zealand.

Jalia Kangave is Research Fellow, International Centre for Tax and Development (ICTD) at the Institute of Development Studies, UK.

Tracy Kaye is Professor of Law at Seton Hall University Law School, Newark, New Jersey, USA.

Nataša Žunić Kovačević, JSD, is Associate Professor and Head of the Department of Financial Law at the Faculty of Law, University of Rijeka (Croatia). She holds a Law Degree from the University of Rijeka and Masters of Law (LL.M.) and Ph.D. in Law from the University of Zagreb (Croatia). She teaches courses in undergraduate, graduate, postgraduate and doctoral studies and her areas of interest include tax procedural law as well as European tax law.

Dr. Sagit Leviner holds dual appointments at Ono Academic College Faculty of Law and Ono Academic College Faculty of Business Administration, Israel.

Raymond H.C. Luja is Professor of Comparative Tax Law, Maastricht University, the Netherlands, and counsel to Loyens & Loeff N.V., Amsterdam.

Yoshihiro Masui is Professor of Law, the University of Tokyo. He has taught tax law since 1990.

André Mendes Moreira is Associate Professor of Tax Law at the Federal University of Minas Gerais. He holds a Ph.D. in Tax Law from the University of Sao Paulo.

Włodzimierz Nykiel is Professor of Law, University of Lodz, Poland.

Michal Radvan is Assistant Professor, Department of Financial Law and National Economy, Brno, Czech Republic.

Fernando Rocha Andrade is a member of the Faculty of Law, University of Coimbra, Portugal.

Jennifer Roeleveld is a Professor of Taxation in the Department of Finance and Tax and the Director of the UCT Tax Institute for Fiscal Research at the University of Cape Town. She is the South African project head for the research project "Sustainable Tax Governance in Developing Countries through Fiscal Tax Transparency" (DeSTaT) funded by the Research Council of Norway. Jennifer holds an LL.M. and is a Chartered Accountant (SA) and registered Tax Practitioner.

Claudio Sacchetto is Professor Emeritus of Tax Law and International, European and Comparative Tax Law, University of Turin, Italy. He is President of International European and Telematic Law in Turin and former teacher at Accademia della Guardia di Finanza in Italy. He has lectured at numerous universities in Europe, North and South America and China. He is Director of Scientific Reviews in the field of taxation and author of over 450 publications in the field of international taxation. He is also author of *Tax Aspects of Fiscal Federalism: A Comparative Analysis* (IBFD, with Bizioli, 2011). He is a founding member and former Vice President of the European Association of Tax Law Professors (EATLP). He is a member of the Scientific Committee of the EATLP. His is a practising tax lawyer at the Italian Supreme Court.

Dr. Tamir Shanan is Lecturer, Haim Striks School of Law – The College of Management Academic Studies, Israel.

Dr. Dana Šramková, Ph.D., MBA is Assistant Professor at the Masaryk University, Faculty of Law, and a member of the Legislative Council of the Czech Government. She completed her *rigorosum* and Ph.D. in the field of financial law (Masaryk University, Brno, 2005). She specializes mostly in tax and customs law and administration. She offers numerous graduate and postgraduate level courses both in the Czech Republic and abroad. She was certified by the World Customs Organization (WCO) as the first Knowledge Academy for Customs and Trade participant (WCO, Brussels, 2011). She regularly presents the results of her research at international conferences and publishes in monographs, journals and proceedings. For her work, she was awarded the Badge of Honour of the Czech Customs in 2013. She is a member of the International Network of Customs Universities (based in Canberra, Australia) and has been also a member of the Centre of Information and Organization of Public Finance and Tax Law Research in Central and Eastern Europe (based in Bialystok, Poland) since 2002.

Miranda Stewart is Professor and Director at the Tax and Transfer Policy Institute, Crawford School at the Australian National University, and Professor at the University of Melbourne.

Edoardo Traversa is Professor of Tax Law, Vice Dean of International Relations, and Faculty of Law and Criminology (CRIDES – Jean Renauld), Catholic University of Louvain, Belgium.

Craig West holds a Ph.D. and is an Associate Professor of Taxation for the UCT Tax Institute for Fiscal Research and the Department of Finance and Tax, University of Cape Town. He is a member of the South African Antenna for the research project "Sustainable Tax Governance in Developing Countries through Fiscal Tax Transparency" (DeSTaT) funded by the Research Council of Norway. Craig is a Chartered Accountant (SA) and registered Tax Practitioner.

Michał Wilk is Professor of Law, University of Lodz, Poland.

Gaëtan Zeyen is Attorney at Law at the Brussels Bar and a Ph.D. candidate in International Taxation (focusing on the OECD Model Convention, and in particular on its Article 21) at the Tax Institute, under the supervision of both Professor Isabelle Richelle (Tax Institute) and Professor Edoardo Traversa (UCL).

Introduction

Increasingly, the impact of individual state actors on the quality of life on the more than seven billion people on planet earth, even those separated by thousands of miles, is of note. This was one of the lessons and causes of the environmental colloquium, the UN Climate Change Summit, held in Paris, France, in November and December 2015. The work of the conference, as that of previous world convocations, concluded that the environmental policies of one country affected all. In particular, the policies instituted by the leaders of the more industrialized, higher-income nations in their quest to produce and prosper helped to create the environmental degradation plaguing everyone, particularly nations which are geographically and economically vulnerable. The accords finally reached acknowledged that agreement to climate control concessions by developing countries placed them in a position not to benefit from the kind of economic expansion they could enjoy from production unrestrained by environmental concerns. Moreover, the accords further acknowledged that, under such circumstances, these nations could not be expected to shoulder the expense of the required technological innovations to achieve climate goals while maintaining the ability to compete effectively in the global marketplace, without financial and other kinds of assistance from richer nations.

A similar interconnection is found in the international tax policies of the more highly developed nations. This has led groups like the Organisation for Economic Cooperation and Development (OECD) among others, to call for increased cooperation among nations to combat the type of tax arbitrage (or manipulation of the differences in countries' laws to gain tax advantages) that results in a world where each sovereign establishes its tax regime independently of the concerns of others. This resulted in the issuance of the 1998 OECD reports on Harmful Tax Competition and Tax Sparing, establishment of the OECD Global Tax Forum on Transparency and Exchange of Information on Tax Matters and promulgation of the final Base Erosion and Profit Shifting (BEPS) report by the OECD in October 2015. The goal of this work has been to move nations to voluntarily agree to conform their tax regimes to certain "internationally accepted" standards and principles. Yet, unlike those setting climate control policies, the tax policymakers have not given sufficient thought to the ways in which the tax systems and regime choices established by the more highly developed, higher-income nations affect more vulnerable nations. Developed nations have condemned many of the tax regimes developing nations have put in place in order to attract investment and revenue to fuel development without acknowledging that many of these strategies have been dictated as a response to the tax strategies of multinational enterprises incentivized by developed -world regimes. Without input from developing nations, the tax reform strategies of higher-income countries will operate primarily to protect the latter countries' own tax bases and will fail to appropriately consider the obstacles faced by resource-limited nations as they struggle to meet international standards they had little opportunity to shape.[1]

This is the phenomenon that caused the International Academy of Comparative Law (IACL) to convene tax scholars from around the world to consider these issues at the 19th World Congress held in Vienna, Austria, in July 2014. This meeting resulted in submission of 19 national reports that consider the international tax regimes of the covered countries and their impact on developing country regimes. The Appendix at the end of Chapter 1, Taxation and Development – Overview, which serves as the General Report for this topic for the 19th Congress, lists the reporters and their affiliations. Each of these national reports, preceded by a synopsis, appears in the following chapters. You will note that every one of these reports is thought-provoking, thorough and insightful. Can tax incentives be an appropriate policy tool in the international marketplace?[2] What is harmful tax competition? How do the tax regimes of higher-income nations affect the ability of developing countries to collect essential fiscal resources? What are the essential non-tax supports for investment? While the reports do not definitively answer all of these questions, they deal with the complexity of the issues and report no easy solutions to the problems confronting countries as they individually and collectively work to determine the appropriate parameters for shaping future international tax policy.

---

[1] See, e.g. Organisation for Cooperation and Development, Part 1 of a Report to G20 Development Working Group on the Impact of BEPS in Low Income Countries 34 (July 2014) ("[W]e encourage international and regional organisations and all stakeholders to take further steps to ensure that developing countries' voices are taken into account in the international efforts to counter BEPS and strengthen domestic resource mobilisation") and Part 2 of a Report to G20 Development Working Group on the Impact of BEPS in Low Income Countries (13 August 2014).

[2] Resolution Adopted by the General Assembly on 27 July 2015, 69/313. Addis Ababa Action Agenda of the Third International Conference on Financing for Development (Addis Ababa Action Agenda) ¶ 27.

Part I
General Report

Chapter 1
Taxation and Development: Overview

Karen B. Brown

Abstract In an effort to promote internationally accepted standards that embody principles underlying their own systems, developed countries have, in some respects, ignored the spill-over effect of their tax regimes on the viability of strategies of countries in the developing world to attract much needed investment. A reconsideration of the principles underlying the decisions made by higher-income countries concerning the proper allocation of taxing jurisdiction over income arising from global operations of multinationals could and should result in a re-examination of the ways in which countries, particularly developing ones, are able to build economies. This chapter provides an overview of contributions that consider whether 19 different countries use their tax laws to attract foreign investment or to encourage investment in developing countries.

Introduction

In general, economists, academics, and other policy analysts maintain that the tax laws of a given economy should not distort the business decisions of its constituents. This is taken to mean that tax laws should be neutral, providing an offset against the income tax base for expenses of producing income, but not allowing for special incentives designed to encourage or discourage specified taxpayer behavior. At the domestic level, examples of special tax breaks include accelerated depreciation allowances for investments in production assets, tax rate preferences for specified types of income, and accelerated recovery of research and development costs. At the international taxation level, neutrality implies a tax regime that would not favor or

---

IV.E, La fiscalité et le développement. General Report for the International Academy for Comparative Law 19th Congress held in Vienna, Austria in 2014. While most of the national reports detail the rules governing taxation of individuals as well as corporations, this General Report refers only to income taxation of corporations and certain other business entities.

K.B. Brown (✉)
George Washington University Law School, Washington, DC, USA
e-mail: karenbrown@law.gwu.edu

© Springer International Publishing Switzerland 2017   3
K.B. Brown (ed.), *Taxation and Development - A Comparative Study*,
Ius Comparatum - Global Studies in Comparative Law 21,
DOI 10.1007/978-3-319-42157-5_1

disfavor investment abroad if there are economically sound reasons (apart from income tax consequences) for doing so. This type of neutrality has been embodied in the principle of capital export neutrality, dictating that a country tax the world-wide income of its residents, but provide a mechanism (usually a foreign tax credit) to relieve the double taxation that may ensue. Although the majority of countries purport to ground their respective tax systems upon the worldwide taxation princi-ple, a number have adopted a variant on capital export neutrality, such as capital import neutrality, in which a country opts not to tax income which its residents derive abroad. An example of this approach is the territorial system of taxation. Such a system allows a country's residents to compete abroad with residents of other countries. The justification for promoting what is known as "tax competition" is that it provides the resident the opportunity to translate the lower rate of taxation operative abroad into lower overall production costs, which would allow it to sell the goods at competitive prices worldwide. Because certain types of tax competition have become widely viewed as harmful to worldwide productivity, they have fallen into disfavor, particularly after the Organisation for Economic Cooperation and Development's (OECD's) 1998 Report on Harmful Tax Competition and, more recently, its October, 2015 Final Report on Base Erosion Profit Shifting (BEPS).

Despite the ostensible hegemony of the neutrality principle, countries have opted both at the domestic and international levels, to provide tax incentives. This depar-ture derives from a practical reality – national leaders find it legitimate to use their respective tax laws to achieve results far beyond that of providing a sufficient infra-structure and social network to support the citizenry. Many of these incentives, such as lowered income tax rates for certain types of production or industries and rapid methods of cost recovery, are designed to encourage production within the coun-try's borders, while others are designed to support (or have the effect of supporting) production activity outside of the country's borders through application of partici-pation exemptions and other means of taxing profits derived abroad more favorably. One of the motives for providing preferential treatment for foreign income can be seen as a competitive move to be the country of choice of multinational enterprises with the hope of attracting business activity and investment.

As competition among the more developed, higher income countries persists, little attention is paid to the impact of these international tax regimes on the fiscal strategies of the developing world. Intergovernmental organizations, like the OECD, have worked to promote internationally accepted standards relating to tax adminis-tration, such as information exchange, transparency, and enforcement, and anti-base erosion techniques, but these have tended to place an imprimatur on the tax com-petitive features of some regimes and condemned features of others traditionally designed to provide an incentive for investment in developing countries. And while some disfavored incentives may have resulted in no real benefit to poorer countries without proper safeguards, there has been no move to encourage safeguards or even to promote resort to other incentives that might hold promise to support developing world initiatives. Increasing income inequality in developing countries, has fre-quently led to political instability, threats to safety, and eventually exodus to more stable locales, with little prospect of increased aid in the form of overseas development assistance through important international organizations like the United Nations. Whether or not the developed world feels called to affirmatively use tax law to spark investment it is clear that a strategy is needed to disrupt the current disincentive for investment in the developing world provided by the tax regimes of higher income countries. In the absence of support for tax incentives, a more effective project would seek to dismantle the current hodgepodge of country approaches and to advocate a common tax base for all nations that would allow developing countries a reasonable share of tax revenue.

This chapter examines on a comparative basis whether, and the extent to which, countries support the use of tax laws to encourage economic activity within their own borders as well as in developing countries, emerging or low-income nations. To varying degrees most of the countries covered in this volume use their tax laws to provide a stimulus for investment within their borders. While most of them do not provide tax benefits designed to encourage investment in developing or poorer countries, the competitive features of some tax regimes actually remove any incentive to invest in these countries. A comparative approach invites a look at the ways in which higher-income countries could offset the harmful spill-over effect of their regimes on the developing world.

National Reports

In preparation for the 19th Congress of the International Academy of Comparative Law held in Vienna, Austria in 2014, national Reports were submitted for 19 countries: Australia, Belgium, Brazil, Croatia, Czech Republic, France, Hong Kong, Israel, Italy, Japan, Maldives, Netherlands, Poland, Portugal, South Africa, Uganda, United Kingdom, United States, and Venezuela.[1] These Reports are contained in the chapters that follow and are discussed below.

International Tax Norms

Sovereign nations are free to enact tax laws designed to meet duly constituted tax policy goals without restriction by the laws or policies of other nations. Although each nation has the power to fashion a tax regime free from interference by the laws of others, international cooperation among jurisdictions has evolved and internationally accepted standards have taken hold. Such group action is essential in a global marketplace in which multinationals unrestricted could exploit incompatible tax laws of separate nations in order to gain an unintended tax advantage. This phenomenon, sometimes known as "tax arbitrage," cannot be prevented without joint action by affected countries.

---

[1] A list of the National Reporters is appended to this General Report.

In addition to collective action through international organizations, such as the United Nations, tax authorities have also resorted to cooperation through inter-governmental organizations, such as the OECD, in order to develop strategies for addressing international tax avoidance, among other matters. The first of the OECD reports relating to strategies to prevent unfair tax competition, the Harmful Tax Competition Report, was published in 1998.[2] This Report condemned certain competitive strategies employed by some nations to attract investment. The most egregious of these was the establishment of preferential regimes that reduced or eliminated tax on specified types of income. However, the competitive practice of overall rate reduction to attract investment, such as Ireland's decision at the time of the Report's publication to reduce its overall tax rate to a level well below that of its peers, was not (for reasons not disclosed) labeled anti-competitive.

After publication of the Harmful Tax Competition report, and partly in response to complaints that the high-income members were imposing their views of appropriate tax policy on non-member countries, in particular, developing nations, the OECD constituted the Global Forum on Transparency and Exchange of Information in Tax Matters (Global Forum). The Global Forum has conducted systematic review of the tax systems of the 130 members to determine compliance with an internationally accepted standard.

While the Global Forum dealt with best practices in the area of tax administration and treaty practices, the OECD began work in 2013 on a project that became known as the BEPS project. In 2014 a G-20 Development Working Group issued its report on the impact of BEPS in low-income countries. In addition to detailing the obstacles to implementation of BEPS by developing countries, the G-20 report noted that "[t]ax incentives…are still a top priority concern for developing countries"[3] and that "risk to their tax base [occasioned by implementation of some of the BEPS proposals] will need to be addressed."[4] The final BEPS report issued in October, 2015 offered recommended action items in 15 areas, including harmful tax competition. The decision not to recommend replacement of the current system with a wholesale revision like worldwide formulary apportionment, in which worldwide income is allocated to jurisdictions in a manner not susceptible to manipulation by sophisticated multinationals, has been critiqued.[5] A radical revision of the prototype for the modern international tax regime would have required developed nations to relinquish competitive features of their systems and provide an opening for developing countries to implement strategies to attract investment.

---

[2] Organisation for Economic Cooperation and Development (OECD), HARMFUL TAX COMPETITION (1998).

[3] OECD, Part 2 of a Report to G20 Development Working Group on the Impact of BEPS in Low Income Countries 4 (Aug 13 2014) (BEPS DWG Pt 2).

[4] OECD, Part 1 of a Report to G20 Development Working Group on the Impact of BEPS in Low Income Countries 25 (July 2014).

[5] Lee A. Sheppard, BEPS Action 2: The Hybrid Hydra, 149 TAX NOTES 183 (Oct 12 2015).

Competitive Features of International Tax Regimes: Tax Base

The majority of reported countries, in keeping with the international trend, feature a worldwide tax regime, subjecting all income of their residents from domestic and foreign sources to taxation and providing a foreign tax credit of varying types to avoid double taxation. The minority report territorial regimes in which only the income of its residents from domestic sources is taxed. A territorial system is generally viewed as one that fosters competition, allowing resident multinationals to go offshore to enjoy the benefits offered by lower-tax jurisdictions. Closer scrutiny, however, reveals that jurisdictions purporting to have a worldwide system nonetheless have competitive features.

Sixteen of 19 reported countries purport to found their tax regimes on the worldwide taxation principle.[6] Of these, however, all but three (Brazil, Uganda, and United States) have some form of participation exemption, or other tax-exemption for dividends (and sometimes other income) paid by foreign subsidiaries of resident corporations.[7] This exemption converts a worldwide regime into a territorial one by exempting from tax (or greatly reducing the tax rate on) income derived offshore through foreign operations. Thus, although the governing international tax principle appears to be that of capital export neutrality – asserting the sovereign's right to tax income from all sources – capital import neutrality, a principle acknowledging the need of resident multinationals to compete in foreign jurisdictions under the prevailing advantageous terms, also guides tax policy.[8]

Two countries, Israel and Venezuela, moved from a territorial to a worldwide system of taxation.[9] The reporters for Israel indicated that this shift represented a decision by Israel to accommodate the realities of "economic globalization" and to conform to commonly accepted tax policy principles. This suggests that the trend among countries is to accommodate certain internationally recognized standards,

---

[6] These are Australia, Belgium, Brazil, Croatia, Czech Republic, Israel, Italy, Japan, Netherlands, Poland, Portugal, South Africa, Uganda, United Kingdom, United States, and Venezuela.

[7] The U.S. regime briefly featured a participation exemption-type regime when a special provision enacted in 2004 provided an 85 % deduction for certain dividends received from controlled corporations. Although Uganda has a worldwide tax regime, the government does grant tax holidays on an ad hoc basis. Although the governing principles under Brazilian law continue to be re-evaluated by the courts, it appears that Brazil provides no exemption for earnings of controlled foreign corporations, but may provide one for non-controlled foreign affiliates in certain cases. Poland and Portugal provide a participation exemption for corporations organized in EU or EEA member states or Switzerland.

[8] This may also suggest that "capital ownership neutrality," a principle that evolved from the work of two economists, Mihir Desai and James Hines, who argued that evaluations by multinationals of the appropriate location for investment should not be impeded by countries' tax laws, has gained acceptance. Some argue that this principle is served only if there is uniformity in the international tax regimes of all countries. See, e.g., C. Gustafson, R. Peroni & R. Pugh, TAXATION OF INTERNATIONAL TRANSACTIONS 22 (2011).

[9] One important country not covered in this volume, China, recently moved from a territorial to a worldwide system of taxation. This move was designed to crack down on certain tax avoidance schemes using special purpose vehicles owned by foreign residents.

which appears to derive force from the collective judgment of inter-governmental organizations. Decisions of these bodies concerning the direction of international tax policy has considerable influence whether or not a country is an official member of participant.

Three countries, France, Hong Kong, and Maldives, have resisted the international trend and continue to embrace a territorial tax regime. France taxes its resident corporations on income derived from operating in France. Only active income derived abroad (that is, not passive income like interest, dividends, royalties, and similar income) is excluded from French taxation. France also has a participation exemption for foreign source dividends received by a qualified French parent. This exemption only exists if the subsidiary is subject to a tax at the French rates or the prevailing rate in the country of organization. Thus, although the rate of tax imposed on an Irish subsidiary (12.5 %) is lower that the French rate of (33.33 %), dividends from an Irish subsidiary would nonetheless be eligible for the participation exemption because the subsidiary is taxed at the prevailing rate of its country of residence. The French participation exemption also extends to gain on the sale of the subsidiary's stock when eligibility requirements are met.[10]

Hong Kong has a territorial regime under which only business profits derived from Hong Kong sources are subject to tax. A dividend paid to a Hong Kong company by an offshore company is deemed to derive from foreign sources and is not subject to Hong Kong tax. According to the reporter, the Hong Kong regime is not intended to encourage investment abroad, but it may be viewed by taxpayers as incentivizing foreign investment. Although it has a territorial system, Hong Kong maintains conformity to mainstream OECD policy by maintaining a large network of comprehensive tax treaties.

The Maldives taxes its resident individuals on a territorial basis. Although corporations are taxed on a worldwide basis, they may enter into an agreement under the Law of Foreign Investments that confers an exemption from the business profits tax. The Maldives is considered a former "tax haven," but it has been building its regime into one that conforms to internationally accepted standards of taxation. This is demonstrated by its intention to increase its entry into Tax Information Exchange Agreements (TIEAs).

Although the Netherlands nominally has a worldwide system of taxation, since 2012, foreign profits and losses are excluded from the tax base either by treaty or under internal law. This exemption extends to foreign passive income derived by a foreign company if the income is subject to a tax of at least 10 % (thus exempting passive income derived through an Irish company because the Irish tax rate is 12.5 %). In addition, the participation exemption is available for dividends received from a 5 %-owned foreign corporation and from gains on the sale of the stock. This exemption applies to a subsidiary with passive income as long as the subsidiary is subject to an effective rate of tax of at least 10 %.

---

[10] Ninety-five percent of the dividend is excluded under the participation exemption, while eighty-eight percent of capital gain is excluded from tax.

As the reporter for the Netherlands indicates, the Dutch tax system would not prevent developing countries from "creating an attractive tax regime aimed at substantial foreign direct investment by or via Dutch companies." It is fair to note, however, that Dutch system is open to all competitors. It is not certain whether a developing country would have an advantage over a developed country, such as Ireland or other low-tax, high income countries, that offers the kind of industrial infrastructure, labor force, and other amenities unavailable in a low-tax developing country.

Other Modes of Competition: Tax Rates

A notable development in international taxation is the race among higher-income countries to compete for investment by lowering tax rates. The reports indicated that there has been some rate competition. The top statutory corporate tax rate for the reported countries is as follows:

United States:	35 %
Brazil:	34 %
Venezuela:	34 % [50 % for some industries]
Belgium:	33 % [plus a 3.3 % emergency contribution]
France:	33 % [plus a 3.3 % social contribution]
Australia:	30 %
Uganda:	30 %
South Africa:	28 %
Italy:	27.5 %
Israel:	26.5 %
Netherlands:	25 %
Portugal:	25 %
Japan:	23.9 %
Croatia:	20 %
United Kingdom:	20 %
Czech Republic:	19 %
Poland:	19 %
Hong Kong:	15 %
Maldives:	15 %

In addition to a competitive rate structure, some countries have adopted special low-tax regimes for prescribed income which is designed to attract business activity to the jurisdiction. The United Kingdom has adopted a competitive Patent Box regime in which profits from the development and exploitation of patents and their equivalents are taxed at a 10 % rate. The Netherlands has implemented an "innovation box" regime in which specified income from patents and other research and development is taxed at a 5 % rate. France applies a special reduced tax rate of 15 %

to income derived from exploitation of intellectual property (IP), including royalties and capital gain resulting from IP transfer. These preferential regimes may be under review by the European Union because they are believed to violate anti-state aid restrictions and code of conduct requirements under EU directives.

Other countries have adopted a special regime to provide advantageous treatment (in the form of lower tax rates) for income from targeted business activities. The United States provides a lower corporate tax rate for specified domestic production activities. Emerging nations, like Croatia, Czech Republic, and Poland offer tax advantages to foreign investors in certain industries or under-developed economic areas. France has offered a special tax regime to encourage companies to establish headquarters or logistics centers in France. These devices to attract investment are typical of countries transitioning from developing to developed country status. It is not certain whether these incentives will violate EU restrictions on state aid.

Israel has offered investment incentives, including a reduced tax rate for income from activities having a demonstrable impact on imports, but these have been viewed as either unfairly competitive by the OECD or in violation of pertinent trade agreements.

Finally, several reports have noted that the existence of approachable tax officials and the ability to obtain reliable guidance in advance of entering into transactions causes many higher income countries to be considered attractive investment destinations. This was noted in particular in the reports on Hong Kong, Maldives, and the Netherlands. When multinationals employ tax-minimizing strategies, predictability of results gains the confidence of investors. To the extent the approachability of tax officials translates into a vehicle to obtain special tax advantages, however, at least for EU member states, the arrangement may be challenged by EU officials as prohibited state aid.[11]

Incentives for Investment in Developing Countries

In the past, a practice of some high-income countries was to grant tax sparing credits to developing, emerging, or lower-income nations. Tax sparing occurs when a multinational's home country allows an offset against the home country tax otherwise due for fictional income taxes deemed paid (but not actually paid) to the lower-income nation. This tax sparing credit allows the capital-seeking nation to offer the multinational enterprise a lower-than-home country tax rate in order to attract foreign investment. In this fashion the higher income nation provided an incentive for investment in the lower-income nation. While the Harmful Tax Competition Report did not expressly address tax sparing, a separate report issued in the same year,

[11] See, e.g., Apple May Owe $8 Billion in European Taxes from Use of Irish Subsidiaries to Shelter Profits, Bloomberg News, Jan 15, 2016 (referring to certain favorable transfer pricing methodologies allowed by Ireland).

recommended an end to the practice.[12] The primary objections were that it was harmful to competition and it created a "race to the bottom" in which the lower-income nation faced pressure to reduce tax rates below a level that would sustain its revenue needs.

After issuance of the Tax Sparing Report, many countries abandoned tax sparing provisions in treaties with developing countries in order to align themselves with acceptable practices. Several of the reported countries have abandoned tax sparing, having terminated these agreements or phased them out. These include Australia, Belgium, Italy, and Japan. The United States has never entered into tax sparing arrangements.[13]

France has continued to use double taxation agreements to provide a tax sparing credit to certain developing countries, including French-speaking Africa, but because the credit provided no incentive for French companies to re-invest their tax savings into the local economy, these agreements are in decline. Japan has also continued to conclude tax sparing agreements with developing countries, like China, Brazil, Thailand, Zambia, and Bangladesh. Agreements with other countries are set to expire or have been negotiated for a limited time period. The reporter for Japan noted that, in lieu of tax sparing, Japan's participation exemption may provide a vehicle for investment in developing countries.

The United Kingdom has promoted investment in emerging economies by concluding tax sparing agreements in 37 treaties. While most of the agreements terminate after 10 years, such agreements in treaties with Belize, Israel, Cyprus, and Sudan do not expire.

It is apparent that the abuse of a tax sparing treaty provision offers the possibility of no real investment in the developing country and this explains, in part, the reason these arrangements are in decline. A well-crafted arrangement that safeguarded returns to the low-income treaty partner and offered other anti-abuse protections could hold promise to circumvent potential problems. It appears that no reported country abandoning tax sparing sought ways to prevent abuse.

As noted by the reporter for the Netherlands, the extensive Dutch treaty network may provide opportunities to attract investment. Special purpose entities (SPEs) may be organized under Dutch law for investment in developing countries. These are appealing because SPEs can pass on dividends and interest at favorable rates to corporate parents in third countries lacking advantageous treaties. The reporter believes that the substantially larger inflow of investment to developing countries through Dutch SPEs may outweigh the revenue loss from routing income out of the developing country to the parents. In addition the unilateral credit provided by Dutch law, for dividends distributed by and interest and royalties received from entities in developing countries provides an incentive for investment in low-income countries.

---

[12] OECD, TAX SPARING (1998).

[13] The U.S. national report indicates that the U.S. has provided relief similar to tax sparing in its internal law. Relief for certain investments in Puerto Rico, a U.S. possession was provided in § 936 of the Internal Revenue Code until its phase-out for years after 2006.

Italy has founded its international tax system upon the capital export neutrality principle. This means that it has opted not to provide tax incentives for investment in developing countries. Instead, it has employed non-tax strategies to assist these nations. In particular, it has taken initiatives in the area of customs duties through the "Cotonou Agreement" with African, Caribbean, and Pacific states. These actions have led to maritime accords, structural accords, and free trade zones. It has aligned itself with the OECD and other strategists that believe that developing nations are more appropriately helped by measures enabling them to create a stable market economy rather than by unilateral investments, aid, or tax benefits.

Tax Treaties with Developing Countries

A robust treaty network can provide considerable support for investment in developing countries. Double taxation agreements have been concluded with developing countries by Australia, Belgium, Brazil, Croatia, France, Hong Kong, Israel, Italy, Japan, the Netherlands, Poland, South Africa, Uganda, United Kingdom, and Venezuela. Some of these countries, like the Netherlands, have an extensive treaty network with developing countries, while others, like Belgium and Croatia, have very few.[14] Others, such as the Czech Republic and the United States, have negotiated Tax Information Exchange Agreements (TIEAs), but not full treaties.

Developing Country Efforts to Attract Investment

Among the reported countries that fall into the category of developing, emerging, or low-income, all employed some type of tax exemption or rate reduction for designated activities.[15] Most of the rate reductions were for activities deemed to bring development, such as building of infrastructure through construction, tourism, research and development, increasing export of goods, foreign film production, and manufacturing, of importance to the country's economy.

A low-tax strategy will be effective to attract investment only from companies resident in countries like France, Hong Kong, the Maldives, the Netherlands, and the United Kingdom which have regimes with territorial features. These tax systems would exempt resident multinationals from home country tax and not interfere with

---

[14] Belgium's only full double taxation treaty (not limited to information exchange like a TIEA) with a developing country is with Burundi, a former colony.

[15] Croatia, Czech Republic, Poland, South Africa, and Uganda, ranging along the spectrum from developed to developing country, all offered some type of rate reduction for specified activities. Uganda offers tax holidays on an ad hoc basis depending upon the merits of a particular project. Israel, while not a developing country, is a small country with special reasons for encouraging investment within its own borders.

a developing country's low-tax incentive. Of these countries, those entering into treaty tax sparing agreements also support the ability to attract investment by offsetting the home country tax liability by a fictional credit that cedes taxing jurisdiction to the developing country.

In addition, the participation exemption regimes of many of the reported countries, described in the section above entitled "Competitive features of international Tax Regimes: Tax Base", also support these low-tax strategies by exempting offshore profits of subsidiaries organized in developing countries and dividends distributed. In view of the rate competition by developed countries, however, these countries may need to reduce rates to a level that will not sustain the needs of the population.

Yet even those regimes that support tax-rate incentives of developing country provide limited effect because these countries are nonetheless competing in a set of market conditions that continue to favor the developed world. Providing a set of factors effective in attracting foreign investment is no easy task. Academics have noted that the most important components of success in attracting foreign investment are: economic determinants (quality of a country's infrastructure, growth of the market, availability of skills, and technological capacity), regulatory framework (whether the legal framework is transparent, stable, and reliable), and investment promotion (capacity to target foreign investors and to provide ongoing follow-up services post-investment).[16] Tax incentives alone are not sufficient because these elements of success cannot exist without the willingness of the developed world to dedicate development assistance in the form of monetary aid and technical expertise and guidance that can help the poorer nation to solidify its economic foundation.[17]

A real contribution to the economic viability and investment-attracting ability of developing countries would be a coordinated overhaul of the current system of separate country tax regimes. This system operates to the detriment of developing countries that are relegated to looking for ways in which to compensate for the spill-over effects of the regimes of the developed world. Yet these are marginal strategies which may not sustain their economies in the global marketplace. A worldwide system of coordinated taxation, such as that described in proposals for formulary apportionment,[18] devised with full input from developing nations, is one example of the type of innovative plan that might provide an effective tool. With this type of regime in place, innovation in the global allocation of corporate income may hold promise to support developing country strategies for economic viability. One example of the type of forward thinking called for is a recent project headed by Professor Reuven Avi-Yonah proposing to further a regulatory goal of the corporate income tax by connecting the overall effective corporate tax rate to corporate performance

---

[16] Karl P. Sauvant, Attracting Foreign Direct Investment and Benefiting from it: Challenges for the Least Developed Countries, 7 Transn'l Corporations Rev. 125–126 (June 2015) (available on line at www.tnc-online.net).

[17] Id. at 125.

[18] Reuven Avi-Yonah, Kimberly Clausing, and Michael C. Durst, Allocating Business Profits for Tax Purposes: A Proposal to Adopt a Formulary Profit Split, 9 Fla. Tax Rev. 497 (2009).

(using factors such as profitability, employment, social and environmental sustainability, and 'wealth redistribution' within a locality).[19] Implementation of this proposal would allow a developing country to structure its tax regime in a way that would further development goals (job training, environmental sustainability, job creation), attract investment, and begin to build the type of social and technological infrastructure that would strengthen and build its economy.

Appendix

National Reporters

AUSTRALIA – Miranda Stewart
BELGIUM – Edoardo Traversa, Gaëtan Zeyen
BRAZIL – André Mendes Moreira, Misabel Abreu Machado Derzi, Fernando Daniel de Moura Fonseca
CROATIA – Nataša Žunić Kovačević
CZECH REPUBLIC – Michal Radvan, Dana Šramková
FRANCE – Thomas Dubut
HONG KONG – Andrew Halkyard
ISRAEL – Tamir Shanan, Sagit Leviner, Moran Harari
ITALY – Claudio Sacchetto
JAPAN – Yoshihiro Masui
MALDIVES – Kevin Holmes
NETHERLANDS – Raymond H.C. Luja
POLAND – Wlodzimierz Nykiel, Michal Wilk
PORTUGAL – Fernando Rocha Andrade
SOUTH AFRICA – Craig West, Jennifer Roeleveld
UGANDA – Jalia Kangave
UNITED KINGDOM – Rita Cunha
UNITED STATES – Tracy Kaye
VENEZUELA – Serviliano Abache Carvajal

---

[19] A corporation successful according to these measures would be awarded a low tax rate.

Part II
National Reports

Chapter 2
Australia's Hybrid International Tax System: Limited Focus on Tax and Development

Miranda Stewart

Abstract Australia does not provide tax incentives for investment abroad. However, Australia's participation exemption regime, which exempts business profits returned to Australia, may be viewed as an incentive to invest offshore. The participation exemption allows a tax exemption for active foreign business income of a corporation resident in Australia and for dividends received by an Australian corporation from foreign subsidiaries actively engaged in foreign business. Buttressed by anti-tax avoidance rules, this regime may provide some incentive for investment in developing countries hoping to attract investment by use of various tax incentives. Australia's main inbound and outbound investment is with the United States and the United Kingdom; its main outbound investment in developing countries has been primarily in BRICS, Mexico, and the ASEAN regions.

Synopsis Australia has historically been a capital importing country, but today there is significant investment by Australian companies abroad. Miranda Stewart notes that, although Australia does not generally provide tax incentives for investment abroad, its participation exemption regime, providing exempt income tax treatment for business profits returned to Australia, may be viewed as an incentive to invest offshore. However, the corporate-shareholder imputation credit claws back the benefit of the participation exemption for profits distributed to Australian shareholders. The imputation credit does not apply to dividends received from foreign corporations or from Australian corporations out of profits not subject to tax in Australia.

The participation exemption regime in Australia, effective since 2004, allows an exemption for active foreign business income of Australian resident corporations as well as for dividends received by Australian corporations from foreign subsidiaries actively engaged in a foreign business. It also provides an exclusion from tax for capital gains derived on the sale of shares of a foreign subsidiary (where ownership is at least 10 %). Stewart notes that this regime operates as a "true territorial system"

M. Stewart (✉)
Tax and Transfer Policy Institute, Crawford School of Public Policy,
The Australian National University, Canberra, Australia
e-mail: miranda.stewart@anu.edu.au

© Springer International Publishing Switzerland 2017   17
K.B. Brown (ed.), *Taxation and Development - A Comparative Study*,
Ius Comparatum - Global Studies in Comparative Law 21,
DOI 10.1007/978-3-319-42157-5_2

when profits are retained offshore. If these profits are distributed to foreign shareholders, there is no further Australian tax on either the corporation or the shareholder. When these profits are distributed to Australian shareholders, as noted above, there is no imputation credit and the shareholder pays Australian tax on the dividend (although the actual amount of the dividend would be diminished by any foreign tax paid by the distributing corporation – in effect allowing the shareholder a deduction for any foreign tax paid).

The participation exemption, buttressed by anti-avoidance rules with differing levels of success, does provide some incentives to invest in developing countries hoping to use various incentives to attract foreign investment. The regime was also intended to support inbound investment into Australian companies.

Most Australian outbound investment is into the United States and United Kingdom. Australian outbound investment in developing countries has been primarily in the BRICS (China, Brazil, India, Russia, and South Africa), Mexico and the ASEAN region (Hong Kong, Indonesia, South Korea, Malaysia, Philippines, Singapore, Taiwan, Thailand, and Vietnam) and tax havens, including the Bahamas, Bermuda, Cayman Islands and British Virgin Islands. There is very little outbound investment into Latin and South America (other than Brazil), Africa, the Pacific, Middle and Eastern Europe.

Historically, Australia has alternated between a territorial system in which foreign source income was exempt from tax and a worldwide system. Australia currently has a worldwide system taxing residents on income from all sources whether inside or outside Australia and allowing a foreign income tax offset (FITO) for taxes paid to another country on foreign source income, except for the corporate business profit participation exemption described above.

Australia has 45 double tax agreements (DTAs) with OECD countries, EU nations, and certain other countries, such as Argentina, Chile, China, Fiji, India, Indonesia, South Korea, Malaysia, Papua New Guinea, Singapore, Philippines, Thailand, Turkey, and Vietnam. Although Australia has negotiated treaties with developing countries which are significant trading or investment partners, it does not use them as a tool for international aid and development policy. Australia had in the past provided tax sparing in all of its DTAs with developing countries. It discontinued that practice in light of the OECD 1998 decision to urge abandonment of this practice among member nations. The current Australia-Papua New Guinea (a former colony) DTA does contain a tax sparing provision, which allows Australian residents to benefit from a tax exemption for investment in that jurisdiction.

Australia relies on its Controlled Foreign Corporation (CFC) rules to prevent avoidance of tax on passive-type income, but, apart from this, it has no special rules that target investment in tax havens. It relies upon its treaty-based information exchange provisions and its General Anti-Avoidance Rules (GAAR) to deny treaty benefits in cases of abuse.

Australia is party to numerous free trade and bilateral trade agreements. For the most part, these have limited application to income tax measures.

Introduction

This chapter discusses the Australian income tax treatment of cross-border investment and addresses the question as to whether Australia uses its tax laws to encourage either domestic or foreign investment, and to counter or implement tax
competition or the use of tax havens.[1] As a general rule, Australia does not provide
tax concessions to encourage investment into or out of developing countries. There
are some exceptions in Australia's Double Tax Agreements (DTAs), however
Australia has only a few DTAs with developing countries. Australia does have some
tax concessions for certain types of investment in Australia, including for research
and development (R&D), certain capital plant and equipment, mineral exploration,
some financial sector activities and concessions in fuel taxes for certain industries.

The Australian company tax rate is 30 %, however following a recent reform,
companies with a turnover of less than $2 million each year have a 28.5 % rate. A
Bill to reduce the company tax rate to 25 % for all companies over a 10 year transition period to 2026–27 is in the Australian Parliament but is unlikely to pass.

Australia operates a participation exemption regime for corporate business profits returned to Australia, which may be perceived by some as an incentive for
Australian companies to invest offshore. However, when combined with Australia's
corporate-shareholder imputation credit system, this regime is less generous than it
first appears.

Australia is very active in engaging in international tax information exchange
and cooperation to counter tax avoidance and the use of tax havens, including assistance to and engagement with developing countries and in relation to the OECD
Base Erosion and Profit Shifting (BEPS) project. As Chair of the G20 in 2014,
Australia led the report on developing country BEPS issues.[2]

Australia's International Investment Profile

Historically, Australia has been a capital importing country (like many developing
countries today), while until the 1980s Australia had a fixed currency and various
capital controls. However, since the floating of the Australian dollar and removal of
most capital controls during the 1980s, Australian companies have increasingly
invested offshore. On a net basis, today Australia remains a capital importer, but
there is now a significant share of foreign investment by Australian companies.

---

[1] Australia has a single income tax, levied by the federal (Commonwealth) government. The
income tax rules referred to in this report are contained in two tax statutes: *Income Tax Assessment
Act 1997 (Cth)* (ITAA97) and *Income Tax Assessment Act 1936 (Cth)* (ITAA36). These statutory
provisions and other sources are referred to where relevant in this report.

[2] OECD, Report to G20 Developing Working Group on the Impact of BEPS in Low Income
Countries (2014)

Most cross-border direct investment into and out of Australia takes place through corporations, the focus of this report is on corporate tax.[3] However, corporations, like trusts and partnerships, are intermediaries and all tax is ultimately paid by individuals. Australia has an imputation credit system in which Australian shareholders receive credit for Australian tax paid by corporations, if certain conditions are satisfied. In addition, a significant amount of cross-border portfolio investment takes place through managed funds which are treated in general as flow-through trusts for Australian tax purposes, and pension ("superannuation") funds which are taxed as entities at 15 %. A substantial proportion of investment into developing countries from Australia is portfolio investment through funds which manage exposure to share investments in diverse regional and industry investment sectors globally.

More than half of Australia's inbound and outbound investment takes place with only two countries: the US and the UK. However, the remaining cross-border investment is spread across a wide range of jurisdictions. As at 31 December 2015, the level of foreign investment into Australia was approximately $3 trillion; leading investor countries were the US (28 %), UK (17 %), Belgium (8 %), Japan (7 %), Singapore (3 %) and Hong Kong (3 %), with the remaining 36 % from other countries around the world.[4] Borrowing by Australian companies on international capital markets (e.g., Eurobonds) was 1 % of this. The level of Australian investment abroad was $2 trillion, an increase of $150 billion over the previous year. The leading investment destination countries were the US (29 %), UK (17 %), New Zealand (5 %), Japan (4 %), China (3 %) and Singapore (3 %), with the remaining 39 % again spread across other countries.

As regards inbound or outbound investment from Australia with respect to developing countries, primary statistics indicate[5] that Australian outbound investment of more than $1 billion was made into the following regions or countries:

- BRICS: mainland China ($70 billion); India ($10.6 billion); Brazil ($7.6 billion); Russia ($1.1 billion); South Africa ($4.2 billion)
- Mexico ($4.2 billion);
- ASEAN region: Hong Kong (SAR) ($50.7 billion); Indonesia ($8.4 billion); South Korea ($15 billion); Malaysia ($5.5 billion); Philippines ($10 billion); Singapore ($67 billion); Taiwan ($5.6 billion); Thailand ($5.5 billion); Vietnam ($1.5 billion);
- Latin and South America (other than Brazil): Chile ($2.9 billion);
- Africa (other than South Africa): None over $1 billion
- Pacific: Fiji ($1.9 billion); Papua New Guinea ($18.4 billion)

[3] This report draws on primary and secondary sources and relies in part on the book, Burgess Cooper Stewart Vann, *Cooper Krever and Vann's Income Taxation Commentary and Materials* (7th ed, 2012) (*Income Taxation Text*) in particular on the corporate tax chapters (contributed by the author) and international tax chapters (contributed by Richard Vann).

[4] ABS Cat. 5352.0 (11 May 2016) available from www.abs.gov.au.

[5] Ibid., Table 5: Australian Investment Abroad by Country and Country groups (including direct, portfolio, equity and debt). All figures are for 2015.

- Middle East and Eastern Europe: United Arab Emirates ($2.4 billion)
- Tax havens: Bahamas, Bermuda ($9.6 billion); Cayman Islands ($32.2 billion); British Virgin Islands ($2.4 billion)

Much investment into other countries is going through "hub" or intermediary companies, e.g., through Hong Kong, Singapore, South Africa or various tax havens. Overall, levels of inbound and outbound equity investment are roughly the same, however Australians borrow more from overseas than they lend, that is, foreign debt is significantly greater than outbound debt held by Australian creditors.

Benchmarks for Assessing International Tax Policy

Australian tax policy makers, like those around the world, tend to refer to generally accepted international tax "neutrality benchmarks" described in one government *Review* as follows:[6]

> *Capital export neutrality* [CEN], which aims for neutrality in international investment deci-
> sions, with pre-tax rates of return on investments equal between countries. To achieve
> this benchmark, an investor would need to face the same effective tax rate on an invest-
> ment regardless of the country of investment.
> *Capital import neutrality* [CIN], which aims for neutrality in international savings deci-
> sions, with the after-tax rate of return on an investment in any particular country the
> same for all investors both domestic and foreign. To achieve this benchmark, the effec-
> tive rate of tax on an investment would need to be the same regardless of investors' place
> of residence.
> *National neutrality*, which aims for neutrality in residents' investment decisions on the
> gross return to their country of residence, with the pre-tax return on domestic invest-
> ments matching the post-foreign tax return on foreign investments. To achieve this
> benchmark, the foreign investment income of a resident investor would need to be taxed
> without deferral at the same domestic tax rate as domestic income and with foreign tax
> treated as a deductible expense

In general, CEN equates to worldwide (residence) based taxation, but in practice this would only be achieved if the foreign taxes are equal to or lower than Australian tax, as Australia like other countries would not refund higher foreign taxes. CIN (sometimes called "capital ownership neutrality" appears to be equivalent to source taxation, except that to prevent tax avoidance or use of havens, generally some level of taxation is expected in the other jurisdiction before the exemption from domestic tax will be granted. National neutrality treats foreign taxes as a cost of doing business and, "this principle presumes that taxes paid to foreign governments yield no direct benefits to Australia, and Australian welfare will be maximized if no offset is provided for any foreign taxes levied on foreign-source income derived by Australians. Instead, foreign taxes should simply be treated as another cost of doing

---

[6]Australian Treasury, Board of Taxation, Review of international Tax Arrangement (RITA) Consultation Paper, 2002, p. 92.

business [overseas]."[7] Thus, "national neutrality" ignores global welfare, and the welfare of other countries around the world.

Australia's international tax policy, including its approach to negotiating DTAs, historically emphasized Australia's source country taxation of foreign investment as befits a capital importing country. The shift of the last few decades towards Australia being both a capital importer and capital exporter was a particular focus of the Board of Taxation's Review of International Tax Arrangements conducted in 2002 and of subsequent tax reforms. Australian international and corporate tax policy is fairly pragmatic and seeks to balance various interests and outcomes, especially in the current era given the Australian investment profile as both a capital importing and capital exporting jurisdiction. The Board of Taxation accepted that country tax systems could not achieve all of the above neutrality benchmarks and that, even though traditionally economists may have favoured capital export neutrality (as it maximizes global welfare), these benchmarks are hotly contested.

Australia does not adopt any tax policy of supporting or favouring investment into developing or poor countries. Australia has only a few former colonies, with Papua New Guinea being the most important of them. Australia has strong intergovernmental arrangements with PNG, but this is supported more by government aid and private investment than by tax measures. Australia has historically had strong alliances with other British Commonwealth countries, evidenced by Australia's treaty network to some extent. Today the Commonwealth alliance is less strong than in past years. Australia has few DTAs with African countries even where they are members of the Commonwealth and there is very little Australian investment into Africa. Today, Australia focuses considerable investment (and aid) policy attention in the local region including the ASEAN (Association of South East Asian Nations) region and Pacific neighbours.

Following some of the Board of Tax Review's recommendations, Australia's tax policy since 2004 has explicitly addressed two objectives: to facilitate Australian companies to expand and invest offshore, and to increase the attractiveness of Australia as a location for foreign investment and especially as an international holding company and financial centre. These objectives were summarized as follows:

> As Australia has integrated into the global marketplace, investment by Australian firms in other countries has increased sharply. This is part of a worldwide trend. ... It is thus becoming increasingly important that the Australian domestic economy offer an attractive investment location for foreign companies. It is also becoming increasingly important that Australian companies are able to invest competitively in international markets. The taxation system should not impede either of these objectives.[8]

---

[7] *Income Tax Text*, above n. 2, [17.10] p. 892.

[8] Board of Taxation Report, above n. 5, Vol 1 para [1.4] p. 29.

Australia's International Tax System

Residence-Based Taxation

Australia levies income tax on a resident basis. The definition of "resident" for individuals includes a person who resides in Australia in the ordinary meaning of the word, whose domicile is in Australia, who has actually been in Australia for more than 6 months in any fiscal year, unless his or her permanent or usual place of abode is outside Australia, or who is a member of a government superannuation fund.[9] The definition of "resident" for companies is based on either incorporation in Australia; central management or control in Australia; or voting control by share-holders who are residents of Australia.[10]

Basic Worldwide Tax System

Since the first federal income tax established in 1915, Australia's international tax system has oscillated between a territorial (exemption) system and a worldwide (foreign tax credit) style system. From 1915 to 1930, Australia had a fully territorial income tax system that only applied to income that had an Australian source. In 1930, seeking increased revenue, the tax law was amended to apply to worldwide income of Australian residents. This led to the possibility of international double taxation, however Australia's first DTA was not signed until 1946 (with the UK). Australia's historical relation with the United Kingdom (UK) as its "former colonial master," led to the enactment of a general exemption for foreign source income from any jurisdiction provided that income had been subject to some income tax.[11] That provision applied (with various exceptions introduced over time) until 1987, when the foreign tax credit system was introduced.

Today, Australia levies income tax on a worldwide basis for most foreign source income derived by individual residents and as the basic rule for taxation of other business and investment intermediary entities. The core assessing provisions in the income tax law include all income of residents, derived directly or indirectly from all sources, whether in or outside Australia, during the income year.[12] For foreign residents, the core rules include only ordinary income or statutory income derived

---

[9] Section 6(1) "resident" (a) ITAA36.

[10] Section 6(1) "resident" (b) ITAA36.

[11] Former s 23(q) of ITAA36, repealed in 1987, was enacted in response to concerns expressed by the UK in 1930, which argued that it should retain exclusive taxing rights over UK-source income: *Income Tax Text*, above n. 2, [17.10] p. 923.

[12] Section 6-5(2), 6-10(4) of ITAA97.

from Australian sources during the income year, except if some specific provision overrides this basic rule.[13]

Where foreign income tax has been paid on amounts included in assessable income in a year, the taxpayer may be entitled to a Foreign Income Tax Offset (FITO) in that year.[14] The FITO applies to foreign taxes on income, profits or gains, or another tax for which a credit is allowed under a DTA to which Australia is a party.[15]

The basic amount of the FITO is the foreign income tax paid.[16] This is subject to a limit calculated as the amount of income tax that would have been paid had the taxpayer's income not included the foreign income, and the taxpayer was not allowed any deductions in relation to that foreign income.[17]

However, as explained further below in 4.1, since 2004, the basic worldwide tax regime is altered for most foreign business income or dividends derived by Australian resident corporations so that an exemption or territorial system applies for foreign source business profits. The ultimate economic outcome of this regime for Australian investors is affected by Australia's corporate-shareholder imputation credit system, also explained further below.

No Tax Incentives for Investment in Poor Countries

Australia does not provide any tax incentives for investment in emerging or developing countries, or countries with low incomes, high poverty rates or high rates of economic inequality. Until this year, income earned by the few residents of Norfolk Island, a small territory of Australia, was exempt from Australian income tax; even this has now ceased.[18] It was estimated that the exemption resulted in revenue foregone of $7 million in 2014–2015.[19]

Exemption System for Foreign Aid and Defence Workers

Australia exempts foreign employment income for Australian tax residents who work abroad for not less than 3 months, for an Australian government aid agency, non-government international aid or disaster relief organisation (such as Oxfam),

---

[13] Section 6-5(3), 6-10(5) of ITAA97.

[14] Div 770 of ITAA97.

[15] Section 770-15 of ITAA97.

[16] Section 770-70 of ITAA97.

[17] Section 770-75 of ITAA97.

[18] Warren Truss MP, Minister for Infrastructure and Regional Development, Media Release 'Delivering a stronger and more prosperous Norfolk Island', JF022/2015 (19 March 2015), http://minister.infrastructure.gov.au/jb/releases/2015/March/jb022_2015.aspx.

[19] Section 251T and 251U of ITAA36; Australian Treasury, Tax Expenditures Statement 2014, Item A5, p. 11.

international institution, or in foreign service for the Australian defence force.[20] The exemption applies so that these workers do not need to pay tax on the income and claim the FITO to eliminate the taxation. This exemption operates largely as a subsidy for Australians working in developing or poor countries. The Australian Treasury estimates the revenue foregone as a result of this tax expenditure to be approximately $55 million in the 2013–2014 tax year.[21]

An exemption is also provided for a range of defence force allowances and payments; for payments to Australian federal police working for the United Nations; and for the income of Australian resident officers of the Asian Development Bank, as part of the arrangement for running the ADB office that services Pacific Island nations.[22]

Double Tax Agreements (DTAs)

Australia is currently a signatory to 45 DTAs.[23] Most are with OECD countries and are based on the OECD Model. Historically, Australia drew on some elements of the UN Model Treaty especially regarding permanent establishment, high royalty withholding tax and business profits articles, to ensure its taxing rights over inbound investment into Australia. Under Australia's DTAs, the foreign tax credit is relied upon for relief of double taxation. However, domestically a limited exemption is provided for labour income (see 3.2, above), and a participation exemption for most corporate profits or dividends.

Outside the OECD and EU, Australia has DTAs with Argentina, Chile, China, Fiji, India, Indonesia, Kiribati, South Korea, Malaysia, Papua New Guinea, Philippines, Singapore, Sri Lanka, Taipei, Thailand, Turkey and Vietnam. The Australian Treasury has a conservative approach to treaty negotiation and does not intend to expand this number of DTAs significantly. It does not see DTA negotiation as a part of international aid and development policy, and is more likely to focus on renegotiating those DTAs with significant trading or investment partners, as needed, for Australia's national benefit.

Australia's former colonial relationship with PNG is acknowledged in the Preamble to the Australia-PNG DTA, which unusually recognizes "the importance of measures to strengthen their relationship in accordance with the Joint Declaration of Principles Guiding Relations between Papua New Guinea and Australia, including the principle that cooperation and exchanges between the two countries shall be mutually beneficial and based on full participation by both countries." The Australia-PNG DTA contains some concessions to support PNG in taxing or seeking to

---

[20] Section 23AF and 23AG of ITAA36.

[21] Australian Treasury, Tax Expenditure Statement 2014, Item A2 p. 10.

[22] Ibid, Item A38 p. 33.

[23] See   http://www.treasury.gov.au/Policy-Topics/Taxation/Tax-Treaties/HTML/Income-Tax-Treaties for full text, dates etc. of Australia's DTAs.

encourage outbound investment from Australia. For example, Art. 5 states that a permanent enterprise includes any assembly project, building site, supervisory activities or consultancy services, in excess of 3 months, or using substantial equipment. This expansive provision facilitates PNG taxation of Australian investment or construction projects carried on in PNG. The Australia-PNG DTA also contains a tax sparing provision, so that if PNG provides a tax concession or exemption for investment, this is not "recaptured" by the Australian fisc under the foreign tax credit rule.

More generally, Australia historically provided tax sparing in all its DTAs with developing countries.[24] However, in 1997, Australia announced a change of policy following the OECD review of tax sparing which decided that member countries should not support it.[25] Consequently, Australia does not include tax sparing in DTAs since 1997 and has also said it will not extend the existing tax sparing provisions, which generally refer to or rely on the developing country's investment laws referred to by Exchange of Letters.

Australia's Corporate-Shareholder Tax System

Australia has had, since 1987, an imputation credit corporate-shareholder tax system. Dividends may be paid "franked" with a credit reflecting company tax, which offsets the shareholder's tax on the dividend. The general policy is that there should be a single layer of taxation on company profits. Individual investors and large institutional investors in Australian companies (primarily, superannuation funds that are taxed at 15 %), have a preference for franked dividends and build the imputation tax offset into their investment portfolios.

The imputation credit applies only for Australian resident companies that pay Australian company tax on profits and then distribute the profit to resident shareholders.[26] A resident company which pays tax on its taxable income (assessable income less deductions) can pay a "franked" dividend to its shareholders out of taxed profits. The shareholder includes the dividend and amount of the franking credit in their assessable income,[27] so being treated as receiving the pre-tax amount of distributed profit. The resident shareholder can apply the "franking credit" reflecting tax paid by the company to offset their own income tax liability on the dividend.

---

[24] See, e.g., Australia-Vietnam DTA (1982), Art. 23(3) and (4) and related Exchange of Letters; Australia-Thailand DTA (1989), Art 24(3), (4) referring to tax foregone by the Thai government under its Investment Promotion Act or subsequent provision as agreed.

[25] OECD, *Tax Sparing: A Reconsideration* (OECD: 1997). For a critique of this OECD approach from a Brazilian perspective, see Luis Schoueri, 'A Reconsideration of the Reconsideration' in Brauner Y and Stewart M (eds) *Tax, Law and Economic Development* (2013).

[26] See [14.70] et seq. *Income Tax Text*, above n. 2.

[27] Section 44 of ITAA36.

For example, a company that derives taxable income of $100 and pays tax of $30 can distribute a "franked dividend" of $70 to a resident shareholder. The shareholder is treated as having assessable income of $100 calculated as the franked dividend of $70 plus an "imputation" credit of $30 for the company tax. If the shareholder is on the top individual marginal rate of 47 %, this rate is then applied to the "grossed up" dividend income of $100, but the imputation credit of $30 is applied against the personal tax liability of $47, leaving $17 further tax to be paid by the individual.[28] If the individual had a lower tax rate, say, 15 %, and was liable to pay tax of $15 on the "grossed up" dividend income of $100, they could apply $15 of the imputation credit to reduce the tax owed to nil, and claim a tax refund for the balance of $15. That is, the imputation tax offset is "refundable." The end result is that the overall rate of tax on the distributed company profit equates to the shareholder's individual marginal tax rate.

However, where a dividend is sourced directly or indirectly from *foreign profit* of an Australian company, the franking credit will not apply. Foreign taxed profit distributed by the Australian company to resident shareholders is paid as an "unfranked" dividend. The shareholder is not entitled to a franking credit, so the full dividend is subject to Australian income tax at the shareholder's individual marginal tax rate. This means that the Australian company tax rate of 30 % is a final tax on foreign profits or companies or for non-resident shareholders.

Diagrams Illustrating Imputation Credit System for Residents

Credit for resident individual (1)

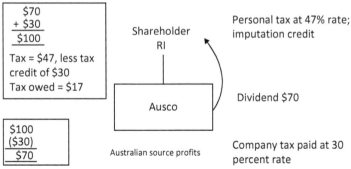

A dividend paid by an Australian company to a foreign shareholder would be subject to dividend withholding tax (WHT) at a rate of 30 % (generally reduced to 15 % or 10 % under an applicable DTA).[29] The imputation credit does not apply for

---

[28] Section 207-20 of ITAA97.
[29] Section 128A of ITAA36.

foreign shareholders or for foreign source profits of Australian companies. Instead, a foreign shareholder is merely relieved from paying any further Australian income tax or dividend WHT on the franked dividend (they may, of course, still be subject to tax on the dividends in their home country).

For example, assume a company derives taxable income of $100, pays tax of $30, and distributes a franked dividend of $70 to a foreign shareholder (see next diagram). Assume that dividend WHT of 15 % (reduced by DTA) would normally apply. As the dividend is franked, no WHT will apply.[30] The shareholder receives the $70 dividend free from any further Australian tax. The effect is that the overall rate of Australian tax on the distributed corporate profit is 30 %, which is effectively a final payment of tax on the foreign share of the taxable Australian profit of resident companies.

Nonresident receives dividend

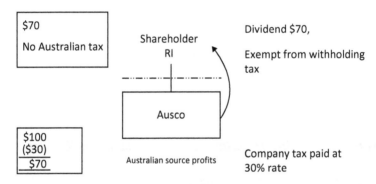

A different result applies for a foreign shareholder receiving a dividend out of foreign sourced and foreign taxed profit from an Australian company. Such a dividend is generally exempt from further Australian income tax or dividend WHT in the hands of the foreign shareholder. Only one level of (foreign) tax will apply to these *conduit* type dividends passed through an Australian company.[31]

Participation Exemption

Since 2004, Australia has operated a participation exemption regime for foreign business income and gains. The Australian income tax law provides for:

- an exclusion from tax for active business income derived by foreign branches of Australian companies.[32]

---

[30] Section 128B of ITAA36.

[31] Division 802 of ITAA97.

[32] Section 23AH and section 23AJ of ITAA36.

- an exclusion from tax for foreign-source dividends paid to an Australian parent company which has a "non-portfolio" shareholding in the foreign subsidiary (a 10 % or greater voting interest).[33]
- an exclusion from capital gains taxation for gains on the sale of a non-portfolio shareholding interest by an Australian company.[34]

Prior to 1987, foreign corporate branch income would have been exempt as long as it was subject to some tax (however slight) in the foreign jurisdiction. However, foreign source dividends of Australian residents (companies or individuals) were made subject to Australian income tax in 1941, and an allowance (in the form of a deduction) provided for foreign tax on the dividend when received by an individual. In 1947, individuals were allowed a credit for the amount of foreign tax on the dividend, and if received by an Australian company, a full rebate equivalent to an exemption from Australian company tax was provided for the dividend.[35]

There was increasing concern in subsequent decades that the exemption for foreign income provided a significant incentive for tax avoidance using tax havens. One of the most important cases concerning Australia's general anti-avoidance rule involved a company that derived interest from investing in the tax haven of the Cook Islands, at a low pre-tax rate of return but high after-tax rate of return, taking into account the low tax rate in the Cook Islands.[36] During the 1980s, when the Hawke-Keating Labor government removed most capital controls, enabling free movement of investments across the border. There was a fear that this could lead to a tax haven "free for all".[37]

To address this concern, for a short period from 1987 to 1991, the foreign tax credit (worldwide taxation) regime applied to all foreign source branch income and dividends. Thus, in 1987, the government applied a CEN approach. However, this regime did not last long, as exemptions were reintroduced in 1991. At this time, the government also introduced a Controlled Foreign Corporations (CFC) regime and Foreign Investment Fund (FIF) regime which both apply accrual taxation of low taxed foreign income, taking inspiration in some respects from the US CFC and PFIC regimes. The CFC regime remains as an integrity measure, as discussed further below.

When (re)introduced in 1991, the branch profits and dividend exemptions were limited to foreign-source profits or dividends from listed countries perceived as having comparable tax rates to Australia. A "broad exemption" was applied to foreign income in listed countries that had been subject to comparable tax, or to dividends from foreign subsidiaries where the foreign profits were considered to have been subject to comparable tax. A "narrow exemption" applied to branch income or dividends received from other countries. Although an exemption system, this regime

---

[33] Section 23AJ of ITAA36.

[34] Division 768 of ITAA97.

[35] Former s 46 of ITAA36.

[36] FCT v Spotless Services (1996) 186 CLR 404.

[37] *Income Tax Text*, above n 2.

required the profits or dividend to be taxed at a comparable rate to the Australian company tax rate and so approximately continued the "capital export neutrality" approach.

Participation Exemption

The exemptions from Australian income tax for foreign source branch profits and dividends were significantly widened in 2004 in a move to CIN or "ownership neutrality" for foreign business income of Australian resident companies. The legislative change followed recommendations resulting from a review by the Board of Taxation including representatives from the business sector, tax and legal professions and the government.[38]

The branch profits exemption applies to "active foreign branch income" derived through a permanent establishment in any country.[39] The provision excludes from tax "foreign income derived by a company, at a time when the company is a resident in carrying on a business, at or through a PE of the company [in the foreign jurisdiction] ...."[40] A parallel rule applies for foreign source non-portfolio (10 % interest or more) dividends.

An exclusion from capital gains taxation was also enacted for gains on the sale of a foreign non-portfolio shareholding interest by an Australian company.[41] The exemption is proportionate to the extent to which the assets of the foreign company (in which shares are sold) are used in an active business. Previously, capital gains of Australian residents on foreign share dealings were subject to tax in Australia, leading to an incentive for Australian companies to realize income from foreign subsidiaries as (tax-free) dividends rather than as capital gains.

For foreign source profits, dividends or capital gains made by the Australian corporation that are retained and reinvested overseas or in Australia, the participation exemption operates as a true territorial system that provides CIN. However, a different result follows once profits are distributed to Australian shareholders. If a dividend out of foreign taxed profit subject to the participation exemption is paid to the ultimate Australian resident shareholders, then no imputation credit is available and the shareholder pays their Australian marginal tax rate on the dividend (as explained above). The effect is twofold.

First, from a corporate tax policy perspective, the foreign source corporate profit is "double taxed," in the sense that both foreign tax has applied at the corporate level, and shareholder-level tax applies to the Australian shareholder.

---

[38] Australian Treasury, Board of Taxation, Review of International Taxation: A Report to the Treasurer (2003) Vol 1 (RITA Report).

[39] Section 23AH(1)(a) of ITAA36.

[40] Section 23AH(2) of ITAA36.

[41] Division 768 of ITAA97.

Second, from the perspective of international tax policy, the effect is that Australia provides the equivalent of a *deduction system* ("national neutrality") for foreign source income of Australian companies distributed to Australian shareholders. Treating the company as an agent of the domestic shareholder, after, say, $25 of foreign tax is deducted on foreign source profit of $100, the balance of $75 is included in the shareholder's income and subject to their individual marginal tax rate. This is the same as if the shareholder had derived $100 of foreign source business profit and was allowed to deduct the foreign tax in calculating their Australian taxable income. The Board of Taxation recommended that a partial or capped imputation credit be allowed in respect of foreign corporate tax. However, this recommendation was rejected by the government, mostly for revenue reasons (it refuses to relieve company tax paid to a foreign government). A small concession is allowed for trans-Tasman (with New Zealand) distributions of corporate profit.[42]

A different result follows if foreign taxed profit is distributed by an Australian company to a foreign shareholder. In this case, the Australian company operates as a conduit and Australia levies no further tax at either company or shareholder level. Thus, there is an incentive built into the corporate-international tax system for Australian companies to stream foreign profits to foreign shareholders, and Australian profits to Australian shareholders. There is also an incentive for Australian companies to raise foreign capital as debt not equity. A range of specific anti-avoidance rules are intended to limit both of these planning opportunities, with variable success.

Effects on Investment in Developing Countries

The participation exemption facilitates Australian business investment through branches or subsidiaries, into developing countries which have lower tax rates or specific incentives for foreign investment. It essentially supports source-based taxation and the exemption was introduced with the specific policy of enabling Australian companies to expand offshore. However, as indicated above, the effect is eliminated for profits distributed to the ultimate Australian shareholders. The participation exemption, together with amendments to the Australian CFC and conduit foreign income rules, was also seen as a way to facilitate inbound foreign investment into companies in Australia, including finance and regional headquarter companies.

Anti-deferral and Integrity Rules

Australia has CFC rules that tax some foreign low taxed income on an accrual basis but does not have specific rules to prohibit or discourage investment in tax havens. It relies on tax information exchange laws requiring full disclosure of investments

---

[42] Div 220 of ITAA97.

and its general income tax law that applies to tax most income of residents on a worldwide basis, apart from the participation exemption explained above. In its DTAs, Australia reserves the right to apply its General Anti-Avoidance Rule (GAAR) and to deny treaty benefits on the basis of abuse of the Treaty.[43] In a few DTAs, Australia adopts a limitation of benefits article, but this is generally because of the counterparty's tax policy (e.g., the US); however, such articles do not reflect general Australian tax policy. Australia recently strengthened its GAAR, in part as a response to successful cross-border corporate tax transactions.[44] The Government proposes to introduce a targeted "multinationals anti-avoidance law" for foreign multinationals supplying goods into Australia but without a permanent establishment; it has not yet been legislated.[45]

OECD Base Erosion and Profit Shifting (BEPS) Project

Australia was the President of the G20 in 2014 and is a strong supporter of the BEPS project.[46] The Australian Taxation Office and Treasury are actively working in the various OECD working parties on BEPS issues. Measures that are being targeted by the Australian Treasury include tax measures to neutralize cross-border arbitrage which leads to global non-taxation, through the use of hybrid entities, hybrid financial instruments (debt/equity) or double dips; transfer pricing; increased transparency and country by country reporting (starting 2016) of multinationals; anti-abuse rules and tightening rules to address the "digital economy," for example concerning permanent establishment and intangible property.

Transfer Pricing

Australia adopts the OECD "arm's length" pricing approach to transfer pricing. Australia has recently updated and strengthened its transfer pricing rules to bring them into line with updates to the OECD Model Guidelines that allow countries to apply the most suitable transfer pricing method including profit split methods.[47]

---

[43] Part IVA of ITAA36; International Tax Agreements Act 1986, s. 4.

[44] Part IVA of ITAA36, amended in Tax Laws Amendment (Countering Tax Avoidance and Multinational Profit Shifting) Act 2013.

[45] Australian Treasury, Tax Integrity: Multinational Anti-Avoidance Law, Exposure Draft http://www.treasury.gov.au/ConsultationsandReviews/Consultations/2015/Tax-Integrity-Law.

[46] Australian Treasury, *Risks to the Sustainability of Australia's Corporate Tax Base* Scoping Paper, July 2013, available from www.treasury.gov.au; OECD, *Addressing Base Erosion and Profit Shifting* (2013); see M Stewart, https://theconversation.com/the-g20-and-the-taxing-issue-of-making-big-business-pay-21466 for a short discussion.

[47] Division 820 of ITAA97. Changes to the legislation allowing application of updated OECD Transfer Pricing guidelines are retrospective, so can apply to past years of Australian companies; the considerable opposition to this reform of 2013 indicates that many corporate taxpayers consider this could lead to increased taxation.

Currently, key enforcement action by the ATO is directed at international profit shifting. It seeks to increase cooperation with tax authorities around the world, while the government has increased specific funding on this issue.

Thin Capitalization

Australia has rules to limit deduction of interest on cross-border debt.[48] Australia has recently legislated to reduce its fairly generous debt-to-assets ratio of 3:1 in its thin capitalization rules to a ratio of 2:1, which is in line with the basic rule in the US and other jurisdictions.[49] Thin capitalization is also a focus of the BEPS project but proposals to adopt a worldwide debt-to-assets test have not yet been accepted in Australia.

Domestic Accrual Rules for Offshore Income

Australia has a range of tax regimes that seek to tax offshore income or gains made in tax haven or low tax jurisdictions, or which are passive rather than active business income, on an accrual basis, to the Australian resident owner or controller of the offshore income.

Australia introduced Controlled Foreign Company (CFC) rules in 1990.[50] At the same time, Australia introduced a "transferor trust" regime applicable to Australian residents that have transferred value to foreign discretionary trusts. In 1993, Australia enacted a foreign investment fund (FIF) regime, which applied to portfolio (non-control) interests in foreign companies and fixed trusts, and additional rules for Australian beneficiaries of closely held fixed trusts.[51] However, these latter two regimes were repealed effective 2010.

The CFC rules apply to tax income in a foreign company controlled by Australian residents under a strict legal 50 % or broader de facto control test. If a company is a CFC, the relevant proportion of its income will be attributed to Australian companies with at least a 10 % interest in the CFC (determined directly and indirectly

---

[48] Division 820 of ITAA97.

[49] Joe Hockey, Treasurer, Media Release *Restoring integrity in the Australian tax system* (6 November 2013), http://jbh.ministers.treasury.gov.au/media-release/017-2013/.

[50] Part X of ITAA36. This section relies on the detailed examination of all Australia's specific anti-avoidance rules (SAARs) relating to cross-border investment by Lee Burns, Australia National Report, *The Taxation of Foreign Passive Income for Groups of Companies* International Fiscal Association Cahier vol. 98a (2013), 95.

[51] Former Part XI and ss 96A-96C of ITAA36.

through tiers of companies). If foreign income is attributed and taxed, then a subsequent dividend from the CFC is tax-free.[52]

Active business income is generally excluded from attribution, which applies mainly to "passive income" and "tainted income" such as rental or royalty income, or sales or services income where essentially no substantial value is added by the CFC, e.g., a "base" company located in a tax haven. The determination of passive and tainted income depends partly on the country where the CFC is resident. The CFC regime lists 7 "white list" countries as being comparably taxed to Australia: Canada, France, Germany, Japan, New Zealand, the UK and the US.[53] A broader definition of attributable income applies to all remaining unlisted countries. However, even for the seven listed countries, if income is derived by the CFC that benefits from tax concessions in that country or from a gap in the tax base, then it will potentially be taxable.[54]

The CEN policy behind the CFC regime as adopted in Australia allows, as a compromise, deferral of tax for foreign active business income. This is similar to the US approach in Subpart F. However, Australia's participation exemption for foreign business income or non-portfolio dividends from any country shifts Australia to a system of CIN. The CFC regime remains as an integrity rule, applicable mainly to passive income or to use of havens or concessional regimes to avoid taxation. As noted by Burns, income derived in a foreign controlled company will be either taxed under the CFC rules, or not taxed at all because it can be returned to the Australian parent company free of tax. This puts significant pressure on the "active/passive" divide in Australia's CFC rules and it is important to modernize the definition of "passive" income in those rules. This has not been done to date.[55]

Proposal for Foreign Accumulation Fund (FAF) Regime

Since the abolition of the FIF and transferor trust rules, the previous government proposed to enact a general tax integrity rule to address the accrual of income in foreign trusts or companies not covered by the CFC rules.[56] This would act as a SAAR or backstop to protect the worldwide tax system applied in Australia for individuals. However, this has not yet been enacted. Consequently, there are some gaps in Australia's taxation of offshore income regime, which may indirectly act as a subsidy for some kinds of offshore funds management activity.

---

[52] Section 23AI of ITAA36.

[53] Income Tax Regulations 1936, Schedule 10, Part I.

[54] So-called "eligible designated concession income;" e.g., New Zealand does not tax capital gains, so these are potentially taxable under the CFC rules.

[55] Burns, above n 52, p. 101.

[56] *Exposure Draft* Tax Laws Amendment (Foreign Source Income Deferral) Bill 2011: Foreign Accumulation Funds.

Global Tax Forum and International Tax Cooperation and Enforcement

Australia is an enthusiastic member of the Global Forum (it Chaired the Forum in 2011–2012). It has been suggested that "Australia is at the forefront of developments in exchange of information and cross-border cooperation between tax authorities."[57] Australia is also a signatory of the Multilateral Convention on Mutual Assistance in Tax Matters which came into force for Australia on 31 December 2012, and on which Australia is increasingly likely to rely for cross-border tax cooperation.

All of Australia's DTAs have an exchange of information (EOI) Article based in general on the OECD Model Tax Convention (Art. 26). The EOI article for treaties concluded prior to 2005 is generally based on the earlier 1977 Model, however some of these treaties have been since updated with Protocols that implement the newer Model Article 26. These updated DTAs and new DTAs have EOI articles based on the 2005/2008 OECD model, including DTAs with South Africa, India, Malaysia and Singapore. The new EOI Articles are broader in terms of taxes covered; apply a standard of "foreseeable relevance" to a tax assessment; provide that the providing country must use its own powers to obtain information it does not have; and override bank secrecy laws.

Australia is a signatory to 36 Tax Information Exchange Agreements (TIEAs).[58] Australia uses the indicators of lack of transparency and lack of effective information exchange to identify tax havens, and on this basis identified in 2012 Cyprus, Hong Kong, Luxembourg, Panama and the Seychelles among some others as tax havens.[59] Most TIEAs are with current (or former) tax havens, but some are with emerging or developing countries with which Australia does not have a DTA, such as Guatemala, Uruguay or Samoa. The TIEAs follow the Global Forum OECD Model in terms of information provided and overriding bank secrecy, although a limit of the TIEAs (and the Model) is that it requires information to be requested about a specific taxpayer. Australia and New Zealand have cooperated in negotiating TIEAs in the Pacific region.

Australia has actively supported the work of the Global Forum in peer review of member country tax laws. The Global Forum has conducted a Peer Review Report of Australia.[60] The report observed that "currently about 75 % of requests for EOI made to Australia come from just seven countries which account for more than half of foreign investment into Australia and receive more than two thirds of Australian

---

[57] Piotr Klank and Terry P Murphy, "Australia" National Report, *Exchange of Information and Cross-border Cooperation Between Tax Authorities* International Fiscal Association *Cahier* vol. 98b (2013), p. 87.

[58] See http://www.treasury.gov.au/Policy-Topics/Taxation/Tax-Treaties/HTML/TIEA .

[59] Australian Taxation Office, *Tax havens and tax administration* (2012).

[60] http://www.oecd.org/australia/peerreviewreportofaustralia-combinedphase1phase2.htm (November 2013).

foreign investment."[61] It found Australia, not surprisingly, to be generally compliant. However, Australia has some weaknesses in terms of information about trusts, nominee companies and their beneficial ownership and control.

The ATO collaborates with other revenue agencies through a range of groups and forums in addition to the OECD and Global Forum, including: The Coordinating Body for the Multilateral Convention; Study Group on Asian Tax Administration and Research (SGATAR); Joint International Tax Shelter Information Centre (JITSIC); and Commonwealth Association of Tax Administrators (CATA).

International Tax Enforcement and Amnesties

Since 2006, Australia has focused enforcement attention on use of tax havens mostly by Australian high wealth individuals. A major cross-agency cooperative project called *Project Wickenby* was established bringing together the ATO, federal police and prosecutors, Australian Securities and Insurance Commission and other agencies for data collection, audit, enforcement and prosecution.[62] In general, if taxpayers make early disclosures, a significant reduction in penalties can be obtained.

In respect of tax liability for unpaid past taxes, as part of Project Wickenby, a limited amnesty including protection from prosecution was provided for individual taxpayers who came forward and declared past years offshore income that had not previously been declared. It was proposed by Commissioner of Taxation Chris Jordan that a new amnesty may be created, enabling individuals not to pay tax on evaded income beyond four prior years, and to avoid prosecution, if they voluntarily declare offshore income.[63]

Public Reporting of Multinationals

In 2013, the government announced it would aim for "greater transparency of tax paid by large and multinational enterprises."[64] The announcement was welcomed by the Australian Council for International Development.[65] New legislative measures were enacted by the previous government, effective from the 2013 to 2014 tax year,

---

[61] OECD Global Forum, Peer Review, Executive Summary, p. 7.

[62] See   https://www.ato.gov.au/General/The-fight-against-tax-crime/In-detail/Tax-crime/Project-Wickenby/.

[63] See, e.g., Business Review Weekly *ATO Amnesty: Rich urged to come forward on stashed Swiss millions*(14November2013):http:// www. brw. com. au/p/ professions/ ato_amnesty_rich_urged_millions_izYWZC7h8nQnZ0gNHx QU0M.

[64] Assistant Treasurer David Bradbury (ALP), *Greater Transparency of Tax Paid by Large and Multinational Businesses* (PR No. 005, 4 February 2013).

[65] ACFID, *Focus on Multinational Transparency Welcome*, 4 February 2013, available http://www.acfid.asn.au/media/files/focus-on-multinational-tax-transparency-welcome/view.

that will require the Commissioner of Taxation to publish certain tax information of large corporate taxpayers with 'total income' of $100 million.[66]

The Commissioner is required to publish the company name, total reported income, taxable income and income tax payable from the company's (self-assessed) annual corporate tax return. The first year's information from the 2013 to 2014 fiscal year has now been published on the ATO website.

Tax Incentives for Investment in Australia

Australia has a range of tax concessions for investment in particular industries and activities in Australia. Generally, these tax concessions apply only to Australian resident companies. There is not scope in this report for a detailed discussion of Australian industry tax incentives; a recent estimate of revenue foregone from these incentives is in the Tax Expenditures Statement 2013.[67] The largest investment tax incentives include: research and development tax concessions; film tax concessions; concessional fuel tax excise for aviation; certain agricultural concessions; and building and heavy equipment accelerated depreciation.

Some concessions aim to make Australia more attractive as a regional headquarters or financial hub. The exclusion of foreign branch profits, combined with the conduit income regime, abolition of the foreign investment fund integrity rules, and tax concessions for venture capital limited partnerships and for venture capital and investment fund managers, all aim to support the financial investment business in Australia. These measures do not go as far as some policy recommendations which had aimed to promote Australia as a global financial services centre.[68] It is also not clear that they have been successful in increasing Australia's role in this regard.

Investment and Trade Agreements

Free Trade Agreements

Australia has become an enthusiastic proponent of bilateral or regional free trade agreements (FTAs) but most such agreements have only limited relevance for direct taxes including the income tax. Australia is a member of the General Agreement on Tariffs and Trade (GATT), World Trade Organisation (WTO), which provides some limits on the ability of members to provide tax incentives for trade or investment activities.

---

[66] New s 3C, 3D, 3E of Taxation Administration Act 1953, introduced by Tax Laws Amendment (2013 Measures No. 2) Act 2013 Schedule 5.

[67] For a summary, see Table 1.3, Large measured tax expenditures for 2013–2014, Australian Treasury Tax Expenditures Statement 2013, p. 12.

[68] Board of Taxation RITA Report, above n 40, pp. 5–6.

The GATT restricts members from imposing tariffs (taxes on imported goods) and quotas (on the quantity of imported goods).[69] Article I deals with general most-favoured-nation treatment, such that concessions made bilaterally must be extended to all other GATT nations. Article III deals with national treatment on internal taxation and regulation: "The products of the territory of any contracting party imported into the territory of any other contracting party shall not be subject, directly or indirectly, to internal taxes or other internal charges of any kind in excess of those applied, directly or indirectly, to like domestic products."[70] There are exceptions to these obligations, in Articles XVII (state trading enterprises), XVIII (Governmental Assistance to Economic Development), XX (general), XXI (security) and XXIV (regional/free trade agreements). However, as is made clear in Article XVIII, a contracting party the economy of which can only support low standards of living and is in the early stages of development, shall be free to deviate temporarily from the provisions of the other Articles of GATT.[71]

Other WTO multilateral agreements include the Agreement on Technical Barriers to Trade, Agreement on Trade Related Aspects of Investment Measures (TRIMS), and General Agreement on Trade in Services (GATS). These agreements generally provide for a basic most-favoured-nation obligation, but for example, GATS provides a general exception in Article XIV relating to the effective and equitable imposition and collection of direct taxes, and for DTAs. The WTO Subsidies Code prohibits certain types of incentives, whether tax or otherwise, regarding export industries.

Australia has FTAs currently in force with New Zealand, Singapore, Thailand, US, Chile, the Association of South East Asian Nations (ASEAN) (together with New Zealand), Malaysia, Korea and Japan. The countries covered by these FTAs account for 42 % of Australia's total trade.[72] The ASEAN-Australia-New Zealand FTA is now in force for all 12 signatories. It generally excludes direct tax measures from the scope of the agreement. Chapter 15 Article 3:1 states:

> Except as provided in this Article, nothing in this Agreement shall apply to taxation measures. This Agreement shall only grant rights or impose obligations with respect to taxation measures where:
>
> a. corresponding rights and obligations are also granted or imposed under the WTO Agreement;
> b. they are granted or imposed under Article 8 (Transfers) of Chapter 11 (Investment); or
> c. they are granted or imposed under Article 9 (Expropriation and Compensation) of Chapter 11 (Investment).

---

[69] WTO Legal Texts < http://wto.org/english/docs_e/legal_e/legal_e.htm>.

[70] *The General Agreement on Tariffs and Trade*, GATT Doc LT/UR/A-1A/1/GATT/2; 55 UNTS 187 (signed 30 October 1947) ('GATT 1947'), Article III:2 http://wto.org/english/docs_e/legal_e/gatt47_01_e.htm.

[71] GATT 1947, Article XVII:4.

[72] Department of Foreign Affairs and Trade, 'Australia's Trade Agreements' http://www.dfat.gov.au/fta/.

Under Chapter 11 Article 8 of the ASEAN-Australia-NZ FTA, a party may prevent or delay a transfer through the equitable, non-discriminatory, and good faith application of its laws and regulations relating to taxation.[73] However, under Chapter 11 Article 9, a Party shall not expropriate or nationalise a covered investment either directly or through measures equivalent to expropriation or nationalisation (expropriation), except for a public purpose; in a non-discriminatory manner; on payment of prompt, adequate, and effective compensation; and in accordance with due process of law.

The Australia-US FTA contains a provision dealing with taxation, essentially ensuring national treatment, non-discrimination and most-favoured-nation treatment for various tax measures.[74] Article 22.3(4) states generally that:

(a) Article 10.2 (National Treatment), Article 13.2 (National Treatment), and Article 13.5.1 (Cross-Border Trade) shall apply to taxation measures on income, capital gains, or on the taxable capital of corporations that relate to the purchase or consumption of particular services except that nothing in this sub-paragraph shall prevent a Party from conditioning the receipt or continued receipt of an advantage relating to the purchase or consumption of particular services on requirements to provide the service in its territory; and

(b) Articles 11.3, 11.4 (Most-Favoured-Nation Treatment), 10.2 (National Treatment), 10.3 (Most-Favoured-Nation Treatment), 13.2, 13.3 (Most-Favoured-Nation Treatment), and 13.5.1 shall apply to all taxation measures, other than those on income, capital gains, or on the taxable capital of corporations, taxes on estates, inheritances, gifts, and generation-skipping transfers;

The provision carves out existing DTAs and most existing tax measures of each country and has a special exception for tax advantages relating to pension or superannuation funds.

The China-Australia FTA is now in force effective 20 December 2015. Australia is currently engaged in bilateral economic partnership negotiations with India and Indonesia; and multilateral FTA negotiations on the Trans-Pacific Partnership Agreement (TPP), the Gulf Cooperation Council (GCC), the Pacific Trade and Economic Agreement (PACER Plus), and the Regional Comprehensive Economic Partnership Agreement (RCEP). In addition, Australia is jointly leading, with the United States and the European Union, negotiations on a services-only free trade agreement known as the Trade in Services Agreement (TiSA).[75] The 26 TiSA parties currently comprise: Australia, Canada, Chile, Chinese Taipei, Colombia, Costa Rica, European Union (representing its 28 Member States), Hong Kong, Iceland, Israel, Japan, Liechtenstein, Mauritius, Mexico, New Zealand, Norway, Pakistan, Panama, Paraguay, Peru, Korea, Switzerland, Taiwan, Turkey, the United States and Uruguay.

---

[73] AANZFTA Chapter 11 Article 8:3(f).

[74] Australia-US FTA, Article 22.3.

[75] Department of Foreign Affairs and Trade, 'Trade in Services Agreement (TiSA)' http://dfat.gov. au/trade/agreements/trade-in-services-agreement/pages/trade-in-services-agreement.aspx.

Investment Treaties

Australia has entered into 23 Bilateral Investment Treaties (BITs) which, together
with FTA investment chapters are providing the most specific treaty provisions
dealing with national treatment, 'fair and equitable treatment,' expropriation and
dispute resolution (arbitration) with foreign investors. Australia's position in general
accords with the general principle advanced by the OECD that foreign investment
should be treated in the same way as domestic investment.[76] Treaties may apply pre-
or post-establishment of investment. For example, the Singapore-Australia FTA in
force on 28 July 2003, applies to both phases (Chapter 8: Investment, article 2):
'investments made, in the process of being made, or sought to be made'.

Australia's current BITs are listed in the table below:[77]

Partner	Date of entry into force
Argentina	11-Jan-97
China	11-Jul-88
Czech Republic	29-Jun-94
Egypt	5-Sep-02
Hong Kong	15-Oct-93
Hungary	10-May-92
India	4-May-00
Indonesia	29-Jul-93
Laos	8-Apr-95
Lithuania	10-May-02
Mexico	21-Jul-07
Pakistan	14-Oct-98
Papua New Guinea	20-Oct-91
Peru	2-Feb-97
Philippines	8-Dec-95
Poland	27-Mar-92
Romania	22-Apr-94
Sri Lanka	14-Mar-07
Turkey	29-Jun-09
Uruguay	12-Dec-02
Vietnam	11-Sep-91

---

[76] *OECD Code of Liberalisation of Capital Movements of 1961* and the *OECD Declaration on International Investment and Multinational Enterprises of 1976.*

[77] *Australia's bilateral investment treaties concluded by Australia*, at 24 August 2015, http://dfat. gov.au/trade/topics/investment/Pages/australias-bilateral-investment-treaties.aspx.

Some BITs contain specific provisions either relating to or excluding relevance of tax laws. For example, the Australia-Hong Kong BIT Article 7 provides that MFN and national treatment rules do not apply so as to extend any special treatment under international agreements or arrangements "relating wholly or mainly to taxation."[78] A similar provision applies in the Australia-Turkey BIT.

---

[78] Australia-HK BIT, Article 7(b) 'Exceptions.'

Chapter 3
Recent Trends in Belgium's International Tax Policy

Edoardo Traversa and Gaëtan Zeyen

Abstract La Belgique est une petite économie ouverte orientée vers les échanges internationaux. Ceci se reflète dans son système fiscal, qui se caractérise par de nombreuses conventions internationales, des règles d'origine européenne et par les dispositions de droit interne spécifiques pour les situations transfrontières. Traditionnellement, la lutte contre l'évasion fiscale internationale et pour la transparence n'étaient pas des objectifs prioritaires de la politique fiscale de la Belgique. Ceci est toutefois en train de changer sous la pression d'organismes internationaux comme l'OCDE et l'Union Européenne et pourrait avoir des répercussions négatives sur les relations avec les pays en voie de développement.

Synopsis Belgian residents are taxed on a worldwide basis. A credit for taxes imposed by another country on the same income is allowed as a credit against the Belgium tax liability. In some cases, however, certain specified items of foreign source income are excluded from Belgian tax.

For example, in certain cases, a corporation is eligible for a participation exemption which allows it to exclude 95% of a dividend received from another corporation (organized in Belgium, an EU member state, or other states) if it owns at least 10% of the stock of the distributing corporation. The participation exemption is only available if the payor is subject to a corporate income tax (the Belgium corporate tax or an analogous foreign tax) with a base that is not more favorable than the one prescribed under Belgian law. While existence of a nominal tax rate less than 15% leads to a presumption of a "more favorable tax regime," EU member states, even if imposing a tax rate below 15%, are presumed to meet the minimum-level-of-tax requirement. This requirement has the effect of discouraging investment in so-called tax havens. Some exceptions apply, including, for instance, qualification of the

E. Traversa (✉)
Catholic University of Louvain, Brussels, Belgium
e-mail: edoardo.traversa@uclouvain.be

G. Zeyen
University of Liège, Brussels, Belgium
e-mail: gzeyen@zeyenlawoffice.com

© Springer International Publishing Switzerland 2017   43
K.B. Brown (ed.), *Taxation and Development - A Comparative Study*,
Ius Comparatum - Global Studies in Comparative Law 21,
DOI 10.1007/978-3-319-42157-5_3

Tunisian tax regime even though it provides a ten-year tax holiday on profits from exports. Notably, Belgium's former colony, Burundi, is presumed to have a more favorable tax regime.

Additional anti-tax haven initiatives include a requirement to disclose large payments to persons in no- or low-tax jurisdictions or in jurisdictions not in substantial compliance with the international standard for exchange of information set by the OECD Global Forum and a requirement that individuals disclose ownership in a corporation, partnership, or other non-resident entity not subject to Belgian income tax or subject to a more favorable tax regime or appearing on a special list published by the tax authorities. The list currently includes entities resident in Caribbean countries, among others. A "Cayman tax," effective in 2016, will allow the tax administration to attribute to Belgian residents tax revenue derived by foreign juridical entities (trusts or companies subject to a tax rate below 15%) by associating it with the creator of the enterprise, his heirs, third-party beneficiaries, or shareholders who are Belgian residents.

Internal Belgian law may discourage transaction of business with nonresidents, including those resident in developing countries. One limits deductions to Belgian residents for payments of interest, royalties, and other mobile income, including professional expenses, to resident subject to tax in a regime notably more advantageous than that in Belgium (more favorable regime), with the exception of EU members. The other, an anti-abuse initiative, allows the Belgian tax authority to ignore transactions (sales, loans, intellectual property transfers, capital contributions, etc.) between Belgian taxpayers and those resident in more favorable regimes unless a legitimate business purpose is demonstrated.

Although there is no notion of "harmful tax regime" in Belgium law, there is targeting of certain tax regimes with more favorable or more advantageous tax regimes than in Belgium. As demonstrated above, certain Belgian tax advantages or benefits may be denied for transactions with entities resident in regimes view to be "unfairly competing for Belgian revenue or investment."

Because of its membership in the European Union, Belgium is prohibited from favoring certain investments. The prohibitions on state aid, as well as the EU Code of Conduct, have been interpreted to restrict tax-competitive measures among the member states. As a result, Belgium was forced to abandon the favorable tax regime it had provided for its Centers of Coordination.

Belgium is party to a large number of tax treaties. This in keeping with its goal to strengthen transparency and exchange of information in tax matters. It has also signed on to a number of agreements designed to reinforce administrative cooperation in tax matters. It has entered into Tax Information Exchange Agreements (TIEAs) with a number of countries, including those considered tax havens, such as Andorra, the Bahamas, Belize, Liechtenstein, Saint Kitts and Nevis, and the Grenadines.

Tax incentives for investment in emerging or developing countries have been eliminated. In the past, tax sparing agreements were contained in treaties with Brazil, India, China, Malaysia, Singapore, and others. Internal law also provided for a *Quotité Forfaitaire d'Impôt Etranger* (Q.F.I.E.), or an imputed tax on foreign source income tax, which often had the effect of tax sparing, but this provision has also been repealed.

Belgian's interest in supporting emerging, developing, or transitional countries has been demonstrated in treaty negotiations. It has acceded to requests by these countries (e.g., Brazil and India) to allow them to tax payments to Belgian residents for technical assistance or services at their source even when they are not attributable to a permanent establishment or services performed within the jurisdiction.

Belgium has adopted incentives to attract foreign investment. The participation exemption regime described in 1.1 excludes from taxation 95% of dividends received by a Belgium parent from an eligible foreign subsidiary. There is a special deduction of notional interest on risk capital. In addition, there are incentives for income from patents (a type of patent box) that allows businesses to deduct 80% of royalty income from the tax base and a special tax shelter regime for investments in cinematography and audiovisual industries. There are numerous exceptions from the withholding tax for dividends, royalties, and interest payments for non-resident investors. Finally, there are special incentives for research and development.

The corporate tax rate is 33%, plus an additional 3% consisting of a complementary emergency contribution, which brings the rate to 33.99%. The rates are reduced for small corporations. A deduction for at-risk capital, a deduction for so-called notional interest is available for all corporations whether resident or non-resident.

Belgium is party to multilateral investment agreements that either prevent discrimination in fiscal matters or provide tax immunity (particularly in the case of international organizations or banks). It is also signatory to numerous bilateral investment treaties which do not relate to tax matters.

Le système fiscal international

Les résidents fiscaux belges sont soumis à l'impôt sur leurs revenus mondiaux, c'est-à-dire non seulement sur les revenus d'origine belge visés au Code des Impôts sur les Revenus 1992 (ci-après en abrégé 'CIR/92'), mais aussi sur les revenus produits ou recueillis à l'étranger.[1] En droit fiscal belge, le principe de territorialité revoie donc davantage à l'idée que l'exercice des compétences fiscales des autorités belges est limité au territoire national.[2] Ceci ne fait pas obstacle a ce que la Belgique soit « *souverainement libre de définir les critères de rattachement qui* lui *conviennent* »,[3] ce qui peut facilement engendrer des situations de double (ou multiple) imposition.

---

[1] Cf. Article 5 CIR/92.

[2] Cour d'appel de Bruxelles, arrêt du 04 juin 1974 (arrêt dit 'Prince de Ligne'), in J.D.F., 1975, p.82 et confirmé par Cour d'appel de Bruxelles, arrêt du 07 novembre 2002, in www.fiscalnet.be

[3] Prof. E. TRAVERSA et B. VINTRAS, « La prévention de la double imposition des revenus dans les conventions bilatérales : enjeux, modalités et limites », in Fiscalité internationale en Belgique – Tendances récentes, Bruxelles, Larcier, 2013, p. 282.

En l'absence d'une convention préventive de double imposition, une exonération forfaitaire – à concurrence de 50 % – est accordée à l'impôt des personnes physiques sur (i) les revenus de biens immobiliers sis à l'étranger, (ii) les revenus professionnels (à condition que lesdits revenus aient été « réalisés et imposés à l'étranger »), à l'exclusion des revenus de capitaux et biens mobiliers que le contribuable a affectés à l'exercice de son activité professionnelle dans les établissements dont il dispose en Belgique et (iii) certains revenus divers (tels que par exemple les prix, subsides, rentes alimentaires à charge de non-habitants du Royaume de Belgique).[4]

Dans les conventions préventives de la double imposition,[5] la Belgique élimine généralement la double imposition des revenus autres que les dividendes, intérêts et redevances, en exonérant avec réserve de progressivité les revenus imposables dans l'Etat de la source. Ainsi, les revenus imposables dans l'Etat de la source (conformément à la convention préventive de la double imposition applicable) seront d'abord intégrés dans la base imposable en Belgique, puis exonérés à concurrence (c'est-à-dire proportionnellement) d'un montant calculé selon les règles prévues par la législation fiscale belge. Ce mécanisme est consacré à l'article 155 du CIR/92, dont l'application suppose l'existence d'une convention préventive de la double imposition entre les Etats concernés.

En pratique, pour pouvoir bénéficier de l'exonération, le contribuable concerné doit adresser à l'Administration fiscale belge une demande motivée (par le biais d'une annexe à sa déclaration) et prouver qu'il répond bien aux conditions pour bénéficier de cette exonération. Jusqu'il y a peu, l'exonération était accordée 'automatiquement'. Toutefois, dans une circulaire du 6 avril 2010,[6] l'Administration fiscale belge remet en question le caractère « automatique » de cette exonération et précise les principes (notamment au niveau de la charge de la preuve) qui, selon elle, doivent présider à l'octroi (ou non) de l'exemption accordée par les conventions préventives de la double imposition.

En ce qui concerne les dividendes, la Belgique applique un système assimilable à une exemption à 95 % pour certaines participations substantielles : le dividende est dans un premier temps inclus dans le bénéfice imposable de la société bénéficiaire (i.e., la société mère), puis déduit de la base imposable à concurrence de 95 %, au titre de « revenus définitivement taxés » (en abrégé, 'R.D.T.'). Le système appliqué par la Belgique, bien que constituant une transposition au niveau belge de la

---

[4] Article 156 du Code des impôts sur les revenus (ci-après CIR).

[5] Au 1 janvier 2014, la Belgique avait conclu des conventions préventives de la double imposition avec environ 100 pays, dont 90 étaient en vigueur. La liste et le texte des conventions sont disponibles sur http://ccff02.minfin.fgov.be/KMWeb/document.do?method=view&id=27c5818d-7978-4749-a1ee-4f4816d3306d#findHighlighted.

[6] Circulaire AAF n°4/2010 du 06 avril 2010 (addendum à la circulaire AFER n°Ci.R9.Div./577.956 du 11 mai 2006).

directive mère-filiale du 23 juillet 1990,[7] aujourd'hui la directive 2011/96/UE[8] est d'applicable générale. Il ne fait donc en principe pas de distinction selon que le dividende provient d'une société belge, d'une société d'un autre Etat membre de l'Union européenne ou d'une société d'un Etat tiers.

Pour bénéficier de l'exemption à concurrence de 95 %, il faut remplir et respecter non seulement des conditions dites de 'participation,' mais également des conditions dites de 'taxation'. Ainsi, s'agissant d'abord des conditions dites de 'participation', il faut (i) qu'à la date d'attribution ou de mise en paiement des dividendes, la société 'bénéficiaire' (par hypothèse, une société 'résidente') détienne dans le capital de la société 'distributrice' (par hypothèse, une société 'étrangère') une participation de 10 % au moins ou une participation pour un montant minimum de € (EUR) 2.500.000,00.- (depuis le 1er janvier 2010)[9] et (ii) une détention en pleine propriété des actions, de manière ininterrompue, pendant une période d'au moins un an[10] (la période de détention doit s'apprécier au moment de la cession des titres). Ensuite, s'agissant des conditions dites de 'taxation',[11] et pour pouvoir bénéficier de l'exemption à concurrence de 95 %, il faut en premier lieu que la société 'distributrice' étrangère soit assujettie à l'Impôt des Sociétés ou à un impôt étranger analogue à l'Impôt des Sociétés et que ses dispositions du droit commun en matière d'impôts ne soient pas notablement plus avantageuses qu'en Belgique (ce sera légalement présumé être le cas, lorsque le taux nominal de droit commun de l'impôt sur les bénéfices de la société est inférieur à 15 %[12] ou lorsque la société 'distributrice' relève d'un des pays figurant sur la liste établie par le législateur belge).[13] Il convient de noter qu'outre cette première condition de taxation, les dividendes distribués doivent également satisfaire à d'autres conditions spécifiques de taxation, conçues comme des 'tests anti-abus'.[14] Enfin, il convient de remarquer que les

---

[7] Directive du Conseil n° 90/435/CEE, concernant le régime fiscal commun applicable aux sociétés mères et filiales d'Etats membres différents, in J.O. L., 255/6 du 20 août 1990, et modifiée par la directive du 22 décembre 2003 (Directive du Conseil n° 2003/123, in J.O. L. du 31 janvier 2004).

[8] Directive 2011/96/UE du Conseil du 30 novembre 2011 concernant le régime fiscal commun applicable aux sociétés mères et filiales d'États membres différents, JO L 345, 29 décembre 2011, p. 8–16.

[9] Cf. Article 202, §2, 1° CIR/92.

[10] Cf. Article 202, §2, 2° CIR/92.

[11] Cf. Article 203, §1, 1° CIR/92.

[12] Cf. Article 203, §1, alinéa 3 CIR/92.

[13] Cf. Article 73/4quater AR/CIR92. Cette liste comprend environ 50 pays : 1. Afghanistan, 2. Aldernay, 3. Belize, 4. Bosnie-Herzégovine, 5. Burundi, 6. Cap Vert, 7. République Centrafricaine, 8. Comores, 9. Iles Cook, 10. Cuba, 11. Dominique, 12. Guinée équatoriale, 13. …, 14. Gibraltar, 15. Grenade, 16. Guernesey, 17. Guinée-Bissau, 18. Haïti, 19. Herm, 20. Iran, 21. Irak, 22. Jersey, 23. Kiribati, 24. Corée du Nord, 25. Laos, 26. Liberia, 27. Liechtenstein, 28. Macao, 29. Maldives, 30. Ile de Man, 31. Iles Marshall, 32. Mayotte, 33. Fédération de Micronésie, 34. Monaco, 35. Montserrat, 36. Namibie, 37. Niue, 38. Oman, 39. Panama, 40. Saint Christopher et Nevis, 41. Sainte-Lucie, 42. Saint-Pierre-et-Miquelon, 43. Saint-Vincent-et-les-Grenadines, 44. Samoa, 45. Samoa américaines; 46. …; 47. Sao Tomé et Principe; 48. Seychelles; 49. Somalie; 50. Tuvalu; 51. Ouzbékistan; 52. Iles Vierges britanniques, 53. Iles Vierges américaines.

[14] Cf. Article 203, §1, alinéa 1, 2° à 5° CIR/92.

dividendes distribués par des sociétés établies dans un Etat membre de l'Union européenne sont présumées satisfaire à cette condition dite 'de taxation'.[15] Lorsque ces conditions ne sont pas remplies, le dividende est taxé comme un bénéfice ordinaire, sans aucun remède à la double imposition économique.

En cette matière, il convient de noter que le Service des Décisions Anticipées (en abrégé, 'S.D.A.'), service autonome à l'intérieur de l'administration fiscale belge chargé d'octroyer des rulings, a considéré que des dividendes distribués par une société soumise au régime fiscal de droit commun de Curaçao entrent en ligne de compte pour l'application du régime fiscal des 'R.D.T.'.[16] De même, le 'S.D.A.' a considéré que des dividendes distribués par une filiale tunisienne à une société belge ne pouvaient être exclus de l'application du régime fiscal des 'R.D.T.,' et ce alors même que le régime fiscal tunisien prévoit une exonération temporaire (dix ans) d'impôt sur les bénéfices réalisés provenant de l'exportation de biens.[17]

Les mesures fiscales destinées à décourager les investissements dans des paradis fiscaux

En plus de la condition de taxation imposée pour bénéficier de l'exemption à 95 % des dividendes reçus de sociétés étrangères (voir ci-dessus), le législateur belge a pris des initiatives assez récentes visant à décourager l'investissement dans certaines juridictions spécifiques. Ainsi, une obligation de déclaration pour les paiements à des paradis fiscaux a été instaurée par la Loi-programme du 23 décembre 2009.[18] Depuis 1er janvier 2010, les sociétés résidentes (contribuables soumis à l'Impôt des Sociétés) ou non-résidentes (soumises à l'Impôt belge des Non-Résidents/Sociétés) doivent déclarer les paiements de plus de 100.000€ effectués directement ou indirectement, à des personnes établies dans des Etats qui, au terme d'un examen approfondi par le Forum mondial de l'OCDE sur la transparence et l'échange d'informations n'ont pas « mis substantiellement et effectivement en Œuvre » le standard de l'OCDE d'échange d'informations ou relèvent de la catégorie des « *Etats à fiscalité inexistante ou peu élevée* ».[19] C'est le cas si un bénéficiaire est établi dans un état où le taux nominal de l'Impôt des Sociétés est inférieur à 10 %. A titre de sanction, les paiements non déclarés ne sont pas déductibles.[20] En

---

[15] Cf. Article 203,§1er, alinéa 3.

[16] Cf. Décision anticipée n°2011.426 du 22 novembre 2011. La décision indique que le régime du droit commun à Curaçao prévoit un Impôt des Sociétés au tarif nominal de 34, 5 %, mais que la société 'bénéficiaire' pourra profiter d'un '*tax holiday*' destiné à favoriser le développement économique, les investissements et l'emploi à Curaçao.

[17] Cf. Décisions anticipées n°2012.146 du 5 juin 2012 ('tax holiday') et n°2012.273 du 28 août 2012 ('tax holiday').

[18] Cf. Article 307, §1, alinéa 3 CIR/92.

[19] Cf. Article 307, §1, alinéa 6 CIR/92.

[20] Cf. Article 198, alinéa 1, 10° CIR/92.

revanche, les paiements déclarés ne seront toutefois admis en déduction qu'à la condition que le contribuable puisse justifier qu'il s'agit *"d'opérations réelles et sincères"* avec des *"personnes autres que des constructions artificielles"*. Une liste des Etats qualifiés d'Etats « *à fiscalité inexistante ou peu élevée* », qui comprend a ce jour 30 juridictions,[21] est fixée par Arrêté Royal et en principe mise à jour tous les deux ans.

Par ailleurs, les contribuables soumis à l'Impôt des Personnes Physiques (I.P.P.) doivent déclarer, à partir de l'exercice d'imposition 2014, l'existence d'une « *construction juridique* »[22]. Cette notion est définie à l'article 2, §1er, 13°, b) du CIR/92, et vise – notamment – une 'entité' disposant ou non de la personnalité juridique (sous forme de société, d'association ou d'une autre personne morale), qui a la qualité de non-résident (au regard du droit belge) et qui n'est pas soumise à un impôt sur les revenus ou y est soumise à un 'régime de taxation notablement plus avantageux' que celui auquel ces revenus sont soumis en Belgique. Un Arrêté Royal du 19 mars 2014 a d'ores et déjà déterminé une liste de 69 'formes juridiques', dont la déclaration est obligatoire.[23] A titre d'exemple, on y retrouve la Limited Liability Company de l'Etat de Delaware (Etats-Unis), la fondation suisse, l'International Business Company des Bahamas et de nombreux autres Etats des Caraïbes ou encore la Stiftung et l'Anstalt du Liechtenstein. Cette liste est susceptible d'évoluer. Il convient de noter que la loi ne prévoit aucune sanction spécifique en cas de non-respect de cette obligation nouvelle de déclaration. Toutefois, en vertu des règles générales en matière de 'sanctions' inscrites au CIR/92 (cf. articles 444 et suivants du CIR/92), l'absence de déclaration pourra être sanctionnée par une amende administrative, voire le cas échéant par des accroissements d'impôts.

Enfin, depuis 2016, est en vigueur une mesure, appelée « taxe de transparence » ou plus familièrement « taxe Caïman ». Celle-ci permet à l'administration fiscale de taxer les revenus perçus par ces constructions juridiques étrangères (trusts ou sociétés soumises à un taux de 15 %) dans le chef du fondateur, de ses héritiers, des tiers bénéficiaires ou des actionnaires résidents belges. Une telle mesure découragera très probablement le recours à des paradis fiscaux à l'avenir.

Par ailleurs, outre ces interventions législatives récentes, il convient de signaler deux dispositions de droit interne belge, qui –sans viser spécifiquement certaines juridictions- peuvent avoir pour effet de dissuader un contribuable belge de 'contracter' avec un non-résident. La première de ces deux dispositions est l'article 54 du CIR/92,[24] qui permet à l'administration fiscale belge de refuser la déduction, à

---

[21] Il s'agit de 1. Abu Dhabi ; 2. Ajman ; 3. Andorre ; 4. Anguilla ; 5. Bahamas ; 6. Bahreïn ; 7. Bermudes ; 8. Iles Vierges britanniques ; 9. Iles Cayman ; 10. Dubaï ; 11. Fujairah ; 12. Guernesey ; 13. Jersey ; 14. Jéthou ; 15. Maldives ; 16. Ile de Man ; 17. Micronésie (Fédération de) ; 18. Moldavie ; 19. Monaco ; 20. Monténégro ; 21. Nauru ; 22. Palau ; 23. Ras al Khaimah ; 24. Saint-Barthélemy ; 25. Sercq, 26. Sharjah, 27. Iles Turks-et-Caicos, 28. Umm al Quwain, 29. Vanuatu, 30. Wallis-et-Futuna. Voir art. 179 AR/CIR 92.

[22] Loi-programme du 27 décembre 2012 (article 36). Cf. Article 307, §1 CIR/92.

[23] AR d'exécution de l'article 2, §1er, 13°, b du CIR/92. du 19 mars 2014, M.B. ; 2 avril 2014.

[24] Sur cette disposition particulière : voir E. CECI, « Le manque de clarté et de prévisibilité du législateur à nouveau pointé du doigt par la CJUE », in Actualités fiscales, 2012, n°44, pp.1 – 4;

titre de 'frais professionnels', de certains paiements de revenus mobiliers (des intérêts et redevances, principalement) lorsque ceux-ci sont payés (ou attribués) à un
non-résident (plus précisément, un contribuable visé à l'article 227 du CIR/92) qui
soit n'est pas soumis à un impôt sur les revenus, soit bénéficie d'un « *régime de
taxation notablement plus avantageux que celui auquel ces revenus sont soumis en
Belgique* ». L'article 54 du CIR/92 peut avoir un effet dissuasif, dans la mesure où
il repose sur une présomption – certes réfragable[25] – de non-déduction de certains
frais professionnels (alors que la déduction des 'frais professionnels' est en principe
admise sur base de l'article 49 du CIR/92, moyennant le respect des conditions
légales), ce qui peut inciter un contribuable belge à préférer contracter avec un 'résident', afin de ne pas tomber précisément dans le champ d'application de l'article 54
du CIR/92.[26] Cette disposition a été considérée incompatible avec la libre prestation
de services par la Cour de justice de l'Union européenne, dans la mesure où elle
s'applique entre Etats membres de l'UE.[27] La Cour a en effet considéré que « une
telle règle ne permet pas de déterminer au préalable et avec la précision suffisante le
champ d'application de celle-ci et laisse subsister des incertitudes quant à son appli-
cabilité » (para. 57).

La deuxième de ces dispositions, analysée comme une disposition 'anti-abus'[28]
dite 'préventive' (et n'ayant pas encore donné lieu à un *véritable* contrôle juridic-
tionnel), est l'article 344, §2 du CIR/92, lequel dispose que:

> « *N'est pas non plus opposable à l'Administration des contributions directes, la vente, le
> cession ou l'apport d'actions, d'obligations, de créances ou d'autres titres constitutifs
> d'emprunts, de brevets d'invention, de procédés de fabrication, de marques de fabrique ou
> de commerce, ou de tous autres droits analogues ou de sommes d'argent, à un contribuable
> visé à l'article 227, qui, en vertu des dispositions de la législation du pays où il est établi
> n'y est pas soumis à un impôt sur les revenus ou y est soumis, du chef des revenus produits
> par les biens et droits aliénés, à un régime de taxation notablement plus avantageux que
> celui auquel les revenus de l'espèce sont soumis en Belgique, à moins que le contribuable
> ne prouve soit que l'opération répond à des besoins légitimes de caractère financier ou
> économique, soit qu'il à reçu pour l'opération une contrevaleur réelle produisant un*

---

[25] Cette présomption peut être renversée si le contribuable arrive à établir « *par toutes voies de droit* »
que de tels paiements répondent à des « *opérations réelles et sincères* » et qu'ils ne « *dépassent pas
les limites normales* ». Selon une partie de la doctrine (cf. A. NOLLET, « L'article 344, §2 du
CIR/92 : essai de contrôle de 'constitutionnalité' et de 'conventionnalité' d'une disposition fiscale
belge 'anti-abus' », in Revue Générale du Contentieux Fiscal (R.G.C.F.), 2011/6 (novembre–
décembre), p.494), « *la seule preuve de la 'réalité juridique' des opérations suspectées ne suffirait
point ; celles-ci seraient aussi examinées en termes de 'nécessite' et de 'normalité' au plan
économique.* »

[26] Il convient de noter que cette disposition a été 'condamnée' par la C.J.U.E. comme portant
atteinte (i) au principe de libre circulation des services et (ii) aux exigences de sécurité juridique:
cf. C.J.U.E., 5 juillet 2012, Société d'investissement pour l'agriculture tropicale SA (« SIAT ») c.
Etat belge, C-318/10 (www.curia.europa.eu).

[27] C.J.U.E., 5 juillet 2012, C-318/10, SIAT.

[28] Pour un aperçu des différentes mesures 'anti-abus' belges: voir M. BOURGEOIS et
E. TRAVERSA, « Tax Treaties and Tax Avoidance: application of anti-avoidance provisions –
Belgian Report », in Cahiers de Droit Fiscal International (I.F.A.), Rotterdam, Kluwer, 2010, vol.
95a, pp.127–148.

montant de revenus soumis effectivement en Belgique à une charge fiscale normale par rapport à celle qui aurait subsisté si cette opération n'avait pas eu lieu.»

L'objectif de cette disposition est de lutter contre les comportements d' «*évasion fiscale*», qui consistent « *à transférer la propriété d'avoirs mobiliers (aisément délocalisables et productifs de revenus) à destination de pays étrangers où les revenus découlant de ces biens seront soumis à un régime beaucoup plus favorable qu'en Belgique.*»[29] Pour ce faire, comme le souligne A. NOLLET, cette disposition « *combine dans une seule disposition plusieurs techniques législatives qui sont symptomatiques du fonctionnement des mesures anti-abus rencontrées dans le CIR/92: présomption réfragable d'évasion fiscale, fiction d'inopposabilité d'actes juridiques non simulés, stigmatisation de régimes fiscaux étrangers, réattribution de revenus entre différents contribuables.*».[30] Pour des raisons identiques à celles invoquées supra au sujet de l'article 54 CIR, il apparait qu'une telle disposition ne puisse être appliquée dans les relations avec d'autres Etats membres de l'Union européenne.

Les mesures fiscales destinées à décourager les investissements dans les régimes fiscaux dommageables

Le droit fiscal belge ne connaît pas la notion en tant que telle de régime fiscal 'dommageable' (« *harmful tax regime* »). Toutefois, parallèlement à celle d'« *Etat à fiscalité inexistante ou peu élevée* » (cf. ci-dessus), le droit fiscal belge connaît également la notion de régime fiscal « *notablement plus avantageux* ». Cette dernière terminologie est utilisée par exemples en relation (i) avec l'obligation de déclaration de l'existence d'une « *construction juridique* » (cf. ci-dessus), (ii) avec le régime fiscal des « *revenus définitivement taxés* » ('R.D.T.') décrit ci-dessus ou (iii) avec certaines dispositions 'anti-abus' (cf. article 344, §2 du CIR/92 : voir ci-dessus 1. et 2.).

Par ailleurs, il convient de noter que même en présence d'une convention préventive de la double imposition certains investissements dans des Etats à fiscalité (relativement) favorable peuvent être découragés par l'existence de conditions de taxation prévues pour l'octroi de l'exonération conventionnelle. Dans certaines conventions conclues par la Belgique, il est prévu que l'exemption ne s'applique que s'il est « *imposé* » (c'est par exemple le cas de la Convention conclue avec le Maroc) ou « *effectivement imposé* »[31] (c'est par exemples le cas des Conventions conclues

---

[29] A. NOLLET, op.cit (note 25)., p. 505.

[30] A. NOLLET, op.cit (note 25)., p. 505.

[31] Sur ces différentes notions: voir E. TRAVERSA et B. VINTRAS, « La prévention de la double imposition des revenus dans les conventions bilatérales: enjeux, modalités et limites », in *Fiscalité internationale en Belgique*, Bruxelles, Larcier, 2013, pp.294–304.

respectivement avec Hong Kong[32] ou le Rwanda[33]) dans l'Etat de la source,[34] ce qui généralement exclut le cas où le revenu bénéfice d'un régime favorable particulier..

Les accords régionaux/ou conventions internationales, des codes de conduite régulant la concurrence déloyale

La Belgique est l'un des membres fondateurs de l'Union européenne. En cette qualité, il est lié non seulement par le droit européen dit 'primaire' (et en particulier le Traité sur l'Union européenne et le Traité sur le Fonctionnement de l'Union européenne), mais aussi par le droit communautaire dit 'dérivé' (et en particulier, les règlements, directives, décisions, avis et recommandations).

Le Traité sur le Fonctionnement de l'Union européenne (en abrégé, 'T.F.U.E.') consacre -notamment- le principe de non-discrimination (sur base de la nationalité)[35] et comporte des règles spécifiques en matière de libre circulation, notamment des capitaux et paiements (cf. articles 63 à 66 T.F.U.E.) et (ii) d'aides d'Etats (cf. articles 107 à 109 T.F.U.E.).

En ce qui concerne le principe de la libre circulation des capitaux, il convient de noter qu'il s'applique sous certaines conditions également aux relations avec pays tiers,[36] en vertu duquel les Etats membres ne peuvent notamment via des mesures

---

[32] Cf. Point 7 (a) du Protocole additionnel de l'accord fiscal conclu avec Hong Kong, qui dispose que « (…) *les éléments de revenu qu'un résident de la Belgique reçoit ne sont pas considérés comme imposés dans la Région administrative spéciale de Hong Kong lorsque ces éléments de revenu ne sont pas compris dans la base sur laquelle l'impôt de la Région administrative spéciale de Hong Kong est dû. En conséquence, les éléments de revenu qui sont considérés comme non imposables par la législation en vigueur dans la Région administrative spéciale de Hong Kong, ou qui sont exemptés de l'impôt de la Région administrative spéciale de Hong Kong par cette même législation, ne sont pas considérés comme imposés.* » Comme le soulignent TRAVERSA et VINTRAS (op.cit., p.301), « *certaines conventions fiscales signées par la Belgique prévoient ainsi une définition particulière du terme 'imposé', qui acquiert alors le sens de 'effectivement imposé'* ».

[33] Le Protocole précise tant pour l'article 21 que pour l'article 23 qu' « *un revenu est imposé lorsqu'il est effectivement compris dans la base imposable sur laquelle l'impôt est calculé. Par conséquent, un revenu n'est pas imposé lorsque, bien qu'étant soumis au régime fiscal normalement applicable à ce revenu, il est soit non imposable, soit exempté d'impôt.* » Cette limite est renforcée par la possibilité prévue par la Convention pour la Belgique de refuser l'exemption pour les bénéfices de source rwandaise imposés à un taux inférieur à 15 % (cf. TRAVERSA et VINTRAS, op.cit., p.302).

[34] Circulaire AAF n°4/2010 du 06 avril 2010 (addendum à la circulaire AFER n°Ci.R9.Div./577.956 du 11 mai 2006).

[35] Cf. Article 18 T.F.U.E.

[36] L'article 63, alinéa 1 T.F.U.E. dispose : « *Dans le cadre des dispositions du présent chapitre, toutes les restrictions aux mouvements de capitaux entre les Etats membres et entre les Etats membres et les pays tiers sont interdites.* »

fiscales rendre moins attractif l'investissement dans les autres Etats par rapport à un investissement domestique.[37]

En ce qui concerne les règles en matière d'aides accordées par les Etats (ou au moyen de ressources d'Etats), le T.F.U.E. consacre le principe selon lequel de telles aides – sous quelque forme que ce soit – sont incompatibles avec le marché intérieur, « *dans la mesure où elles affectent les échanges entre Etats membres* » ou « *faussent ou menacent de fausser la concurrence en favorisant certaines entreprises ou certaines productions*».[38] Cette interdiction de principe s'applique aussi aux mesures fiscales.[39] Il existe par ailleurs certaines dérogations, la plupart prévues par le Traité et mises en œuvre par la Commission européenne, sous le contrôle de la Cour de justice.[40]

Parallèlement aux dispositions de 'Hard Law' (notamment en matière d'aides d'Etat), les institutions de l'Union européenne recourent également au 'Soft Law'- pour lutter contre la «concurrence fiscale dommageable » que se livrent les Etats membres (pour attirer ou maintenir des investissements étrangers sur leur territoire respectif) : elles ont ainsi adopté en 1997 un 'Code de Conduite' dans le domaine de la fiscalité des entreprises.[41] D'une manière générale, ce 'Code de Conduite' « *vise les mesures ayant, ou pouvant avoir, une incidence sensible sur la localisation des activités économiques au sein de la Communauté*».[42] Il impose aux Etats membres de cesser d'appliquer des mesures fiscales dommageables existantes (« *démantèlement* ») et de ne pas introduire de nouvelles mesures fiscales dommageables (« *gel* »), telles que définies par ce 'Code de Conduite'[43] et par un groupe *ad hoc*, dit

---

[37] Sur l'application par la Cour de justice des libertés de circulation-, voir notamment J. MALHERBE, Ph. MALHERBE, I. RICHELLE and E. TRAVERSA, The impact of the Rulings of the European Court of Justice in the area of direct taxation, requested by the European Parliament's Committee on Economic and Monetary Affairs, 1st edition: April 2008, 2nd edition : November 2011, available on www.europarl.eu.

[38] Cf. Article 107, §1 T.F.U.E.

[39] Sur les aides d'état fiscales, voir Rust/Micheau (eds.), State aid and Tax Law, 2013; Micheau, Droit des aides d'État et des subventions en fiscalité, 2013; Kube, Nationales Steuerrecht und europäisches Beihilfenrecht, in Becker/Schoen (eds.), Steuer- und Sozialstaat im europäischen Systemwettbewerb, 2005, p. 99 à 117; Panayi, State aid and tax : the third way?, Intertax , 6-7/2004, p. 283; Waelbroeck, La compatibilité des systèmes fiscaux généraux avec les règles en matière d'aides d'État dans le Traité CE, Mélanges John Kirkpatrick, 2004, p. 1023 ; Luja, Assessment and Recovery of Tax Incentives in the EC and the WTO: A View on State Aids, Trade Subsidies and Direct Taxation, 2003; Wouters/Van Hees, Les règles communautaires en matière d'aides d'Etat et la fiscalité directe : quelques observations critiques, C.D.E., 2001, p. 655 ; Schön, Taxation and State aid in the European Union, CMLR., 1999, pp. 927–928.

[40] Cf. Article 107, §§2 et 3 T.F.U.E., qui énumèrent certaines mesures qui 'sont' comptables ou 'peuvent être' compatibles avec le marché intérieur.

[41] Conclusions du Conseil Ecofin du 1er décembre 1997 en matière de politique fiscale, in *J.O.*, 6 janvier 1998, C 2, p.1 (ci-après, « Code de conduite »). Sur la concurrence fiscale dans l'UE et sur le Code de conduite, voir notamment A. C. DOS SANTOS, *L'union européenne et la régulation de la concurrence fiscale*, Bruxelles, Bruylant, 2009; C. PINTO, *Tax competition and EU law*, La Haye, Kluwer, 2003 ; W. SCHÖN (éd.), *Tax Competition in Europe*, Amsterdam, IBFD, 2003.

[42] Code de conduite en matière de fiscalité des entreprises, point A.

[43] Code de conduite en matière de fiscalité des entreprises, point C.

'groupe Primarolo'.[44] C'est notamment à la suite de l'application du 'Code de Conduite' (mais aussi du régime des aides d'Etats) que la Belgique a été contraint d'abandonner le régime fiscal particulier des centres de coordination et a adopté le régime des intérêts notionnels.[45]

Plus récemment, ces dispositions dites de 'Soft Law' ont été étendues, en vue de lutter plus efficacement contre les mécanismes qualifiés de 'planification fiscale agressive', lesquels se concrétisent par exemple tantôt par une double déduction de la même perte (i.e., dans l'Etat de la source et dans celui de résidence), tantôt par une double non-imposition. Dans le cadre de cette lutte spécifique contre la fraude et l'évasion fiscales, il convient ainsi de mentionner la communication de la Commission du 6 décembre 2012 sur un plan d'action pour renforcer la lutte contre la fraude et l'évasion fiscales (COM(2012)0722) et les recommandations qui l'accompagnent notamment en ce qui concerne les relations des pays de l'Union européenne avec les pays tiers.[46] Le Parlement européen a soutenu ces initiatives.[47]

Participation au Forum fiscal mondial de l'OCDE?

A l'instar de la majorité des pays, la Belgique participe au Forum mondial (dans le cadre de l'O.C.D.E.) sur la Transparence et l'Echange de renseignements. D'une manière générale, les Conventions préventives de la double imposition conclues (et ratifiées) par la Belgique suivent de (très) près la Convention-modèle O.C.D.E. Toutefois, en matière d'échange de renseignements en relation avec pré-cisément le 'secret bancaire' – matérialisé par l'insertion d'un (nouveau) paragraphe 5 à l'article 26 de la Convention-modèle O.C.D.E. (version 2004) – la Belgique a, du moins dans un premier temps, émis une réserve à cet égard, n'intégrant pas l'article 26, §5 de la Convention-modèle O.C.D.E. Cette attitude valut au Royaume de Belgique d'être placé sur la 'liste grise' des paradis fiscaux de l'O.C.D.E. Sous une pression internationale croissante, la Belgique modifia son point de vue et retira

---

[44] Rapport du Groupe 'Code de conduite' (fiscalité des entreprises) au Conseil ECOFIN du 29 novembre 1999, rendu public le 28 février 2000, disponible sur le site de la DG TAXUD de la Commission européenne (« Rapport PRIMAROLO »).

[45] Cf. E. TRAVERSA et A. LECOCQ, « Les intérêts notionnels en droit belge », in *Revue de Droit fiscal*, n°9, 2009, pp. 9–16; J. MALHERBE., M. DE WOLF et C. SCHOTTE, « Les centres de coordination après la réforme fiscale belge pour 2003 », in *L'année fiscale*, Paris, P.U.F., 2003, pp. 177–191.

[46] Voir aussi la Recommandation relative à la bonne gouvernance dans le domaine fiscal dans les pays tiers (Doc.17669/12) adoptée par le Conseil ECOFIN le 14 mai 2013.

[47] Résolution du Parlement européen du 21mai 2013 sur la lutte contre la fraude fiscale, l'évasion fiscale et les paradis fiscaux (2013/2060(INI)), Doc. T7-0205/2013. Voir aussi PE, Commission des affaires économiques et monétaires, Rapport du 3 mai 2013 sur la lutte contre la fraude fiscale, l'évasion fiscale et les paradis fiscaux (2013/2060(INI), Doc. A7-0162/2013.

sa réserve à la disposition précitée (article 26, §5 O.C.D.E.).[48] Dès lors, la Belgique a conclu, depuis 2009, de nouvelles conventions préventives de double imposition et surtout de nombreux protocoles additionnels à des conventions préventives existantes, qui intègrent cette clause particulière.[49] Ce changement d'attitude permit au Royaume de Belgique d'être retiré de cette 'liste grise' à l'automne 2009.

Les Accords d'échange d'informations

En tant qu'Etat membre de l'Union européenne, la Belgique est lié par le droit de L'union européenne 'primaire' et 'dérivé'. Au cours des quelques dernières années, plusieurs instruments juridiques relevant du droit européen 'dérivé' ont été adoptés, en vue de renforcer la 'transparence' et les échanges d'informations sur le plan fiscal entre les Etats membres.

Tel est le cas de la directive 2011/16/UE du Conseil du 15 février 2011 relative à la coopération administrative dans le domaine fiscal[50] (et abrogeant la directive 77/799/CEE avec effet au 1er janvier 2013). Cette dernière directive s'applique (cf. article 2) à tous les types de taxes et impôts prélevés par un Etat membre (ou en son nom) ou par ses entités territoriales ou administratives (ou en leur nom), y compris les autorités locales, à l'exception toutefois de la taxe sur la valeur ajoutée, des droits de douane ou d'accises, ainsi que des cotisations. Elle prévoit les modes d'échanges d'informations « *sur demande* » (cf. articles 5 à 7), « *automatique et obligatoire* » (cf. article 8) ou « *spontané* » (cf. articles 9 et 10). Il convient par ailleurs de noter que la directive du 15 février 2011 contient une clause dite de la « *nation la plus favorisée* » (cf. article 19), en vertu de laquelle « *lorsqu'un Etat membre offre à un pays tiers une coopération plus étendue que celle prévue par la présente Directive, il ne peut pas refuser cette coopération étendue à un autre Etat membre souhaitant prendre part à une telle forme de coopération mutuelle plus étendue.* » Cette clause n'avait pas d'équivalent dans la directive 77/799/CEE du 19 décembre 1977.

En matière de recouvrement, la directive n°2010/24/UE du 16 mars 2010 concernant l'assistance mutuelle en matière de recouvrement des créances relatives aux taxes, impôts, droits et autres mesures (remplaçant la directive n°2008/55/CE du 26 mai 2008, abrogée avec effet au 1er janvier 2012), qui prévoit plusieurs formes d'assistance mutuelle, plus particulièrement en matière d'échange d'informations (soit, sans demande préalable, soit « à la demande »).

---

[48] Voir aussi la 'nouvelle' Convention-modèle belge (version de juin 2010) comporte désormais une disposition spécifique en matière d'échange de renseignements en relation avec le 'secret bancaire' (article 25, §5).

[49] Cf. C. DOCCLO et S. KNAEPEN, « Exchange of Information and Cross-border Cooperation between Tax Authorities », Rapport belge, in Cahiers de droit fiscal international (I.F.A.), 2013, vol.98b, pp.133 et suivants.

[50] Cf. J.O., L.64/12 du 11 mars 2011.

En matière de TVA, l'objectif du règlement du 31 janvier 2012 qui fixe les modalités d'application des articles 14, 32, 48, 49 et 51, §1 du règlement (UE) n°904/2010 est de renforcer la coopération administrative et la lutte contre la fraude fiscale en matière de T.V.A. par le biais d'une 'facilitation' des échanges d'informations (échanges automatiques), essentiellement sous forme électronique, entre les Etats membres. Ainsi, les articles 2 et 3 du règlement déterminent respectivement les catégories et sous-catégories d'informations faisant l'objet d'un échange automatique: les informations concernant des assujettis non établis et les informations sur les moyens de transport neufs. Si un Etat membre ne souhaite pas participer à l'échange automatique d'informations portant sur les catégories/sous-catégories visées aux articles 2 et 3 précités, il doit le notifier par écrit à la Commission, et au plus tard pour le 20 mai 2012 (cf. article 4).

Il convient également de signaler que depuis le 1er janvier 2010, la Belgique a cessé de bénéficier du régime particulier qu'elle avait négocié dans le cadre de la directive du Conseil 2003/48/CE du 3 juin 2003, en matière de fiscalité des revenus de l'épargne sous forme de paiements d'intérêts (directive dite « épargne »), aujourd'hui abrogée, et a appliqué la procédure d'échange automatique de renseignements à ces revenus.

Au niveau belge également, comme cela a déjà été évoqué ci-dessus, la Belgique s'est livré -plus particulièrement en 2009 et 2010- à un véritable 'marathon' de négociations avec ses partenaires, qui s'est concrétisé par la conclusion d'environ une quarantaine de protocoles additionnels d'échanges d'informations (sur base de l'article 26, §5 de la Convention-modèle O.C.D.E)[51] et/ou de conventions d'échange d'informations fiscales ('*Tax Exchange Information Agreements*', en abrégé 'T.I.E.A.') y compris avec des pays considérés comme paradis fiscaux , tels que Andorre, les Bahamas, Belize, le Liechtenstein, Saint Kitts et Nevis, les îles Grenadine, etc.[52]

Pour terminer, il convient de signaler que la Belgique a conclu avec les Etats-Unis d'Amérique, en avril 2014, l'accord dit 'F.A.T.C.A.' (« *Foreign Account Tax Compliance Act* »),[53] lequel fixe le cadre pour la mise en place d'un échange automatique d'informations financières entre la Belgique et les Etats-Unis. Il décrit les informations qui doivent être obtenues et échangées, et indique le calendrier et les modalités pratiques de l'échange. Cet accord a déjà été ratifié par la Belgique.

---

[51] D. van BORTEL et R. NEYT, Rapport belge, in « Tax Survey and Tax Transparency. The relevance of Confidentiality in Tax Law », ed. Eleonor Kristoffersson, Michael Lang, Pasquale Pistone, Josef Schuch, Claus Staringer et Alfred Storck, 2013, Part 1, pp.156–157; Sur la question générale des échanges d'informations, voir aussi notamment: C. DOCCLO et S. KNAEPEN, « Exchange of Information and Cross-border Cooperation between Tax Authorities », Rapport belge, in Cahiers de droit fiscal international (I.F.A.), 2013, vol.98b, pp.137–138.

[52] Il convient toutefois de noter que la plupart de ces 'conventions d'échange d'informations fiscales' n'ont pas encore été ratifiées et ne sont pas encore entrées en vigueur : D. van BORTEL et R. NEYT, op.cit., p.157.

[53] Cf. C.P. TELLO, « Practical Aspects of FATCA preparation for investment funds and their advisors », in Revue Générale du Contentieux Fiscal (R.G.C.F.), Bruxelles, Larcier, 2013/5-6, septembre–décembre, pp. 373–381.

Les incitants fiscaux à l'investissement dans les pays émergents ou les pays en développement

La législation belge ne prévoit pas d'incitants fiscaux destinés spécifiquement à des investissements dans des pays dits 'émergents', 'en développement', 'en transition' ou 'à faibles revenus'. Toutefois, par le passé, certaines dispositions conventionnelles et internes adoptés dans un tel but ont existé. On retrouve ainsi des clauses de *tax sparing* (crédits d'impôt fictif) dans les anciennes conventions avec le Brésil (supprimées pour partie en 2002 et pour un autre en 2012),[54] l'Inde, la Chine, la Malaysie, les Philippines,[55] la Corée du Sud,[56] la Grèce, la Turquie, l'Espagne, le Portugal[57] ou encore avec Singapour.[58]

En droit interne, le mécanisme dit de '*Quotité Forfaitaire d'Impôt Etranger*'[59] (en abrégé, 'Q.F.I.E.') visait à remédie (partiellement) à la double imposition en permettant d'imputer sur l'impôt belge (I.Soc.) une quotité du revenu (et non de l'impôt) payé à l'étranger. A l'origine, la 'Q.F.I.E.' sur les intérêts avait un caractère forfaitaire (une imposition de 15 % -parfois davantage en cas d'application d'une convention préventive de la double imposition- dans l'Etat de la source était présumée). Par voie de conséquence, la 'Q.F.I.E.' pouvait, dans certains cas, être supérieure au montant de l'impôt étranger réellement payé et constituait un incitant à l'investissement international, notamment dans des pays en développement. Toutefois, cette mesure a également favorisé la mise en place de nombreuses opérations d' « optimisation fiscale » et provoqué de nombreux litiges devant les

---

[54] a) En ce qui concerne les dividendes imposables conformément à l'article 10, § 2, et non visés sub 3* ci-après, les intérêts imposables conformément à l'article 11, § 2, 3, b ou 8 et les redevances imposables conformément à l'article 12, § 2 ou 6,la Belgique accorde sur l'impôt belge dû par ledit résident une déduction égale à 20 p.c. du montant brut des revenus susvisés qui est compris dans la base imposable au nom de ce résident.

b) Dans l'éventualité où le Brésil réduirait la charge fiscale normale applicable aux revenus susvisés attribués à des non-résidents, à un taux inférieur à 14 p.c. du montant brut de ces revenus la Belgique réduirait de 20 à 15 p.c. le taux de cette déduction; dans le cas où le Brésil éliminerait ladite charge fiscale,la Belgiquelimiterait à 5 p.c. le taux de cette déduction.

c) Par dérogation aux dispositions de sa législation,la Belgique accorde également la déduction de 20 p.c. prévue à l'alinéa a) à raison des revenus susvisés qui sont imposables au Brésil en vertu dela Conventionet des dispositions générales de la législation brésilienne, lorsqu'ils y sont temporairement exemptés d'impôt par des dispositions légales particulières tendant à favoriser les investissements nécessaires au développement de l'économie du Brésil. Les autorités compétentes des Etats contractants déterminent d'un commun accord les revenus à admettre au bénéfice de cette disposition.

[55] Convention du 2 octobre 1976, dans sa version antérieure à1996, article 23.

[56] Convention entre la Belgique et la Corée du Sud dans sa version du 29 aout 1977, article 23.

[57] Convention entre la Belgique et le Portugal du 16 juillet 1969 dans sa version antérieure à 1995, article 23.

[58] Convention entre la Belgique et Singapour du 8 février 1972, dans sa version antérieure à 1996, article 23.

[59] Cf. Article 285 et suivants du CIR/92.

juridictions belges. Elle donc été adaptée et a perdu son caractère forfaitaire.[60] Ces abus ont également eu un impact en matière de politique conventionnelle, la Belgique suivant le scepticisme de l'OCDE sur l'efficacité des clauses de *tax sparing*.[61]

Toutefois, on observe dans la politique fiscale internationale de la Belgique une prise en considération grandissante (et forcée) pour mes intérêts des Etats dits 'émergents', 'en développement' ou 'en transition' (particulièrement le Brésil, la Russie, l'Inde et la Chine), qui se reflète dans la pratique conventionnelle par une extension de la compétence fiscale accordée en faveur des 'pays de la source'. Cette influence se traduit également au niveau de la Convention-modèle O.C.D.E., Par exemple, en ce qui concerne les questions liées à l'« *assistance technique* » et/ou aux « *services techniques* », les pays 'en développement' ou 'en transition' souhaitent pouvoir imposer 'à la source' ces rémunérations (en règle comme des « *redevances* », sur base de l'article 12), même lorsque ces rémunérations ne sont pas attribuables à un établissement stable situé sur leur territoire ou même lorsque de tels services ne sont pas prestés *concrètement* dans cet Etat.[62] Bien que l'administration fiscale belge juge cette position des Etats 'en développement' ou 'en transition' contraire à l'article 12, la Belgique a accordé une telle compétence fiscale notamment au Brésil (qui peut appliquer une retenue 'à la source' de 10 % pour les droits d'auteur, une de 20 % pour les marques de fabrique ou de commerce

---

[60] Par la suite, et pour lutter précisément contre certains 'abus' résultant d'une planification fiscale jugée trop agressive, la quotité « forfaitaire » a été remplacée par l'imputation d'une quotité « réelle » de l'impôt étranger, qui s'obtient (article 287 du CIR/92) en multipliant le revenu net frontière par une fraction dont le numérateur est égal à l'impôt étranger effectivement retenu (exprimé en %, avec un maximum de 15 %) et le dénominateur est égal à 100 moins le numérateur. Cette quotité est ajoutée au revenu imposable de la société (à titre de dépense non admise) ; elle est imputable sur l'Impôt des Sociétés et n'est pas remboursable, si elle excède l'impôt dû. Par ailleurs, la possibilité de se prévaloir de la 'Q.F.I.E.' a été « balisée » par certains mécanismes :

– une disposition anti-abus, dite « anti-channeling » (article 289 du CIR/92) ;
– une imputation prorata temporis, c'est-à-dire proportionnellement à la période pendant laquelle une société a eu la pleine propriété des capitaux, titres ou créances (article 288 du CIR/92) ; et.
– elle est limitée au montant net des intérêts d'origine étrangère, après déduction des charges financières qui se rapportent proportionnellement aux intérêts (article 287 du CIR/92).

La 'Q.F.I.E.' sur les brevets doit être calculée conformément à l'article 286, alinéas 2 à 4 du CIR/92.

Il convient enfin de signaler que cette technique d'élimination de la double imposition est inscrite dans la Convention-modèle belge (version de Juin 2010) et donc reprise dans la très grande majorité des conventions préventives de la double imposition conclues par la Belgique. Cf. Article 22, §2, g), lequel dispose: « Sous réserve des dispositions de la législation belge relatives à l'imputation sur l'impôt belge des impôts payés à l'étranger, lorsqu'un résident de la Belgique reçoit des éléments de revenu qui sont compris dans son revenu global soumis à l'impôt belge et qui consistent en intérêts ou redevances, l'impôt … établi sur ces revenus est imputé sur l'impôt belge afférent auxdits revenus.»

[61] OCDE, *Les crédits d'impôt fictif Un réexamen de la question*, 1998.

[62] Cl. DEVILLET, « Autour et au-delà de la notion de redevance: le traitement fiscal des revenus générés par l'exploitation des droits de propriété intellectuelle dans un contexte international », in Fiscalité internationale en Belgique, Bruxelles, Larcier, 2013, p.227.

et une de 15 % pour les autres « redevances ») ou à l'Inde (au taux de 20 % en vertu de la convention applicable, mais ramené à 10 % suite à l'existence d'une clause dite de la 'nation la plus favorisée').[63]

Les incitants fiscaux ou des régimes fiscaux spéciaux pour les anciennes colonies, territoires, possessions ou protectorats

La Belgique n'a pas institué de régime fiscal favorable ou des incitants fiscaux en matière d'investissements spécifiquement en faveur de son ex-colonie (République Démocratique du Congo) ou de ses anciens protectorats (Burundi et Rwanda). Au contraire, il convient de noter que la Convention préventive de double imposition avec la République Démocratique du Congo n'est entrée en vigueur qu'en décembre 2011.[64] En ce qui concerne le Burundi, il convient de remarquer que cet Etat figure sur la liste des pays[65] présumés bénéficier d'un régime fiscal « *notablement plus avantageux* » que la Belgique en relation avec le régime fiscal à l'Impôt des Sociétés des « *revenus définitivement taxés* » (cf. ci-dessus).

Les mesures visant à attirer l'investissement étranger

Malgré la suppression du régime fiscal favorable aux « centres de coordination », la Belgique conserve plusieurs déductions fiscaux 'spécifiques' à l'Impôt des Sociétés (régimes dits '*extra-comptables*') et/ou de dispositions fiscales 'attractives' destinés à favoriser les investissements (étrangers) sur son territoire.

Parmi les régimes fiscaux 'spécifiques' à l'Impôt des Sociétés, il convient de mentionner – outre le régime des 'R.D.T.' déjà exposé (cf. point 3 ci-dessus) – plus particulièrement (i) le régime dit de la déduction pour capital à risque (ou déduction des intérêts dits 'notionnels'),[66] qui permet aux sociétés de déduire 'fictivement' de leur base imposable des intérêts censés rémunérer les capitaux propres investis, intérêts qualifiés de « notionnels » (cf. également point 12 ci-dessous), (ii) le régime de la déduction pour revenus de brevets,[67] qui permet aux entreprises de déduire de leur base imposable 80 % des revenus provenant de brevets[68] et (iii) le régime dit du

---

[63] Cl. DEVILLET, op.cit., pp. 238–241.

[64] Cf. Loi d'assentiment du 13 février 2009, in Mon.b du 10 février 2012.

[65] Cf. Article 73/4*quater* AR/CIR92.

[66] Cf. Articles 205*bis* à 205*novies* du CIR/92.

[67] Cf. Articles 205/1 à 205*novies* du CIR/92.

[68] Ce régime fiscal 'spécifique' fut introduit par la Loi-programme du 27 avril 2007 et avait pour objectifs évidents, d'une part, d'encourager l'innovation technologique (dans des secteurs tels que notamment la chimie, la biotechnologie, etc.) et, d'autre part, d'inciter les entreprises, soit à dével-

'tax shelter,'[69] dont l'objectif général est de favoriser la production d' «*œuvres audiovisuelles*» (cette mesure fiscal est donc destinée plus particulièrement à l''industrie' cinématographique et/ou 'audio-visuelle').

Parallèlement à ces régimes fiscaux à l'Impôt des sociétés, il convient de noter que la Belgique organise, par le biais d'une 'simple' circulaire administrative du 8 août 1983, un régime d'imposition particulièrement favorable aux 'cadres étrangers'[70] non-résidents, dans la mesure où ceux-ci bénéficient, d'une part, d'un remboursement des dépenses/frais liés à l'expatriation (tant les dépenses dites 'non répétitives', c'est-à-dire par exemple celles en relation avec le déménagement en Belgique et l'aménagement du logement en Belgique, que celles dites 'répétitives', telles que par exemple les frais de scolarité des enfants) et, d'autre part, d'une imposition sur les seuls revenus de source belge (en d'autres termes, les rémunérations afférentes aux activités exercées 'à l'étranger' sont en principe exclues de la base imposable).

Il convient également de signaler que le régime fiscal belge applicable aux sociétés 'holdings' est plutôt favorable et qu'en matière de précompte mobilier (retenu à la source sur revenus mobilier, tels dividendes, intérêts et redevances), il existe de (très) nombreuses exonérations qui résultent soit des dispositions mêmes du CIR/92 (cf. article 264 du CIR/92), soit de l'A.R.(Arrêté Royal)/CIR92, et en particulier des articles 105 et sv. AR/CIR92. Ainsi, les articles 105 et 106 de l'A.R./CIR92 énumèrent différentes catégories de contribuables susceptibles de bénéficier d'une exonération du précompte mobilier. L'une des catégories ainsi 'favorisée' par le législateur belge est celle des « épargnants non-résidents ».

Concernant la recherche, outre la déduction pour revenus de brevets, La Belgique prévoit d'autres mesures favorables, tels qu'une déduction pour investissement dans la recherche,[71] un crédit d'impôt,[72] et un régime de dispense – partielle – de versement au Trésor du précompte professionnel (impôt sur le revenu) retenu sur la rémunération des chercheurs scientifiques.

Amnistie fiscale

Entre 2004 et 2014, la Belgique a organisé trois 'rounds' successifs de régularisations fiscales, sous la forme de trois 'Déclarations Libératoires Uniques' (en abrégé, 'D.L.U.'). La première 'D.L.U.' fut d'application du 1er janvier au 31 décembre

---

opper des brevets « en propre », soit à en acquérir auprès de tiers, puis à les exploiter à partir de la Belgique.

[69] Cf. Article 194*ter* du CIR/92.

[70] L'expression de 'cadres étrangers' vise plus précisément les employés de nationalité étrangère qui exercent au sein d'entreprises (souvent multinationales) installées sur le territoire de l'Etat belge des fonctions de direction exigeant des connaissances et responsabilités spéciales.

[71] Article 69 CIR.

[72] Article 289quater CIR.

2004 et avait pour objectif de rapatrier certains avoirs 'non déclarés' (placés, le cas échéant, dans des « paradis fiscaux ») dans l'économie belge. La seconde (ou 'D.L.U.*bis)*' fut organisée à partir de 2006 sous la forme d'une procédure de régularisation dite 'permanente', prenant toutefois fin le 14 juillet 2013. Cette 'D.L.U.*bis*' pouvait bénéficier tant aux personnes physiques que morales et visait, d'une manière générale, *tous* les revenus, c'est-à-dire pour l'essentiel des revenus mobiliers (par exemples, des intérêts, dividendes ou autres capitaux issus d'une succession) et professionnels, mais également des revenus provenant d'opérations TVA.[73] Enfin, du 15 juillet au 31 décembre 2013 (c'est-à-dire pendant une période strictement limitée dans le temps), une troisième régularisation fiscale et sociale (ou 'D.L.U.*ter*') fut organisée. Elle visait non seulement les mêmes revenus que la 'D.L.U.*bis*', mais aussi les revenus fiscalement prescrits, ceux issus de la fraude fiscale dite 'grave et organisée', ainsi que les revenus professionnels qui auraient dû être soumis au paiement de cotisations sociales. En 2016, une procédure permanente de régularisation a été introduite, avec une centralisation des demandes auprès du point de contact Régularisations de l'administration fiscale.

Pour terminer, il convient de noter que le mécanisme de « *transaction fiscale pénale*»[74] (article *216bis* du Code d'Instruction Criminelle) a été élargi par les lois des 14 avril et 11 juillet 2011. Désormais, l'article 216*bis* du C.I.C. dispose que:

> « *Pour les infractions fiscales ou sociales qui ont permis d'éluder des impôts ou des cotisations sociales, la transaction n'est possible qu'après le paiement des impôts ou des cotisations sociales éludés dont l'auteur est redevable, en ce compris les intérêts, et moyennant l'accord de l'administration fiscale ou sociale.* »

Structure des taux d'impôt sur les sociétés

En principe, le taux (de base) de l'Impôt des Sociétés ('I.Soc.') est de 33 %,[75] auquel il convient d'ajouter trois (3) centimes additionnels à titre de 'contribution complémentaire de crise',[76] soit au total un taux de 33,99 %. Toutefois, pour les 'petites'[77] sociétés, le CIR/92 prévoit des taux progressifs par tranches 'réduits.'[78]

---

[73] Sur les amnisties fiscales, notamment en Belgique, voir Jacques Malherbe (ed.), Tax Amnesties, Kluwer Law International, 2011.

[74] Sur cette question, voir notamment Sonja VAN DUERM, « La transaction pénale, coté fiscal », in Revue Générale du Contentieux Fiscal (R.G.C.F.), Bruxelles, Larcier, 2012/5, septembre–octobre 2012, pp. 351–356.

[75] Cf. Article 215, alinéa 1 CIR/92.

[76] Cf. Article 463bis, §1, alinéa 1 CIR/92.

[77] La notion de « petites » sociétés est définie à l'article 15 du Code des Sociétés, en fonction de certains critères spécifiques tels que (i) le nombre de travailleurs occupés, (ii) le chiffre d'affaires annuel (hors TVA) ou (iii) le total du bilan

[78] Cf. Article 215, alinéa 2 CIR/92.

Ces taux 'de base' peuvent toutefois faire l'objet d'une correction 'à la baisse' par l'application d'une déduction extra-comptable 'fictive' intitulée déduction (fiscale) pour capital à risque[79] (ou encore déduction des intérêts dits 'notionnels'). En effet, la mesure précitée permet aux sociétés de déduire 'fictivement' de leur base imposable des intérêts censés rémunérer les capitaux propres investis, intérêts qualifiés de « notionnels ».

La déduction pour capital à risque (ou déduction des intérêts dits 'notionnels') s'applique à tous les contribuables soumis à l'Impôt des Sociétés, c'est-à-dire toutes les sociétés belges, mais aussi les associations, établissements (i) qui ont la personnalité juridique, (ii) se livrent à une exploitation ou à des opérations de caractère lucratif et (iii) ont en Belgique leur siège social, leur principal établissement ou leur siège de direction ou d'administration. La loi du 22 juin 2005 vise également les *autres* personnes morales soumises à l'Impôt des Sociétés en vertu des articles 179 à 182 du CIR/92, à savoir notamment les « fausses » ASBL ou les sociétés civiles ayant emprunté la forme d'une société commerciale. Enfin, les « petites » sociétés sont également visées (pour autant qu'elles renoncent à la possibilité qui leur est offerte de ne pas établir des comptes annuels), ainsi que les sociétés étrangères ayant un établissement stable en Belgique.

Interdictions d'incitants fiscaux pour investissement à l'étranger

Comme déjà indiqué ci-dessus (cf. Point 4), en ce qui concerne les aides accordées par les Etats (ou au moyen de ressources d'Etats), le T.F.U.E. consacre le principe selon lequel de telles aides – sous quelque forme que ce soit – sont en principe incompatibles avec le marché intérieur, « *dans la mesure où elles affectent les échanges entre Etats membres* » ou « *faussent ou menacent de fausser la concurrence en favorisant certaines entreprises ou certaines productions.* Nous avons également indiqué que ce principe général pouvait toutefois connaître certaines dérogations. Toutefois, le régime des aides d'état à vocation à s'appliquer principalement à l'intérieur de l'Union européenne (et de l'Etat membre considéré), des lors que son objectif premier est d'empêcher que des mesures protectionnistes favorables aux opérateurs nationaux ne faussent la concurrence entre entreprises.

---

[79] Cette mesure fut introduite par la loi du 22 juin 2005 (in <u>Mon.b.</u> du 30 juin 2005), afin d'atténuer la discrimination existant d'un point de vue fiscal entre, d'une part, le financement par capital à risque (dont la rémunération est entièrement taxée) et, d'autre part, le financement par capitaux empruntés (dont la rémunération est en règle déductible fiscalement). L'objectif de cette mesure législative consiste donc à promouvoir le « capital à risque », c'est-à-dire les capitaux propres investis par les actionnaires ou associés d'une société.

Par ailleurs, les libertés de circulation du Traité s'opposent à ce que les Etats membres réservent des incitants fiscaux à des situations internes[80] par rapport à des situations transfrontalières. Un exemple particulièrement intéressant au regard du thème de ce rapport cest constitué par un arrêt de la C.J.U.E.('Petersen'), en relation avec l'exercice d'une activité salariée par un résident fiscal allemand (M. Petersen) en dehors du territoire de l'Union européenne (en l'occurrence, au Bénin), dans le cadre d'un projet d'aide au développement financé par l'Agence danoise pour le développement international. Dans le cas d'espèce, M. Petersen se voyait refuser par les autorités fiscales allemandes l'exonération d'impôt sur ses revenus ainsi perçus sous prétexte, d'une part, que son employeur n'est pas un 'résident' et, d'autre part, que ni lui-même, ni son employeur ne relèvent de l'aide publique allemande au développement. L'arrêt en question a permis à la C.J.U.E. de rappeler que les dispositions de droit de l'Union européenne (dont le principe de non-discrimination) peuvent s'appliquer à des activités professionnelles exercées également en dehors du territoire de l'Union, pour autant que la relation de travail garde un rattachement suffisamment étroit avec ce territoire. Dans le cas d'espèce, elle a également jugé que : « L'article 45 TFUE doit être interprété en ce sens qu'il s'oppose à une réglementation nationale d'un État membre selon laquelle des revenus perçus au titre d'activités salariées par un contribuable résident de cet État membre et assujetti de manière illimitée sont exonérés d'impôt sur le revenu lorsque l'employeur est établi dans ledit État membre, mais ne le sont pas lorsqu'il est établi dans un autre État membre.»[81]

Dans le cadre de sa politique de la bonne gouvernance dans le domaine fiscal dans les pays tiers, la Commission européenne par ailleurs recommande aux Etats membres de prendre des mesures contre les paradis fiscaux qui ne respecteraient pas des normes minimales de bonne gouvernance fiscale.[82] Dans une recommandation de 2012,[83] la Commission établit des critères permettant de déterminer quels sont ces pays tiers, notamment en référence aux critères fixés par la Code de conduite en matière de fiscalité des entreprises (voir supra). Sont ainsi visées « les mesures fiscales prévoyant des taux réels d'imposition sensiblement inférieurs à ceux qui sont générale-

---

[80] E. TRAVERSA AND B. VINTRAS, "The territoriality of tax incentives within the single market", in I. RICHELLE, W. SCHÖN and E. TRAVERSA (eds.) Allocating Taxing Powers within the European Union, Series: MPI Studies in Tax Law and Public Finance, Springer, Vol. 2, 2013, pp. 171–196.

[81] C.J.UE., 28 février 2013, Petersen.

[82] Voir a ce sujet Fiscalité et développement. Coopérer avec les pays en développement afin d'encourager la bonne gouvernance dans le domaine fiscal COM(2010) 263, avec commission staff working document SEC (2010) 426 . Voir aussi COM(2009)201 et European Parliament's Report on Tax and Development – Cooperating with Developing Countries on Promoting Good Governance in Tax Matters (2010/2101(INI)) , 8 mars 2011 (Joly Report).

[83] Recommandation de la Commission du 6.12.2012 relative à des mesures visant à encourager les pays tiers à appliquer des normes minimales de bonne gouvernance dans le domaine fiscal, C(2012) 8805 final.

ment appliqués dans le pays tiers concerné, et notamment un taux d'imposition nul, doivent être considérées comme potentiellement dommageables. Un tel niveau d'imposition peut résulter du taux d'imposition nominal, de l'assiette fiscale ou de tout autre facteur pertinent ». La Commission recommande d'examiner entre autres:

a) *si les avantages sont accordés exclusivement à des non-résidents ou pour des transactions conclues avec des non-résidents;*
b) *si les avantages sont totalement isolés de l'économie domestique, de sorte qu'ils n'ont pas d'incidence sur l'assiette fiscale nationale;*
c) *si les avantages sont accordés même en l'absence de toute activité économique réelle et de présence économique substantielle à l'intérieur du pays tiers offrant ces avantages fiscaux;*
d) *si les règles de détermination des bénéfices issus des activités internes d'un groupe multinational divergent des principes généralement admis sur le plan international, notamment les règles approuvées par l'Organisation de coopération et de développement économiques; ou*
e) *si les mesures fiscales manquent de transparence, et notamment si les dispositions légales sont assouplies d'une façon non transparente au niveau administratif.*

Accords en matière de protection des investissements

Sur le plan multilatéral, et en matière de protection des investissements étrangers, la Belgique a signé et ratifié la Convention de Washington du 18 mars 1965 pour le règlement des différends relatifs aux investissements entre Etats et ressortissants d'autres Etats. Cette convention est entrée en vigueur pour la Belgique le 29 septembre 1970. Bien que l'objectif premier d'une telle convention ne soit pas d'ordre fiscal, certaines mesures adoptées (par voie législative) en relation avec des investissements étrangers nécessitent d'être examinées précisément sous un angle 'purement' fiscal: il en va par exemples ainsi de la question de savoir si une mesure législative – à portée fiscale – à l'égard d'un investisseur étranger peut s'analyser comme une 'expropriation' indirecte ou déguisée (et partant, en principe prohibée) ou constitue une discrimination prohibée (en relation avec la clause dite de la 'nation la plus favorisée').

Outre la Convention de Washington précitée, il convient de signaler que dans le domaine énergétique, la Belgique est membre de la '*Energy Charter Conference*' dont le traité multilatéral (le '*Energy Charter Treaty*', en abrégé, 'E.C.T.') comporte une disposition fiscale spécifique (cf. Article 21 ECT).

La Belgique est également un Etat signataire de différents accords créant des organisations internationales qui comprennent des clauses d'immunité fiscale. Par exemple, l'Accord portant création de la Banque Asiatique de Développement; cet accord comporte une disposition l'article 56, §1 prévoyant que: « *La Banque, ses avoirs, ses biens, ses revenus et ses opérations de transaction sont exonérés de tous impôts nationaux ou locaux et de tous droits de douane (…).*»[84]

---

[84] Voir à ce sujet, I. RICHELLE, E. TRAVERSA and B. VINTRAS, "Belgian Report" in M. LANG, P. PISTONE, J. SCHUCH and C. STARINGER (ed.), Tax rules in non-tax agreements, IBFD, 2012, p. 115–148/.

Parallèlement à ces instruments juridiques multilatéraux, il convient de noter que la Belgique a également conclu de nombreux traités d'investissements réciproques bilatéraux: tel est par exemple le cas de la signature, en date du 6 novembre 2007, d'un « *Accord concernant l'encouragement et la protection réciproques des investissements* » entre l'Union économique belgo-luxembourgeoise ('U.E.B.L.') et le Quatar.[85] Tel est également le cas des accords conclus assez récemment entre l'U.E.B.L. et respectivement la République du Tadjikistan (en date du 10 février 2009), la République Togolaise (en date du 06 juin 2009), le Monténégro (en date du 16 février 2010) et le Gouvernement de la République du Kosovo (en date du 09 mars 2010). Il convient toutefois de noter que ces accords d'investissements bilatéraux, qui suivent actuellement le processus parlementaire[86] en matière de ratification, ne prévoient pas de dispositions fiscales.[87]

Sur un plan strictement institutionnel, il convient de noter que depuis l'entrée en vigueur du traité de Lisbonne (1er décembre 2009), l'Union européenne est en principe la seule compétente pour la politique commerciale commune, en ce compris pour les investissements directs étrangers. Par voie de conséquence, il appartient en principe à l'UE de négocier de tels accords en la matière, les États membres devant demander à l'UE l'autorisation – soumise à des conditions strictes – de pouvoir mener eux-mêmes de telles négociations. Toutefois, l'Union européenne n'ayant pas de compétence spécifique en matière fiscale (et certainement pas en matière d'impôt sur le revenu), les accords commerciaux négociés ne devraient pas affecter les conventions fiscales conclues par les Etats membres.

Recent Trends in Belgium's International Tax Policy

Edoardo Traversa and Gaëtan Zeyen
Université Catholique de Louvain
Louvain-la-Neuve, Belgium

Université de Liège
Liège, Belgium
edoardo.traversa@uclouvain.be
gzeyen@zeyenlawoffice.com

(Translated from the French by Karen B. Brown. Most footnotes in original omitted.)

---

[85] Cf. Documents parlementaires, Sénat, session 2011–2012, 5-1529/1 (projet de loi portant assentiment de l'accord entre l'Union économique belgo-luxembourgeoise et le Quatar).

[86] Docs parl. Chambre des Représentants, Rapport du 12 juillet 2012 (Herman De Croo), Doc.53, 2336-002.

[87] La liste des accords d'investissment conclus par la Belgique est disponible sur http://investment-policyhub.unctad.org/IIA/CountryBits/19#iiaInnerMenu (accédé le 5 septembre 2015). Voir à ce sujet, E. TRAVERSA/I.RICHELLE « Belgium », in M. LANG et alii, *The Relationship between Taxation and Bilateral Investment Agreements* (provisional title), Linde, 2016 (forthcoming).

International Tax System

Belgian residents are subject to tax on a worldwide basis. This means that they are taxed not only on income derived from Belgian sources, but also on income produced or collected abroad under the Income Tax Code of 1992 (CIR/92). Therefore, in Belgian tax law, the principle of territoriality suggests only that the Belgian authority to exert control over tax matters is limited to its own national borders. Because Belgium has the sovereign right to define the criteria for taxation, including tax on income from sources outside Belgium, there is the opportunity for double, or even multiple, taxation.

In the absence of a treaty, there is an exemption for certain income derived abroad, including income from immobile assets located outside of Belgium, income from professional activities abroad unless conducted with the support of Belgian establishments, and certain other income (such as prizes, subsidies, and rental income from persons who are not Belgian inhabitants).

When conventions for the prevention of double taxation (double taxation conventions) apply, Belgium generally eliminates double taxation of most revenue, except dividends, interest, and royalties. Although income determined to be sourced in the other contracting state under the treaty is exempt from Belgian tax, the exempted foreign source income is included in the tax base for the purpose of determining the top tax rate to be imposed on the remaining income subject to tax in Belgium.

In order to qualify for the exemption, the taxpayer must establish entitlement by presenting the appropriate documents to the Belgian tax administration. The exemption was automatic until 2010 when the government promulgated rules requiring demonstration of satisfaction of the conditions necessary for exemption prescribed by the applicable double taxation convention.

For a corporate shareholder with substantial holdings, there is a type of participation exemption for dividends received from its subsidiary. Although the dividend is included in the income tax base of the parent-recipient of the dividend, there is a 95 % deduction (*revenus définitivement taxés* or "RDT"). This deduction is available for dividends distributed by Belgian corporations, corporations organized in member states of the European Union (EU) or corporations organized in other jurisdictions. Eligibility for the participation exemption is detailed below.

The participation exemption is available only if the parent corporation meets certain ownership requirements and the subsidiary's profits are subject to a minimum level of taxation. In order to meet the ownership requirement, the corporation receiving the dividend (*la société bénéficiaire*), for example, a resident corporation, must own i) at least 10 % of the stock of the distributing corporation (*la société distributrice*), for example, a foreign corporation, or a number of shares with a minimum cost of 2,500,000 euros (since 1 January 2010), and ii) establish ownership of the shares for at least one year before receipt of the distribution. In order to meet the minimum-level-of-taxation requirement, the profits of the foreign distributing subsidiary must be subject to a corporate income tax (either the Belgian *l'impôt des*

Sociétés or an analogous foreign-imposed tax) with a base that is not more favorable than the one prescribed by Belgian law. The existence of a more favorable tax base in a foreign country is presumed if the nominal tax rate imposed on corporate profits is less than 15 % or if the country is listed as one with a more favorable regime by Belgian regulation.[88] In order to qualify for the participation exemption, dividends must also meet certain "anti-abuse" tests. Corporations resident in an EU Member State are presumed not to have a more favorable regime and therefore presumed to meet the minimum-level-of-tax requirement.

If the above conditions are not met, the dividend is taxed in the same fashion as ordinary profits, resulting in double taxation of distributed profits.

The *Service des Décisions Anticipées* (SDA) has ruled that dividends paid by a corporation subject to the tax regime of Curaçao qualify for the participation exemption because that country's tax regime is analogous to that in Belgium. In addition, it has determined that a dividend distributed by a Tunisian subsidiary to it Belgian parent is not ineligible for the participation exemption even though the Tunisian tax regime provides a ten-year tax holiday on profits realized from exporting goods.

Tax Havens

The unavailability of the participation exemption, described above, for dividends paid by corporations resident in low-tax jurisdictions is one anti-tax haven initiative. There are additional initiatives to discourage investment in certain designated tax havens. The first is a requirement, effective 1 January, 2010, that all resident and nonresident corporations disclose all payments in excess of 100,000 euros directly or indirectly to persons established in jurisdictions found by the OECD Global Forum not to have substantially complied with the international standard for exchange of information or in jurisdictions with no- or low-taxation. A low- or no-tax regime is one in which the nominal tax rate is below 10 %. Payments that are not disclosed are not deductible. Even disclosed payments are not deductible if the tax-payer cannot establish that the transactions are real and that the payments are not to artificial entities employed to camouflage an arrangement constructed to avoid taxation. The list of no- or low-tax jurisdictions, consisting of about 30 countries,[89] is updated every two years.

---

[88] More than 50 countries are on the list, including: Afghanistan, Aldernay, Belize, Bosnia-Herzegovina, Burundi, Cape Verde, Central African Republic, Comoras, Cook Islands, Cuba, Dominica, Equatorial Guinea, Gibraltar, Grenada, Guernesey, Guinea-Bisau, Haiti, Iran, Iraq, Jersey, North Korea, Laos, Liberia, Liechtenstein, Macao, Maldives, Isle of Man, Marshall Islands, Micronesia, Monaco, Montserrat, Namibia, Oman, Panama, St. Christopher and Nevis, Saint Lucia, Samoa, American Samoa, Sao Tomé and Principe, Seychelles, Somalia, Uzbekistan, American Virgin Islands, and British Virgin Islands.

[89] These include: Abu Dhabi, Amman, Andorra, Anguilla, Bahamas, Bahrain, Bermuda, British Virgin Islands, Cayman Islands, Dubai, Guernsey, Jersey, Maldives, Isle of Man, Micronesia, Moldavia, Monaco, Montenegro, St. Bartholomew, Turks and Caicos, and Vanuatu.

Since 2014, taxpayers subject to *l'impôt des Personnes Physiques* (IPP) must disclose ownership in a *construction juridique*. The term encompasses a legal entity (whether a corporation, partnership, or other entity which is a non-resident of Belgium which is not subject to Belgian income tax or is subject to a regime with a tax system more favorable than Belgium's regime. This latter category includes any *Stiftungen* or any corporation with its residence in a tax haven. Ownership in any entity appearing on a special list issued by decree (*l'Arrêté Royal*) must be disclosed. This list, which will be updated, includes the Delaware Limited Liability Company, *la foundation Suisse*, the Bahamian International Business Company, entities resident in a number of Caribbean countries, and *la Stiftung et l'Anstalt du Liechtenstein*. There is no penalty for failure to make the required disclosure under the new law, but under general regulations, non-disclosure may be penalized by an administrative fine or even an increase in tax liability.

In 2016, a transparency tax ("taxe de transparence"), informally known as the Cayman tax, entered into effect. This measure will permit the fiscal administration to tax revenue derived by foreign juridical entities (trusts or companies subject to a tax rate below 15 %) by associating it with the creator of the enterprise, his heirs, third-party beneficiaries, or shareholders who are Belgian residents.

In addition to the legislative initiatives noted above, there are two developments in internal tax law, which, although not aimed specifically at particular jurisdictions, may provide a disincentive to Belgian taxpayers to transact business with non-residents. The first is under *l'article 54 du CIR/92* (Article 54), which allows the Belgian tax administration to deny deductions for payments of interest, royalties and other mobile income, such as professional expenses, when paid to a non-resident (targeted by *l'article 227 du CIR/92*) (Article 227) which is either not subject to an income tax or subject to an income tax regime which is notably more advantageous than that to which revenue derived in Belgium is subject. Article 54 may have the effect of encouraging investment in a resident company in order not to fall within the purview of these limitations on deductions. The European Court of Justice found this scheme incompatible with the free movement of services and not applicable to member states of the EU in particular because of uncertainty in the application of the regulation.

The second is an anti-abuse initiative which is preventative in nature. This rule, set forth in *l'article 344, §2 du CIR/92* (Article 344), generally, for purposes of the income tax and other direct taxes, allows the tax authority to ignore sales, loans, capital contributions, transfers of patents, trademarks, and other intellectual property, or sums of money between a Belgian taxpayer and an entity not subject to an income tax or subject to a tax regime considerably more advantageous than that in Belgium unless the taxpayer establishes either legitimate business, financial, or economic reasons for entering into the transaction or demonstrates receipt of substantial profit effectively subject to tax in Belgium that otherwise would not have been derived if the transaction had not taken place.

The point of the anti-abuse initiative is to battle tax avoidance consisting of the transfer of ownership of mobile assets to destinations outside the reach of the Belgium tax system. According to A. Nollet, this article combines a number of anti-evasion techniques found in Belgian law: rebuttable presumption of tax avoidance purpose, the fiction that the tax administration may not disregard or re-characterize actions taken primarily to avoid tax and not for a business reason, stigmatization of foreign tax regimes, and reallocation of income between related taxpayers. As discussed above and for the same reasons, the anti-abuse initiative may not be applied to residents of member states of the EU.

Tax Measures to Discourage Investment in Harmful Tax Jurisdictions

There is no notion of "harmful tax regime" in Belgian law. However, paralleling the idea of the state with no- or low-taxation is the tax regime notably more advantageous than that in Belgium, which might be termed a regime "unfairly competing for Belgian revenue or investment." This latter type of regime is targeted in provisions concerning: disclosure requirements, requirements for minimum levels of taxation in order to receive certain tax benefits, and certain anti-abuse requirements.

In addition, tax treaties concluded by Belgium also anticipate the existence of conditions similar to those present in harmful tax regimes. In these treaties, such as those with Morocco, Hong Kong, and Rawanda, certain exemptions are not available unless the income in question is subject to tax in the source country. This would exclude exemptions under treaties with countries with so-called harmful regimes.

Rules or Agreements Prohibiting Discrimination in Favor of Certain Kinds of Investment

Belgium was one of the founding members of the EU. It is, therefore, bound not only by the European law derived from the Treaty founding the European Union (*le Traité sur l'Union européenne*) and the Treaty governing the operation of the EU (*le Traité sur le Fonctionnement de l'Union européenne* – T.F.U.E), but also by derivative community law (regulations, directives, decisions, advice and recommendations).

The T.F.U.E. is founded on the principle of nondiscrimination on the basis of nationality and includes specific rules on the free circulation of capital and payments (Articles 63 to 66 of T.F.U.E.) and State aid. The rules concerning the free movement of capital apply equally to EU members as well as non-members. Under these rules member states may not enact fiscal measures that make investment in a covered country less attractive than investment in the home country.

In matters of State aid, the T.F.U.E. adopts the principle that such measures, in whatever form, are incompatible with the common market to the extent that they affect transactions between member states or distort competition by favoring certain enterprises or modes of production. There are exceptions anticipated by the treaty and interpreted by the European Commission's Court of Justice. The State aid prohibition also applies to tax provisions.

In addition to the above "hard law" concerning State aid, there is also "soft law" employed by the EU institutions to battle unfair competition among member states to attract investment into their respective territories. In 1997, the EU adopted a Code of Conduct concerning taxation of enterprises aimed at measures within the community having the effect of localizing economic activity. Under the Code, member states must begin to dismantle existing competitive fiscal measures and refrain from introduction new measures of this type. Whether measures are forbidden by the Code is determined by an *ad hoc* Primarolo group (*groupe Primarolo*). Notably, Belgium was forced to abandon its centers of coordination and to adopt its notional interest regime (*le régime des intérêts notionnels*) after adoption of the Code of Conduct as well as the State aid prohibitions.

Instances of application of "soft law" have extended to actions taken against aggressive tax planning, for example, by techniques resulting in double non-taxation, such as twice deducting the same loss (in the country of source as well as the country of residence). In connection with the battle against tax avoidance or evasion, the Commission issued a plan of action on 6 December 2012 to reinforce its efforts and to make recommendations concerning relationships between member and non-member states. The European Parliament sustained these initiatives 21 May 2013.

OECD Global Forum

Following the example of most other countries, Belgium participates in the OECD's Global Forum on Transparency and Exchange of Information. The Belgian anti-double taxation conventions generally follow the OECD Model treaty. However, Belgium initially did not accept the clause requiring exchange of information covered by bank secrecy (¶5 of Article 26 of the 2004 version of the Model treaty) and did not integrate it into its treaties. This caused the OECD to place Belgium on the "grey list" of tax havens. After international pressure, Belgium relented and began to include this clause in its treaties. Since 2009, new treaties and protocols integrate this clause, causing Belgium to be removed from the "grey list" in autumn of 2009.

Exchange of Information

In the course of the past several years, many secondary legal documents have been adopted which aim to reinforce the transparency and exchange of information in fiscal matters among the member states of the EU. This includes Directive 2011/16/UE, of 15 February 2011, relating to administrative cooperation in fiscal affairs (abrogating Directive 77/799/CEE, effective 1 January 2013). This directive applies to all types of taxes imposed by member states (or in the name of a member state) or by territorial or administrative entities, including local authorities (with the exception of VAT, customs duties or excises, and mandatory contributions). The Directive references three types of exchange: on demand, automatic, and spontaneous. It also includes a "most favored nation" clause requiring a member state to extend to another member state more extensive cooperation measures if they are provided to a non-member state. This clause did not appear in Directive 77/799/CEE.

Concerning collection, Directive 2010/24/UE of 16 March 2010, concerning mutual assistance in recovery of debts relating to taxes, duties, and other measures, allows several forms of mutual assistance more particularly regarding exchange of information (either on demand or with prior notice).

Since 2011, Belgium no longer proceeds in accordance with the Savings Directive of 2 June 2003 (2003/48/UE) which was repealed in 2015 concerning reporting obligations for interest payments. Instead, it engages in automatic exchange of information regarding this type of revenue.

After a flurry of activity in 2009 and 2010, Belgium has negotiated about 40 treaty protocols based on the exchange of information provisions of the OECD Model Treaty (Article 26, §5) or Tax Information Exchange Agreements (TIEAs), including those with countries considered tax havens, including Andorra, the Bahamas, Belize, Liechtenstein, Saint Kitts and Nevis and the Grenadines.

In April, 2014, Belgium concluded an accord with the U.S. under the Foreign Account Tax Compliance Act ("FATCA"), which put into place automatic exchange of financial information between the two countries. This agreement, which has already been ratified by Belgium, details the types of information that must be exchanged, as well as the timing and practical mechanisms for the exchange.

Tax Incentives for Investment in Developing Countries

While Belgian legislation no longer provides tax incentives for investment in emerging or developing countries, such provisions existed in the past. Tax sparing clauses (providing for a fictional tax credit for taxes not paid) appeared in former treaties with Brazil, India, China, Malaysia, Philippines, South Korea, Greece, Turkey, Spain, Portugal and Singapore.

In internal law, the *Quotité Forfaitaire d'Impôt Etranger* (Q.F.I.E.) attempted to partially remedy double taxation by allowing, in certain cases, imputation of foreign tax for purposes of the Belgian tax. Originally, the Q.F.I.E. applied to foreign source interest and had a tax sparing-like quality presuming payment of a tax of 15 % or more (depending on the applicable anti-double taxation convention) to the source country. As a result, because the presumptive tax, in certain cases, exceeded the actual foreign tax paid, this provided an incentive to invest abroad, notably in developing countries. However, this provision supported establishment of a number of tax-avoidance schemes and caused much litigation in Belgium regarding these operations. It was, therefore, modified to eliminate the presumptive tax element. The abuses it generated had an impact in the realm of politics, as Belgium suffered the criticism of the OECD on the effectiveness of such tax sparing clauses.

However, one observes in Belgian international fiscal policy, a growing interest in emerging, developing, or transitional countries (particularly Brazil, Russia, India and China) which is reflected in the treaty practice to accord jurisdictional preference to tax to source countries. This influence is also found in the OECD Model Treaty, for example, in matters of "technical assistance" or "technical services." Developing or transitional countries desire the power to tax these payments at their source (such as royalties under article 12 of the treaty) even when they are not attributable to a permanent establishment situated within their territory or even when such services are not physically performed in the state. While the Belgian tax administration finds this position taken by developing or transitional countries to be contrary to article 12, Belgium has acceded to such a provision, notably with Brazil (which may apply a withholding tax at the source of 10 % for copyrights, 20 % for trademarks or service marks, and 15 % for other intellectual property payments) or with India (20 % rate applicable under the convention, but reduced to 10 % under a "most favored nation" clause).

Fiscal Incentives for Former Colonies or Protectorates

Belgium has not instituted a favorable tax regime or tax incentives for investment in favor of its former colony, Democratic Republic of Congo ("Congo"), or its former protectorates, Burundi and Rwanda. Moreover, the anti-double taxation convention with the Congo did not even come into force until December, 2011. Burundi was placed on the list of countries presumed to have a competitive fiscal regime in relation to Belgian corporate tax, *les revenus définitivement taxes*, as described above.

Tax Measures to Attract Foreign Investment

Despite the repeal of the favorable tax regime for Centers of Coordination, Belgium has retained several special tax deductions relative to the corporate tax (*l'Impôt des Sociétés*) and incentives designed to attract foreign investment.

Among the tax regimes applicable to *l'Impôt des Sociétés* – apart from the R.D.T. regime – there is: (i) the deduction for risk capital (deduction of notional interest) that permits corporation to claim a fictitious deduction from the tax base of invested capital property for notional interest (see section "Corporate Tax Rates" below), (ii) the deduction for income from patents, which allows enterprises to deduct from their tax base 80 % of royalty income, and (iii) a tax shelter regime that favors production of audiovisual works (a fiscal measure aimed at the cinematography and or audiovisual industries).

Paralleling these tax regimes relating to the corporate tax, Belgium has organized, through issuing a simple administrative circular on 8 August 1983, a tax regime particularly favorable to a specialized group of non-resident managers who benefit on the one hand from reimbursement of expenses tied to expatriation (nonrepetitive expenses, such as those relating to moving to Belgium and settling into Belgian lodging, as well as repetitive expenses such as the cost of child schooling) and on the other hand, from tax solely on Belgian source revenue (that is to say that remuneration connected to activities exercised outside of Belgium are in principal excluded from the tax base).

It should also be noted that the Belgian tax regime applicable to holding companies is rather favorable and concerning the withholding tax (on mobile income such as dividends, interest, and royalties) there are numerous exceptions resulting either from CIR/92 (compare article 264) or from articles 102 *et. seq.* of the AR (*Arrêté Royal*)/CIR92. Thus, articles 105 and 106 of AR/CIR92 enumerate different categories of taxpayers eligible for an exemption from the withholding tax. One of the categories so favored by the Belgian legislature is that of nonresident investors.

Concerning research, apart from the deduction for revenue from patents, Belgium has provided other favorable measures, such as a deduction for investment in research, a tax credit, and a regime of partial exemption from payment of the professional withholding tax retained from the remuneration of scientific researchers.

Tax Amnesty

Between 2004 and 2014, Belgian has held three successful rounds of tax regularizations in the form of three Free Tax Declarations (*Déclarations Libératoires Uniques* or D.L.U.). The first, applicable 1 January to 31 December 2004, had the goal of repatriating certain assets not declared (placed in tax havens) in Belgium. The second (D.L.U. *bis*) was organized in 2006 under the form of a procedure of tax regularization said to be permanent, which ended, however, 14 July 2013. This D.L.U. *bis* benefited physical as well as moral taxpayers and targeted all revenue, mobile revenue (such as interest, dividends, and other capital issued from an estate), professional revenue, as well as revenue arising from the value added tax (TVA). Finally, from 15 July 2013 (during a strictly limited time period) to 31 December 2013, a third tax and social regularization (D.L.U. *ter*) was organized. It targeted not only the revenue sought by D.L.U. *bis*, but also certain prescribed revenue – that resulting from serious and organized tax fraud as well as professional revenue which should have been paid as social security contributions. A new permanent regularization scheme has been introduced in 2016.

In conclusion, it is notable that the mechanism for addressing the criminal tax transaction has been broadened by the laws of 14 April and 11 July 2011. Article 216*bis* of the Code of Criminal Instruction (*le Code d'Instruction Criminelle*). Henceforth, that article provides that:

For tax or social infractions that have allowed avoidance of obligations to pay tax or make a social contribution, the transaction is not allowed until payment is made by the perpetrator of the tax due or social contributions owed, plus interest, if the tax or social administration agree.

Corporate Tax Rates

In general, the rate of tax imposed on corporations (*l'Impôt des Sociétés*) is 33 %, plus a 3 % addition entitled "complementary emergency contribution," bringing the total rate to 33.99 %. However, for small corporations, the CIR/92 provides progressive reduced rates. These base rates are reduced for a fictional accounting deduction for at-risk capital (or deductions for notional interest). This measure, in effect, allows corporations to deduct from the tax base, fictionally, interest supposedly paid on capital stock, which is interest qualified as "notional."

The deduction for at-risk capital (or for so-called notional interest) is available for all taxpayers subject to the corporate tax. This includes Belgian corporations, but also associations, which are establishments (i) with a juridical personality, (ii) engaged in an enterprise or in lucrative operations, and (iii) have in Belgium their head office, principal establishment, or their seat or direction or administration. A law, dated 22 June 2005 covers other persons subject to the corporate tax (*l'Impôt des Sociétés*) by virtue of articles 179 through 182 of CIR/92, notably the false "ASBLs," or civil corporations, taking the form of a commercial corporation. Finally, small corporations are equally covered (to the extent they renounce the option of not reporting annual accounts), as well as foreign corporations having a permanent establishment in Belgium.

Limitations on Tax Incentives for Foreign Investment

The EU prohibitions on State Aid found in the Treaty on the Functioning of the European Union make any foreign investment incentives incompatible with the internal market to the extent that they affect transactions between member states or threaten competition by favoring certain enterprises or modes of production. The State Aid prohibitions primarily have application inside the EU (and the member state in question) because its main goal is to prevent protectionist measures relating to national operators so that they do not limit competition between enterprises.

Moreover, the freedoms of movement guaranteed by the Treaty opposes anti-competitive actions of member states concerning internal situations versus transactions outside the EU. A particularly interesting example is a ruling (*arrêt*) by the European Court of Justice (C.J.U.E) regarding a salaried activity by a German tax resident (M. Petersen) outside of the EU territory (in Benin) for a foreign development aid project by the Danish Agency for International Development. In this case, the German tax authorities refused to grant M. Petersen an exemption from tax on this income derived in Benin on the ground that his employer was not a resident and neither M. Petersen nor the employer came under the jurisdiction of German public development aid. The ruling in question permitted the C.J.U.E. to affirm that legal measures of the EU (including the principle of nondiscrimination) may apply equally to professional activities exercised outside of the EU territory, considering that the work relationship holds a sufficiently direct connection to the territory. In this case, the court also ruled that "article 45 of the T.F.U.E. must be interpreted in the sense that it opposes a national regulation by a member state according to which revenue, collected for a salaried activity by a taxpayer resident in this member state and subject to unlimited taxation, is excused from income tax when the employer is resident of that state, but not when the employer is resident in another member state."

In connection with its policies concerning tax governance in non-member countries, the European Commission recommends that member states take measures against tax havens which do not respect minimum standards of good governance. In a 2012 recommendation, the Commission established criteria to determine which non-member states do not meet the standards, notably in reference to the criteria fixed by the Code of Conduct regarding taxation of corporations (see 4.1 above). Tax measures providing for tax rates considerably lower than those generally applied in the country in question, and especially a tax rate of zero, must be considered potentially harmful. Harmful tax competition may result from the imposition of a nominal base rate of taxation or any other pertinent factor. The Commission recommends scrutiny of the following factors, among others:

(i) tax advantages are provided exclusively to non-residents or for transactions concluded with non-residents,
(ii) tax advantages are totally removed from the domestic economy so that there is no effect on the national base tax rate,
(iii) tax advantages are provided even in absence of real economic activity or a substantial economic presence within the country offering them,
(iv) the rules for determining profits resulting from internal activities of a multinational group depart from those generally accepted on the international level, particularly the rules approved by the OECD, or
(v) tax measures are not transparent, especially if legal issues are resolved flexibly in a nontransparent way on the administrative level.

Foreign Investment Protection

On the multilateral level, concerning protection of foreign investment, Belgium has signed and ratified the Washington Convention of 18 March 1965 for the regulation of investment between the signatory States and their nationals. This Convention entered into force for Belgium on 29 September 1970. While the first objective of such a convention is not tax matters, certain measures adopted (by legislation) in relation to foreign investment must be examined precisely under a purely fiscal lens, including, for example, the question whether legislation with a fiscal scope may be treated as a direct or disguised expropriation (and consequently, prohibited in principle) from the perspective of the foreign investor or as prohibited discrimination (in connection with the so-called "most favored nation clause").

In addition to the Washington Convention, noted above, in the area of energy, Belgium is a member of the Energy Charter Conference of which the multilateral treaty (Energy Charter Treaty, E.C.T.) contains a specific tax provision (cf. Article 21 ECT).

Belgium is equally a signatory state to different agreements creating international organizations which contain tax immunity clauses. For example, the Agreement creating the Asian Development Bank contains a provision, Article 56, §1, providing that: The Bank, its assets, possessions, revenue and business transactions are exempted from all national or local taxes as well as customs duties.

Paralleling these multilateral agreements, Belgium has concluded in the course of the last few years certain reciprocal bilateral investment treaties, which is the case of the signing on 6 November 2007 of an Agreement Concerning the Reciprocal Encouragement and Protection of Investments between the Belgium-Luxembourg Economic Union (*l'Union économique belgo-luxembourgeoise* (U.E.B.L.) and Qatar. Similarly, agreements recently concluded between U.E.B.L. and the Republic of Tadjikistan (dated 10 February 2009), Montenegro (dated 16 February 2010), and the Republic of Kosovo (dated 9 March 2010). These bilateral investment accords, which must be ratified by the Parliament, do not include tax measures.

On a strictly institutional level, it must be noted that since the advent of the Lisbon Treaty (1 December 2009), the European Union is in principle sovereign over common commercial policy, including those relating to foreign direct investment. Consequently, it is within the province of the EU to negotiate such accords, with the member states required to request permission from the EU, given only under strict conditions, to be able to lead their own negotiations. However, with the EU having no specific expertise in tax matters (and certainly not in matters of income tax), the commercial accords should not affect tax treaties concluded by member states.

Chapter 4
Income Taxation in Brazil: A Comparative Law Approach

Misabel Abreu Machado Derzi, André Mendes Moreira, and Fernando Daniel de Moura Fonseca

Abstract Brazil taxes the income of its residents on a worldwide basis and allows a foreign tax credit to avoid double taxation. Taxation of controlled foreign corporations in Brazil is complex and depends upon judicial guidance. In general, the ability to defer income derived by Brazilian-owned subsidiaries is very limited. This makes the prospect of investment in any foreign country, including developing, low-income, or emerging countries, difficult because the income will nonetheless be taxed by Brazil. In countries without a low-tax regime, it is possible to defer Brazilian tax on the profits of non-controlled foreign affiliates until they are made available to the owner. There are special consequences for transactions with companies resident in low- or no-tax jurisdictions which may make investment in developing countries unappealing.

Synopsis A distinguishing characteristic of the Brazilian tax system is that most of the fundamental rights and guarantees regarding taxation are based in the Federal Constitution of 1988 (CF/88). Accordingly, most of the important (but not large in number) international tax issues relating to the proper income tax base are decided

M.A.M. Derzi (✉)
Full Professor of Tax Law at the Federal University of Minas Gerais (UFMG).
Ph.D. in Public Law from the Federal University of Minas Gerais (UFMG). Lawyer
Tax Law, Federal University of Minas Gerais, Minas Gerais, Brazil
e-mail: mderzi@sachacalmon.com.br

A.M. Moreira
Associate Professor of Tax Law at the Federal University of Minas Gerais (UFMG). LL.M.
Degree in Tax Law from the Federal University of Minas Gerais (UFMG). Ph.D. in
Economic and Financial Law from the University of São Paulo (USP), Lawyer
Tax Law, Federal University of Minas Gerais, Minas Gerais, Brazil
e-mail: mendesmoreira@ufmg.br

F.D. de Moura Fonseca
LL.M. Degree in Economic and Financial Law from the University of São Paulo (USP).
LL.M. Degree in International Taxation from the New York University (NYU).
Lawyer and Accountant Taxation, New York University,
Sacha Calmon, Misabel, Derzi, Brazil
e-mail: fernando.moura@sachacalmon.com.br

© Springer International Publishing Switzerland 2017
K.B. Brown (ed.), *Taxation and Development - A Comparative Study*,
Ius Comparatum - Global Studies in Comparative Law 21,
DOI 10.1007/978-3-319-42157-5_4

by the Federal Supreme Court. Regarding administrative decisions, however, the Administrative Federal Court of Appeals (CARF) is in charge of disputes relating to federal tax planning transactions. Its rulings have been more numerous, varied and wide ranging.

The proliferation of tax minimizing transactions has brought considerable tension in the development of the law. The taxpayer-friendly principle of free enterprise embedded in the CF/88 has been in conflict with the federal government's design to invalidate transactions undertaken solely to reduce taxes and lacking in a legitimate business purpose. This gave rise to a type of general anti-avoidance rule (GAAR) in the Brazilian Tax Code which allows the Brazilian Internal Revenue Service (RFB) to re-characterize for tax purposes a transaction entered into solely for tax purposes.

Brazil taxes resident individuals and legal entities on their worldwide income. In order to avoid double taxation, a credit is available for foreign taxes paid, if there is reciprocity or a double tax convention between Brazil and the other country. Regarding legal entities, in some instances, Brazilian tax may be avoided if payment of the income is outside of Brazil even if production remains within its jurisdictional limits. For example, a foreign parent may in some cases arrange for its Brazilian subsidiary to acquire stock in another Brazilian company (as controlled by a foreign parent) simply by making payment outside of Brazil which is tax-free to the target's foreign owner.

Taxation of the income of foreign controlled corporations is complex. Initially, the rules required that a Brazilian parent report the income of its controlled subsidiary on December 31 of each year regardless of actual receipt of a payment or distribution from the subsidiary. There were questions concerning the constitutionality of these rules, viewed to require taxation of income not yet realized. In addition, they were held to be in violation of Brazil's treaty obligations (prohibiting income derived by a resident of a treaty country which was not earned through a permanent establishment in Brazil), except in a case where the entity did not have economic substance and was used simply to avoid tax through application of the treaty. CARF subsequently determined that these rules involved no treaty violation because the law was intended to tax the income of the Brazilian corporation and not that of the foreign company.

A special rule for foreign affiliates (those not controlled by the Brazilian corporation) defers taxation of their profits until they are shown on the affiliate's balance sheet as made available (as a dividend, credit against a liability, transfer of assets, etc.) to the Brazilian owner. This rule applies only if the affiliate is not resident in a country with a low-tax or "favorable" tax regime.

Dividends paid to individuals or legal entities are, generally, exempt from Brazilian tax on the theory that it avoids double taxation of corporate profits. There is a question, however, whether dividends computed in accordance with new accounting rules will be subject to taxation.

Dividends paid by foreign companies to certain Brazilian resident companies (those using the cost basis versus asset equivalent method) are not exempt from Brazilian tax.

Nonresident individuals and corporations are subject to a withholding tax of 15 or 25 % on certain income derived from Brazilian sources and to a net-basis tax on income derived from a Brazilian permanent establishment. Capital gain, including gain on the sale of an equity stake in a Brazilian company (even if the buyer and seller are located outside Brazil), is subject to tax in Brazil at the rates applied to residents.

There are special consequences for transactions undertaken with a company resident in a jurisdiction with a tax-favored or privileged (no-tax or tax imposed at rate below 20 %, ring fencing, or taxpayer information secrecy) tax system. These include: application of transfer pricing rules, loss of residency, thin capitalization rules, or certain limitations on deductions, among others.

Introduction to the Brazilian Tax System

Any paper that discusses a particular aspect of taxation in Brazil and that is intended to be consulted by professionals and scholars from other countries must begin with the Federal Constitution of 1988 (CF/88). In contrast with other countries, the Brazilian tax system is dealt with in detail in the constitutional text. This is quite possibly the greatest peculiarity of the Brazilian taxation system.

An analysis of the Brazilian Constitution reveals to what degree taxation is dealt with in its text, moving from the distribution of the power to tax among members of the federation to detailing the content of this power. Thus, it is with the Federal Constitution that one must begin the search for the definition of income, revenues, services, and finally, what has been classified as subject to taxation by legislators.

The CF/88 was undeniably intended to grant greater stability and certainty to taxpayers who, following the military dictatorship (which began with a coup d'état in 1964), saw in the new constitution a chance to guarantee their most basic rights, founded on a State that respects and obeys its laws. Given the rigidity of the Brazilian constitutional regime,[1] it was reasonable for one to defend the inclusion in the Constitution of the greatest number of rights and guarantees possible.

However, if on the one hand the rigidity of a constitution means a guarantee of stability, then on the other hand it means that the text can fail to keep up with the times, given that social changes are not immediately followed by an alteration in the constitutional text. This is an example of the old tension between dynamic and static interpretation of the law and between evolution and stability.

But what is the relevance of such questions in a study of worldwide income taxation? The importance resides precisely in the fact that important international tax issues in Brazil, such as the taxation of income of foreign controlled and affiliated corporations, are still handled by the Federal Supreme Court (STF) whenever an argument is made that a particular decision contradicts the constitutional concept of taxable income. It is precisely this concept of taxable income that is behind the majority of issues that involve taxation on a worldwide basis.

---

[1] The Constitution is difficult to change due to a prescribed process of amendment.

In truth, these debates rage on eternally precisely because the STF has not yet been able to put an end to the discussion and to establish a precise concept of income for tax purposes. Despite innumerable decisions dealing with the issue (there are even decisions that question the very existence of a concept of income at the constitutional level), no decision has resolved this issue once and for all.

This means that important questions regarding international tax law, although they may seem simple to the eyes of practitioners in most countries, have yet to be ruled on by the Judiciary in Brazil. This important feature of Brazilian law must be shared with the international tax community.

One final limitation must be expressed here. International tax law is a highly visible topic in Brazil, as it is the object of new laws, revenue rulings, administrative and judicial decisions. For obvious reasons, it is not possible to deal with all these issues in a single text. Nevertheless, this paper will provide foreign readers an efficient overview of this subject in the current Brazilian context.

The Brazilian Point of View with Regard to Tax Planning

Issues related to tax planning have been the subject of broad discussion in Brazil for some time now. Even though it is not possible to find a large number of judicial precedents in this area, the same cannot be said for administrative decisions. The Administrative Federal Court of Appeals (CARF), the body in charge of ruling on disputes related to federal taxes, has taken a variety of positions with regard to tax planning and it is possible to find decisions that vary widely.

In recent decades, various rulings have considered the validity of transactions with no economic substance, defended by taxpayers on the ground that the "principle of free enterprise," guaranteed by the CF/88, allows them to take advantage of any non-illicit business arrangement, provided that the transaction occurs independently of tax considerations. Evidently, all manner of abuses occurred, which led to placement of enormous pressure by the Federal Government and scholars on CARF to adopt a restrictive understanding, invalidating transactions that have the sole purpose of reducing taxes. Basically, taxpayers must demonstrate a non-tax related economic reason for the transaction. This involves the adoption of the "business purpose test" as the legitimizing factor for tax planning, as is the case in many other countries.

In their defense, however, taxpayers claim that there is no legal mechanism that allows tax authorities to disregard transactions. For example, in their view, there is no legal instrument that gives a tax authority the power to reclassify a sale and repurchase agreement constructed solely for tax purposes as a financing transaction.

In this context, legislators included a rule in the Brazilian Tax Code that would confer greater autonomy on the Brazilian Internal Revenue Service (RFB). This took the form of the adoption of the single paragraph of article 116 of the Brazilian

Tax Code (CTN),[2] referred to by some as the Brazilian general anti-avoidance rule. This rule is dependent on regulations that have not yet been drafted. In general, the precise purpose of the rule is to allow specific legal transactions to be disregarded/ reclassified for exclusively tax-related purposes, whenever the taxpayer's goal is to avoid a taxable event.

However, the absence of regulations has not prevented an about-face in the administrative jurisprudence. Influenced by scholars who support the application of such theories as substance over form and the business purpose test, CARF has become extremely strict with regard to the issue of tax planning, disallowing many transactions with the simple argument that the purpose of the transaction was solely to incur a lesser tax burden, as if such goal were prohibited.

The current trend seems to be heading towards a greater degree of equilibrium and a middle ground between total permissiveness and generalized prohibition. Recent decisions continue to require that the economic substance of transactions be demonstrated, allowing taxpayers the goal of reducing taxes, but also requiring that the transactions be more than a succession of acts with no economic substance. Nothing can yet be said regarding a convergence of jurisprudence with regard to such an intricate subject, but it is expected that a balance will be struck quickly.

Despite this controversial general anti-avoidance rule, Brazil has included in its legislation various mechanisms that target closing the door on specific abusive transactions as have many other countries. As will be seen further in this chapter, Brazil imposes certain restrictions on transactions undertaken with corporations located in tax havens or in countries with favorable tax regimes and has been establishing rules regarding the identification of beneficial ownership in order to eliminate the effects resulting from the interposition of conduit companies and similar transactions used as vehicles to avoid taxes.

Income Taxation in Brazil

Global Income Taxation

In Brazil, income tax is a Federal tax (CF/88, article 153, II). This power is directly established in the Constitution, with legislation represented by the Brazilian Tax Code (CTN), implementing the definition of a taxable event, and other legislation instituting the actual tax.

Generally speaking, income is understood to be a means of increasing the taxpayer's net worth within a particular period of time – as a rule, 1 year – as the result of capital, labor or a combination of both (CTN, article 43). There is no consensus in the doctrine as to whether Brazilian legislation has adopted a concept of income that encompasses merely an increase in the taxpayer's net worth or that results from

---

[2] This inclusion took effect through Complementary Law No. 104/01.

a specific operation or event during the taxable year.[3] Either way, it is undeniable that many provisions establish that taxation of the economic flow from a particular source, independently of an increase in the taxpayer's net worth, constitutes the taxation of property and not income.[4]

With regard to income earned abroad, individuals and legal entities are taxed on a worldwide basis. For individuals, this determination is contained in article 3, § 4 of Law No. 7.713/88. With regard to legal entities, the rule is found in article 25 of Law No. 9.249/95, which establishes the taxation of direct and indirect activities that occur abroad. Regarding basic questions of international tax law, it must be said that Brazil, like many other countries, has adopted both the source and residence principles.

Specifically in relation to the source principle, scholars diverge regarding the requirements that must be met in a specific case. There are those who maintain that the source principle presupposes the verification, in Brazil, in a cumulative manner, of production and payment sources. On the other hand, there are scholars who defend the possibility of a payment source being located outside of Brazil, with the location of the production source inside Brazil being sufficient. Regardless of the doctrinal divergence, a careful analysis of Brazilian legislation reveals that both criteria have been adopted (production and payment), though not always in a cumulative manner.

Given the complexity of the current business dynamics in an ever more integrated economic environment, it seems difficult to continue arguing that a payment source must always be present when determining the presence of the source of production. This situation leaves room for the utilization of simple corporate structures with the sole purpose to avoid taxes even when the production source is clearly located in Brazil.

An example illustrates this point. It is quite common for Brazilian companies to be directly controlled by foreign corporations. Imagine that a Brazilian company, controlled by a foreign company, wishes to acquire shares in another Brazilian company, also controlled by a foreign company. This transaction is undertaken directly by the controlling entities, and thus, outside of Brazil, in the location where the payment is made. If the production and payment sources must be both be in Brazil, this transaction will not be taxed in Brazil, despite the fact that the production is clearly Brazilian, solely because the parties involved are controlled by foreign corporations, with the payment occurring abroad.

Thus, regarding worldwide income taxation, Brazilian legislation's reliance on the source of payment to determine taxation unconnected with the source of production shows greater attention to the economic relevance of the income. This practice

---

[3] The main difference lies in the fact that with the income-product concept taxation depends on the increase of the taxpayer's net worth at the end of the taxable period, with it being sufficient that a particular source of income has borne fruit (products) over the same period regardless of the occurrence of an actual event resulting in realization of the income.

[4] This situation occurs mainly in the taxation of financial investments by individuals.

is in theory consistent with views expressed in the OECD's 1998 Report on Harmful Tax Competition.

In other words, when deciding whether to tax a particular transaction, an effort is made to take into account the degree to which there is a connection between the income generated and Brazilian territory. The determination of source through scrutiny of production and payment serves as a means of implementing this tax policy.

Credit for Tax Paid Abroad

In a manner similar to that of many countries that have adopted a tax system based on worldwide income, Brazilian legislation establishes a foreign tax credit, provided that certain conditions are met. As a general rule, the credit is allowed when Brazil has a convention to avoid double taxation with the source country, or when there is reciprocity of treatment between the two countries.[5]

As a means of regulating the foreign tax credit, the Brazilian Revenue Services (RFB) drafted IN/RFB No. 213/02, which deals with the taxation of profits, income and capital gains earned abroad by legal entities that are residents in Brazil. This legislation limits the foreign tax credit to the amount that would be due in the event the income was taxed in Brazil. In other words, the foreign tax credit may not exceed the amount that would be due based on the application of the Brazilian rate to this same income.

The rule is logical. Income earned abroad continues to be taxed in Brazil based on a worldwide basis with the foreign tax credit serving merely as a means of offering relief from the double taxation that results whenever the source country taxes this same income. Therefore, this credit cannot exceed the amount that would be owed in the event the income was taxed solely in Brazil.

The credit is not lost in the event that a Brazilian company has not earned taxable income. The amount paid abroad may be used in subsequent years, provided that some operational and control rules established in the legislation are followed.

This regime seems to be applicable to situations in which a Brazilian company had tax collected in addition to that imposed on income realized in Brazil and abroad. This situation is relatively common in Brazil, since, in certain cases, legislation determines that companies must make monthly pre-payments, even if the taxable event occurs only on December 31. In this context, the foreign tax credit may be redeemed using the tax owed in Brazil in subsequent periods, following the same logic for treatment conferred upon excess local credit.

Another important question is related to the name of the tax paid abroad. Brazilian legislation, with no regard for the name given to the tax by each country, establishes that creditable income tax paid abroad must be related to income and capital gains.

---

[5] Although Brazil has entered into many conventions to prevent double taxation, countries that are of great importance to Brazil lie outside of this group, such as the USA and Germany. However, in these cases the RFB itself recognizes reciprocity of treatment and allows the foreign tax credit.

Taxation of Affiliated and Controlled Foreign Corporations

One of the most controversial issues in Brazil's international tax law is related to the taxation of the income of affiliated and controlled foreign corporations. The question has become the subject of billion-dollar disputes between tax authorities and taxpayers and it was only recently, as a result of both a decision handed down by the STF in 2013 and the new Law No. 12.973, enacted in 2014, that it began to be more clearly defined.

The taxation of affiliated and controlled foreign corporations falls, necessarily, within two important concepts that involve income taxation in Brazil: realization and recognition, both of which are present in the law of many other countries. In Brazil, income taxation is based on realization,[6] which does not occur when the income earned abroad is not made available to the Brazilian corporation, through the distribution of dividends, for example.

Within this context, it was possible for Brazilian corporations to define the moment at which the income would be made available, especially when the income was related to one of their foreign controlled corporations. It was sufficient to decide against distributing profits, and taxation would thus be deferred.

As a means of combating this strategy, a paragraph was added to article 43 of the CTN. This rule determined that the law may establish the time at which income from abroad would be considered available for income tax purposes. It then became possible for the law to determine when the realization occurred, thus allowing legislators to do so by presumption, through choosing a time prior to the actual distribution of dividends, for example.

Based on this authorization for presumed realization, Provisory Measure No. 2.158/01, beginning with its 35th reissuance, came to establish the rule of automatic recognition of income earned abroad on December 31. That is to say, independent of any act on the part of those who earn the income, the Brazilian corporation is deemed to realize income (the income is deemed to be made available) on the date of the foreign corporation's balance sheet.[7] The constitutionality of this rule has been questioned.

The main argument of those that oppose the rule is a supposed violation of the constitutional concept of income. In addition, they maintain that if there is no act that makes the income earned abroad available, it is not possible for the Brazilian company to incorporate it into its assets. Therefore, the date of the balance sheet

---

[6]Although opinions differ with respect to this issue, a large number of scholars regard juridical realization as accrual basis and economic realization as a cash flow regime. Although we are of a different opinion, the scope of this paper does not allow us to delve deeper into this issue.

[7]Another point in the Brazilian rule attracts even more attention: the special treatment given to foreign losses. In this case, in contrast with income, which is considered to have been made available on the date of the balance sheet, the legislation expressly restricts compensation, which seems to be blatantly anti-isonomic. While this subject has not been conclusively resolved by the STF, it should be noted that this prohibition has been upheld in decisions handed down by the STJ (Superior Court of Justice).

cannot be considered a reasonable reference for the purposes of characterizing income realization.

In addition, considering that foreign legal entities have a juridical personality that is distinct from that of a Brazilian affiliate or controlled corporation, the taxation would end up being levied on the income of a third party. Only realization is appropriate for determining the addition to the assets of the Brazilian legal entity.

In our opinion, however, the true reason for the invalidity of the rule is not mentioned in the arguments presented above. Within the context of combating harmful tax competition, it is entirely reasonable that countries should seek to restrict transactions that have the sole objective of arbitrarily deferring the taxation of income earned abroad. This is in accordance with the recommendation of the OECD.

However, precisely because this is a measure that tends to limit abusive structures, it should not be applied broadly and without restrictions,[8] as was prior Brazilian law governing the taxation of controlled and affiliated foreign corporations. That rule was aimed at the taxation of any and all profits earned abroad, independently of the circumstances, such as the nature of the income.

It is precisely for this reason that the Brazilian rule also may not be classified as a CFC rule. Although it attempts to achieve fiscal transparency, the new Brazilian rule goes beyond this scope when it presumes all income of any character to be made available to the Brazilian parent on the date of the publication of balance sheet of the foreign controlled or affiliated corporation. Therefore, the problem that could be seen in Brazilian legislation consists not of the establishment of the hypothesis of international fiscal transparency, but rather in it having broadened the scope of the rule.

The effects of this rule must also be analyzed considering the treaties to prevent double taxation that Brazil has signed. Though Brazil is not a member of the OECD, it has broadly adopted its Model Tax Convention on Income and on Capital. As a result, all treaties entered into by Brazil contain Article 7, which deals with the taxation of business profits.[9]

Article 7 establishes that income earned by a corporation in a contracting State may only be taxed in that State, unless the company conducts its business in another

---

[8] The OECD recommends that the CFC rules be utilized only when there is evidence of harmful tax competition. Note that, among OECD members, two types of measures have been adopted that, individually or in conjunction, form the CFC norms of the member countries: (i) the transactional approach to taxation, applicable, in the majority of cases, to specified income, such as passive income (interest, dividends, rents, royalties, etc.); and (ii) the jurisdictional approach to taxation, which applies to income from subsidiaries domiciled in tax havens or countries with favorable tax regimes. As has already been seen, Brazil adopted, extensively, both types of measures when it inserted into its CFC legislation taxation of all the income earned by a subsidiary (active and passive income), independent of the subsidiary's is domicile (including countries with normal tax regimes, tax havens and countries with favorable tax regimes).

[9] "Article 7. BUSINESS PROFITS. 1. The profits of an enterprise of a Contracting State shall be taxable only in that State unless the enterprise carries on business in the other Contracting State through a permanent establishment situated therein. If the enterprise carries on business as aforesaid, the profits that are attributable to the permanent establishment in accordance with the provisions of paragraph 2 may be taxed in that other State."

contracting State through a permanent establishment there located. If the company conducts its business through a permanent establishment, the profits attributed to it may be taxed.

Despite the Model Convention, article 74 of Provisory Measure No. 2.158-35 makes clear that income earned abroad should be taxed in Brazil, even if the affiliate or controlled company is established in a country with which Brazil has signed a convention to avoid double taxation.

This issue has become the subject of heated discussion, both in the Judiciary and in the administrative realm. Some cases have also become widely known and deserve to be highlighted.

The first of these is known as the "Eagle I" Case[10] and was ruled on by the former Taxpayer Court of Appeals, today known as CARF.[11] In this case, the Court discussed the supremacy (or lack thereof) of treaties entered into by Brazil over domestic legislation. The case involved the taxation of the income of a Spanish corporation which was not attributable to a permanent establishment located in Brazil. Based on a treaty signed by Brazil and Spain, the Court ruled that Brazil did not have the authority to tax the Spanish corporation's profits or dividends received by a taxpayer residing in Brazil, since, in accordance with the Convention, these would only be taxable in Spain. In other words, it was ruled that the treaties should prevail.

The issue later came to be analyzed by CARF, in a matter that came to be known as the "Eagle II" Case.[12] In this second ruling, the understanding that Brazil did not have the authority to tax the profits of the Spanish company, as established in the "Eagle I" Case, was upheld. However, it was ruled that the Spanish company did not possess any economic substance, as it acted merely as a conduit between Brazil and a third country with which Brazil did not have a convention to avoid double taxation. In the end, the Spanish company had been constituted with the sole purpose of deferring the taxation of profits by means of the Brazil-Spain Treaty. With this in mind, CARF ruled that article 74 of Provisory Measure No. 2.158-35 was applicable.

In 2011, CARF again considered this issue in a case involving the Brazilian company, Normus, and one of its Hungarian controlled corporations. In this case, the understanding was the opposite. CARF asserted that the Brazilian rule required taxation of income earned abroad by Brazilian companies (considered to be made available on the date of the foreign company's balance sheet) as that of the Brazilian parent and not that of its foreign subsidiaries. Therefore, the income earned by the Hungarian companies, when added to the results of the Brazilian owner, was not income of the Hungarian corporations, but rather that of its Brazilian owner, thus preventing the application of the Treaty's prohibition on taxation of the Hungarian company's income.

---

[10] Ruling No. 101-95802, session of October 19, 2006.

[11] This is an administrative court tasked with ruling on disputes involving Tax Authorities and taxpayers within the federal realm. The change mentioned in the text was merely one of nomenclature.

[12] Ruling 101-97.070, Session of December 17, 2008.

Within the realm of the Judiciary, following years of discussion, a partial solution was reached for this issue by the STF. This occurred in the Writ of Unconstitutionality (ADI) case No. 2.588 and in Extraordinary Appeals cases No. 611.586 ("Coamo" Case) and No. 541.090 ("Embraco' Case").

In these cases, when analyzing the constitutionality of article 74 of Provisory Measure No. 2.158-35, the STF reached different conclusions for foreign affiliated companies located abroad as compared to foreign controlled corporations. With regard to the former, the Court decided that the rule was invalid, since a Brazilian company would not have the decision-making authority to determine the deferment of taxation through the non-distribution of dividends, except in cases where the foreign company was located in a tax haven. As for controlled companies, the Court concluded that rule was constitutional regardless of the place of incorporation of the foreign corporation.

The law is unsettled concerning situations involving a foreign controlled corporation, not resident or incorporated in a country that is not classified as a tax haven, and with which Brazil has entered into a valid treaty. Although the STF's decision was that the rule was constitutional in the case of controlled companies resident in non-tax haven countries, there has been no ruling on situations that involve active treaties. Based on the STF's understanding regarding cases of conflict between international treaties and domestic law, informed thinking suggests that the treaties will prevail.

Following the cases cited above the RFB hurried to consolidate its understanding of the "Coamo" and "Embraco" cases through COSIT (General Taxation Coordination Office) Revenue Ruling No. 18. In an analysis of the treaty issue, the administrative authority upheld its understanding through the application of article 74 of Provisory Measure No. 2.158-35, arguing simply that the Brazilian rule was intended not to tax the income of foreign companies, but rather to tax the income of Brazilian corporations deemed to have been made available on the date of the foreign companies' balance sheets. According to the RFB, double taxation would be eliminated due to the permission granted to use the taxes paid by the CFC as credit.

This chaotic situation was partially resolved by Law No. 12.973/14. With regard to foreign affiliated corporations, article 81 established that income earned abroad may only be included in the calculation base for Corporate Income Tax (IRPJ) and Social Contribution Tax, a federal tax on net profits (CSLL), for Brazilian owners based on the balance sheet prepared on December 31st of the calendar year in which said profits were deemed to be made available to a Brazilian resident corporation. This rule applies provided that the affiliated company:

(i) is not subject to a low tax regime, which is considered to be a regime that taxes profit by applying nominal rates lower than twenty per cent, and

(ii) is not resident in a country with a favorable tax regime, or is not the beneficiary of a privileged tax regime, in the manner stipulated in articles 24 and 24-A of Law No. 9.430/96, and

(iii) is not controlled, directly or indirectly, by a legal entity subject to the regime described under (i) above..

In the case where a foreign affiliated corporation violates any of the conditions described above, the positive portion of the adjustment to the amount invested must be included in the calculation of income tax for the investing legal entity in Brazil, in the balance sheet from December 31st of the calendar year in which the profits were calculated by the foreign corporation.

In the event of a drop in the value of an investment, future income tax liability may be reduced by future profits of the same foreign legal entity from which they originated, during the five subsequent calendar years.

In a generic manner, the new rule established that profits shall be considered to have been made available by the affiliated company in Brazil (i) on the date of the payment of dividends; (ii) on the date of a credit to the liabilities account in the foreign company's books; (iii) in the event of the transfer of fungible assets, if the transferring party, an affiliate, has profits or profit reserves, or, even, (iv) in the event of an advance transfer of resources by the affiliate, related to future sales, the realization of which, through the transfer of the sold good or service, is to occur within a period that exceeds the production cycle of the good or service.

Under the terms of article 77 of Law No. 12.973/14, profits made by the Brazilian controlling corporation (or similar) shall continue to be added to the income tax calculation for the calendar year in which they were included in the balance sheet of the foreign corporation in accordance with the proportion of its equity stake in each controlled company, either directly or indirectly.

It should be noted that it is possible up to the 2022 calendar year to consolidate profits from affiliates with active income to determine the profits of a Brazilian company, with the exception of portions related to invested legal entities that are (i) residents in countries with which Brazil does not have a tax treaty in force for the exchange of information for tax purposes; or (ii) resident in a country that is tax-favored or has a privileged tax regime or under-taxation regime.

The taxation of affiliated or controlled foreign corporations certainly remains the subject of heated discussion and changes within the scope of Brazilian tax law.

Dividend Taxation in Brazil

Brazilian legislators, in contrast with many others around the world, have exempted dividend payments from income tax, regardless of whether the beneficiary is a natural person or a legal entity or resident in Brazil or abroad. This is established in article 10 of Law No. 9.249/95, which links the exemption to the corporate results.

It is an incontrovertible fact that since the drafting of Law No. 9.249/95 tax law has been based on accounting results using the generally accepted accounting principles and other accounting rules established in Law No. 6.404/76 (the Corporate Law).

However, with the advent of Laws No. 11.638/07 and No. 11.941/09, which govern the convergence of Brazilian accounting with the standard dictated by the IASB (International Accounting Standards Board), the RFB has understood, based on a transitional tax regime (RTT), that only distributions determined on the basis of the old accounting rules (accounting standards in existence on December 31 of 2007) are exempt from income tax and that any differences resulting from the application of the new accounting standard should be taxed.[13]

It does not seem to us that there is any foundation for this rationale. The exemption of dividends from income tax is based on the premise that such incidence would generate an instance of economic double taxation, since the profit taxed from the distribution of dividends would be the same as that which the legal entity had already been taxed, with the means of calculating this to be dealt with in corporate law.

Thus, dividends distributed under the new accounting rules should be exempt in the same manner as those calculated based on the regime in force on December 31 of 2007, respecting the decision made by legislators in Law No. 9.249/95.

Therefore, with alteration of the accounting/corporate concept of profits, which is the basis for the payment of dividends, the tax effects should be seen immediately. In reality, there is only an indirect tax effect, since Law No. 9.249/95 continues to be applied in the manner in which it was conceived (exempting from income tax dividends paid based on corporate accounting results).

Finally, it should be noted that this exemption does not apply to dividends paid by nonresident companies. The taxation of dividends received by Brazilian companies (paid by foreign companies) only occurs for those taxpayers whose investments in these companies are assessed using the cost basis method. For investments assessed using the asset equivalence method, the legislation contains a specific rule, described above, under which dividends are not separately taxed.

In the case of natural persons, dividends received from abroad are subject to taxation in the form of obligatory monthly collection, similar to a withholding tax. In both cases, the taxes paid abroad may be credited in Brazil, under the terms explained in section "Credit for Tax Paid Abroad" above.

The Taxation of Nonresidents

In general, nonresidents (corporations or individuals) are subject to withholding tax on the gross income sourced in Brazil at a rate of 15 or 25%, depending on the nature of the income and/or upon the domicile of the recipient. In some specific situations, nonresidents may be deemed to have a permanent establishment in Brazil and thus are taxed on a net basis (e.g., when having an agent-PE). In the first case (i.e., when taxed on the gross income), the Brazilian payor must withhold the income tax on any capital gains or other types of income verified on payments, credits or transfers made to nonresidents (Article 685 of Income Tax Regulations).

---

[13] The RTT was revoked by Law No. 12.973/14 and did not change, from our point of view, the tax treatment for dividends.

Specifically with regard to capital gains, the abovementioned article 685 was altered by Law No. 9.249/95 and now imposes tax on nonresidents in the same rate as for residents of Brazil.

Another point that deserves mention, though it has already been dealt with above, is related to capital gains recorded by nonresidents in situations where the income is paid from a foreign source. Prior to the enactment of Law No. 10.833/03, this transaction was not taxed, because it was necessary for the source of the payment to be located within Brazil.

However, the law was amended to remove the requirement that the payment source be located in Brazil, with the new criteria being that the income must be economically connected to Brazil. This means that capital gain arising from a payment from a foreign source is taxed if the production source is Brazilian. This would occur in the case of payments for purchases of equity stakes in a Brazilian company between parties located abroad even though the payment source is not present in Brazil.

In no case does the rule described above allow the taxation of indirect sales, such as the sale of an equity stake in a foreign company between nonresident buyers and sellers. Under these circumstances there would be a Brazilian tax liability only in the event that the foreign company were considered a mere conduit for the sale of an equity stake in a Brazilian company with the goal of avoiding taxes.

Special Tax Rules

Countries with Favored Taxation and Privileged Tax Systems

Brazilian legislation has included a definition of countries with favored taxation since the passing of Law No. 9.430/96. At that time, legislators sought to subject companies located in tax havens to transfer pricing controls, even though they did not constitute related parties, as previously required.[14]

Brazilian legislation does not state which countries are tax-favored or have privileged tax systems. Simply in order to allow greater openness in the regime, the drafters of the legislation[15] opted to list a series of characteristics.

Generally speaking, in Brazilian legislation a country with favored taxation is one: (i) that does not tax income or that taxes at a rate below 20 %, (ii) that grants preferential tax treatment to nonresidents (ring fencing), (iii) in which profit is not taxed or is taxed at a rate below 20 % because earned outside of the country in question, or (iv) that practices secrecy with respect to information related to the share-

---

[14] Transfer pricing legislation is also applied to transactions realized in countries whose domestic legislation impedes secrecy in relation to the shareholder composition of legal entities or their ownership.

[15] Law No. 9.430/96, articles 24 and 24-A.

holder composition of legal entities, their ownership, or the identification of the beneficial ownership of income attributed to nonresidents.

Countries that feature the characteristics mentioned above are added to a list prepared by the RFB in Brazil by way of a normative instruction. Currently, this instruction is in IN/RFB No. 1.037/10. Although changes occur in the realm of tax law around the world, in order to support clarity, taxpayers are entitled to rely on the list when undertaking a particular transaction.

The list is updated to reflect important changes in a country's practices that would warrant removal of a country from the list. Once the need to alter the list has been recognized, a new normative instruction is prepared. It is precisely for this reason that the drafting of the list is the responsibility of the Executive Power and not the Legislative Power. Since its publication, the list has been amended three times.

According to the tax legislation, the classification of a transaction as having been undertaken with countries with favored taxation or one with a privileged tax system may result in any of the following consequences: (i) the application of transfer pricing rules, (ii) the application of a special regime resulting in a loss of residence in Brazil for natural persons residing in or domiciled in Brazil that transfer their residency to a country or dependency that is tax-favored or has a privileged tax system, (iii) the application of special thin capitalization rules for interest paid or credited to a source located in Brazil for natural persons or legal entities residing or domiciled there, or (iv) the application of special deductibility rules for payment made, directly or indirectly, to natural persons or legal entities residing or domiciled in such countries.

Thin Capitalization

Brazilian thin capitalization rules arose from the same concerns found around the world, that is, to address an attempt to artificially increase indebtedness with the objective of achieving a more beneficial tax regime than that allowed for of payment of dividends. These transactions are intended to convert nondeductible dividends into deductible interest payments that reduce the payor's tax liability in its country of residence while simultaneously shifting distributed profits to a low- or no-tax jurisdiction.

Thin capitalization rules were first adopted in Brazil on December 15, 2009, through Provisory Measure No. 472. Because dividends are exempt from taxation in Brazil, these rules were not deemed necessary. Legislators have nonetheless identified certain cases of inadequate capitalization that justify the utilization of thin capitalization rules.

These rules apply only if the creditor is located abroad, the creditor is related to the debtor, and the indebtedness is excessive. To be excessive the debtor's capital/

debt ratio must exceed a prescribed level.[16] The portion of debt deemed excessive is not deductible.

The legislation eliminates the requirement of relationship between the creditor and debtor when the former is domiciled in a country with favored taxation (i.e., it is the beneficiary of a privileged tax system).

The Definition of a Permanent Establishment in Brazilian Legislation

The concept of permanent establishment has always been illusive in most tax systems and Brazil's regime is no exception.

Brazilian legislation does not contain a concept of permanent establishment, but the issue is usually dealt with in Brazilian conventions to avoid double taxation. The absence of the concept seems to result from a particularity of Brazil's own legislation covering foreign companies. Although allowed to under Brazilian law, companies rarely choose to conduct operations in the country directly. The requirements imposed by Brazilian legislation simply make this model of doing business not viable.

Therefore, foreign corporations that wish to conduct business in Brazil do so by means of controlled legal entities incorporated in Brazil. This corporate model means that the taxation of these "branches" occurs in the same manner as for any Brazilian company, because these "branches" are actually separate legal entities incorporated in Brazil.

Beneficial Ownership Rules

As has been seen, Brazil is constantly amending its legislation as it pertains to international taxation. Noteworthy among recent modifications is the concept of beneficial ownership, inserted into article 26, § 1, of Law No. 12.249/10 within a context of the determination of deductibility, for corporate income tax purposes, of payments made to natural persons or legal entities residing in countries with favored taxation or classified as having privileged fiscal regimes.

Generally speaking, legislators sought to restrict the effects of the utilization of vehicles to obtain a deduction for expenses not normally deductible. Deductibility is permissible only if the beneficial owner, which is the person who ultimately receives the payment, is not resident in a country with a favored or privileged tax

---

[16] The indebtedness may not be greater than twice the value of the creditor's equity stake in the net assets of the Brazilian company and the total indebtedness with related persons domiciled abroad may not be greater than twice the value of the equity stakes held by these related parties in the net assets of the Brazilian company.

regime. Payment of the item directly to a mere agent, fiduciary or mandatory administrator who is not operating on the beneficial owner does not qualify for deduction. The Brazilian rule follows global trends in this area.

Conclusion

Brazilian legislators have shown themselves to be concerned with the fiscal effects resulting from international tax competition, in line with the great nations of the world. We expect this concern to grow in coming decades, because the Brazilian capital markets have gained increased importance. Increasingly Brazilian companies are establishing themselves abroad, maintaining a link with a Brazilian parent company and foreign companies are operating in Brazil through controlled Brazilian subsidiaries.

The effects of internationalization mean that, in a certain manner, the focus of tax legislation is being altered. This translates into a concern with the regulation of transactions that involve more than one country, which leads to the need to adopt uniform measures among countries, often in the form of bilateral agreements. This situation increases the importance of bodies such as the OECD, along with international discussions, and an exchange of experiences between tax authorities and taxpayers. Only an international policy to combat the effects of the base erosion and profit shifting is capable of allowing economic development to reach its maximum level of efficiency, provided that the taxation aspects, whenever possible, remain neutral.

Brazil, while not a member of the OECD, has, to a large degree, adopted its Model Convention with Respect to Taxes On Income and On Capital and has been implementing internal measures to combat abusive tax planning, the recording of artificial profits through transactions with connected parties, and excessive indebtedness, among other targets.

The most important issue related to international taxation in Brazil, however, is certainly the taxation of the profits of affiliates and controlled foreign corporations. It is shocking that an issue of such importance has not yet been resolved in a definitive manner by the judiciary and remains the subject of controversy in business transactions that involve many billions of dollars.

It is to be hoped that, in addition to the convergence of Brazilian accounting rules with the IFRS standard, there will be many more updates to Brazilian legislation with regard to developments in international tax law.

Chapter 5
Taxation and Development in Croatia

Nataša Žunić Kovačević

Abstract Although Croatia does not provide incentives for investment in developing countries, it does employ some measures to attract investment into its own jurisdiction. These include tax and customs relief for companies making investments for a specified period to provide jobs and to make other contributions to the Croatian economy. It is expected that with accession to the European Union (EU) the practice of providing investment incentives will diminish. Croatia taxes its residents on worldwide income and provides a foreign tax credit to avoid double taxation. Although there are no explicit incentives for investment in developing countries, the tax exemption for dividends paid to a Croatian corporation may have the effect of encouraging such investment if other favorable conditions are present.

Synopsis Individuals and corporations resident in Croatia are taxed on worldwide income. For residents there is a credit for foreign taxes paid to a foreign corporation limited to the amount of tax that would have been paid in Croatia. Non-residents are taxed only on income from Croatian sources.

There is an exemption for dividends paid to a Croatian resident corporation or any other legal entity. Dividends paid to a nonresident entity are subject to a 12 % withholding tax, unless the rate is reduced by treaty or the distribution is exempt from tax under the EU Parent-Subsidiary Directive. A withholding tax at the rate of 15 % is imposed on interest (with some exceptions), royalties and other payments relating to the exploitation of intellectual property rights.

For payments made to residents of jurisdictions deemed to be tax havens or to have harmful tax regimes (other than EU members) with a corporate tax rate lower than 12.5 %, the withholding rate on the above payments is increased to 20 %. This increased withholding applies only when the country is listed and by the Ministry of Finance and this list published on the appropriate website.

Although Croatia does not provide tax incentives for investment in developing countries, it does employ measures to attract investment within its own jurisdiction. There are tax and customs advantages provided to micro- and other enterprises that

N.Z. Kovačević (✉)
Faculty of Law, University of Rijeka, Rijeka, Croatia
e-mail: zunic@pravri.hr

© Springer International Publishing Switzerland 2017
K.B. Brown (ed.), *Taxation and Development - A Comparative Study*,
Ius Comparatum - Global Studies in Comparative Law 21,
DOI 10.1007/978-3-319-42157-5_5

invest a minimum amount for a specified period, create new jobs for workers, and make other contributions to the Croatian economy. Investments in certain Free Zone Areas enjoy the benefits of exemption from customs duties and a corporate income tax rate reduction of 50 %. There is a complete tax exemption for all profits that are reinvested in the project until they are distributed in a manner that reduces the total amount of investment.

The practice of providing regional tax holidays, distinct from the capital investment incentives described above, has ended with Croatia's accession to the European Union. It is expected that the general practice of providing investment incentives will diminish in order to meet EU expectations.

Croatia imposes corporate tax at the rate of 20 % on taxable profits.

Overview of Croatian International Tax System

Residents (corporations and individuals) are taxed on their worldwide income, while non-residents are taxed only on Croatia-source income. The Income Tax Act (*hereinafter:* ITA) prescribes that the income tax *base* of a resident includes the total amount of income (from employment, from self-employment, from property and property rights, from capital, from insuring risks, and from certain other sources) acquired by a resident from sources in Croatia and abroad reduced by certain personal and other allowances (a world-wide income principle). The income tax base of a non-resident is the total amount of income (from employment, from self-employment, from property and property rights, from capital, from insuring risks and other from certain other sources) acquired by a non-resident from sources in Croatia (the domestic-source income principle).[1] Similarly, the Profit Tax Act (PTA) (Corporate Income Tax Act) provides that the tax base of a resident taxpayer is the profit earned in Croatia and abroad, while the tax base of a non-resident is only the profit earned in Croatia. Resulting tax is assessed in accordance with the PTA.[2]

---

[1] Reduced by the personal allowances or decreased by personal allowance referred to in article 36 of the ITA for natural persons who are residents of the European Union Member States and the European Economic Area, with the exception of the Republic of Croatia, in accordance with Article 36, paragraph 14 of the ITA. The ITA was published in the Official Gazette of the Republic of Croatia "Narodne Novine" No. 177/04, 73/08, 80/10, 114/11, 22/12, 144/12, 120/12 – Decision of the Constitutional Court of the Republic of Croatia, 125/13. *(hereinafter: ITA).*, defines resident and non-resident as follows: A resident is a natural person who has a domicile or habitual residence in the Republic of Croatia. A resident is also a natural person who has neither a domicile nor habitual residence in the Republic of Croatia but is employed in the civil service of the Republic of Croatia and receives a salary on that basis. A non-resident shall be a natural person who has neither domicile nor habitual residence in the Republic of Croatia, but acquires an income from sources within the Republic of Croatia which in subject to taxation pursuant to the ITA.

[2] Profit Tax Act (Corporate Income Tax Act), published in the Official Gazette of the Republic of Croatia "Narodne novine" No. 177/04, 90/05, 57/06, 146/08, 146/08, 80/10, 22/12. *(hereinafter: PTA).* In terms of this Act, residents are legal or natural persons whose seat shall been enrolled in

Foreign tax paid may be credited against the domestic tax liability up to the amount of tax that would have been paid to Croatia on such income if the taxpayer is able to establish that the foreign tax was paid.[3] There is an absolute prevalence of the ordinary credit method, both in the unilateral measures to avoid international double taxation and in the double tax conventions.[4] This means that it is treated as a method for the avoidance of double taxation in the ITA, regulating the taxation of individuals, and in the PTA, mostly regulating the taxation of legal entities and some categories of individual entrepreneurs.

Dividends are subject to tax in Croatia, except for dividends paid to a resident entity. Dividends paid to a non-resident entity are subject to a 12 % withholding tax unless the rate is reduced under a tax treaty or the dividends are qualified for an exemption under the European Union's Parent-Subsidiary Directive. Similarly, a 15 % withholding tax is levied on interest paid to a non-resident unless the rate is reduced under a tax treaty or an interest and royalties directive. A mandatory 20 % withholding tax applies to dividends and interest paid to entities resident in non-EU countries that have an average corporate tax rate of less than 12 % if Croatia and the country in question have not concluded a tax treaty.[5] The tax rate for the payments of royalties to a non-resident is the same as the interest payments – 15 % withholding tax levied on royalties paid to non-residents and 20 % withholding mandatory tax for entities located in jurisdictions specified by Minister of Finance, listed and published in official gazette.

Provisions Targeting Investment Incentives in Tax Haven Jurisdictions

The legal measures directed at hindering the outflow of capital, which involve unfavourable tax treatment of investments in tax havens, are rare in Croatian law and not very explicit. There is no strong and categorical criterion that is used to determine whether a country is a tax haven or a country with a harmful tax regime. Under the PTA, one criterion for positioning a country on a kind of "grey list" is a low tax rate, which is defined as a general or average nominal profit tax rate lower that 12.5 %. The existence of the low tax rate changes the "standard" rules governing imposition of the withholding tax (corporate income tax) on the profit derived by a non-resident

---

the Register of Companies or another register in the Republic of Croatia, or whose place of effective management and control of business is in the Republic of Croatia. Residents are also entrepreneurs-natural persons with domicile or habitual residence in the Republic of Croatia, whose business activity is enrolled in a register or other records. A non-resident shall be any person who does not satisfy one of the requirements referred to in previous paragraphs of this Act.

[3] DTCs that Croatia concluded as an independent state abandoned the exemption method and provide for the credit method in the variety of ordinary credit.

[4] Fifty-seven DTCs are in force.

[5] A List of these jurisdictions was published in the Official Gazette of the Republic of Croatia.

from sources within the Republic of Croatia. Under the "standard/normal rules," the withholding tax collected by the payer is imposed on the gross amount paid by a resident payer to a non-resident recipient. The withholding tax is imposed on interest, dividends, shares of profit, royalties and other receipts from exploiting intellectual property rights (copyrights, patents, licenses, trademarks, designs or models, production processes, formulas, blueprints, plans, industrial or scientific knowhow and other similar rights) payable to foreign entities other than natural persons.

Both the ITA or PTA, provide by way of derogation of the rule described above that the withholding tax is not imposed on interest paid: (i) on commodity loans for the purchase of goods used for carrying out of a taxpayer's business activity, (ii) on loans granted by non-resident bank or other financial institution, or (iii) to holders of government or corporate bonds, who are non-resident legal persons. The withholding tax is imposed, however, in respect of market research services, tax and business counselling and auditor services paid to non-residents.

The prescribed rate of withholding tax is 15 %, except for dividends and shares of profit which are subject to withholding tax at a rate of 12 %. The withholding tax must also be collected by a permanent establishment of a non-resident entrepreneur, when it pays consideration such as interest, dividends, shares of profit, royalties and other payments on exploitation of intellectual property rights (copyrights, patents, licenses, trademarks, design or model, production processes, formulas, blueprints, plans, industrial or scientific knowhow and other similar rights) to the parent company. There is no withholding tax if the payment is recognised as the revenue of a resident permanent establishment of a non-resident entrepreneur.

Regarding tax haven jurisdictions or jurisdictions with harmful tax regimes, the withholding tax is imposed at the higher rate of 20 % for all payments to persons having their permanent establishment or headquarters in those countries, except for the European Union Member States, when the general or average nominal profit taxation rate is lower that 12.5 % and the country is on a list of countries issued by the Finance Minister and published on the web pages of the Ministry of Finance and the Tax Administration of the Republic of Croatia. This list includes 50 countries: US Virgin Islands, Andorra, Anguilla, Antigua and Barbuda, Aruba, Bahamas, Bahrain, Barbados, Belize, Bermuda, Christmas Island, British Virgin Islands, Brunei Darussalam, Dominican Republic, Falkland Islands, Fiji, Gibraltar, Grenada, Guam, Guernsey, Guyana, Hong Kong, Jersey,[6] Cayman Islands, Cook Islands, Liberia, Liechtenstein, Macao, Maldives, Marshall Islands, Monaco, Montserrat, Nauru, Netherlands Antilles, Niue, Turks and Caicos Islands, Isle of Man, Palau, Panama, Samoa, Seychelles, Saint Kitts and Nevis, Saint Lucia, Saint Vincent and the Grenadines, Solomon Islands, Tonga, Trinidad and Tobago, Tuvalu, Vanuatu, and Commonwealth of Dominica. While the jurisdictions of Nauru and Niue are considered tax havens stricto sensu are on the "Croatian list," the other jurisdictions are considered to have regimes with characteristics of tax havens and other harmful tax regimes.

---

[6] Guatemala, not appearing on the list, is classified as an "other financial centre" according to the so-called "grey list" of the OECD, see: http://www.oecd.org/dataoecd/50/0/43606256.pdf.

Croatia is not a party to any regional or international agreements conventions or codes of conduct regarding countries deemed to unfairly compete for capital or to discriminate against or favour certain types of investment.

The Republic of Croatia does not formally participate in the OECD Global Tax Forum. Although not a member of the OECD, it has participated in a number of other initiatives, including the OECD's SIGMA[7] program, which promotes public administration reform. Croatia also participates in the regional Investment Compact for South East Europe program, intended to improve the investment climate and private sector development. Further involvement in the work of the OECD is one of the strategic orientations of Croatia.

In addition, Croatia has also modelled some of its tax treaties on the OECD Model Convention. Although some changes are done on the initiative of member countries, Croatia accepted the modifications provided by the double tax convention on taxation on income and on capital signed in Vienna in 2000.[8] A 2012 amendment of Article 26 of the Austria-Croatia treaty, concerning the exchange of information, extends that provision to cover all taxes. This change resulted from the effort of the Republic of Austria to implement the OECD standards on transparency and exchange of information. The Republic of Croatia relies on the OECD Model and Commentary to fashion its own Model treaty.

Information Exchange

In 2013, Croatia signed the Multilateral Convention on Mutual Administrative Assistance in Tax Matters as amended by the Protocol of 2010, which was developed jointly by the Council of Europe and the OECD.[9] This Convention as multilateral agreement enables enhanced international cooperation between tax administrations in order to fight against tax evasion and avoidance and to ensure full implementation of national tax legislation, while respecting the fundamental rights of taxpayers.

Croatia's Minister of Finance believes that the Convention establishes the necessary international legal framework for mutual assistance in tax matters and supports the mutual exchange of tax information as an important tool in the fight against tax evasion. It is in line with internationally accepted standards on exchange tax information and the fight against tax evasion in Croatia. The Convention allows the exchange of tax information with countries with which Croatia has not concluded an agreement on the avoidance of double taxation. Signing was a precondition for

[7] SIGMA – Support for Improvement in Governance and Management, is a joint initiative of the European Union and the OECD.

[8] See Agreement between the Republic of Austria and the Republic of Croatia for the avoidance of double taxation with respect to taxes on income and on capital, published in the Official Gazette of the Republic of Croatia "Narodne novine – Međunarodni ugovori" No. 3/01.

[9] Croatia signed the Multilateral Convention on October 11, 2013.

the conclusion of the Agreement between the Croatian Government and the Government of the United States in order to improve the performance of tax obligations at the international level and enforcement of the Foreign Account Tax Compliance Act (FATCA) in accordance with the recommendation of the European Commission. The Convention has been signed by 55 countries of the world, opening exchange of information between the Republic of Croatia and countries with whom such exchange was not previously possible. In addition to exchange of tax information, the Convention opens possibilities for simultaneous tax audit and overseas tax audits and interstate cooperation in tax collection.

The European Union's Savings Directive is another example of multilateral agreement on mutual administrative assistance in tax matters. It guarantees mandatory and automatic exchange of information between competent tax authorities of the EU Member States. The Croatian General Tax Act (GTA)[10] has enacted the following European Union Directives into the legal system of the Republic of Croatia: Council Directive 2003/48/EC of 3 June 2003 on taxation of savings income in the form of interest payments,[11] Council Directive 2010/24/EU of 16 March 2010 concerning mutual assistance for the recovery of claims relating to taxes, duties and other measures[12] and Council Directive 2011/16/EU of 15 February 2011 on administrative cooperation in the field of taxation (repealing Directive 77/799/EEC). This Act also established the authority responsible for the implementation of Council Regulation (EU) No. 904/2010 of 7 October 2010 on administrative cooperation and combating fraud in the field of value added tax.[13]

The GTA defines international legal assistance as the right of the tax authority to request assistance of a foreign tax authority in the investigation of a specific tax case. It provides that international legal assistance normally is available only if pursuant to an existing tax treaty, but if a treaty has not been concluded, international legal assistance may be provided under the following terms: (i) there is reciprocity, (ii) the state receiving legal assistance commits itself to use the received information and documentation only for the purposes of tax, criminal, contravention and misdemeanour proceedings and agrees that it will be available only to those persons, governmental bodies or courts that have jurisdiction over a certain tax case or for the purpose of prosecution of tax, criminal, contravention or misdemeanour acts, (iii) the state which has been provided assistance displays willingness to enter into an agreement to avoid possible double taxation in respect to income tax, profit tax and property by way of adequately apportioning the basis of taxation, (iv) compliance with the request does not endanger public order, or other essential interests of the Republic of Croatia, there is no risk of disclosing trade, industrial, technical, or professional secrets or business processes, and (v) domestic taxable persons will not incur injury incompatible with the purpose of the legal assistance.

---

[10] General Tax Act, *Official Gazette, No. 147/08, 18/11, 78/12, 136/12, 73/13., (hereinafter: GTA).*
[11] OJ, L 157, 26.6.2003.
[12] OJ, L 84, 31.3. 2010.
[13] OJ. L 268, 12.10.2010.

Investment Incentives

While Croatia provides no tax incentives for investment in countries with low incomes, high poverty rates or high rates of economic inequality, it has taken many different measures to attract economic activity to its own jurisdiction.

Investors in Croatia may benefit from various types of incentives as defined by the Act on Investments Promotion and Enhancement of Investment Environment.[14] These include incentives for microenterprises, tax and custom advantages, incentives for eligible costs of new jobs linked to the investment project, incentives for eligible costs of training linked to the investment projects, incentive measures for development and innovation activities, incentive measures for the business support activities, incentive measures for the high added value service, incentive measures for capital costs of an investment project, and incentive measures for labour intensive investment projects. All mentioned incentives may be used by foreign and domestic investors investing at least 150.000 EUR (50.000 EUR for micro entrepreneurs)[15] and creating at least five new jobs (places of employment) for workers (three for micro entrepreneurs). These incentives relate to manufacturing and processing activities, development and innovation activities, business support activities, and high-added value activities.

The minimum period for maintaining the investment is 5 years for large enterprises and 3 years for small and medium-sized enterprises after the completion of the project. In any event, the period of investment must equal or exceed the period the incentive measure is provided under the Act.

Thirteen free zone locations are currently in Croatia, ranging from sea port-based ones at Pula, Rijeka, Split and Ploče to other strategically located zones in Krapina, Zagorje, Kukuljanovo, Osijek, Ribnik, Slavonski Brod, Split-Dalmacija, Varaždin, Vukovar and Zagreb. The Free Zones Act was adopted in 1996 and introduced dual zones: zones established on the basis of concessions and zones established on the basis of specific decisions or giving consent. All the zones have the same requirements regarding their structure, governance and compliance with the conditions for the start of work, relationships with customers, customs control, and payment of taxes. The main benefits for users are the exemption from customs duties on imports of goods and lowering the corporate income tax in the amount of 50 % of the prescribed rate (and exemption from this tax for the first 5 years for investment in the construction of infrastructural facilities in the zone of more than one million Croatian Kunas (kn).[16]

---

[14] Act on Investments promotion and Enhancement of Investment Environment, Official Gazette, No. 11/12 and 28/13, and Regulation on Investments promotion and Enhancement of Investment Environment, Official Gazette, No. 40/13.

[15] Article 8, Act on Investments promotion and Enhancement of Investment Environment.

[16] Free Zones Act, Official Gazette "Narodne novine", No. 44/96, 92/05, 85/08, 148/13; Rules on how to calculate the investments made and used to support investment and how to achieve tax advantages for users of free zones, Official Gazette 122/08, 33/10, 05/10; Act on Implementing the EU Customs Regulations, Official Gazette 54/13. The users of the Free Zone are obliged to pay the

Advantages and benefits of operating in a free zone were promoted by the incentive measures regulated by the Act on Investment Promotion and Development of Investment Climate. These measures include incentives for micro enterprises, profit tax incentives, aid to cover eligible costs of the job creation linked to an investment project, aid to cover eligible costs of training linked to an investment project; incentive measures for development-innovation activities, business support activities, and high value added service activities, incentive measures for capital expenditures of investment project, and incentives for labour intensive investment projects.

Tax deferral for reinvested profits is one of the key elements of the amended Croatian corporate taxation regime. The PTA provides a tax exemption (with the same effect as tax deferral) for reinvested profits. The taxpayer is exempted from all taxes on profits that are reinvested, but in the case of a distribution of profits in any way affecting the nominal worth of the reinvested profit, the earlier exempted profit becomes taxable. The procedure for obtaining such treatment is regulated through the provisions of Art. 12A, Profit Tax Regulation.[17]

Tax Holidays and Accession to the European Union

While Croatia has introduced a number of tax holidays, a distinction must be made between general tax holidays (so-called capital investment incentives) applicable to the entire territory of Croatia and regional tax holidays which applied only in certain parts of the country and were abandoned with the Croatian accession to the EU. General tax holidays are allowed for 10-year periods during which a reduced tax rate (10 %, 7 %, 3 %) or a full tax exemption (0 %) is applied, depending on the investment amount and the number of new employees. The stipulated conditions must be met within a time period (3 years) from the beginning of investment (for details see: Šimović 2008).

Regional tax holidays were allowed similarly, but under even more favourable conditions, for investment in underdeveloped Croatian regions. Such tax holidays included tax relief, allowances and incentives which applied to the area of the City of Vukovar, in areas of special national concern, hilly and mountain areas, and in free zones. Due to the requirement related to adjustment to the European Union *acquis communautaire*,[18] Croatia has over the last few years made significant

---

corporate income tax – profit tax in the amount of 50 % of the prescribed rate, and if they are taking part in the construction of the infrastructure buildings in the Free Zone in an amount greater than 1.000.000 kn (approximate 130.000 Euro) they are tax-free (exempt from corporate income tax payments) during the first 5 years of business dealings in the Free Zone, but until the end of 2016 year.

[17] Profit Tax Regulation, Official Gazette "Narodne novine", No. 95/05, 133/07, 156/08, 146/09, 123/10, 137/11, 61/12, 146/12, 160/13, 12/14.

[18] Šimović, Bratović, Efficiency of tax incentives in Croatia, Economic Policy and Global Recession, (2009), in: A. Praščević et al. (ed.), Economic Policy and Global Recession, Beograd: Faculty of Economics (2009).

reforms and adjustments of the legislation related to tax holidays. Some of the mentioned tax holidays were amended and a certain number of incentives were completely suspended.

The legislation provides for a gradual decrease in the level of tax incentive and the duration of tax holidays. Complete suspension of tax holidays is mostly connected with Croatia's accession to the EU.

Out of the list of standard investment incentives in the broader sense only accelerated depreciation is used in Croatia, which allows for the depreciation rate to be doubled. In addition to accelerated depreciation, other tax incentives exist which are not classic investment allowances. Such incentives include tax base deductions for certain costs and tax loss relief (Šimović 2008).

Regarding tax base deductions, additional allowances reducing the tax base are possible for costs of research and development (R&D) projects as well as for education and training costs of employees. In case of tax loss relief, tax losses may be carried forward for up to five consecutive years. The carry- back of losses is not permitted.

Croatia, as a typical transition country, implemented a relatively large number of corporate income tax incentives with the purpose of stimulating economic activity, with tax holidays as the predominant form of corporate income tax incentives. Presently, other types of corporate income tax incentives play a significant role. Croatia implements various tax incentives as instruments of stimulating economic activity.

Corporate Tax Rate Structure

The profit tax is imposed at the rate of 20 % of the assessed tax base (the corporate tax rate). Taxable income is determined by adjusting accounting profit in accordance with the provisions of the PTA. The corporate tax base is the difference between revenue and expenditure assessed in the profit and loss statement under the accounting rules, which is then increased or reduced for tax-specific items under the tax provisions. Dividends are subject to tax in Croatia, except for dividends paid to a resident entity. Dividends paid to a non-resident entity are subject to a 12 % withholding tax unless previously mentioned conditions apply – the rate is reduced or exempt under tax treaty or the dividends are qualified for an exemption under the EU legislation (Parent-Subsidiary directive). Also, a 15 % withholding tax is levied on interest paid to a non-resident unless the rate is reduced (or exempt) either under a tax treaty or the EU legislation (Interest and Royalties (I & R) Directive). A 15 % withholding tax is levied on royalties paid to a non-resident unless the rate is reduced or exempt under a tax treaty or the EU (I & R) Directive. The withholding tax is imposed at a rate of 20 % on all services paid to persons having their permanent establishment or headquarters in countries, except for the European Union Member States, in which a general or average nominal profit taxation rate is lower that 12.5 % and the country is published in the list of countries issued by the Finance Minister and published on the web pages of the Ministry of Finance and the Tax Administration of the Republic of Croatia.

Trade Agreements

Croatia was a party to the Central European Free Trade Agreement (CEFTA), an agreement between non-EU countries in Southeast Europe. When Croatia became a member of the EU in 2013, the CEFTA participation ended. Subsequent to establishment of membership in the International Centre for Settlement of Investment Disputes – ICSID, Croatia concluded 56 bilateral investment treaties:

	Signature date	Entry into force date
Zimbabwe	Feb 18, 2000	
United States of America	Jul 13, 1996	Jun 20, 2001
United Kingdom of Great Britain and Northern Ireland	Mar 11, 1997	Apr 16, 1998
Ukraine	Dec 15, 1997	
Turkey	Feb 12, 1996	Apr 21, 1998
Thailand	Feb 18, 2000	
Switzerland	Oct 30, 1996	Jun 17, 1997
Sweden	Nov 23, 2000	Aug 01, 2002
Spain	Jul 21, 1997	Sep 17, 1998
Slovenia	Dec 12, 1997	Jul 08, 2004
Slovak Republic	Feb 12, 1996	Feb 06, 1997
Serbia	Aug 18, 1998	Jan 31, 2002
San Marino	May 07, 2004	Jul 27, 2005
Russian Federation	May 20, 1996	
Romania	Jun 08, 1994	Sep 09, 1995
Qatar	Nov 12, 2001	
Portugal	May 10, 1995	Nov 27, 1997
Poland	Feb 21, 1995	Oct 04, 1995
Oman	May 04, 2004	
Netherlands	Apr 28, 1998	Jun 01, 1999
Morocco	Sep 29, 2004	
Mongolia	Aug 08, 2006	
Moldova	Dec 05, 2001	Mar 20, 2007
Malta	Jul 11, 2001	May 10, 2002
Malaysia	Dec 16, 1994	
Libya	Dec 20, 2002	Jun 21, 2006
Latvia	Apr 04, 2002	May 25, 2005
Kuwait	Mar 08, 1997	Jul 02, 1998
Korea, Republic of	Jul 19, 2005	
Jordan	Oct 10, 1999	Apr 27, 2000
Italy	Nov 05, 1996	Jun 12, 1998
Israel	Aug 01, 2000	Jul 18, 2003
Iran, Islamic Republic of	May 17, 2000	Jul 20, 2005
Indonesia	Sep 10, 2002	

(continued)

	Signature date	Entry into force date
India	May 04, 2001	Jan 19, 2002
Hungary	May 15, 1996	Mar 01, 2002
Greece	Oct 18, 1996	Oct 21, 1998
Germany	Mar 21, 1997	Sep 28, 2000
France	Jun 03, 1996	Mar 05, 1998
Finland	Jun 01, 1999	Nov 01, 2002
Egypt, Arab Republic of	Oct 27, 1997	May 02, 1999
Denmark	Jul 05, 2000	Jan 12, 2002
Czech Republic	Mar 05, 1996	May 15, 1997
Cuba	Feb 16, 2001	
China	Jun 07, 1993	Jul 01, 1994
Chile	Nov 28, 1994	Jul 31, 1996
Canada	Feb 03, 1997	Jan 30, 2001
Cambodia	May 18, 2001	Jun 15, 2002
Bulgaria	Jun 25, 1996	Feb 20, 1998
Bosnia and Herzegovina	Jul 23, 2002	Jan 03, 2005
Bosnia and Herzegovina	Feb 26, 1996	
Belgium-Luxembourg	Oct 31, 2001	Dec 28, 2003
Belarus	Jun 26, 2001	Jul 14, 2005
Austria	Feb 19, 1997	Nov 01, 1999
Argentina	Dec 02, 1994	Jun 01, 1996
Albania	Mar 05, 1993	Apr 16, 1994

The ICSID convention entered into force for Croatia on October 22, 1998. These agreements do not contain tax provisions[19] or concessions.

Reference

Šimović, H. 2008. *Porezni poticaji za izgradnju konkurentnosti*. Faculty of Economics and Business Zagreb, Working Paper Series, 08-03, 1–19. http://web.efzg.hr/RePEc/pdf/Clanak%2008-03.pdf.

[19]The one exception, a clause containing taxation terminology in the Croatia-Austria agreement: "The provisions of paragraph 1 of this Article shall not be construed as to oblige one Contracting Party to extend to the investors of the other Contracting Party and their investments the present or future benefit of any treatment, preference or privilege resulting from (a) any customs union, common market, free trade area or membership in an economic community; (b) any international agreement, international arrangement or domestic legislation regarding taxation;…".

Chapter 6
Tax Law Components to Provide Incentives for Investment

Michal Radvan and Dana Šramková

Abstract Although the Czech Republic does not have a territorial tax regime, its participation exemption allows deferral of tax on income of certain foreign subsidiaries. With EU approval, the Czech Republic provides incentives to attract investment. These incentives support manufacturing, job creation, and employee training in the Czech Republic. There is special high withholding tax on dividends, interest, and royalties paid to off-shore tax haven jurisdictions. The Czech Republic is committed to information exchange and the latest standard of information exchange.

Synopsis The Czech Republic, a member of the European Union (EU) since 2004, taxes its residents on their worldwide income, allowing a credit against Czech income tax liability for taxes paid to a foreign country (foreign tax credit). A corporation with a registered office or headquarters in the Czech Republic is subject to worldwide taxation. When a treaty applies, a foreign tax credit may be allowed under the full credit method (allowing a refund of taxes paid if the tax liability in the foreign country exceeds the Czech liability) or the ordinary credit method (allowing offset of the worldwide tax liability only for foreign tax computed on foreign source income at a rate no higher than the Czech effective rate). Some Czech treaties, such as the one with Brazil, follow the exemption method in which specified foreign source income (but not passive income) is exempted from taxation. The Czech Republic is signatory to more than 42 double taxation treaties. In the absence of a treaty, a deduction is allowed for foreign taxes paid which reduces the Czech tax base, but does not provide a dollar-for-dollar tax reduction.

Nonresidents are taxed only on income from Czech sources.

Although, the Czech Republic does not have a territorial tax regime, the operation of the EU Parent-Subsidiary Directive provides exemptions for dividends derived from profits earned abroad. The participation exemption, based on principles established in the Directive, allows for deferral of tax on the income of foreign subsidiaries (resident in EU member nations as well as Norway, Switzerland, and Iceland) as well as an exemption when the profits are returned to the Czech parent

M. Radvan (✉) • D. Šramková
Department of Financial Law and Economics, Faculty of Law, Masaryk University, Brno, Czech Republic
e-mail: michal.radvan@law.muni.cz; dana.sramkova@law.muni.cz

© Springer International Publishing Switzerland 2017   107
K.B. Brown (ed.), *Taxation and Development - A Comparative Study*,
Ius Comparatum - Global Studies in Comparative Law 21,
DOI 10.1007/978-3-319-42157-5_6

in the form of a dividend or other profit share. This regime also exempts from taxation payments from permanent establishments resident in any foreign country to tax non-residents.

One provision that may impact tax havens is the introduction of a withholding tax on dividends, interest, royalties paid to off-shore jurisdictions. In 2013, a special tax rate of 35 % was introduced for payments to taxpayers not resident in EU member states and to those resident in any other country that is not a signatory to certain treaties or international agreements (to which the Czech Republic is a party) that do not contain an acceptable exchange of information provision.

As a member of the EU and OECD, the Czech Republic participates in Harmful Tax Competition projects sponsored by these organizations. In particular, the EU Code of Conduct for Business Taxation, adopted in 1997. The Code of Conduct identifies potentially harmful tax measures, such as tax benefits reserved for non-residents, tax incentives isolated from the domestic economy, grant of tax advantages in the absence of real economic activity, and lack of transparency. Guidelines concerning restrictions on provision of State Aid, defined as any aid granted by a member state that distorts competition by favoring certain production or other undertakings. A subsequent EU Communication, adopted in 2004 and further detailed in 2009, identifies actions to be taken by member states to promote 'good governance' in tax matters. The Czech Republic also participates in the OECD's Global Tax Forum.

In addition to the double taxation treaties described above, the Czech Republic has also concluded seven Tax Information Exchange Agreements (TIEAs) with jurisdictions commonly identified as tax havens (Bermuda, British Virgin Islands, Jersey, Isle of Man, Bahamas. It is also signatory to the Convention on Mutual Administrative Assistance in Tax Matters (which has gained more than 60 signers). The Convention, which meets the OECD's latest standard, provides for all forms of administrative cooperation, including spontaneous, automatic, and "upon request" information exchange, concurrent inquiries, tax examination abroad, requests for enforcement, and document delivery. With EU approval, the Czech Republic offers incentives to attract domestic and foreign investment. These incentives relate to support of manufacturing, creation of jobs, and employee training. They may be provided only in the processing and servicing industries, technology (software) centres, and strategic service centers (accounting, finance, human resources administration, marketing, and information system management). Typically, a minimum level of investment is required. Application for these incentives, including tax relief, is made to Czechinvest through the Ministry of Industry and Trade, which makes the final determination. The Czech Republic has entered into a number of agreements with other countries for the promotion of reciprocal protection of investments, including a small number with developing countries.

The corporate tax rate is 19 % of net income. A reduced tax rate of 5 % is provided for domestic and foreign investment funds and retirement pension funds established in EU member states, Norway, and Iceland.

Overview of International Tax System

The Czech Republic is an economically developed country with strong economic links to other countries, mainly those of the European Union (EU). The right to collect taxes and to set the conditions for tax collection are among the main elements constituting national sovereignty. However, the entry of the Czech Republic into the EU in 2004 resulted in a limitation of the country's sovereignty because fiscal jurisdiction over certain matters was handed over to the EU. Unpopular as the surrender of the tax sovereignty is among the member states of the EU, it is a crucial prerequisite helping to support the free movement of persons, goods, services and capital. Despite these goals, however, the unification of direct taxes (namely income and property taxes) has not progressed in any significant manner, except for the joint system of taxation of parent and subsidiary companies in the area of dividends and licensing fees and the taxation of deposits and savings. By contrast, the unification is almost complete as regards indirect taxes (value added tax and select excise taxes), with the exception of tax rates which are not unified yet.

The limitation of sovereignty, which occurs when imposing tax liabilities, operates not only at the level of the EU but also at the level of the individual countries, typically in the form of bilateral treaties preventing double taxation. The Czech Republic is one of the countries with the highest number of double taxation treaties in the world. The primary aim of such treaties is to prevent undesirable double taxation, though this only affects the situation in the international context. On the national level, the prevention of double taxation is primarily addressed by internal (national) law. In spite of that, however, double taxation often results from political decision.

The legal regulation of taxation in the Czech Republic is, in many respects, quite standard and does not differ from other advanced countries. The Czech Republic follows the worldwide tax liability approach for its tax residents. Natural persons domiciled or usually staying within the territory of the Czech Republic (i.e. Czech tax residents) are liable for tax on incomes generated from sources in the Czech Republic as well as from foreign sources. Non-residents, by contrast, have a tax liability only on income generated from sources in the Czech Republic. The liability does not apply to taxpayers who stay in the Czech Republic only for the purposes of study or medical treatment: these individuals are liable for tax on income generated from sources in the Czech Republic only if they are habitually present within the territory of the Czech Republic. Legal persons that have their registered offices or headquarters in the Czech Republic have a tax liability on both income generated from sources in the Czech Republic and from foreign sources. Those taxpayers that do not have their registered offices or headquarters in the Czech Republic have a tax liability only on income generated from sources in the Czech Republic. Since double taxation is not economically desirable, it is eliminated by use of the credit or exemption method in accordance with each particular double taxation treaty.[1]

The full credit method allows taxpayers to reduce the tax calculated on the basis of their world-wide incomes by the amount of tax already paid abroad. The full credit method is applied in the same manner as the withholding tax on interest, as provided for in the European Council Directive No. 2003/48/EC on taxation of savings income in the form of interest payments. The directive is reflected in the Czech system in the rule stipulating that where a resident has had a tax on income in the form of interest payment withheld abroad in an amount higher than provided in the relevant treaty, it can be used to reduce Czech tax liability as long as the tax is withheld abroad in accordance with Directive No. 2003/48/EC. Where the total tax liability is lower than the tax withheld in accordance with Directive No. 2003/48/EC, the difference constitutes overpaid tax. The full credit method also appears in the international treaty on the prevention of double taxation between the Czech Republic and Sri Lanka. In practice, however, the full credit method results in quite paradoxical situations, e.g., when the reduction of tax paid in the country where the income is generated reduces the tax payable from quite unrelated incomes in the resident's country.

For this reason, double taxation treaties usually provide for the ordinary credit method. This method likewise anticipates the inclusion of foreign source income in the tax base and the crediting of the tax paid abroad. However, the worldwide tax liability may be offset by the foreign tax imposed on the foreign source portion of income computed at a rate no higher than the Czech rate. New double taxation treaties concluded between the Czech Republic and other countries operate with the method of ordinary credit most often.

Formerly, however, the exemption method (deduction) was preferred, as in the case of treaties between the Czech Republic and the Federal Republic of Germany, Great Britain, etc. The exemption method does not apply to dividends, interest, and royalty payments. Under this method, the country of the taxpayer's residence exempts some foreign source income from taxation. Full exemption is found, for instance, in the treaty between the Czech Republic and Brazil. Because of the linear rate of tax on the income of legal persons, which was applicable to natural persons until 2012 as well, the Czech Republic essentially applies full exemption of tax on foreign source income whenever the exemption method is used. This is also the case with other double taxation treaties that do not provide for the credit method (except for some income generated in Brazil).

The treaties presuppose the application of the credit method and exemption with progression. The significance of the latter has increased since 2013 due to the introduction in the Czech Republic of the so-called solidarity increase of income tax of natural persons in the amount of 7 %. As a result of the application of the method of exemption with progression, the exempted income is not included in the tax base in

---

[1] SOJKA, Vlastimil. Mezinárodní zdanění příjmů (International Income Taxation). Prague: Wolters Kluwer, 2013.

the country of the taxpayer's residence. However, it is taken into account when determining the tax rate imposed on the remaining income.

The national law in the Czech Republic provides for the elimination of double taxation of income of natural persons generated from dependent activities. The law makes it possible (thus allowing for discretion) to apply the exemption method in all other situations where any double taxation treaty exists, i.e., also where a given treaty specifies that the credit method be used (cf. treaties between the Czech Republic and Slovakia, Austria and Poland).

In the absence of a double taxation treaty between the Czech Republic and any other country, double taxation is eliminated based on the deduction method provided by national law. Under the Act No. 586/1992 Sb. on Income Taxes, as subsequently amended, any tax paid abroad is treated as a cost that reduces the tax base in the Czech Republic. Thus, this phenomenon concerns the alleviation of the effects of double taxation rather than the elimination of double taxation in the proper sense of the word. A deduction, unlike a credit, does not provide a dollar-for-dollar reduction in tax liability and is less valuable.

Below is the list of double taxation prevention treaties between the Czech Republic and other states[2]:

Country	Valid since	Act no.[a]	Country	Valid since	Act no.[b]
Albania	10.9.1996	270/1996 Sb.	Lichtenstein	22.12.2015	8/2016 Sb. I. T.
Armenia	15.7.2009	86/2009 Sb. I. T.	Lithuania	8.8.1995	230/1995 Sb.
Australia	27.11.1995	5/1996 Sb.	Luxembourg	31.7.2014	51/2014 Sb.
Austria	22.3.2007	31/2007 Sb. I. T.	Macedonia	17.6.2002	88/2002 Sb. I. T.
Azerbaijan	16.6.2006	74/2006 Sb. I. T.	Malaysia	9.3.1998	71/1998 Sb.
Bahrain	10.4.2012	59/2012 Sb. I. T.	Malta	6.6.1997	164/1997 Sb.
Barbados	6.6.2012	69/2012 Sb. I. T.	Morocco	18.7.2006	83/2006 Sb. I. T.
Belarus	15.1.1998	31/1998 Sb.	Mexico	27.12.2002	7/2003 Sb. I. T.
Belgium	24.7.2000	95/2000 Sb. I. T.	Moldavia	26.4.2000	88/2000 Sb. I. T.
Bosnia and Herzegovina	12.5.2010	58/2010 Sb. I.T.	Mongolia	22.6.1998	18/1999 Sb.
Brazil	24.11.1990	200/1991 Sb.	Netherlands	5.11.1974	138/1974 Sb.
Bulgaria	2.7.1999	203/1999 Sb.	New Zeeland	29.8.2008	75/2008 Sb. I. T.
Canada	28.5.2002	83/2002 Sb. I. T.	Nigeria	2.12.1990	339/1991 Sb.

(continued)

[2] For more details, see http://www.mfcr.cz/cs/legislativa/dvoji-zdaneni. Accessed on 20 October 2016.

Country	Valid since	Act no.[a]	Country	Valid since	Act no.[b]
China	23.12.1987	41/1988 Sb.	Norway	9.9.2005	121/2005 Sb. I. T.
CMEA (legal entities)	1.1.1979	49/1979 Sb.	Pakistan	30.10.2015	58/2015 Sb. I. T.
CMEA (natural persons)	1.1.1979	30/1979 Sb.	Panama	25.2.2013	91/2013 Sb. I. T.
Colombia	4.8.2016	47/2016 Sb. I. T.	Peoples Rep. of Korea	7.12.2005	3/2006 Sb. I. T.
Croatia	28.12.1999	42/2000 Sb. I. T.	Philippines	23.9.2003	132/2003 Sb. I. T.
Cyprus	26.11.2009	120/2009 Sb. I. T.	Poland	20.12.1993	31/1994 Sb.
Denmark	27.12.1982	53/1983 Sb.	Portugal	1.10.1997	275/1997 Sb.
Egypt	4.10.1995	283/1995 Sb.	Romania	11.8.1994	180/1994 Sb.
Estonia	26.5.1995	184/1995 Sb.	Russia	18.7.1997	278/1997 Sb.
Ethiopia	30.5.2008	54/2008 Sb. I. T.	Saudi Arabia	1.5.2013	42/2013 Sb. I. T.
Finland	12.12.1995	43/1996 Sb.	Serbia and MN	27.6.2005	88/2005 Sb. I. T.
France	1.7.2005	79/2005 Sb. I. T.	Slovenia	28.4.1998	214/1998 Sb.
Georgia	4.5.2007	40/2007 Sb. I. T.	Slovakia	14.7.2003	100/2003 Sb. I. T.
Germany	17.11.1983	18/1984 Sb.	Republic of South Africa	3.12.1997	7/1998 Sb.
Greece	23.5.1989	98/1989 Sb.	Singapore	21.8.1998	224/1998 Sb.
Hong Kong	24.1.2012	49/2012 Sb. I. T.	Spain	5.6.1981	23/1982 Sb.
Hungary	27.12.1994	22/1995 Sb.	Sri Lanka	19.6.1979	132/1979 Sb.
Iceland	28.12.2000	11/2001 Sb. I. T.	Sweden	8.10.1980	9/1981 Sb.
India	27.9.1999	301/1999 Sb.	Switzerland	23.10.1996	281/1996 Sb.
Indonesia	26.1.1996	67/1996 Sb.	Syria	12.11.2009	115/2009 Sb. I. T.
Ireland	21.4.1996	163/1996 Sb.	Tajikistan	19.10.2007	89/2007 Sb. I. T.
Iran	4.8.2016	47/2016 Sb. I. T.	Thailand	14.8.1995	229/1995 Sb.
Israel	23.12.1994	21/1995 Sb.	Tunisia	25.10.1991	419/1992 Sb.
Italy	26.6.1984	17/1985 Sb.	Turkey	16.12.2003	19/2004 Sb. I. T.

(continued)

Country	Valid since	Act no.[a]	Country	Valid since	Act no.[b]
Japan	25.11.1978	46/1979 Sb.	Ukraine	20.4.1999	103/1999 Sb.
Jordan	7.11.2007	88/2007 Sb. I. T.	United Arab Emirates	9.8.1997	276/1997 Sb.
Kazakhstan	29.10.1999	3/2002 Sb. I. T.	United Kingdom	20.12.1991	89/1992 Sb.
Korea	3.3.1995	124/1995 Sb.	USA	23.12.1993	32/1994 Sb.
Kuwait	3.3.2004	48/2004 Sb. I. T.	Uzbekistan	15.1.2001	28/2001 Sb. I. T.
Latvia	22.5.1995	170/1995 Sb.	Venezuela	12.11.1997	6/1998 Sb.
Lebanon	24.1.2000	30/2000 Sb. I. T.	Vietnam	3.2.1998	108/1998 Sb.

[a]In Collection (Sb.) or in Collection of International Treaties (Sb. I. T.)
[b]In Collection (Sb.) or in Collection of International Treaties (Sb. I. T.)

The Czech Republic has not in the past and currently does not offer a territorial tax regime. In some cases, however, it may exempt inbound dividends based on the principles arising from the Parent-Subsidiary Directive (Directive No. 2011/96/EU on the common system of taxation applicable in the case of parent companies and subsidiaries of different Member States), a practice which may amount functionally to a territorial regime.[3]

Parent-Subsidiary Dividend Relief

The Czech Republic provides for a participation exemption based on the principles arising from the Parent-Subsidiary Directive (2011/96/EU). The aim of the directive is to remove the disadvantage faced by tax residents when repatriating the profits from their subsidiaries in other EU countries. The practical importance consists in the elimination of multiple taxation of corporate distributions on equity and the deferral of tax liability until the distribution of profits to the shareholder. The Czech Republic implements this directive by exempting the transfer of profits between the parent company and its subsidiary from income tax at both the parent and subsidiary levels. The exemption relates to payment by tax residents of the Czech Republic of dividends and other shares of profit for the benefit of parent companies that are registered for tax purposes in other EU countries. It also covers payments made for the benefit of permanent establishments of tax non-residents from any country. The same regime applies to residents of Norway, Switzerland and Iceland.

---

[3] For more details, see below.

Anti-tax Haven Initiatives

In 2012, the Czech Republic introduced a withholding tax on profits in the form of dividends, interest, royalties paid to off-shore jurisdictions.

In 2013, the Czech income tax act introduced a special tax rate of 35 % for tax-payers (both natural and legal persons) who are tax residents neither in any other EU member state (or any state of the European Economic Area) nor in any third country that is a signatory to a valid and effective double taxation treaty with the Czech Republic, some other treaty or international agreement on the exchange of information in income tax matters, or a multilateral international treaty containing a provision on the exchange of information in income tax matters that is valid and in effect for the given country and the Czech Republic. Although this legal regulation is not expressly concerned with the taxation of incomes from so-called tax havens, it affects precisely those incomes.

Anti-harmful Tax Competition Measures

European Union Measures

The Czech Republic, as a member of the OECD and the EU, participates in Harmful Tax Competition projects sponsored by these organizations and generally follows the principles agreed upon by these organizations.

The most important document at the EU level is the Code of Conduct for Business Taxation.[4] It was set out in the conclusions of the Council of Economics and Finance Ministers (ECOFIN) in December 1997. The Code is not a legally binding instrument but it clearly does have political force. By adopting this Code, the Member States have undertaken to roll back existing tax measures that constitute harmful tax competition and to refrain from introducing any such measures in the future.

The criteria for identifying potentially harmful measures include[5]:

- an effective level of taxation which is significantly lower than the general level of taxation in the country concerned;
- tax benefits reserved for non-residents;
- tax incentives for activities which are isolated from the domestic economy and therefore have no impact on the national tax base;
- a grant of tax advantages even in the absence of any real economic activity;

---

[4] See   http://ec.europa.eu/taxation_customs/taxation/company_tax/harmful_tax_practices/index_
en.htm. Accessed on 13 December 2013.
[5] Ibid.

- a basis of profit determination for companies in a multinational group that departs from internationally accepted rules, in particular those approved by the OECD;
- a lack of transparency.

Concerning other EU work related to harmful tax practices, the Communication on Preventing and Combating Financial and Corporate Malpractice adopted in September 2004 by the European Commission is important. It provides a strategy for coordinated action in the areas of financial services, company law, accounting, tax, supervision and enforcement, aimed to reduce the risk of financial wrongdoing. As regards taxation, the Commission suggested more transparency and information exchange in the area of company taxes so that tax systems are more capable of dealing with complex corporate structures. The Commission also wished to ensure coherent EU policies concerning offshore financial centres, as well as to encourage these jurisdictions to move towards transparency and effective exchange of information. In April 2009, the Commission adopted a Communication identifying actions that EU Member States should take in order to promote "good governance" in the area of taxation (i.e. more transparency, exchange of information and fair tax competition). The Communication identified the way in which good governance could be improved within the EU. It also listed the tools that the EU and its Member States had at their disposal to ensure that good governance principles were applied at the international level. Finally, it called on Member States to adopt an approach that was more consonant with good governance principles in their bilateral relations with third countries and in international fora.[6]

In support of the Code of conduct on business taxation, the Commission committed itself to publishing guidelines on the application of State Aid rules to measures relating to direct business taxation. These guidelines were adopted by the Commission in November 1998. According to EU law, any aid granted by a Member State or through State resources in any form whatsoever which distorts or threatens to distort competition by favouring certain undertakings or the production of certain goods is deemed, in so far as it affects trade between Member States, to be incompatible with the common market. State aid rules apply regardless of the form in which the aid is given in, i.e. any kind of tax relief can constitute State aid if the other criteria are fulfilled. However, even if a measure fulfils the criteria for being State aid there are a number of situations in which aid can be deemed compatible with fairness principles. In addition, the Commission issued a large number of regulations, notices, guidelines, frameworks and communications in the area of State aid. In particular, in the area of direct taxation the Commission issued a notice on the application of State aid rules to measures relating to direct business taxation in 1998 and a report in 2004 on the implementation of that notice.[7]

---

[6] Ibid.
[7] Ibid.

OECD Global Forum

The Czech Republic participates in the OECD's Global Tax Forum. In 1998, OECD created the Forum on Harmful Tax Practices. The Forum is focused on three areas[8]:

- harmful tax practices in Member Countries (three progress reports);
- tax havens (together with cooperative tax havens the Forum has produced a Model Tax Agreement on Exchange of Information in Tax Matters);
- participation and input by non-OECD economies.

The Czech tax regime has not been characterized as harmful.

Information Exchange Agreements

The Czech Republic has exchange of information provisions in its bilateral tax agreements. Information exchange concerns not only income taxes, but also other taxes such as VAT, excise duties, property taxes, etc. The exchange is of all information necessary to comply with obligations under provisions of international double taxation treaties as well as national legal regulations concerning taxes on the national and local levels, i.e. including local charges. The agreements bind the signatory states to exchange information as well as to protect the confidentiality of such information.

In this connection, the role of EU law in the Czech Republic bears mention, particularly Council Directive 2011/16/EU of 15 February 2011 on administrative cooperation in the field of taxation (repealing Directive 77/799/EEC) and Council Directive 2010/24/EU of 16 March 2010 concerning mutual assistance for the recovery of claims relating to taxes, duties and other measures. These directives were incorporated into the national legal regulations of the Czech Republic by means of two independent acts: the Act No. 164/2013 Sb., on International Cooperation in Tax Administration amending related acts, and the Act No. 471/2011 Sb., on International Cooperation in the Enforcement of Some Financial Claims.

Since 2012, the Czech Republic has concluded ten Tax Information Exchange Agreements (TIEAs) with countries that are commonly identified as tax havens. The Czech Republic has had a positive experience with this kind of international cooperation, which was previously carried out mainly on the basis of double taxation treaties (see above) and the original Council Directive 77/799/EEC of 19 December 1977 concerning mutual assistance by the competent authorities of the Member States in the field of direct taxation and other memoranda of understandings.[9]

---

[8] Ibid.

[9] Current information available from the web site of the Ministry of Finance, see http://www.mfcr.cz/cs/legislativa/mezinarodni-vymena-info-v-danove-oblasti/platne-smlouvy. Accessed on 20 October 2016.

The Tax Information Exchange Agreements are listed in the following table:

Country	Valid since	Act no.[a]	Country	Valid since	Act no.[b]
Island of Bermuda	14.03.2012	48/2012 Sb. I. T.	Guernsey	09.07.2012	2/2013 Sb. I. T.
British Virgin Islands	19.12.2012	6/2013 Sb. I.T.	Republic of San Marino	06.09.2012	4/2013 Sb. I. T.
Jersey	14.03.2012	51/2012 Sb. I. T.	Cayman Islands	20.09.2013	90/2013 Sb. I. T.
Isle of Man	18.05.2012	3/2013 Sb. I. T.	Andorra	05.06.2014	33/2014 Sb. I. T.
Bahamas	02.04.2015	34/2015 Sb. I. T.	Monaco	2.3.2016	17/2016 Sb. I. T.
Cook Islands	10.5.2016	34/2016 Sb. I. T.	Aruba	1.8.2016	41/2016 Sb. I. T.

[a]In Collection (Sb.) or in Collection of International Treaties (Sb. I. T.)
[b]Ibid.

After the multilateral Convention on Mutual Administrative Assistance in Tax Matters became valid on 1 February 2014, Czech tax administrators gained another tool to combat tax evasion. The convention, drafted under the auspices of the OECD and Council of Europe, is in harmony (as worded in the Protocol of 1 June 2011) with the OECD's new standard for information exchange in the field of taxation. The Convention, which has so far been signed by more than 60 countries, includes all forms of cooperation in tax administration – both on the action and payment levels, including, among other mechanisms, information exchange upon request, automatic and spontaneous information exchange, concurrent tax inquiries, presence at tax examinations abroad, and requests for enforcement, preliminary measures and document delivery. The convention, as formulated in the Protocol, applies to all kinds of taxes identified by national regulations of the contracting countries, including the obligatory contributions to social security. It does not, however, apply to the field of customs. All signatory states may express reservations with respect to the particular forms of administrative cooperation to be provided and received, as well as reservations with respect to the individual categories of taxes to which the Convention applies in a given country. The Czech Republic did not make any such reservation.[10]

Currently several other agreements and other documents are being negotiated, e.g. the negotiations between the United States of America and the Czech Republic concerning application of FATCA (Foreign Account Tax Compliance Act) obligations imposed on financial institutions in the Czech Republic.[11]

---

[10]For more details, see http://www.mfcr.cz/cs/legislativa/mezinarodni-vymena-info-v-danove-oblasti/umluva-o-vzajemne-spravni-pomoci-v-danov and http://www.oecd.org/ctp/exchange-of-tax-information/conventiononmutualadministrativeassistanceintaxmatters.htm. Accessed on 13 December 2013.

[11]Agreement between the United States of America and the Czech Republic to Improve International Tax Compliance and with Respect to the United States Information and Reporting Provisions Commonly Known as the Foreign Account Tax Compliance Act, effective since 18.12.2014.

Tax Incentives for Investment in Emerging, Developing, or Low Income Countries

The Czech Republic has provided no specific incentives for investment in emerging, developing, or low-income countries.

Measures to Attract Economic Activity to Czech Republic

In the past, the Czech Republic offered several incentives aimed at attracting both domestic and foreign investment. Presently, foreign investors have the opportunity to negotiate investment incentives as a part of establishing manufacturing or assembly operations according to the Act No. 72/2000 Sb., on Investment Incentives, as subsequently amended. Being directly linked to the relevant EU regulations (on the provision of regional investment support and the support of employment and education), Act No. 72/2000 Sb. regulates the conditions for the provision of investment incentives for the purpose of enhancing economic development and creating jobs in the Czech Republic. Investment incentives include the transfer of plots of land for favourable prices, material support for the creation of new jobs, material support for employee requalification and training, material support for the purchase of long-term tangible and intangible property, and income tax relief. Investment incentives may be provided only in the fields of processing and servicing industries, technological (software) centres and centres of strategic services (accounting, finance, human resources administration, marketing and information system management). It is usually necessary to meet the requirements of making a certain minimum investment, which includes a minimum investment into machinery, and establishing a certain minimum number of new jobs. Any entrepreneurial entity, be it a legal or a natural person, may apply for an investment incentive regardless of whether it is domestic or foreign. The application for an investment incentive is assessed by Czechinvest, a governmental organization established by the Ministry of Industry and Trade, which prepares an evaluative opinion. The Ministry of Labour and Social Affairs, the Ministry of Finance, and the Ministry of the Environment assess the prerequisites related to the conditions for the investment incentive, while the final decision on the application for an investment incentive is issued by the Ministry of Industry and Trade. The applicant may, on the basis of the decision on the offer of an investment incentive, submit an application for the grant of an investment incentive, issued automatically by the Ministry.

Any taxpayer who has been promised an investment incentive may utilize a tax relief, provided that the taxpayer applies all depreciation and adjusting entries to receivables to the maximum amount when determining its tax base. The tax relief may be used during up to ten consecutive tax periods. The tax relief may not exceed, during the individual tax periods, the amount of public support concerning the actually expended costs and may not, in its sum, exceed the maximum amount of public support specified by the relevant decision.

Additional details on investment incentives in the Czech Republic and the list of investment incentives that have been granted are available online.[12]

The Czech Republic also allows a super-deduction on research and development expenses. This means that expenses on research and development may be applied twice – both when determining one's tax base together with other tax deductible items, and as items reducing the tax base. It is also possible to deduct from the tax base expenses for the support of professional education. Where such deductions cannot be made on account of a low tax base or a tax loss, they may be made no later than in the third tax period.

Below is the current list of agreements for the promotion and reciprocal protection of investments between the Czech Republic and other states[13]:

Country	Valid since	Act no.[a]	Country	Valid since	Act no.[b]
Albania	7. 7. 1995	183/1995 Sb.	Mauritania	27.4. 2000	62/2000 Sb. I. T.
Argentina	23. 7. 1998	297/1998 Sb.	Mexico	13.3. 2004	45/2004 Sb. I. T.
Australia	29. 6. 1994	162/1994 Sb.	Moldavia	21.6. 2000	128/2000 Sb. I. T.
Austria	1. 10. 1991	454/1991 Sb.	Mongolia	7. 5. 1999	104/1999 Sb.
Azerbaijan	9. 2. 2012	14/2012 Sb. I. T.	Montenegro	29. 1. 2001	103/2000 Sb. I. T.
Bahrain	17.11.2009	117/2009 Sb. I. T.	Morocco	30. 1. 2003	15/2003 Sb. I. T.
Belarus	9. 4. 1998	213/1998 Sb.	Netherlands	1.10. 1992	569/1992 Sb.
Belgium (and Luxembourg)	13. 2. 1992	574/1992 Sb.	Nicaragua	24.2. 2004	51/2004 Sb. I. T.
Bosnia and Herzegovina	30. 5. 2004	74/2004 Sb. I. T.	Norway	6. 8. 1992	530/1992 Sb.
Bulgaria	30. 9. 2000	103/2000 Sb. I. T.	Panama	20.10.2000	96/2005 Sb. I. T.
Canada	22. 1. 2012	8/2012 Sb. I. T.	Paraguay	24.3. 2000	38/2000 Sb. I. T.
Cambodia	23.10.2009	104/2009 Sb. I. T.	Peru	6. 3. 1995	181/1995 Sb. I. T.

(continued)

[12] See http://www.czechinvest.org/en/investment-incentives-new. Accessed on 13 December 2013. http://www.czechinvest.org/data/files/3-udulene-investicni-pobidky-investment-incentives-granted-web-k-30-11-2013-1438-cz.xls. Accessed on 13 December 2013.

[13] In the case of multiple treaties and documents there is mentioned the first agreement only. For more details see e.g. http://www.mfcr.cz/cs/legislativa/dohody-o-podpore-a-ochrane-investic/prehled-platnych-dohod-o-podpore-a-ochra. Accessed on 20 October 2016.

Country	Valid since	Act no.[a]	Country	Valid since	Act no.[b]
Chile	5. 10. 1996	41/1997 Sb.	Peoples Rep. of Korea	10.10.1999	250/1999 Sb.
China	9. 1. 2006	89/2006 Sb. I. T.	Philippines	4. 4. 1996	141/1996 Sb.
Costa Rica	5. 3. 2001	68/2001 Sb. I. T.	Poland	29.6. 1994	181/1994 Sb.
Croatia	15. 5. 1997	155/1997 Sb.	Portugal	3. 8. 1994	96/1995 Sb.
Cyprus	25. 9. 2002	115/2002 Sb. I. T.	Republic of SA	17. 9. 1999	294/1999 Sb
Egypt	4. 6. 1994	128/1994 Sb.	Romania	28. 7. 1994	198/1994 Sb.
El Salvador	28. 3. 2001	34/2001 Sb. I. T.	Russia	6. 6. 1996	201/1996 Sb.
Finland	23.10.1991	478/1991 Sb.	Saudi Arabia	13. 3. 2011	15/2011 Sb. I. T.
France	27. 9. 1991	453/1991 Sb.	Singapore	8. 10. 1995	57/1996 Sb.
Georgia	13. 3. 2011	18/2011 Sb. I. T.	Serbia	29. 1. 2001	23/2001 Sb. I. T.
Germany	2. 8. 1992	573/1992 Sb.	Sri Lanka	28. 3. 2011	ratification
Greece	30.12.1992	102/1993 Sb.	Spain	28.11.1991	647/1992 Sb.
Guatemala	29. 4. 2005	86/2005 Sb. I. T.	Sweden	23. 9. 1991	479/1991 Sb.
Hungary	25. 5. 1995	200/1995 Sb.	Switzerland	7. 8. 1991	459/1991 Sb.
India	6. 2. 1998	43/1998 Sb.	Syria	14.8. 2009	62/2009 Sb. I. T.
Indonesia	21. 6. 1999	156/1999 Sb.	Tajikistan	6. 12. 1995	48/1996 Sb.
Israel	16. 3. 1999	73/1999 Sb.	Thailand	4. 5. 1995	180/1995 Sb.
Jordan	25. 4. 2001	62/2001 Sb. I. T.	Tunisia	8. 7. 1998	203/1998 Sb.
Kazakhstan	2. 4. 1998	217/1999 Sb.	Turkey	18. 3. 2012	21/2012 Sb. I. T.
Korea	16.3. 1995	125/1995 Sb.	Ukraine	2. 11. 1995	23/1996 Sb.
Kosovo	29.1. 2001	23/2001 Sb. I. T.	Uruguay	29.12.2000	10/2001 Sb.
Kuwait	21. 1. 1997	42/1997 Sb.	Uzbekistan	6. 4. 1998	202/1998 Sb.
Latvia	1. 8. 1995	204/ 1995 Sb.	United Arab Emirates	25.12.1995	69/1996 Sb.

(continued)

Country	Valid since	Act no.[a]	Country	Valid since	Act no.[b]
Lebanon	24. 1. 2000	106/2001 Sb. I. T.	United Kingdom	26.10.1992	646/1992 Sb.
Lithuania	12. 7.1995	185/1995 Sb.	USA	19.12.1992	187/1993 Sb.
Luxembourg (and Belgium)	13. 2. 1992	574/1992 Sb.	Venezuela	23. 7. 1996	99/1998 Sb.
Macedonia	20. 9.2002	116/2002 Sb. I. T.	Vietnam	9. 7. 1998	212/1998 Sb.
Malaysia	3. 12. 1998	296/1998 Sb.	Yemen	4. 9. 2009	65/2009 Sb. I. T.

[a]In Collection (Sb.) or in Collection of International Treaties (Sb. I. T.)
[b]In Collection (Sb.) or in Collection of International Treaties (Sb. I. T.)

Below is the list of former agreements for the promotion and reciprocal protection of investments between the Czech Republic and other states:

Country	Applicable to	Act no.[a]	Country	Applicable to	Act no.[b]
Denmark	18.11.2009	109/2009 Sb. I. T	Malta	30. 9. 2010	89/2010 Sb. I. T
Estonia	20. 2. 2011	11/2011 Sb. I. T.	Slovakia	1. 5. 2004	105/2009 Sb. I. T.
Ireland	1. 12. 2011	105/2011 Sb. I. T	Slovenia	13. 8. 2010	73/2010 Sb. I. T.
Italy	30. 4. 2009	37/2009 Sb. I. T			

[a]In Collection (Sb.) or in Collection of International Treaties (Sb. I. T.)
[b]In Collection (Sb.) or in Collection of International Treaties (Sb. I. T.)

Corporate Tax Rate Structure

Corporate income tax is levied at the rate of 19 % on the net income earned by resident legal entities and permanent establishments of non-resident legal entities. The net income is calculated as the difference between taxable income (less exempt income) and deductible expenses. Deduction of some expenses may be limited by the statutory provisions – for example, in some cases, interest deductions are limited.

The reduced tax rate of 5 % is set for domestic and foreign investment funds established in any member state of the EU, and in Norway and Iceland, as well as for retirement pension funds organized in these states.

Michal Radvan Author specializes in tax law and local government finance. He is the author of 5 books and the coauthor of almost 40 books. He has presented his scientific research in approximately 70 reviewed articles in prestigious journals and conference proceedings. He is a member of European Association of Tax Law Professors and of Information and Organization Centre for the Research on the Public Finances and Tax Law in the Countries of Central and Eastern Europe.

Dana Šramková Author specializes mainly in tax and customs law and administration. She regularly presents customs and tax related topics at international conferences and publishes the papers as an author or co-author in books or as reviewed articles in prestigious journals and conference proceedings. She is a member of i.n.c.u. (International Network of Customs Universities) and Information and Organization Centre for the Research on the Public Finances and Tax Law in the Countries of Central and Eastern Europe.

Chapter 7
Structural and Temporary Tax Mechanisms to Promote Economic Growth and Development in France

Thomas Dubut

Abstract France has adopted a territorial tax system for corporations. Departing from the prevailing rule of worldwide taxation, France taxes its corporations only on income (other than passive income) derived from operating in France. Under the participation regime, a qualified parent company may exclude from French taxation 95 % of a dividend received from its foreign subsidiary. This exemption is available only if the subsidiary is taxed at the prevailing rate in its country of residence (even if that rate happens to be lower than the top French rate of 33 %). This may provide an incentive for investment in developing or low-income countries wishing to attract investment. France is a party to numerous double taxation agreements and has used these treaties to provide a tax sparing credit to certain developing countries.

Synopsis France has adopted a worldwide tax regime for resident individuals and a territorial tax system for corporations. For individuals, double taxation is alleviated by a foreign tax credit or an exemption of the income provided by a treaty. In the absence of a treaty, only a deduction for foreign taxes is allowed under the French General Tax Code (FTC).

In a departure from the prevailing rule, France taxes its corporations only on income derived from operating in France (and certain other income attributed to France by a bilateral treaty). The territorial regime does not extend to passive income (interest, dividends, royalties, and similar income) unless such income is derived from an asset carried on the books of a foreign enterprise (including a foreign branch of a French company).

Under the participation regime for foreign source dividends, a qualified parent company may exclude from French taxation 95 % of a dividend received from its subsidiaries. In order to qualify, the parent must actively participate in management, requiring ownership of at least 5 % of the capital and the financial and voting rights of the subsidiary. The exemption applies only if the subsidiary is subject to tax in

T. Dubut (✉)
University of Paris-Dauphine, Paris, France
e-mail: thomasdubut@gmail.com

© Springer International Publishing Switzerland 2017
K.B. Brown (ed.), *Taxation and Development - A Comparative Study*,
Ius Comparatum - Global Studies in Comparative Law 21,
DOI 10.1007/978-3-319-42157-5_7

France at the ordinary corporate tax rate or at the prevailing rate abroad (regardless of the actual rate, which would include, for example, Ireland and Cyprus). The parent-subsidiary regime is designed to attract holding companies to France, providing the advantage of a 1.67 % rate (33 % of 5 %) on dividends paid by subsidiaries. Dividends received from subsidiaries operating in so-called "non-cooperative" states, however, are not eligible for the exemption.

In some cases, the participation exemption extends to capital gains on the sale of shares held in a subsidiary. In this case, however, only 88 % of the gain is exempt from taxation.

Under the EU Mergers and Acquisitions regime, capital gain resulting from these transactions between companies subject to French tax and those in other EU member states (and third countries with approval of the French tax administration) is exempt from tax. Registration fees and stamp duties are also eliminated.

As described above, tax disincentives have been provided for taxpayers that engage in transactions with certain "non-cooperative" states or territories (NCST). An exceptionally high withholding tax rate, 75 %, is applied to payments of dividends, interest, and royalties paid to financial institutions located in a NCST. Real estate profits, capital gains from real estate or the sale of shares, and income from artistic or sporting services are subject to the same withholding rate when derived or received by entities established in a NCST. A 60 % rate is applied to trusts, gifts, or transfers made by a settlor if the trustee is established in or a resident of a NCST.

Additional denial of tax benefits includes disqualification from the participation exemption regime for dividends received from (and capital gains from the sale of shares of) subsidiaries established in a NCST. In addition, payments of dividends, interest, royalties and payments for services made to entities located in a NCST may not be deducted from the French income tax base. Special rules apply to CFCs located in a NCST (deemed distribution of dividends to parent) and for purposes of transfer pricing documentation. None of the disincentives applies if the taxpayer can prove that NCST operations were undertaken with a purpose other than to shift benefits. A country may only be a NCST if (i) it is not a member of the EU, (ii) the OECD has analyzed the country's exchange of information practices, (iii) it has not entered into an exchange of information agreement with France containing a mutual assistance clause, and (iv) it has not entered into any mutual agreement or treaty with 12 or more member states. Eight countries are listed as NCSTs by the French Ministry: Botswana, Brunei, Guatemala, the Marshall Islands, the British Virgin Islands, Montserrat, Nauru, and Niue.

France has implemented additional disincentives for preferential tax regimes. A preferential tax regime is one in which the amount of tax imposed on an item of income is 50 % less than the tax that would have been imposed on France. The emphasis is on effective tax rates and not nominal or statutory tax rates.

Operations in countries with preferential tax regimes have significant disadvantages. Deductions for payments made by French companies to individuals or legal entities domiciled in such countries are not allowed unless the taxpayer can establish that the transactions are real and do not involve artificial amounts. If an entity subject to French corporate tax owns a greater-than-50 % interest in any entity established outside of France that benefits from a preferential regime, a proportionate amount (relative to the shares held) of the profits of the entity is taxable in France. Anti-abuse rules relating to CFC apply automatically to entities situated in a preferential regime.

As a member of the OECD, France participates in the Forum on Harmful Tax Practices and the Global Tax Forum (GTF). After phase 1 and phase 2 review by the GTF, France's system has been deemed "compliant."

France has an extensive network of information exchange agreements with 142 partners. These include double tax agreements and TIEAs. Exchange of information generally follows the OECD Model Convention's Article 26, except those concluded with former French colonies which are based on Article 26 of the UN Model Convention. Because of its membership in the OECD and the Council of Europe, France is obligated to provide administrative assistance in tax matters under a number of specific directives and Conventions. The type of information to be exchanged and the types of taxes covered vary from treaty to treaty.

Incentives to Invest Abroad

The French tax system provides some incentives for investment abroad in developing and developed countries. The former "worldwide tax consolidation regime," designed to encourage international development, allowed French multinationals to consolidate the income or losses of their foreign branches or subsidiaries with their French taxable income or losses. It was granted to large enterprises on a case-by-case basis until the resulting heavy budgetary losses and concerns that such benefits were accorded only to multinationals caused it to be repealed in 2011.

Since 2009, a special regime applies to small and medium enterprises (SMEs) which are allowed to deduct (for up to 5 years) losses from 95 %-owned foreign branches or subsidiaries established in EU member states or in countries with which France has concluded a tax treaty containing an administrative assistance clause. This benefit is available only if the branch or subsidiary is subject to a tax equivalent to a corporate tax. Special rules apply this regime to subsidiaries organized in EU states, Norway, or Iceland, even if they are not subject to corporate tax. This measure is designed to encourage French SMEs to go abroad by reducing the initial costs of doing so, allowing these costs to offset the French tax base of the owner.

SMEs are also encouraged to go abroad by benefiting from a special tax credit for up to 50 % of prospecting expenditures incurred in order to permit export outside of the EU market. There is a ceiling on eligible expenditures and a 2-year limit on availability.

In order to encourage investment in developing countries, France has used double taxation agreements to provide a "tax sparing credit" to certain developing countries. This credit applies to passive income and allows an offset against French tax liability for a fictitious tax (or one higher than the French rate of tax) levied in the country in which investment is made. An example of this is the *Décote africaine* contained in the DTCs with French-speaking African countries. Because the tax sparing credit provided no incentive for French companies to re-invest the tax savings in the local economy, these types of agreements have receded.

There are incentives for investment in overseas French departments and territories. These include a reduced income tax rate or a deduction from income subject to French corporate tax. These incentives are available only for investments in important sectors of economic activity for the locality, including tourism, aquaculture, renewable energy, or in some cases, mining.

Incentives to Invest in France

France provides a number of incentives for economic activity within its borders. These include incentives built into the general tax base, such as generous depreciation rules, carry back and forward of losses, and generous research and jobs creation tax credits. A special regime to encourage companies to establish headquarters or logistics centers in France (to coordinate provision of management, auditing, and other administrative services to a group of companies) is also provided. This also involves tax exemptions of limited duration for income paid to certain employees of these companies.

Companies that locate in certain disadvantaged or otherwise targeted areas may benefit from corporate tax exemptions for specified periods. Innovative new companies that are SMEs may also enjoy a tax exemption.

Corporate Tax Rate Structure

The corporate tax rate is 33.33 %, with an additional 3.3 % social contribution imposed on companies with income exceeding a certain level. Large enterprises must pay an additional "exceptional contribution" for a limited period.

A reduced rate of 15 % applies to income from intellectual property, including royalties and capital gains derived on the transfer, held for at least 2 years.

SMEs are taxed at the reduced rate of 15 % on a first level of income and 33.33 % on the remainder.

Trade and Investment Agreements

France is a party to a number of bilateral and multilateral trade and investment agreements.

The French International Tax System: In General

While worldwide taxation applies to individuals with residence in France, the French tax system adopts the territoriality principle for the taxation of corporations. This is an exception, since presently the majority of countries purports to adopt the principle of worldwide taxation for corporate taxation.

As a preliminary point, it should be underlined that the French domestic (internal non-treaty based) rules of international taxation described below only apply if an international agreement concluded by France does not contain contrary provisions. In fact, according to the French Constitution,[1] as interpreted by the case law of the French Constitutional Council, the provisions of international agreements concluded

---

[1] Article 55 of the French Constitution of 4 October 1958.

by France prevail over statutory law (but not over the Constitution). This implies that the provisions of double tax treaties also prevail over domestic tax law and in particular over the relevant provisions of the French General Code of Taxes (FTC).

However, the French Council of State has clarified that the application of double tax treaties shall respect the "subsidiarity principle."[2] According to this principle, during a judicial review, the domestic law provisions should be examined before the provisions of international agreements. Taxation should be based directly on the provisions of double tax treaties only if the application of domestic rules results in a violation of the provisions of such an agreement.

Worldwide Taxation for Individuals

Individuals with a tax residence in France are subject to worldwide taxation,[3] i.e. they are taxed in France on all income, even if from foreign sources,[4] unless this is precluded by a double tax convention (DTC) concluded by France with the State in which the foreign income has its source. The type of income (business income, salary, capital gains) is irrelevant.

DTCs concluded by France alleviate potential double taxation through the credit or the exemption method. In the absence of a tax treaty, taxes paid abroad are merely deducted from the taxable income.

Territoriality Principle for Corporate Taxation

The Statutory Base of the Territoriality Principle

For corporate taxation, France is one of the very few countries in the world to apply the principle of territoriality for the assessment of the amount of taxes due. According to article 209-I FTC, French companies are subject to corporate tax on their benefits "derived from enterprises operating in France and on their income the taxation of which is attributed to France by a bilateral tax treaty." The territoriality principle of corporate taxation has never been seriously contested by French groups and remains one of the cornerstones of the French corporate tax system. It dates back to the origins of the French schedular tax system, when French enterprises had a very strong national character.

---

[2] See Council of State (CE), judgment of 28 June 2002, n° 232276, Schneider Electric (RJF 10/02 n° 1080).

[3] Articles 4A and 4B of the French General Tax Code (FTC).

[4] Article 12 FTC.

Today, there is one significant statutory exception to the territoriality principle: small and medium enterprises ("SMEs") are allowed to offset their foreign tax losses against their French taxable profits, as explained below.[5]

Furthermore, within the framework of intra-group support measures, article 39 FTC allows, under specific conditions, the deductibility of trade related aids in the form of debt waivers (*abandons de créance*) given by a parent company to a subsidiary or a PE and explicitly excludes the deductibility of all other aids regardless their nature.

Territoriality Principle and Foreign Passive Income

The receipt of foreign passive income by a French company does not automatically constitute a trade or business conducted outside of France. Therefore, in principle, interests, dividends, royalties and other relevant items of passive income derived by French companies abroad are part of the French corporate tax base, i.e. subject to corporate income tax in France at the standard rate of 33.33 %.

No corporate income tax is due in France, however, if the passive income results from a financial asset which is recorded on the balance sheet of an enterprise carrying out a business outside of France (for instance a foreign branch of a French company). In addition, as described below, there are some derogatory regimes for intra-group operations.

The French Participation-Exemption Regime

*The Parent-Subsidiary Regime (*régime des sociétés-mères*)*

Under the participation-exemption regime for foreign source dividends,[6] qualifying parent companies subject to French corporate income tax at the full standard rate on all or part of their business activities, benefit from a 95 % tax exemption on dividends received from their subsidiaries. The remaining 5 % is deemed to correspond to a "management charge" (*quote-part de frais et charges*) and is taxed.

In order to benefit from the exemption, the parent company should own at least 5 % of the capital of the subsidiary and this participation should confer at least 5 % of financial rights and voting rights. The parent-subsidiary regime is therefore reserved to the companies that actively participate in the management of their subsidiary. The exemption applies only if the subsidiary is taxed at the ordinary corporate tax rate in France or at the rate prevailing abroad. This means that the subsidiary may not be tax exempt or benefit from a special regime, but must be subject to the

---

[5] Article 209C FTC.

[6] See articles 145 and 216 FTC (introduced by Law of 31 July 1920).

ordinary corporate tax. The rate of the tax is however irrelevant. Therefore subsidiaries located in countries where ordinary corporate tax is very low (for instance, Cyprus or Ireland) may also benefit from the parent-subsidiary regime. French permanent establishments of foreign companies may also benefit from it. By contrast, dividends paid by subsidiaries located in a non-cooperative State or Territory are not eligible for the participation exemption as of 1 January 2011 (for the concept of non-cooperative State or Territory – NCST see below under 4.1).[7]

The objective of the parent-subsidiary regime is to attract holding companies to France. The scheme is intended indeed to offer considerable advantages, since it entails a minimum effective tax rate of 1.67 % (5×33.3 %) on the dividends paid out by subsidiaries.

The Participation-Exemption Regime for Certain Capital Gains

Capital gains on the sale of shareholdings held for at least 2 years are also tax exempt, except for 12 % of the gain, which is deemed to correspond to a "management charge."[8] This exemption no longer applies to transferred securities of companies located in a NCST.

In addition, a loss on the investment (*provision pour dépréciation de titres de participation*) may be deducted from long-term/future capital gains on the sale of shareholdings (but not from the profits).[9] This provision is useful for companies or shareholdings that are not eligible for the above mentioned participation-exemption regime for capital gains and are thus subject to corporate tax for their capital gains on the sale of shareholdings.

The EU Mergers and Acquisitions Regime

Within the European Union, mergers and acquisitions are subject to EU law,[10] which established a common tax regime applicable to all Member States with a view to facilitating the restructuring of groups at the EU level. According to this tax regime as transposed into French law,[11] capital gains resulting from mergers and acquisitions are exempt from corporate tax and registration fees/stamp duties.

The regime applies to operations carried out by companies subject to French corporate tax and operations concerning companies of another EU Member State or

---

[7] Tax Circular of 27 April 2012 (BOI 14A-5-12 of 10 May 2012).

[8] Article 219-I a *quinquies* FTC (introduced by Law n° 2004-1485 of 30 December 2004).

[9] Article 223D FTC.

[10] Directive 2009/133/CE, OJEU L 310/34 of 23 November 2009.

[11] Articles 210-0A, 210A, 210B, 210B bis and 210C FTC.

of a third country with which France has concluded a DTC with an exchange of information clause.

For some operations, however, this regime does not apply without prior authorization by the French tax administration. This is the case in particular for contributions made by a French company to a foreign company.

Investments in Tax Haven Jurisdictions in the French Tax System

The concept of tax haven jurisdiction does not exist as such in the French tax system. Instead, since 2009, the concept of "non-cooperative State or Territory" (NCST) was introduced into the FTC,[12] thereby providing new tax disincentives for taxpayers to engage in transactions with entities located in such jurisdictions.

Disincentives for Investments in NCST

The disincentives to invest in NCST jurisdictions include high withholding tax rates, strong anti-avoidance or disclosure rules and denial of certain exemption regimes.

Increase of Withholding Tax Rate for Certain Payments

As of 1 January 2013, a 75 % withholding tax[13] applies to the distribution of investment income (primarily dividends and interest, but also royalties) by a French resident, when the payment is made to a financial institution located in a NCST, irrespective of the tax residency of the beneficiary. This 75 % withholding tax also applies on real estate profits, real estate capital gains and capital gains on the sale of shares, when these profits or capital gains are realized by entities established in a NCST.[14] In addition, a 75 % withholding tax also applies to income from artistic or sporting services supplied or used in France when the recipient is established in a NCST.[15]

Moreover, for trusts, gifts or transfers made by the settlor, a 60 % withholding tax applies if the trustee is established in or resident of a NCST irrespective of the link between the settlor and the beneficiaries.

---

[12] Article 238-0 A FTC (introduced by Law n°2009-1674 of 30 December 2009).

[13] See articles 187 (for dividends), 125A-III (for interests) and 182B (for royalties) FTC.

[14] Articles 244 bis, 244 bis A and 244 bis B FTC.

[15] Articles 182A bis and 182B FTC.

Denial of Tax Benefits

(i) Exclusion from the participation-exemption regime

Capital gains realized on, and dividends derived from, shares in subsidiaries established in a NCST are excluded from the French participation-exemption regime.

(ii) Deductibility restrictions

Under the French base-erosion rule, certain payments such as interests, royalties and payments for services of any kind, made to entities located in a NCST may not be deduced from the French taxable income.[16]

Facilitated Implementation of Anti-abuse Rules

(i) CFC rules

CFC rules for companies (Section 209B FTC) and for individuals (Section 123 bis FTC) automatically apply when a French resident holds interests or has operations with an entity located in a NCST. In this case, the profits of the foreign entity are deemed to have been distributed as dividends to the French parent company.

(ii) New transfer pricing documentation requirements

New transfer pricing documentation requirements in France are significantly more burdensome for transactions involving entities in NCST. The French entities must produce all tax and accounting documents relating to such foreign entities (i.e., all the documents that a French entity liable to French corporate income tax must keep).

Safeguard Clause

The above mentioned dissuasive tax measures do not apply if the taxpayer can prove that the operations concerned have a purpose other than to shift benefits in a NCST.

The Criteria Used to Determine Whether a Country/Territory Is a NCST

In line with article 238-0A FTC (effective 1 January 2010), all the following four conditions must be met in order to list a country or a territory as a NCST:

1. States and countries considered may not be members of the European Union;

---

[16] Article 238A FTC.

2. The State's situation with respect to the exchange of tax information was analyzed by the OECD;
3. The State did not as of 1 January 2010 enter into an agreement with France containing a mutual assistance clause allowing the exchange of information for purposes of implementing each contracting State's tax legislation, and;
4. The State did not have as of 1 January 2010 entered into any mutual agreement or treaty with 12 or more other States or territories.

The list of NCST is established through ministerial order and is updated annually.

The Countries Listed as NCSTs

- The List of NCSTs set out in the Ministerial Order of 12 February 2010 as last modified by Ministerial Order of 17 January 2014 refers to eight countries and territories: Botswana, Brunei, Guatemala, the Marshall Islands, the British Virgin Islands, Montserrat, Nauru and Niue. As mentioned above, the NCST list is updated annually depending on: the signature of new conventions on mutual administrative assistance with France;
- The evaluation by France of the concrete results of the exchange of information with States with which a convention on mutual administrative assistance has been concluded;
- The evaluation made by the World Forum on Transparency and Exchange of Information in Tax matters.

Disincentives Regarding Investments in Harmful Tax Regimes

Beyond the above mentioned (narrow) NCST concept, the French tax system also has a concept of "preferential tax regime," which is close to that of harmful tax regime in the international tax debate. The related rules and definitions follow.

The Relevant Provisions

The French Base Erosion Rule (Article 238A FTC)

Deduction of payments made to individual or legal entities domiciled or established in a "preferential tax regime" is not allowed unless the taxpayer can prove that these payments correspond to real transactions and that the amount involved is neither outside the company's business interest nor exaggerated.

CFC Rules for Companies (Article 209B FTC)

According to article 209B FTC, if an entity subject to French corporate income tax operates an enterprise outside France or holds, directly or indirectly, more than 50 % of the shares, interest shares, financial rights or voting rights in a company or an entity established outside France and such enterprise, company or entity benefits from a privileged tax regime, the profits of the enterprise, company or entity are taxable in France in proportion to the shares, interest shares or financial rights which that entity, directly or indirectly, holds in the foreign entity.

CFC Rules for Individuals (Article 123 bis FTC)

The general anti-abuse provision of article 123bis FTC specifies that the items of income resulting from financial or voting rights representing at least 10 % of the undistributed profits of entities situated in a preferential tax regime are taxable in France. In 2009, the FTC instituted a presumption providing that the 10 % ownership threshold is presumed to be reached if assets or rights are transferred to a NCST.

The Definition of the Term "Preferential Tax Regime"

In France, a "preferential (harmful) tax regime" is as a tax regime in which a given item of income is subject to an amount of tax, which is 50 % lower than the one that would have been due in France.[17]

The comparison is therefore concrete and the case law of the French Courts has underlined several times that the fact that a foreign tax system has lower nominal rates is not sufficient to conclude the existence of a preferential tax regime. In other words, the only criterion is the concrete amount of taxes effectively paid abroad compared to the taxes that would have been paid in France.[18]

Regional/International Anti-harmful Tax Competition Initiatives

The most important regional/international initiative against countries deemed to unfairly compete for capital in which French participates is the OECD "Forum on Harmful Tax Practices." This forum was created in 1998[19] to identify and recommend the eventual elimination of harmful tax competitive legislation.

---

[17] See Article 238A FTC.

[18] French Council of State (CE), judgment of 21 March 1986, *Auriège*. See also, CE, judgment of 25 January 1989, n° 49847; CE, judgment of 30 September 1992, *Sarl Toul France*.

[19] OECD, "Harmful Tax Competition, An Emerging Global Issue" (1998) (the "1998 Report").

As a contracting party of the OECD, France also participates in the OECD's Global Tax Forum.

France has been subject to the combined – Phase 1 plus Phase 2 – review[20] and has been assigned a rating of "compliant" for each essential element of scrutiny. As a consequence, no substantial modifications have been brought into the French tax system as a result of participation in the OECD's Global Tax Forum.

Information Exchange Agreements Concluded by France

France has one of the oldest and largest networks of international instruments containing provisions on the exchange of tax information with 142 partners. These instruments are either (bilateral or multilateral) treaties, or binding rules produced by the EU.

The Types of Agreements

This network consists mainly of (i) Double Tax Conventions (DTCs) that comprise an exchange of information clause, (ii) Tax Information Exchange Agreements (TIEAs), (iii) EU instruments and (iv) tax agreements concluded within the framework of the Council of Europe.

DTCs with an Exchange of Information Clause

On international exchange of information, the majority of the DTCs concluded by France follow the basic lines of Article 26 of the OECD Model. An alternative standardized formulation is generally used in DTCs concluded with former French colonies,[21] whereas some DTCs are based on article 26 of the UN Model Tax Convention.[22] The DTCs based on the OECD Model usually follow the version available at the time of their conclusion.

---

[20] OECD, Global Forum on Transparency and Exchange of Information for Tax Purposes Peer Reviews: France 2013 Combined: Phase 1 + Phase 2, incorporating Phase 2 ratings.

[21] See DTC with Burkina Faso (11/08/1965), Benin (27/02/1965), Cameroon (21/10/1976), Central African Republic (13/12/1969), Ivory Coast (06/04/1966), Lebanon (24/07/1962), Mali (22/09/1972), Morocco (29/05/1970), Mauritania (15/11/1967), Niger (01/06/1965), Senegal (29/03/1974) and Togo (24/11/1971). Strangely, the same formulation is adopted in the DTC with Ireland (21/03/1968).

[22] These DTCs clarify that the exchange of information is necessary "in particular for the prevention of fraud or evasion of such taxes": see the DTCs with Qatar (04/12/1990), Philippines (09/01/1976), Pakistan (15/06/1994), Malaysia (24/06/1975), India (29/09/1992), South Korea

TIEAs

The first international agreement concluded by France in tax matters was a Mutual Assistance Agreement signed on 12 August 1843 between France and Belgium. This agreement is still in force and concerns taxation of rights *in rem*, inheritance and gifts taxes included. More recently, France has concluded TIEAs with several other countries, and more precisely Liberia, Aruba, Anguilla, Netherlands Antilles, Brunei, Belize, Cook Islands, St Vincent and the Grenadines, Saint Lucia, St Kitts and Nevis, Grenada, Antigua and Barbuda, Uruguay, Vanuatu, Bahamas, Cayman Islands, Bermuda, Turks and Caicos, San Marino, Liechtenstein, Gibraltar, Andorra, British Virgin Islands, Isle of Man, Guernsey and Jersey.[23]

The majority of these agreements follow the basic lines of the Model Agreement on Exchange of Information on Tax Matters developed by the OECD Global Forum Working Group on Effective Exchange of Information in 2002 and they even contain some improvements. For instance, generally speaking, TIEAs concluded by France cover all taxes existing in the contracting States and oblige tax authorities to provide information held both by them directly or by persons situated within the territorial jurisdiction of the State concerned, even if the requesting party does not need it in order to apply its own tax legislation. Personal privileges and professional secrecy cannot justify the refusal of the tax administration to provide the requested data and the contracting States are required to amend their domestic legislation so as to guarantee an effective and quick exchange of tax information. Officials of the requesting State may also be authorized to enter the territory of the other State in order to collect and verify data or make inquiries.

EU Instruments

The European Union has also developed instruments that oblige the Member States' tax administration to collaborate, such as Council Regulation (EC) No 1798/2003 of 7 October 2003 on administrative cooperation in the field of value added tax (repealing Regulation (EEC), Council Regulation (EC) No 2073/2004 of 16 November 2004 on administrative cooperation in the field of excise duties), Council directive 2003/48/EC of 3 June 2003 on taxation of savings income in the form of interest payments, Council Directive 2010/24/EU of 16 March 2010 concerning mutual assistance for the recovery of claims relating to taxes, duties and other measures, or Council Directive 2011/16/EU of 15 February 2011 on administrative cooperation in the field of taxation and repealing Directive 77/799/EEC.[24]

(19/06/1979) China (30/05/1984) and Botswana (15/06/1999), as well as the new DTC with the United Kingdom (19/06/2008).

[23] See the list of TIEAs in force on 1 June 2012: Bulletin Officiel des Finances Publiques-Impôts, BOI-ANNX-000307-20120912 (12 September 2012). For more information, see the OECD Global Forum on Transparency and Exchange of Information for tax purposes.

[24] The provisions of this directive were incorporated in articles L.114A and R*114A-1 to 5 of the French Tax Procedures Book.

Some French overseas territorial collectivities have the status of "overseas countries and territories" of the EU (namely New-Caledonia, French Polynesia, Saint-Pierre-and-Miquelon, Saint Barthélemy and Saint Martin), to which EU legislation on exchange of information does not apply. In order to extend the application of EU legislation to them, specific agreements must be concluded.[25]

Instruments Developed Within the Framework of the Council of Europe

Some important international agreements concerning administrative cooperation in tax matters have also been adopted within the framework of the Council of Europe. This is the case, for instance, for the European Convention on Mutual Assistance in Criminal Matters of 17 March 1978, ratified by France on 23 May 1967, which enables tax administrators to overcome bank secrecy in case of tax offences, since bank secrecy does not apply in criminal matters.

The joint Council of Europe/OECD Convention on Mutual Administrative Assistance in Tax Matters[26] is also noteworthy. This Convention is a comprehensive multilateral instrument available for all forms of tax cooperation to tackle tax evasion and avoidance. The Convention was amended to respond to the call of the G20 at its April 2009 London Summit to align it to the international standard on exchange of information on request and to open it to all countries, in particular to ensure that developing countries could benefit from the new more transparent environment. The amended Convention was opened for signature on 1st June 2011. France has signed and ratified the Protocol of amendment. This Convention also does not cover the above mentioned French Overseas Territorial Communities, because French OTCs have the right to conclude their own bilateral tax treaties and TIEAs with foreign States.[27] Nevertheless, no agreement of this kind has been yet concluded.[28]

---

[25] To this date, only Saint-Bathélemy applies EU legislation on exchange of information. See the Agreement between the European Union and the French Republic concerning the application to the collectivity of Saint-Barthélemy of Union legislation on the taxation of savings and administrative cooperation in the field of taxation signed on 17 February 2014.

[26] The Convention entered into force in France on 1 September 2005 and the Protocol on 1 April 2012.

[27] Article 39 of the Organic Law no. 2004-192 for French Polynesia; Article LO.6351-15 of the French General Code of Territorial Communities (CGCT) for Saint Martin; Article LO.6251-15 CGCT for Saint Barthélemy; Article LO.6461-15 CGCT for Saint Pierre and Miquelon.

[28] On this issue, see Thomas Dubut, 'Brief Critical Observations on the Problem of Horizontal Tax Coordination between 'Overseas Territorial Communities' within the French Republic', in: M. Lang, P. Pistone, J. Schuch and C. Staringer (eds.), Horizontal Tax Coordination within the EU and within States (Amsterdam: IBFD, 2012) pp. 295–308 (p. 299).

The Type of Information Exchanged

Regarding the content of the exchange of information clause, first of all, some DTCs concluded by France determine the practical modalities of the exchange. While the relevant provisions are not always very detailed,[29] some protocols contain procedural rules as well as the interpretation of certain language used in the relevant provision.[30] Furthermore, according to some DTCs,[31] the contracting States have the obligation to obtain the requested information, whereas others[32] contain only an obligation to transmit data that are already available to the tax administration of the other State. Another divergence exists as to the possibility to use the requested data for purposes other than taxation, especially for customs or exchange control purposes. Indeed, some DTCs authorize such a use provided that this is permitted by the domestic law of both contracting States.[33] In addition, the DTC concluded with the United States of America enables the tax administration of each contracting State to proceed to a tax audit within the territory of the other contracting State and to obtain witness statements and copies of the original documents.[34] Given that the majority of DTCs based on the OECD Model do not contain detailed provisions on the exchange of information, France has concluded some specific agreements concretizing the modalities and the forms of the exchange,[35] but in recent years this practice appears to be abandoned.[36]

---

[29] See the DTCs concluded with Algeria (17/10/1999), Finland (11/09/1970), Jamaica (09/08/1995), Sweden (27/11/1990), Trinity and Tobago (05/08/1987), Ukraine (31/01/1997), Panama (30/06/2011), Pakistan (15/06/1994), Madagascar (22/07/1983), Greece (21/08/1963), Finland (Inheritance Tax Treaty: 25/08/1958), Spain (10/10/1995) and Botswana (15/04/1999).

[30] See the protocols of the DTCs concluded with Austria (26/03/1993 amended on 23/05/2011), Hong-Kong (21/10/2010) and Switzerland (09/09/1966 amended on 27/08/2009).

[31] See DTCs concluded with Algeria (17/10/1999), Philippines (09/01/1976), Germany (21/07/1959), Belgium (10/03/1964), Chile (07/06/2004), Mauritius (11/12/1980), Panama (30/06/2011), Switzerland (09/09/1966 amended on 27/08/2009), Switzerland (Inheritance Tax Treaty: 31/12/1953), Sri Lanka (17/09/1981), United Kingdom (Inheritance Tax Treaty: 21/06/1963), Malawi (21/08/1951), Zambia (21/08/1951), Greece (21/08/1963) and the United States of America (31/08/1994).

[32] See the DTCs with the former African French colonies (see supra FN 102) and Ireland (21/03/1968), Lebanon (24/07/1962), the Netherlands (16/03/1973) and Finland (Inheritance Tax Treaty: 25/08/1958).

[33] As provided in the DTCs concluded with Bahrain (10/05/1993 amended on 07/05/2009) and Switzerland (09/09/1966 amended on 27/08/2009).

[34] See the DTC with the United States of America (31/08/1994).

[35] Such an agreement has been concluded with the Netherlands (BOI 13 K-3-96 of 7 August 1996), Sweden (agreement of 17 April 1998, BOI 13 K-6-98 of 19 May 1998), Germany (agreement of 18 October 2001, BOI 13 K-13-01 of 20 November 2001); Belgium (agreement of 10 July 2002, BOI 13 K-10-02 of 7 14 October 2002) and Russia (agreement of 28 January 2004, BOI 13 K-7-04 of 27 October 2004).

[36] B. Gouthière, Les impôts dans les affaires internationales, (Levallois-Perret: Ed. Francis Lefebvre, 2010) No. 74305 (p. 876).

The Limitations on Agreements on Exchange of Information

Regarding the material scope of the exchange of information clause in the French DTCs based on article 26 of the OECD Model in its 1963 and 1977 versions, the exchange of information concerns only the taxes covered by the DTC according to article 2 of the OECD Model. Curiously, the same limitation applies to the DTC with Croatia (19/06/2003), as well as those with Australia (20/06/2006) and Chile (07/06/2004), two OECD members, although these conventions have been adopted more recently. Regarding the personal scope of the exchange of information clause, in the French DTCs based on the 1963 OECD Model as well as in some quite recent DTCs with non-OECD countries,[37] the exchange of information only applies to the residents of the two contracting States. Therefore, the tax administration of the two contracting States cannot obtain information concerning a permanent establishment of a company that is a resident of a third country. It should be underlined here that the potential restrictions of the exchange of information clause in the DTCs concluded between Member States of the European Union are not of great importance, since tax administrations of the EU Member States have a broader obligation to collaborate in tax matters on the basis of the above mentioned directive 2011/16/EU. The same is true for the DTCs concluded between two contracting States of the joint Council of Europe/OECD Convention on Mutual Administrative Assistance in Tax Matters.

Regarding the potential derogations to the obligation to exchange tax information, some DTCs concluded by France, such as the ones with Belgium[38] and Portugal[39] for instance, contain a reciprocity condition, while others exclude any exchange of information when this threatens state sovereignty, public security or strikes a blow at the State's general interests (*intérêts généraux*).[40] These derogations may seriously endanger the efficiency of the exchange of information clauses. The DTC concluded between France and Qatar[41] further excludes any exchange of information when this information concerns the relations between a lawyer and his client; therefore, lawyers' professional tax secrecy justifies derogations to the exchange of information obligation of the relevant DTC.

---

[37] See the DTCs with Turkey (18/02/1987), Namibia (29/05/1996), India (29/09/1992), Indonesia (14/09/1979) and Bolivia (15/12/1994).

[38] 10/03/1964.

[39] 14/01/1971.

[40] This is the case for the DTCs concluded with French speaking African countries (model clause), as well as for the DTCs concluded with Ireland (21/03/1968), Lebanon (24/07/1962), Spain (Inheritance Tax Treaty: 08/01/1963), Finland (Inheritance Tax Treaty: 25/08/1958) and Germany (21/07/1959).

[41] 04/12/1990 amended on 14/01/2008.

Information Relating to Transactions in Tax Haven Jurisdictions or in Countries with a Harmful Tax Regime

In principle, in line with article 26 of the OECD Model Tax Convention, the information received by a contracting State may not be disclosed to a third party, even if the contracting State from which the information comes is deemed to have a harmful tax regime (confidentiality of tax information exchanged). The only DTCs concluded by France that do not guarantee the confidentiality of tax information exchanged are the DTC with Hungary,[42] according to which the sending State has to indicate whether the information exchanged should remain secret and the DTC with the former Soviet Union[43] still applicable to Belarus, Kirgizstan, Tajikistan and Turkmenistan, which does not guarantee the confidentiality of the exchanged information at all. However, there is no published information as to whether information received from these States has been transmitted to a third country by the French tax administration.

Incentives for Investment Abroad

The French tax system contains some incentives for investment abroad, in particular for SMEs. These incentives apply to investments made both to developed and developing or emerging countries.

The (Now Abolished) Worldwide Tax Consolidation Regime (régime du bénéfice mondial ou consolidé)

In the past, according to the so-called "worldwide tax consolidation regime," some large French multinational companies were allowed to consolidate the income (or the losses) of their foreign branches or subsidiaries with their French taxable income (or losses). This regime was first introduced in the French tax system in the 1960s[44] in order to encourage the international development of French companies, by eliminating by tax credit the possibility of international double taxation within a multinational group of companies. It allowed a French parent company to consolidate its French income with the taxable results of its at least 50 %-owned foreign subsidiaries. Another advantage of this regime was to enable French companies to consolidate losses abroad (inherent in any new investment) with their French income and to neutralise transfer pricing. However, the benefit of this regime was granted to

---

[42] 28/04/1980.

[43] 04/10/1985.

[44] Article 209 *quinquies* FTC and articles 103–134 ter A of the Annexe II FTC.

large multinational groups by the French Tax Administration on a case by case basis and only a few groups of companies benefitted from it.[45] It was finally abolished by a statute, adopted in September 2011, because of criticisms raised concerning the heavy budgetary losses that it entailed for the French State and equity concerns expressed in relation to the beneficial treatment reserved only to multinational companies.

Incentives for French SMEs

Special Deduction of Foreign Losses by SME

Since 2009, within a time-limit of five tax periods, SMEs (small and medium enterprises)[46] are permitted to deduct from their income the deficits of their branches or subsidiaries in which they have a direct stake of at least 95 %, if the latter are established in a European Union Member State or in a State that has signed a tax treaty with France containing an administrative assistance clause, and are subject to a tax equivalent to corporate tax.[47] French subsidiaries owned through a European company (located within the European Union, Norway or Iceland) not subject to corporate tax in France may be considered part of a consolidated group, which allows the parent company to take advantage of the above rules.

This deduction is optional and does not require the prior authorisation of the French tax administration.

The objective of this measure is to encourage French SMEs to establish themselves abroad. In fact, such an establishment (new branch or subsidiary) normally generates costs that, in the absence of the special rules, could not be deduced from the French tax base. The above-mentioned derogation temporarily sets aside the French territoriality principle with a view to reducing the costs that an investment abroad may entail for a SME. This is an obvious cash-flow advantage.

Tax Credit for Commercial Prospecting Expenditure Outside France

Prospecting expenditure incurred by French SMEs in order to export outside the EU common market services and goods give, since 2005, rise to a tax credit of up to 50 % of the amount of these expenditures with an upper limit of 40,000 euros for a 24 month period.[48] This incentive encourages SMEs to establish abroad.

---

[45] The French Tax Administration had approved only about ten applications of the most important French groups to be taxed under this regime. In 2011, only five French groups were under this regime.

[46] I.e., companies subject to corporate tax that employ less than 2,000 persons and which are not owned at 25 % or more, directly or indirectly, by another company having more than 2,000 employees.

[47] Article 209C FTC.

[48] Article 244 quater H FTC.

An Extensive Network of Double Tax Treaties

Last but not least, the negotiation of bilateral tax treaties is an important part of French international tax policy that may indirectly promote investment abroad. In fact, France has signed a double tax convention (DTC) with more than 100 countries and thus provides foreign investors with outstanding protection against double taxation.

Most of the DTCs concluded with major industrial nations provide for the application of a withholding tax on dividends with a standard rate of 5 % for companies (subject to a minimum stake in the subsidiary created in France) or 15 % for individuals. The new tax treaties signed by France (with Japan and the United States) provide for no withholding tax to be applied when dividends are paid (subject to specific conditions of stake ownership). If no tax treaty exists, the withholding tax is 30 %.

For interest and royalties paid to foreign countries, DTCs set out rates that vary from 0 to 15 %.

In addition, some DTCs concluded by France with developing countries adopt the exemption method for the elimination of international double taxation so as to encourage French residents to invest in these countries. The income thus generated is not taken into account for the calculation of the French tax base.

Specific Tax Incentives for Investment in Developing or Emerging Countries

In the French domestic tax law, there are no explicit provisions to encourage investment in developing or emerging countries. On the other hand, some DTCs concluded by France with developing and emerging countries contain clauses granting fictitious tax credits. This is a rather old French tax policy choice that is intended to stimulate capital investments in the developing world.[49]

The mechanism depends on the right given to the taxpayer to benefit from a (fictitious) tax credit (regarding passive income) in the residence State, even if no tax was levied in the source State (tax sparing) or to benefit from a tax credit the amount of which is higher than the ordinary rate (domestic or conventional) of the withholding tax (matching credit). For instance, the so-called "Décote africaine" (a « tax sparing » modality) applies to dividends within the framework of DTCs concluded with French-speaking African countries. This method consists in calculating the amount of the tax credit by applying to the gross amount of the dividends the percentage resulting from the application of the formula $[100 - (25t)]/2$, where t = rate of the tax levied abroad.

---

[49] See B. Gouthière, *op. cit.*, No. 8120 (p. 159).

However, recent practice is to reduce the effect of these clauses. Their application today is residual.[50] One of the most negative effects of these mechanisms is that investors are encouraged to repatriate, rather than re-invest, their profits realized in the developing country.

Tax Incentives and Other Special Tax Regimes for Overseas French Possessions

The French tax system also contains tax incentives for investments to overseas French territories. These territories are the five French overseas departments (Guadeloupe, Guyana, Martinique, Mayotte and Reunion),[51] the five French overseas territorial collectivities, which enjoy some degree of autonomy (French Polynesia, Saint-Barthelemy, Saint-Martin, Saint-Pierre and Miquelon, Wallis and Futuna)[52] and New Caledonia, which has an extended tax autonomy in line with the provisions of title XIII of the French Constitution.[53]

Productive investment in the outmost regions can benefit, first of all, from the preferential tax regime of the "Girardin statute" of 2003,[54] either in the form of a reduced income tax[55] or in the form of a deduction from income subject to corporate tax.[56] In order to benefit from this preferential tax regime, the investments must relate to specific sectors of economic activity (tourism, aquaculture, renewable energy) or be important for local development; this is the case, for instance, for the mining or the metallurgical industry.

Furthermore, since 2002, the government of New Caledonia has established a specific tax regime for the metallurgical sector,[57] according to which there is a tax exemption for most of the ordinary taxes during the construction phase and for the first 15 years of the exploitation. Ad hoc tax aids, covered by tax secrecy, may also be granted to the industries concerned.

---

[50] This is in line with the 1986 OECD report on fictitious tax credits (OECD-MTC, Tome II, R(14)).
[51] Article 73 of the French Constitution of 1958.
[52] Article 74 of the French Constitution of 1958.
[53] Article 77 of the French Constitution of 1958.
[54] Law n° 2003-660 of 21 July 2003.
[55] Article 199 undecies B FTC.
[56] Article 217 undecies FTC.
[57] Local statute n° 2002-19 of 29 April 2002.

Measures Intended to Stimulate Economic Activity in France

Globally, in France, tax incentives for economic activity may be divided into four categories: general tax base rules that are drafted with a view to encouraging business investment (General tax base rules encouraging business investment in France), special rules and in particular tax credits that aim at promoting specific sectors of activity (Tax credits for specific sectors activity), rules intended to attract foreign investment and rules improving legal certainty.

General Tax Base Rules Encouraging Business Investment in France

Generous Depreciation Rules

Among OECD Member States, France has one of the most advantageous depreciation regimes, both in terms of duration and in terms of depreciation rates.[58] More precisely, fixed assets are depreciated on a straight-line basis over their expected useful life. In the case of certain production assets bought new with a minimum 3-year depreciation period, acceleration multiples ranging from 1.25 to 2.25 may be applied to the straight-line depreciation rates, depending on the normal useful life of the assets concerned (declining balance scheme). Equipment and tools used for scientific and technical research can be depreciated on an accelerated declining balance basis. In this case, the acceleration multiples go from 1.5 to 2.5.

Allowable Provisions

First of all, allowable provisions for depreciation may be deducted from the tax base if they can be justified and if they relate to clearly identified claims, inventories, securities or tangible and intangible assets. In addition, allowable provisions include provisions for contingencies, work in progress, price increases, annual leave, etc.

Loss Carry Back and Forward

France is one of the very few OECD countries to allow carrying losses both forward and back. Losses recorded in a given year can be carried forward indefinitely against future profits. They can also be carried back against profits made in previous years, but with a 3 years limit. This is also one of the longest carry back periods among OECD Member States.

---

[58] Articles 39, 1–2° and 39 A sq. FTC.

Tonnage Taxation Regime

The optional tax regime of tonnage taxation authorizes businesses of maritime transport to determine their taxable profits resulting from operations linked with the exploitation of some ships on a flat rate basis.[59] Such a regime may be found in several members of the European Union and in particular, Greece, the Netherlands, Denmark, United Kingdom, Germany, Spain, Finland, Ireland and Belgium. It concerns all businesses 75 % of the turnover of which results from the exploitation of commercial ships.

Tax Credits for Specific Sectors Activity

In recent years, a tax credit has become the main instrument for encouraging investment in specific sectors or zones in France. Listed below are the most important tax credits for specific sectors of activity in the French tax system.

Research Tax Credit (*crédit d'impôt recherche*)

The French research tax credit is a scientifically oriented tax measure introduced in 1983.[60] Since 2008, it has become a leading instrument used by the French government to support research and development efforts by companies established in France. This tax credit is available to all businesses subject to either corporate tax or income tax that carry out research and development work, irrespective of their size or business sector. The research tax credit takes the form of a tax claim against the State and is primarily used to pay business taxes. The research tax credit is calculated by applying a rate of 30 % to research expenditure incurred during the calendar year of up to €100 million; above this threshold, the applicable rate is 5 %. Eligible research expenditures are listed in the French General Tax Code.[61] The research tax credit claim is submitted together with the corporate tax return. If a company has no tax to pay, it may, under certain conditions, claim a refund of its research tax credit.

Patronage Tax Credit

This tax credit is equal to 60 % of the amount of donations or subsidies granted to certain specified non-profit organisations, with an upper limit of 5 % of the annual turnover of the enterprise.

---

[59] Article 209-0 B FTC.
[60] Article 244 quater B FTC
[61] Article 244 quater B FTC.

Competitiveness and Employment Tax Credit (*crédit d'impôt pour la compétitivité et l'emploi*: *CECI*)

A new competitiveness and employment tax credit was introduced in the French tax system in 2013.[62] It amounts to 4 % of the remuneration paid in 2013 for all salaries up to 2.5 times the statutory national minimum wage (SMIC) (it will amount to 6 % of remuneration paid out in subsequent years). The CICE is not capped and can be offset against the corporate tax (IS) that a company owes for the year in which the payments were made. The remainder of the tax credit can be used to pay future taxes and may be reimbursed, if it is not used within a specific time frame. Certain companies such as SMEs, innovative new companies, and ailing companies may receive the credit immediately.

Family Tax Credit

Companies may obtain a tax credit equal to 50 % of the cost of child care for children (under 3 years old) paid to reimburse such expenses of the company's employees or 25 % of the cost of issuing universal employment service vouchers (*chèques emplois universels*) to make access to personal services easier (child care at home, domestic help, etc.). The tax credit is capped at €500,000 per company per year. It can be offset against the company's corporate tax liability for the year in which the spending was incurred. If the tax credit is greater than the tax due for the year in question, the difference may be refunded.

Tax Credit for International Productions

In order to improve France's attractiveness for foreign productions, a tax credit is granted to cinematographic or audiovisual productions by companies based outside France.[63] This tax credit applies to expenditures incurred until December 31, 2016. The tax credit amounts to 20 % of expenditures in France, provided that they do not exceed 80 % of the film's total production budget. The tax credit is capped at €10 million per film (and not per company). To qualify, films must be approved by the National Center for Cinema and Animation (*Centre national du cinéma et de l'image animée* – CNC), which ensures that films contain elements of French culture, national heritage or landscape.

---

[62] Law n° 2012-1509 of 29 December 2012. See article 244 quater C nouveau FTC.
[63] Article 220 quaterdecies FTC.

Tax Credit for Video Games Development

Video game development companies subject to corporate tax are entitled to a tax credit for video game development expenses which meet specific criteria and are approved by CNC.[64] To be eligible for the tax credit, games must incur development costs higher than or equal to €150,000, and also contribute to French or European cultural creativity in the video-gaming field and promote variety and quality. The tax credit equals 20% of total eligible expenditures, which essentially includes: depreciation of new assets and expenditures for salaried staff directly assigned to create games, copyrights, other costs, overhead and subcontracting up to €1 million. The tax credit is capped for all companies at €3 million per financial year.

Special Rules to Attract Foreign Investment in France

Special Tax Regime for Headquarters and Logistics Centers (quartiers généraux et centres de logistiques)

In France, there is a special tax regime for certain headquarters and logistics centers. This regime has no statutory basis, but results from a tax circular.[65] According to this circular, the centers must be set up solely for the provision of specialized services. Headquarters may provide only management, administration, coordination and auditing services, while logistics centers handle only packaging, labeling and distribution. To be eligible, services must only be provided to companies of the same group and the majority of these must be located abroad.

The tax rules are based on a fixed cost-plus formula which is determined by agreement with the tax authorities. This agreement eliminates the risk of a change in the cost-plus rate applied by the company during a subsequent tax audit. Tax is assessed at a standard rate on earnings which is derived by applying the agreed cost-plus formula to expenditure incurred by headquarters, logistics centers or research and development coordination centers. The cost-plus rate applied is usually between 6% and 10%; agreements are usually reached for periods of 3–5 years. As part of the tax regulations seeking to eliminate expatriation costs, headquarters and logistics centers may pay supplementary remuneration that is fully or partially exempt from personal income tax to their expatriate employees. Companies must apply to the tax authorities to benefit from these measures, which may not be combined with the new scheme for expatriate employees: potential beneficiaries must opt for one or the other.

---

[64] Art. 220 terdecies FTC.
[65] Tax circular of 21 January 1997 (BOI 13 G-1-97 of 30 January 1997).

Special Tax Regime for Expatriates Coming to France

The special tax regime for expatriate personnel is open to any person, regardless of nationality, coming to work in France, provided that (s)he has not been a French tax resident during the five previous calendar years.[66] The requirement is that the person be called to work for a company in France (even a foreign one) and establish his or her tax residence in France by the 31st December of the year following the year during which work started in France (e.g., by December 2015 at the latest for work in France beginning during the course of 2014).

The expatriate exemption scheme applies for up to 5 years starting in the first full year after expatriates assume their new position. Beneficiaries of the system receive exemption from income tax on any additional remuneration ("expatriation bonuses") directly related to their professional activity, and on bonuses for work undertaken abroad in the direct interest and for the exclusive benefit of the company. Total exemptions are capped at 50 % of all remuneration or, alternatively upon request, 20 % of taxable income earned for work performed abroad, excluding the expatriation bonus.

During the same period, expatriates are subject to the "wealth tax" (*impôt de solidarité sur la fortune – ISF*) only for their assets located in France. Thereafter, expatriates must pay ISF on accumulated assets (barring any exemptions) located in France and abroad. ISF is only payable on net taxable assets over €1,300,000.

Measures Improving Legal Certainty[67]

Development of the Ruling Procedure

Besides the general advance ruling procedure (*rescrits fiscaux*),[68] the French legislator has recently introduced specific advance rulings from the tax authorities for companies regarding the eligibility of investment projects for the granting of specific depreciation rules,[69] for the above-mentioned research tax credit,[70] as well as for the tax holiday offered to the Innovative New Companies (JEI)[71] and the Research and Development Areas (ZDR) Regimes (see below 13.1.2).[72] Moreover, an advance ruling procedure enables any company already set up in France, or planning to do so, to ask the tax authorities to rule whether or not it has (or will have) a

---

[66] Art. 81B FTC.

[67] Bruno Gibert, *Améliorer la sécurité du droit fiscal pour renforcer l'attractivité du territoire*, Ministère de l'économie, des finances et de l'industrie, Novembre 2004.

[68] Article L80B-1° of the Tax Procedures Code (TPC) – *Livre des Procédures Fiscales*.

[69] Article L80B-2°b) TPC.

[70] Article L80B-3° and 3bis TPC.

[71] Article L80B-4° TPC.

[72] Article L80B-5° TPC.

permanent establishment in France.[73] In addition, an advance ruling concerning the assessment of a financial operation as fictitious or not may be requested by the taxpayer.[74]

The French Tax Administration is bound to reply to these advanced rulings within 3 months.

Advance Pricing Agreement (APA)

An APA procedure was finally introduced in 1999.[75] The French tax administration published a detailed circular on the APA procedure,[76] according to which SMEs may also conclude a simplified form of APA.[77]

Tax Amnesty and Tax Holiday for Income from Specific Types of Investments

Tax Amnesty

Although in the past France has made use of tax amnesty statutes,[78] the so-called "repressive" option has finally been maintained in the French tax system together with a procedure of tax regularisation.[79] According to this procedure, the taxpayers have the obligation to submit rectified tax returns for all items of income, of property, of inheritances or gifts not declared since 2006. All such taxes are required to be paid, but a small discount may be granted for the penalties.

Tax Holiday

There are two main tax holiday schemes in French law: (i) specific areas schemes and (ii) a tax exemption for innovative new companies.

---

[73] Article L80B-6° TPC.

[74] Article L64B TPC.

[75] Article L80B-7° TPC.

[76] See tax circular of 7 September 1999 n° 4 A/1211 on the Advance Pricing Arrangement Procedure (Official Tax Bulletin 4 A-8-99 No. 171 of 17 September 1999).

[77] Manual on Transfer Pricing for SMEs, November 2006.

[78] Law of 24 May 1951; Law of 14 April 1952; Law of 21 December 1970; Law of 30 December 1981; Law n° 86-824 of 11 July 1986.

[79] Decree n° 2013-1193 of 19 December 2013 and Ministerial Circular of 12 December 2013.

Specific Area Schemes

Companies located (taken over or created[80]) in certain areas may qualify, subject to certain conditions,[81] for a temporary exemption from corporate or income tax, diminishing over time. They may also be exempt from local taxes and social security contributions. These areas are currently the following: Urban Regeneration Areas (ZRU),[82] Regionally Aided Areas (ZFR),[83] Rural Regeneration Areas (ZRR),[84] Employment Priority Areas (BER),[85] Military Restructuring Areas (ZRD),[86] and, more recently, Research and Development Areas[87] located in a competitiveness cluster (*pôle de compétitivité*).

Foreign residents may also benefit from these schemes, provided that they establish a branch or a subsidiary in the areas concerned.[88]

*The Innovative New Companies Tax Exemption (*Jeune entreprise innovante – JEI*)*

The "Innovative new company" status[89] was established in 2004 and aims at fostering the development of SMEs. To be eligible for the JEI status, a company must be an SME as defined by EU law (enterprises with fewer than 250 employees and either annual turnover of less than €50 million or a balance sheet total of less than €43 million) and must meet certain criteria. In particular, it must be an SME less than 8 years old, independent and genuinely new, with research and development expenditure accounting for at least 15 % of the company's total expenses.

---

[80] Article 44 sexies FTC

[81] As, for example, hiring local residents or conducting a specific activity.

[82] Article 44 octies FTC.

[83] Article 44 sexies FTC.

[84] Article 44 quindecies and 1465A FTC.

[85] Article 44 duodecies FTC.

[86] Art. 44 terdecies FTC.

[87] Article 44 undecies FTC.

[88] See Réponse Decagny, JO AN 30 November 2004 p. 9438 (BF 2/05 n° 110).

[89] Article 44 sexies-O FTC.

The Corporate Tax Rate Structure for Foreign and Domestic Corporations in France

Standard Corporate Tax Rate and Additional "Social Contribution"

For benefits from business carried on by natural persons (with no separate existence as a legal entity) the progressive individual income tax rates apply. The developments that follow concern taxation of corporations.

In France, the standard rate for corporate tax is 33.33 %.[90] For companies with a turnover of over €7,630,000, an additional "social contribution" is added. This contribution is equal to 3.3 % of the corporate tax.[91]

As a matter of principle, the taxation of corporations is territorial and individual. It should be noticed however that, in the French tax system, there is an optional tax consolidation regime, according to which French groups of companies may file a consolidated return for the French income of all their members.[92] Under this regime, profits and losses incurred by the members of the group are aggregated to determine a tax consolidated result (in other words, intra-group transactions are neutralized). To qualify for the tax consolidation regime, the head of the group must be a French company that is not itself owned 95 % or more by another French company subject to corporate income tax. The other members of the group must also be subject to French corporate income tax. This implies that foreign subsidiaries are excluded from the tax consolidation regime, which may constitute a negative discrimination incompatible with EU law. In addition, the French parent must hold at least 95 % in the share capital of the subsidiary, either directly or indirectly through other companies that are members of the same tax consolidated group. According to the ECJ,[93] a French company which is indirectly held for more than 95 % by another French company via a foreign company located in the EU, Norway or Iceland can be part of the French consolidation regime.

The tax consolidation regime is intended to promote buyouts of companies by allowing a deduction for the financial costs of acquisition and the use of other losses and thus encourage the development of enterprises.

For sake of completeness, it should be added here that, since 1 January 2012, companies in corporate groups have been able to choose to apply the optional VAT payment consolidation scheme. Only the head of the group is required to pay the VAT balance on behalf of the group's companies. This balance will be calculated as the difference between taxes owed and any tax credits due on the tax returns filed by

---

[90] Article 219I FTC as amended by article 11 of the Finances Law for 1993 (n° 92-1376 of 30 December 1992), JORF n° 304 of 31 December 1992, p. 18058.

[91] Article 235 ter ZCA du CGI. Contribution at rates of 3.3 % calculated on the standard corporate tax amount (i.e. $3.3 \% \times 33.33 = 1.1 \%$).

[92] Article 223A FTC (introduced by Finance Law 1988).

[93] CJCE, 27 November 2008 aff. C-418/07, Papillon.

the group's members. The parent company must directly or indirectly hold a stake of at least 50 % in the subsidiaries' capital or voting rights. As such, the scope of the VAT payment consolidation will not in theory match the scope of tax consolidation in the corporate tax system.

Reduced Corporate Tax Rate

Rates for SMEs

For small and medium-sized businesses (SMEs), a reduced corporate tax rate of 15 % may apply to profits up to €38,120[94] and the standard 33.33 % rate on the remainder. SMEs are exempt from paying the additional "social contribution".

Rates for Non-profit Organizations

Non-profit organisations also benefit from special rates: 24 % for income from immovable property (rental income, agricultural income etc.), and 10 % for other investment income.

Rates for Intellectual Property Income

Proceeds from intellectual property (royalties and capital gains on the transfer of patents, if they have been held for at least 2 years) are eligible for a reduced corpo-rate rate of 15 %.[95] This affects patents, inventions that can be patented, and manu-facturing processes, as well as improvements made to patents and patentable inventions.

Increased Corporate Tax Rate

Exceptional Contribution for Large Enterprises

For the tax years ending 31 December 2011 to 30 December 2016, companies with over €250 million in turnover must pay an **exceptional contribution**. The rate of this contribution is 5 % until the 31 December 2013 and thereafter 10.7 % of gross corporate tax.[96]

---

[94] Article 219 I FTC. Intended for SMEs with at least 75 % of their shares owned, directly or indi-rectly, by individuals, or for companies satisfying the same conditions with an annual turnover of less than €7,630,000, subject to having fully paid up share capital.

[95] Article 39 terdecies and article 219 I FTC.

[96] Article 235 ter ZAA FTC.

Additional Corporate Tax Contribution on Dividends Distributed by a Company Established in France

As of August 17, 2012, dividends paid out by a company established in France are subject to an additional contribution of 3 %.[97] However, dividends paid out by a SME (as per the European Union definition) or by an entity not subject to corporate tax, dividends paid out as shares, and dividends paid out within consolidated groups (see above under 14.1.1) are all exempt. Foreign companies established in France as branches are subject to the 3 % contribution on sums that cease to be available for operations in France.

Branch Tax

A 30 % branch profits tax is imposed on the profits of branches of non-EU entities, although the tax can be reduced or eliminated by a DTC in force.

Domestic Law, Regional or Multilateral Agreements (Including Prohibitions on State Aid) Prohibiting Tax Incentives for Investment Abroad

Although there are no rules specifically prohibiting tax incentives for investment abroad in French domestic law and in regional/multilateral agreements concluded by France, some tax incentives may infringe EU law (15.1.1) or WTO-GATT rules (15.1.2).

EU Rules That May Prohibit Tax Incentives, Including for Investment Abroad

EU State Aid Rules

In line with article 107 of the Treaty on the functioning of the European Union, any aid granted by a Member State or through State resources in any form whatsoever which distorts or threatens to distort competition by promoting certain undertakings or the production of certain goods shall, in so far as it affects trade between Member States, be incompatible with the common market. Since France is an EU Member

---

[97] Article 235 ter ZCA FTC.

State, it must comply with the EU legal framework on State Aids,[98] according to which any such aid should be authorized by the European Commission.

State aid rules apply regardless of the form in which the aid is given, i.e., any kind of tax relief can constitute State aid if the other criteria are fulfilled. Therefore, some tax incentives, including for investment abroad, may be considered as state aids if they exceed the EU *de minimis* policy cap of 200,000€ for a 3-year sliding period.

The EU Code of Conduct for Business Taxation

The EU Code of Conduct for business taxation was established in March 1998 and is not a legally binding instrument, but it clearly has political force. By adopting this Code, the Member States have undertaken to roll back existing tax measures that constitute harmful tax competition and refrain from introducing any such measures in the future ("standstill"). This instrument may also affect or restrain French tax policy choices.

The WTO Agreements

France is also a party of the WTO-GATT agreement (1947), which prohibits tax subsidies.[99] Some authors consider indeed that certain French tax incentives, such as the headquarters regime, may be considered contrary to the WTO-GATT legal framework.[100]

Bilateral or Multilateral Trade or Investment Agreements Concluded by France

With the entry into force of the Treaty of Lisbon and the establishment of a common commercial policy, the conclusion of (bilateral and multilateral) trade or foreign investment agreements is an exclusive competence of the European Union.[101] As a consequence, the Commission has undertaken the long process of replacement of the bilateral agreements between Member States and third countries, which will have a direct impact on the validity and application of the trade and investment

---

[98] In particular, Regulation (EC) n° 1998/2006 of 15 December 2006 on the application of Articles 87 and 88 of the Treaty to de Minimis aid.

[99] Article XVI of the General Agreement on Tariffs and Trade (GATT 1947).

[100] Cf. Marilyne Sadowsky, *Droit de l'OMC, droit de l'Union européenne et fiscalité directe*, Bruxelles, Larcier, 2013. Kabbaj and Sadowsky, in: Lang (ed.), WTO and Direct Taxation.

[101] Article 3 and 207 of the Treaty on the Functioning of the European Union.

agreements concluded by France with the countries concerned. In addition, the treaties previously concluded with other EU Member States are no longer applicable, since a common market has been put in place.

Keeping these limitations in mind, however, the lists below include all the trade and investment agreements concluded by France. Most of these agreements only contained a clause against tax-discrimination. Some of them could also contain the so-called "most favoured nation" clause, according to which the citizens of the one contracting State should benefit in the other State equal advantages as the "most favoured nation" citizens.[102]

List of Bilateral Trade Agreements Concluded by France

Germany, 27-10-1956 (JO 10-9-1959 p. 8850); Belgium, 6-10-1927 (JO 5-11-1927 p. 11270); Canada, 12-5-1933 (JO 10-11-1936 p. 11700); Colombia, 30-5-1892 (JO 1-11-1893); Congo (Brazzaville), 15-8-1960 (JO 23-11-1960 p. 10473); Costa Rica, 2-6-1955 (JO 2-9-1959 p. 8611); Spain, 7-1-1862; USA, 25-11-1959 (JO 15-12-1960 p. 11220); Greece, 11-3-1929 (JO 27-10-1929 p. 11898); Honduras, 25-11-1959 (JO 15-5-1960 p. 4425); Iran, 24-6-1964 (JO 5-11-1969 p. 10829); Italia, 23-8-1951 (JO 23-4-1958 p. 3820); Lebanon, 6 & 27-12-1934 (JO 25-5-1935 p. 5619); Liberia, 17-4-1852 (entry into force : 14-10-1856); Luxembourg, 31-3-1930 (JO 22-8-1931 p. 9430); Madagascar, 27-6-1960 (JO 20-7-1960 p. 6627); Nicaragua, 4-5-1938 (JO 12-7-1938 p. 8243); Saint-Marin, 15-1-1954 (JO 1-6-1956 p. 5041); Sweden, 16-2-1954 (JO 5-6-1956 p. 5136) and Chad, 11-8-1960 (JO 23-11-1960 p. 10479).

List of Bilateral Investment Agreements Concluded by France (Including a Non-discrimination Clause Covering Tax Matters)

Bolivia (Agreement of 25-10-1989 (JO 5-12-1996 p. 17682), Bulgaria (Agreement of 5-4-1989 (JO 16-8-1990 p. 10054), South Korea (Convention of 22-1-1975 (JO 7-5-1975 p. 4268 and agreement of 28-12-1977 (JO 11-4-1979 p. 834), Costa Rica (Agreement of 8-3-1984 (JO 6-4-2000 p. 5260).), Egypt (Convention of 22-12-1974 (JO 8-11-1975 p.11486), UAE (Agreement of 9-9-1991 (JO 8-4-1995 p. 5597), Haiti (Agreement of 23-5-1984 (JO 10-4-1985,p. 4159), Mauritius (Convention of 22-3-1973 (JO 18-5-1974 p. 5367), Indonesia (Agreement of 14-6-1973 (JO 10-8-1975 p. 7820), Jamaica (Agreement of 25-1-1993 (JO 19-11-1994 p. 16361), Jordan (Convention of 23-2-1978 (JO 7-11-1979 p. 258), Kazakhstan (Agreement of

---

[102] For more details, see Thomas Dubut and Tovony Randriamanalina, 'French Report', in: M. Lang (et alii), The Impact of Bilateral Investment Treaties on Taxation (Amsterdam: IBFD) 2016 (forthcoming).

3-2-1998 (JO 26-9-2000 p. 15155), Kuwait (Agreement of 27-9-1989 (JO 25-6-1991 p. 8193), Laos (Agreement of 12-12-1989 (JO 30-4-1991 p. 5793), Malta (Agreement of 11-8-1976 (JO 31-12-1977 p. 6361), Morocco (Agreement of 13-1-1996 (JO 24-3-2000 p. 4536), Mongolia (Agreement of 8-11-1991 (JO 24-3-1994 p. 4469), Nigeria (Agreement of 27-2-1990 (JO 9-10-1991 p. 13197), Pakistan (Convention of 1-6-1983 (JO 14-3-1985 p. 1923). Pakistan (Convention of 30-11-1978 (JO 7-1-1981 p. 178), Poland (Agreement of 14-2-1989 (JO 5-4-1990 p. 4182), Salvador (Agreement of 20-9-1978 (JO 24-1-1993 p. 1267), Senegal: Agreement of 28-7- 2007 (JO 27-7-2010 p. 13839), Serbia and Montenegro (Convention of 28-3-1974 (JO 13-5-1975 p. 4813), Sudan (Convention of 31-7-1978 (JO 3-10-1980 p. 2295), Syria (Agreement of 28-11-1977 (JO 8-6-1980 p. 1418 and Amendment in JO 22 p. 5403), Czech Republic (Agreement of 13-9-1990 (JO 29-1-1992 p. 1424), Tunisia (Convention of 9-8-1963 (JO 22-9-1965 p. 8411), Uruguay (Agreement of 14-10-1993 (JO 22-3-2001 p. 4476), Vietnam (Agreement of 26-5-1992 (JO 16-11-1994 p. 16222), Yemen (Agreement of 27-4-1984 (JO 19-12-1991 p. 16536), Croatia & Former Yugoslavian Republic of Macedonia (JO 13-8-1996 p. 12280 and JO 20-8-1996 p. 12536), Zaire (Convention of 5-10-1972 (JO 16-9-1975 p. 9507), now applicable to the Democratic Republic of Congo.

Chapter 8
Transparency and Simplicity Support Investment in Hong Kong

Andrew Halkyard

Abstract Hong Kong has a territorial tax system in which, with very few exceptions, business profits from foreign sources are not subject to tax. Accordingly, the regime may be viewed as friendly to foreign investment, even though it was not designed with this intention. In order to attract investment into its own borders, Hong Kong features a regime that minimizes red tape for business and a common law legal system that provides transparency and simplicity.

Synopsis Hong Kong has a territorial tax system. Business profits derived from Hong Kong sources are subject to tax. With very few exceptions, those derived from sources outside Hong Kong are not. Consequently, residence has virtually no role in determining tax liability.

Common law rules determine the source of income. In general, a dividend paid to a Hong Kong company by an offshore company is treated as derived from sources outside Hong Kong and is not subject to tax in Hong Kong.

Although not designed to encourage investment abroad, Hong Kong's territorial regime may be viewed as friendly to taxpayers seeking to do so.

Concerning international matters, Hong Kong's tax policy is consistent with mainstream OECD practice. Exchange of information by Hong Kong can only occur through a treaty or other binding agreement. Accordingly, by the beginning of 2016, Hong Kong had concluded 34 comprehensive double taxation agreements. Recent changes in domestic law allow Hong Kong to exchange information relating to all taxes with a treaty partner and to enter into stand-alone TIEAs. By the beginning of 2016, Hong Kong had concluded seven TIEAs.

Currently, information exchanged must meet the "necessary" or "foreseeably relevant" standard and sharing for non-tax purposes is limited to very high level matters, involving serious crime, drug trafficking, or terrorism financing.

A. Halkyard (✉)
Law Faculty, Hong Kong University, Pok Fu Lam, Hong Kong

University of New South Wales, Sydney, New South Wales, Australia

Taxation Law and Policy Research Group, Monash University, Clayton, Australia
e-mail: andrew.halkyard@gmail.com

© Springer International Publishing Switzerland 2017   157
K.B. Brown (ed.), *Taxation and Development - A Comparative Study*,
Ius Comparatum - Global Studies in Comparative Law 21,
DOI 10.1007/978-3-319-42157-5_8

While Hong Kong exchange of information is currently limited to exchange upon request, it has moved to meet the standard for automatic exchange of information extolled by the OECD. With a simple tax regime based upon territorial source of income, Hong Kong anticipated the need for fundamental changes in policy in order to implement automatic exchange of information. In order to avoid being viewed as an uncooperative regime, it passed legislation to meet the standard in June 2016.

In order to attract investment within its own borders, Hong Kong has adopted a regime that ensures minimal red tape for business and supports a common law legal system that is transparent and simple. With limited exceptions, such as for offshore funds and offshore treasury centres investing in Hong Kong, it does not provide investment incentives through the tax system.

The corporate tax rate on Hong Kong source profits is 16.5 %.

Hong Kong has concluded a number of bilateral and multilateral trade and investment agreements.

International Tax System

The international tax system in Hong Kong is simple and straightforward – Hong Kong has a territorial taxation system under which business profits sourced in Hong Kong are taxable and business profits sourced outside Hong Kong are non-taxable. Although statutory deemed source rules have been enacted (such as for royalties and other payments for intellectual property, and rent of movable property, used in Hong Kong), in the great majority of cases common law rules propounded by the courts determine issues of source (such as for profits derived from trading, manufacturing and the provision of services).

Accordingly, with very limited exceptions (which relate to special category taxpayers such as aircraft owners, ship owners, and offshore funds), residence plays no part in determining liability to tax on business profits.

Under common law rules as applied in Hong Kong, in the great majority of cases dividends paid to a Hong Kong company by an offshore company (whether associated or not) are sourced outside Hong Kong and thus not liable to tax in Hong Kong.

Offshore Investment

Hong Kong has not enacted any tax laws designed to discourage investment in offshore jurisdictions. Hong Kong has a territorial taxation system under which profits arising outside Hong Kong are not subject to taxation in Hong Kong, regardless of whether such profits are liable to tax in the place where they are earned (see section "International Tax System", above).

OECD Global Tax Forum

Hong Kong is a member of the OECD Global Tax Forum. By and large, Hong Kong's taxation policy concerning international matters is fairly consistent with mainstream OECD practice. Two examples illustrate this conclusion. The first relates to taxation of e-commerce (which, according to published Departmental practice, broadly accepts that Hong Kong will follow the guidance contained in various OECD reports on this topic). The second involves exchange of information (EoI) for Double Tax Agreement (DTA) purposes (which, in order to be compliant with OECD developments, has necessitated changes to Hong Kong domestic law, see section "Exchange of Information Agreements" below).

Exchange of Information Agreements

The taxation authority in Hong Kong, the Inland Revenue Department (IRD), cannot provide information to any party without legislative authority. In the international context, this means that Hong Kong can only provide information to parties outside Hong Kong in accordance with a binding agreement or treaty.

In this regard, the three most important sources for providing information are comprehensive DTAs, stand-alone Taxation Information Exchange Agreements, and the Mutual Legal Assistance in Criminal Matters Ordinance (Laws of Hong Kong, Cap. 525) which regulates the provision of assistance in criminal matters between the governments of Hong Kong and other jurisdictions with which Hong Kong has concluded a relevant agreement.

As at January 2016, Hong Kong had concluded 34 comprehensive DTAs. Each contains an EoI provision. A diminishing number of these were based upon the fairly restricted 2004 version of the OECD Model Convention article on EoI. However, recent protocols to earlier DTAs concerning EoI indicate that they are being periodically updated (for example, the fourth protocol to Hong Kong's DTA with Mainland China and Notes exchanged with Japan, which were signed respectively in April 2015 and July 2015). A full report on the status and content of those provisions in DTAs concluded by Hong Kong up to August 2013 is provided by the Global Forum's *Peer Review Report Phase 1: Legal and Regulatory Framework (Hong Kong, China)* (November 2011) and *Phase 2: Implementation of the Standards in Practice (Hong Kong, China)* (November 2013).

Following changes to Hong Kong's domestic law in 2013, Hong Kong (a) expanded its power to exchange information with a treaty partner (e.g., Hong Kong can now provide information relating to "tax of every kind" imposed by the treaty partner rather than simply those taxes specified in the DTA) so that, in law and practice, Hong Kong's future DTAs (when concluded or renegotiated) can be consistent with the 2012 version of the OECD Model Convention article for EoI and (b) has the power to enter into stand-alone Taxation Information Exchange Agreements (TIEAs). As at January 2016, Hong Kong had concluded seven TIEAs (the first being with the U.S.).

It should particularly be noted that the 2014 version of the EoI article in the OECD Model Convention permits the use or sharing of information exchanged for limited non-tax related purposes, provided such use is allowed under the laws of both sides and the competent authority of the supplying party (in Hong Kong's case, the IRD) authorizes such use. A detailed statement of the Hong Kong government's attitude to this issue, which basically accepts the OECD position, is contained in the *Report of the Bills Committee on the Inland Revenue (Amendment) Bill 2013*, LC Paper No CB(1)1385/12-13 at paragraphs 41–45. In this regard, it is important to appreciate that (a) a request for information must first satisfy the previous "necessary" or, more recently, the "foreseeably relevant" condition for exchange and (2) any subsequent sharing of such information is limited to 'high level' matters (under Hong Kong domestic law, the Commissioner of Inland Revenue can disclose information to specified government bodies only in limited circumstances – namely, in relation to organized and serious crime, recovery of proceeds from drug trafficking, and terrorism financing).

The most recent development in this rapidly changing area is best summarized in the following extract from the Consultation Report on Automatic Exchange of Information issued by the Hong Kong Government in April 2015:

> The OECD standard for EOI permits exchange of information upon request or on automatic or spontaneous basis. So far, Hong Kong has only opted for EOI upon request. However, the international landscape on tax cooperation has been evolving rapidly. OECD released in July 2014 the "Standard for Automatic Exchange of Financial Account Information in Tax Matters" (AEOI), calling on governments to collect from their financial institutions financial account information of overseas tax residents and exchange the information with jurisdictions of residence of the relevant account holders on an annual basis.
>
> The Global Forum on Transparency and Exchange of Information for Tax Purposes ("Global Forum"), a 120-strong international organisation pursuing tax transparency, has invited all its members, including Hong Kong, to commit to implementing the new global standard. It has also established a mechanism to monitor and review the progress of implementation amongst members from 2017 onwards. By the end of October 2014, over 90 jurisdictions have expressed commitment to the new standard. As a responsible member of the international community and to avoid being labelled as an "uncooperative" jurisdiction which will affect our position as an international financial centre, we indicated to the Global Forum in September 2014 our support for implementing the new standard on AEOI on a reciprocal basis with appropriate partners which can meet relevant requirements on protection of privacy and confidentiality of information exchanged and ensuring proper use of the data, with a view to commencing the first information exchanges by the end of 2018. We have stated clearly that our commitment was premised on the condition that Hong Kong could put in place necessary domestic legislation by 2017.
>
> Hong Kong has been practising a simple, territorial-based tax regime. Moving towards AEOI requires fundamental changes to our policy and legal framework and to our established position of implementing EOI only on request. In developing the model for AEOI in Hong Kong, we need to ensure that our model meets the international standard without creating undue burden of compliance on the financial institutions and their non-Hong Kong tax resident account holders. We will adopt a *pragmatic approach* to include all essential

requirements of the AEOI standard in our domestic law and will *ensure effective implementation* of the international standard.

The "Consultation Paper on Automatic Exchange of Financial Account Information in Tax Matters in Hong Kong" can be accessed at http://www.fstb.gov.hk/tb/en/docs/AEOI-ConsultationPaper-e.pdf. The law has now been enacted - see Inland Revenue (Amendment) (No. 3) Ordinance 2016, which authorizes automatic EoI with effect from 1 January 2017.

Incentives for Investment in Emerging or Developing Countries

Hong Kong has no specific tax incentives for investment in emerging, developing, or any other countries. It should be reiterated that, given its limited jurisdiction to tax, Hong Kong does not tax any business profits derived outside Hong Kong (see section "International Tax System", above).

Measures to Attract Economic Activity

Hong Kong has taken several measures to attract economic activity, such as striving to ensure minimal red tape for business, adopting a light regulatory touch, and continuing a common law legal system which is both transparent and relatively simple in terms of its laws and compliance obligations. However, with very limited exceptions (which relate to exemption and reduction of tax for offshore funds investing in Hong Kong, and certain profits derived from various debt instruments and reinsurance, offshore treasury centre and captive insurance activity respectively) such measures are not provided through the taxation system.

In short, with very limited exceptions, Hong Kong's tax system does not discriminate in favour of, or against, any particular industry or geographic area. In common parlance, in the taxation sphere 'Hong Kong does not try to pick winners.'

Tax Rate on Business Profits

The rate of tax on business profits earned by a corporation (whether incorporated in Hong Kong or overseas), and sourced in Hong Kong, is 16.5 %. The rate has remained unchanged since the year of assessment 2008/2009.

It is commonly argued that Hong Kong's tax incentives are 'inherent' in its low rate, territorial based, fairly narrow and easily complied with, taxation regime.

Trade Agreements

Hong Kong has entered into several bilateral and multilateral trade and investment agreements (details available from the Trade and Industry Department website, http://www.tid.gov.hk/eindex.html). However, the terms of these agreements exclude provisions relating to taxation measures (apart from those touching upon customs duties). Hong Kong's international agreements relating to taxation measures are contained in the terms of the DTAs it has concluded.

Chapter 9
Current Issues in Cross Border Taxation and Investment in the State of Israel

Tamir Shanan, Sagit Leviner, and Moran Harari

Abstract In order to reconcile forces of economic globalization with commonly accepted distributional principles, in 2003, the State of Israel shifted from a territorial to a worldwide system of taxation. A remnant of the old territorial system was retained in a special, mid-way, regime, that (among other features) exempts foreign source income from Israeli tax for "new immigrants" and "returning residents". This regime and the Investment Law, providing drastically reduced tax rates along side other lucrative benefits, have not been repealed despite on-going national and internatioal pressure to do so. In the case of the Investment Law some revisions have recently been made to tie qualification for benefits to proven measures of industry competitiveness and the demonstration of an impact on exports and on Israel's GDP. Special benefits provided to owners of stock in Israeli holding companies that invest in certain foreign corporations may also offer an interesting, yet underutilized, incentive for investment.

Synopsis In 2003, Israel's international income tax regime sustained a transformation from territorial to one of worldwide taxation. This shift was viewed as a timely one reconciling forces of economic globalization with commonly accepted distributional principles. Under this system, individuals are taxed where they reside and corporations are taxed where incorporated or in the country from which management and control are exercised. A credit is allowed against Israeli tax liability for foreign taxes paid by residents on foreign source income. Since 2003, this is true

T. Shanan (✉)
College of Management, Haim Striks School of Law, Rishon LeZion, Israel
e-mail: tamirsh@colman.ac.il

S. Leviner
Ono Academic College Faculty of Law and Ono Academic College Faculty of Business Administration, Kiryat Ono, Israel
e-mail: sagit.leviner@ono.ac.il

M. Harari
College of Management, The Tax Justice Network, Rishon LeZion, Israel
e-mail: moran@taxjustice.net

© Springer International Publishing Switzerland 2017   163
K.B. Brown (ed.), *Taxation and Development - A Comparative Study*,
Ius Comparatum - Global Studies in Comparative Law 21,
DOI 10.1007/978-3-319-42157-5_9

even when income is produced in a country with which Israel does not have a treaty. As in the case of most countries, the credit is limited to the Israeli tax on foreign source income. While residents are taxed world-wide, nonresidents are taxed only on income earned or produced in Israel. This places considerable importance on the determination of the source of a nonresident's income.

Israel is signatory to 53 bilateral treaties with foreign countries. Most of the treaties follow the OECD Model Convention. These treaties provide Israel a valuable tool in an effort to enhance taxpayer compliance, ease tax collection and advance trade. Although the scope of information exchange, one of the primary benefits derived from treaties, varies from treaty to treaty, Israel commonly provides for information upon request of the other contracting state. Importantly, in view of recent global trends and pressures, the Israeli Tax Authority currently works to amend the Income Tax Ordinance to allow and to exercise ratification of international information-sharing agreements, regardless of whether a bilateral or multilateral treaty exists. Over the long run, this is expected to drastically change the scope and quality of information that the Israeli Tax Authority shares and receives.

Israel has retained the remnants of a territorial regime in the income tax exemption for foreign source income for immigrants and returning Israeli residents. It also exempts these taxpayers from key filing requirements, including income tax returns and capital statements. The exemption is available for a 10–20 year period. The efforts of fellow OECD member countries to force repeal these provisions (designed to attract investments to Israel, but viewed as unfairly competitive by trading partners) have been largely unsuccessful.

A long standing Investment Law, providing government grants and lucrative tax benefits to eligible corporations, was significantly modified in 2010. At that time, incentives failed to provide economic development in targeted areas and often exceeded the benefit obtained by the Israeli government. In the post-2010 Investment Law, qualification for benefits is tied to proven measures of industry competitiveness and the demonstration of an impact on exports and on Israel's GDP. Only time will tell whether and the extent to which these revisions are successful.

Introduction

Since it was established on May 14, 1948,[1] the State of Israel has absorbed millions of immigrants from all over the world. Currently, Israel's population stands at more than eight million citizens and its gross domestic product (GDP) is estimated at approximately USD 250B.[2] To finance the growing needs of Israel's population, the

---

[1] DECLARATION OF THE ESTABLISHMENT OF THE STATE OF ISRAEL, MAY 14, 1948, available at http://main.knesset.gov.il/About/Occasion/Pages/IndDeclaration.aspx (in Hebrew), accessed 20.08.2015; http://www.mfa.gov.il/mfa/foreignpolicy/peace/guide/pages/declaration%20of%20establishment%20of%20state%20of%20israel.aspx (in English), accessed 20.08.15.

[2] ISRAEL STATISTICS BUREAU, STATISTICAL ABSTRACT, ISRAEL 2012, available at http://www.cbs.gov.il/reader/shnaton/templ_shnaton.html?num_tab=st14_04&CYear=2012 (in Hebrew), accessed 20.08.2015.

state issued various debentures over the years, mainly by means of government bonds. These currently amount to approximately USD 180B, one sixth of it in foreign currency.[3] Consequently, Israel spends approximately USD 38B each year servicing its debt, which is equal to about 34 % of its annual budget.[4]

Israel has a limited pool of natural resources, the key natural asset being phosphate. Natural gas was also recently discovered in the Mediterranean Sea, off the coast of Israel.[5] The country generally imports crude oil and other fuels, vehicles, raw materials, military equipment, grain, and consumer goods.[6] The state is prospering, however, owing to its technologically advanced market economy and its exports of software and computerized systems, communications technology, medical equipment, pharmaceuticals, fruits, chemicals, some natural gas, and military technology.[7] Israel's key trading partners include the United States, which accounts for about 37 % of Israeli exports, and the European Union, responsible for approximately 33 % of exports and 35 % of imports.[8] China, India, Japan, and Brazil are also among the country's key trading partners, all of which have double taxation treaties with Israel.[9]

The Israeli judiciary system combines three groups of legal traditions: English common law, civil law, and Jewish law.[10] Israel's income tax system has its origins in British income tax law,[11] but in the last two decades Israeli tax law and jurisprudence have significantly evolved to now more closely mirror the American income tax system.[12] Concurrently, in May 2010 the State of Israel joined the Organisation for Co-operation and Economic Development (OECD) as a full member,[13] while most of its double taxation treaties with key commercial partners were already

---

[3] STATE COMPTROLLER OF ISRAEL, DEFICIT STATISTICS, available at http://www.ag.mof.gov.il/AccountantGeneral/BudgetExecution/BudgetExecutionTopNav/BEGovReports/BEGovReports_2015/?WBCMODE=PresentationUnpublished (in Hebrew), accessed 20.01.2014.

[4] TREASURY OF THE STATE OF ISRAEL, STATE BUDGET STATISTICS, available at http://www.mof.gov.il/BudgetSite/StateBudget/Budget2013-2014/Pages/Budget2013-2014HP.aspx (in Hebrew), accessed 20.1.2014; THE LAW FOR CHANGES IN NATIONAL PRIORITIES (LEGISLATION AMENDMENTS TO ACHIEVE BUDGETARY GOALS FOR FISCAL YEARS 2013 AND 2014), 2013 (in Hebrew), accessed 20.06.2015.

[5] Supra note 3, pp. 34–35.

[6] Ibid.

[7] ORGANISATION FOR ECONOMIC CO-OPERATION AND DEVELOPMENT (OECD), SURVEYS INFORMATION, available at http://www.oecd.org/economy/surveys/2013%20ISRAEL%20Overview.pdf, accessed 20.08.2015.

[8] ISRAEL STATISTICS BUREAU, INTERNATIONAL TRADE DATA, available at http://www.cbs.gov.il/www/hodaot2013n/09_13_038b.doc (in Hebrew), accessed 20.08.2015.

[9] OECD SURVEYS INFORMATION, available at http://www.oecd.org/economy/surveys/2013%20ISRAEL%20Overview.pdf, accessed 20.08.2015.

[10] Accordingly, the Israeli judiciary regime is often viewed neither as a pure common nor a pure civil law system. See AHARON BARAK, JUSTICE IN A DEMOCRATIC SOCIETY 228–236 (2004).

[11] AMNON REFAEL and SHLOMI LAZAR, INCOME TAX, vol. I, 5–21 (4th ed., 2009).

[12] Ibid.

[13] OECD ECONOMIC SURVEYS OVERVIEW REPORT, ISRAEL (DEC., 2013), available at http://www.oecd.org/israel/israelsaccessiontotheoecd.htm, accessed 20.08.2015.

patterned after the OECD Model Tax Convention.[14] The Israeli Income Tax Ordinance (hereinafter, "the Income Tax Ordinance" or "the Tax Ordinance") levies taxation on individuals at progressive rates of up to 50 %, and on capital gains, dividend, and interest income at reduced rates of 25 or 30 %. Corporations are usually taxed at a fixed rate of 26.5 %, with no decreased rates for small and medium-size businesses.[15]

While the term international taxation commonly refers to international or cross-border aspects of national income tax systems, it also derives from an umbrella of international agreements and understandings, including a broad and dynamic treaty network. This chapter adopts this comprehensive interpretation of international taxation to explore the manner in which Israel taxes and exempts cross-border transactions, focusing largely – yet not exclusively – on outbound investments. The chapter contains a critical analysis of the strengths and weaknesses of the Israeli income tax system in this context. Changes carried out in the Israeli income tax system after 2002 take center stage. At that time, the Israeli income tax system underwent an extensive reform with the implementation of Amendment 132 of the Income Tax Ordinance, which came into effect on January 1, 2003.[16] The reform included, among other changes, an important makeover of Israel's international income tax regime, bringing the Israeli income tax system closer to systems of large industrial countries. The remainder of this chapter is structured as follows: Section I reviews Israel's international income tax regime; Section II focuses on Israel's international tax information-exchange and cooperation practices; and Section III explores Israel's income tax incentive regime. The chapter concludes with a brief overview and several suggestions for further improvements of Israel's international tax regime.

Israel's International Income Tax System

Evolution of the Israeli Income Tax System

For more than half a century, the Income Tax Ordinance followed territorial principles under which, with some exceptions, Israeli income tax liability was only levied on income earned or produced in Israel[17]; income generated abroad was nor-

[14] OECD, Exchange of Tax Information Portal, Israel, available at http://www.eoi-tax.org/jurisdictions/IL#agreements, accessed 20.08.2015.

[15] §121, §125B and §125C of Israel Income Tax Ordinance [New Version], 1968 (hereinafter, the "Income Tax Ordinance" or "Tax Ordinance." Also, unless otherwise stated, section numbers and amendments refer to the Income Tax Ordinance.).

[16] Amendment 132 was enacted pursuant to the recommendations of the Rabinovich Committee, which in turn relied on the recommendations of the Ben Bassat Committee, 2000, available at http://ozar.mof.gov.il/reform/basat_report.htm (in Hebrew), accessed 24.08.2015; http://ozar.mof.gov.il/reform2002/index.htm (in Hebrew), accessed 24.08.2015.

[17] §2 and §89, before the 2003 income tax reform.

mally exempted.[18] With the implementation of Amendment 132, the Israeli income tax system underwent a significant transformation, from territorially centered taxation to a worldwide tax approach of Israeli residents, regardless of where income was earned or produced.[19] According to the 2002 Rabinovich Tax Reform Committee, the departure from a broadly-defined territorial approach and the move toward residence-based worldwide income taxation was a timely move in view of key fiscal factors such as "economic globalization and the increase in capital mobility."[20] The committee added that the worldwide income tax approach "best fits with distributional mechanisms universally accepted by most countries as well as the fundamentals of the OECD Model Tax Convention."[21]

Worldwide income taxation means that the key criterion in determining income tax jurisdiction and liability becomes the taxpayer's place of residence or nationality. According to this approach, individual residents are taxed in the country where they reside or of which they are nationals, while corporate residents are taxed in the country where they were incorporated or from which control and management are exercised.[22] Consequently, the decision over the taxpayer's nationality, or in the case of Israel, residence, becomes the key factor.

Determining Residence

With the implementation of Amendment 132, Israel's Income Tax Ordinance was reformed to adopt the principle of residence-based taxation, with residence being broadly defined by utilizing two categories of residence: one for individuals and another for corporations. For individuals, residence is now based on a substantive test for establishing the taxpayer's "Center of Living"[23] Additionally, the Tax Ordinance now provides legal presumptions for proving residence based on a day-count test of

---

[18] Notwithstanding the territorial premise, some exceptions existed even before the 2003 reform. The most important of these were: (1) §5, which specified the circumstances in which income was considered produced in Israel, even when it was generated abroad, and (2) §89, which taxed capital gains based on residence criteria, making it possible to tax Israeli residents on their capital gains regardless of where these gains were created.

[19] *Supra* note 16.

[20] *Ibid; see also* High Court of Justice Petition 477/02 *Kaniel v. The Israeli Government*, Taxes 19/3 5–3 (2005) (in Hebrew).

[21] At the same time, tax systems of countries like Japan have moved from citizenship or residence approach to territorial-based taxation, and a similar change is being contemplated in the United States.

[22] §1.

[23] The "center of living" doctrine is the closest (yet not identical) concept to the domiciliary approach practiced in some tax systems. Domiciliary is commonly established in the country where the taxpayer has her permanent home or a substantial connection to. Most often, once the taxpayer is born, domiciliary it is automatically assigned based on the taxpayer parents' place of domiciliary, until she moves elsewhere. In contrast, residency, whether determined with reference to the "center of living" concept or any other test, is independently and repeatedly established on a yearly basis. The Israeli courts applied the "center of living" doctrine even prior to Amendment

the length of time the taxpayer was physically present in Israel during the tax year in question and, in certain cases, in the preceding 2 years as well.[24] Specifically, §1 of the Income Tax Ordinance determines that an individual taxpayer becomes an Israeli resident when their center of living is in Israel, and provides that:

(A) […], in this context, the following guidelines apply:

1. To determine the center of living of an individual, the totality of family, economic, and social ties are considered, including:

   (a) The place of the taxpayer's permanent home;
   (b) The place where the taxpayer and his or her family reside;
   (c) The taxpayer's regular place of business or employment;
   (d) The place of the taxpayer's active and substantive economic interests;
   (e) the place where the taxpayer is active in organizations, associations, and other establishments.

The residence of Israeli corporations is established when one of the following criteria is met[25]:

1. the corporation is incorporated in Israel; or
2. the control and management of the corporation are exercised from within Israel.[26]

Conversely, §1 of the Income Tax Ordinance defines foreign residents as persons (a) who reside abroad for 183 days or more a year, for at least 2 consecutive years, and (b) whose center of living is established abroad during the subsequent 2 consecutive years, for a 4-year test in total.[27] Consequently, taxpayers who are engaged in multinational transactions may find themselves in ambiguous situations in which they have two or more residences for income tax purposes (e.g., an Israeli and a foreign one). In the absence of a treaty to help provide a definitive residence determination, these taxpayers face a greater risk of double taxation.[28]

---

132. *See*, e.g., Supreme Court Appeal 477/02 *Gonen v. Haifa Tax Assessment officer*, Taxes 20/1 5–1 (2006) (in Hebrew).

[24] §1 determines:

(2) the center of living of an individual is in Israel if –

(a) The taxpayer was physically present in Israel for at least 183 days of the tax year;
(b) The taxpayer was physically present in Israel for at least 30 days of the tax year, and the total number of days the taxpayer was present in Israel in the course of that year and the two preceding tax years is at least 425 days; partial days are counted as full days for this purpose.

[25] Before amendment 132, corporations were considered Israeli residents when one of the following criteria was met: (a) the corporation was registered in Israel and the majority of its activity took place in Israel; (b) the control and management of the corporation were exercised from within Israel.

[26] *See*, e.g., Supreme Court Appeal 3102/12 *Niago v. Kfar Saba Tax Assessment officer*, Taxes 28/4 5–4 (2014) (in Hebrew), where the court established the Israeli residence of a company registered in the Bahamas because of management and control considerations. *See also* Tax Appeal 1090/06 *Yanko Weiss* v. Holon *Tax Assessment officer*, Taxes (2013) (in Hebrew).

[27] §1.

[28] Conversely, there can be situations where taxpayers are classified as nonresidents and face a reduced risk of double taxation (or taxation at all).

Foreign Double Tax Credit Relief

Despite Israel's predisposition toward worldwide taxation, as implemented with Amendment 132, territorial features remain in the reformed law. For example, the amended Income Tax Ordinance imposes liability on the income of foreign residents when it is earned or produced in Israel.[29] To this end, detailed source rules were written into the Tax Ordinance.[30] These rules are of relevance for foreign residents who generate income within Israel's borders; they are also valuable for Israeli residents who earn income abroad and, given the risk of double taxation, consider claiming a double tax relief from the Israeli Tax Authority.[31]

For Israeli residents pursuing a double tax relief, Amendment 132 introduces a thoughtfully worked-out arrangement.[32] As in many other progressive economies, the key mechanism for addressing double taxation of cross-border transactions in Israel is based on a method of credit relief available in section three of the Income Tax Ordinance.[33] Among other things, this section clarifies that Israel normally acquires only a secondary right to tax foreign-source income and gain.[34] The double tax relief introduced with Amendment 132 applies primarily to foreign taxes paid on foreign income, based on Israeli source rules. Conversely, once Israeli source rules determine that income was generated in Israel, Israel's Tax Authority gains the primary right to tax, and its foreign tax credit relief becomes irrelevant.[35]

Provision §200 of the Income Tax Ordinance provides that foreign federal, state, provincial, or cantonal income taxes paid on foreign income subject to Israeli income tax are eligible for the double tax relief, as against the Israeli tax liability.[36] Provision §199 defines foreign taxes as taxes that Israeli residents pay a foreign tax system for income earned or produced abroad. The relief is only available to Israeli (as opposed to foreign) residents, and only for taxes levied on foreign-source income.[37] Furthermore, the size of credit awarded for relief is capped.[38] In other words, the Income Tax Ordinance requires that Israeli tax liability be calculated

---

[29] Territorial features are also common in other countries implementing residence or citizenship taxation.

[30] Before Amendment 132, the Income Tax Ordinance failed to offer clear source rules. The new, more detailed, rules are now provided in §4A and §89.

[31] See §§199–210 for unilateral domestic legislation.

[32] The credit mechanism is elaborated in §§199–210, section three B, offering rules for specific cases such as credit limits for corporations and individuals and instances involving dividends. Prior to Amendment 132, with some exceptions, Israel offered double tax relief only to residents of countries with which it had double tax treaties.

[33] *Ibid.* For a comparative study see REUVEN S. AVI-YONAH ET AL., GLOBAL PERSPECTIVE ON INCOME TAXATION LAW, 158–160 (2011).

[34] §199.

[35] *Ibid.*

[36] §200.

[37] Israeli-source income is fully taxable in Israel, unless statutorily exempted. Accordingly, it is generally not creditable for the purpose of double tax relief. §§199–200.

[38] §204.

based on Israel's tax laws and that the double tax credit relief be limited to the amount of such liability.[39] Foreign tax liability in excess of this measure is ineligible for credit relief in the tax year in which this liability was incurred. However, the Income Tax Ordinance allows, in certain circumstances, that the excess amount will qualify for credit relief as against Israeli tax liability within the subsequent 5 years.[40]

Like tax systems in countries such as the United States and Iceland, the Tax Ordinance computes foreign income and liability based on a worldwide (as opposed to per-country) basis.[41] Accordingly, foreign income tax liability and double tax credit relief are not calculated individually for each country where income is generated, but are based on a global, all-inclusive measure.[42] Income is classified pursuant to its source[43] so that income tax liability and credit eligibility are computed and awarded within each income category or "basket."[44] With some exceptions,[45] credit eligibility and tax liability cannot be transferred between different baskets of income.[46] When cross-border transactions involve countries with which Israel has a tax treaty, this treaty becomes the source of the double tax relief, while the mechanism utilized for executing the relief is drawn from the Income Tax Ordinance.[47] When no treaty exists, the Income Tax Ordinance serves as both the source and the mechanism for the double tax relief.[48] In other words, because Israel's method of relief does not depend on reciprocity, it is binding even when other jurisdictions do not offer similar arrangements.[49]

Conformity with Globally Accepted Corporate Income Tax Practices and Statutory Rates

In addition to adopting a worldwide taxation standard and introducing a detailed double tax credit relief mechanism, Amendment 132 also added four anti-avoidance arrangements, tailored to a worldwide income tax system. These include rules for

---

[39] Therefore, the computation of income tax liability is based on Israeli tax rules. *See* §§1, 2, 199–210.

[40] §205A.

[41] §204.

[42] §199 and §200.

[43] §4A and §89 provide several source rules based on income type. There are 11 types of income, commonly divided into three main categories: income from land, business income, and passive income. Income types, detailed in §4A, include, for example, income from trade, labor, dividend, lottery, and the like. These categories echo, to a large extent, the income categories listed in §2.

[44] §199 and §204.

[45] §205A(b).

[46] §205A(a).

[47] Prior to Amendment 132, such relief was available only for residents of countries with which Israel had a tax treaty. *See supra* note 32 and accompanying text.

[48] §§199–210.

[49] §75B.

controlled foreign corporations, foreign vocation corporations,[50] expatriation tax incidences, and transfer pricing.[51] The amendment also introduced incidences of imputed capital gain arising from the disposition of capital assets upon expatriation from Israel.[52] Lastly, in 2006, Amendment 147 of the Income Tax Ordinance introduced two other important additions to Israel's international tax regime, including measures of participation exemption and the taxation of trusts.[53]

To further enhance Israel's corporate environment appeal to foreign investors, significant legislative changes have also been implemented in that area. In line with global trends, statutory corporate tax rates were drastically reduced over the past three decades: while Israel's corporate tax rate stood at approximately 61 % until the mid-1980s,[54] in the 1990s the rate was reduced to 36 %, dropping to 25 % by the end of the first decade of the new millennium,[55] and the legislative intention was to further reduce it to 18 % by 2016.[56] This last reduction was eventually abandoned, however, and the Israeli statutory corporate tax rate increased slightly to 26.5 % in 2014, and recently decreased again to 25 % in 2016.[57]

Israel's Income Tax Treaty Network

Provision §196 of the Income Tax Ordinance provides that when Israel has an income tax treaty with another country, the rules of the treaty take precedence over Israel's domestic tax legislation.[58] Israel has 53 bilateral income tax treaties with foreign countries.[59] As noted in the introduction, most of these treaties adopt the

---

[50] §5 (introduced with Amendment 132) and, now, §75B1 (as revised by Amendment 198, enacted in 2013).

[51] Borrowing a worldwide practice, the Income Tax Ordinance adopted the "arm's length principle" for evaluating cross-border transactions in §85A (initially enacted in 2003 yet legally set in motion in 2006).

[52] §100A.

[53] Amendment 147, 2006, available in http://fs.knesset.gov.il/%5C16%5Claw%5C16_lsr_299994.pdf (in Hebrew), accessed 24.08.2015.

[54] For a detailed explanation of the taxation of corporate entities in Israel before Amendment 72, 1987, see David Gliksberg, *"The Mini Reform:" The full Integrative Model and Taxation of Corporations in Israel*, 20 MISHPATIM 185 (1990) (In Hebrew).

[55] Amendment 132.

[56] *See* Amendment 147, 2006, available at http://fs.knesset.gov.il/%5C16%5Claw%5C16_lsr_299994.pdf (in Hebrew), accessed 24.08.15; The Law for a Change in the Tax Burden (Legislative Amendments), 2011, available at http://fs.knesset.gov.il/%5C18%5Claw%5C18_lsr_301335.pdf (in Hebrew), accessed 24.08.2015.

[57] §126. Compare with views that the statutory corporate rate in Israel and its recent moderate increase pose an adverse effect to Israel's "competitiveness." OECD, Economic Surveys, Israel (2013), available at http://www.pmo.gov.il/MediaCenter/SecretaryAnnouncements/Documents/OECD2013.pdf.

[58] §196.

[59] According to the GLOBAL FORUM ON TRANSPARENCY AND EXCHANGE OF INFORMATION FOR TAX PURPOSES 2013: PEER REVIEW REPORT – LEGAL AND REGULATORY FRAMEWORK ISRAEL, PARIS,

OECD Model Tax Convention.[60] Prior to the 2003 reform, the Tax Ordinance offered double tax credit relief only to foreign-source income earned or produced in a jurisdiction with which Israel had a bilateral tax treaty. This requirement was relinquished with Amendment 132 and the Tax Ordinance currently provides double tax credit relief regardless of whether an applicable treaty exists or the terms of that treaty.[61] Similarly, the Tax Ordinance exempts foreign residents from capital gains derived from the disposition of holdings in Israeli corporations, even when there is no treaty to rely on.

While the changes detailed above might appear to have weakened the role of Israel's tax treaty network in the framework of the Israeli income tax system, this network remains vital. For example, taxing foreign-source income ultimately depends either on taxpayer compliance with Israeli tax law or on its enforcement by the tax authorities. Such enforcement, especially in the international context, necessitates successful collection and exchange of information among countries and between their tax administrations. In a globalized world, this, in turn, is unattainable without a solid tax treaty network. The next section of this chapter examines Israel's income tax treaty network and the extent to which Israel takes advantage of its network to enhance taxpayer compliance within Israel and abroad.

Information Sharing and Cross-Border Cooperation

Introduction

Detecting tax noncompliance in cross-border transactions can be challenging, especially with respect to complex tax planning transactions.[62] The ability of nations to tax income arising in such circumstances fundamentally derives from effective information exchange among national tax authorities.[63] The main purpose of infor-

---

the agreements with Malta, Panama, and the Former Yugoslav Republic of Macedonia are yet to come into effect. *See* http://www.eoi-tax.org/jurisdictions/IL#peerreview (p. 59), accessed 20.06.2015 (hereinafter, "GF Repot").

[60] OECD, EXCHANGE OF INFORMATION TAX PORTAL, ISRAEL, available at http://www.eoi-tax.org/jurisdictions/IL#agreements, accessed 20.06.2015.

[61] §75B. *See also supra* notes 47–49 and accompanying text.

[62] Steven A. Dean, *More Cooperation, Less Uniformity: Tax Deharmonization and the Future of the International Tax Regime*, 84 Tul. L. Rev. 125 (2009); TSILLY DAGAN, *The Costs of International Tax Cooperation*, THE WELFARE STATE, GLOBALIZATION AND INTERNATIONAL LAW (Benvenisti and Nolte eds., 2004); Reuven S. Avi-Yonah, *Globalization, Tax Competition, and the Fiscal Crisis of the Welfare State*, 113 HARV. L. REV. 1573 (2000); Michael Keen and Jenny E. Ligthart, *Incentives and Information Exchange in International Taxation*, 13 INT'L TAX and PUB. FIN. 163 (2006).

[63] Unfortunately, jurisdictions that tax on a residence basis do not necessarily acquire good access to relevant tax information. At the same time, source countries, which have better access to such data, do not necessarily tax (and collect information on) all types of income. For a helpful discussion, see TONNY SCHENK-GEERS, INTERNATIONAL EXCHANGE OF INFORMATION AND THE PROTECTION OF TAXPAYERS (2009).

mation exchange in this context is to strengthen tax enforcement, on a national as well as international level.[64] This is especially relevant for residence-based jurisdictions that face significant challenges in detecting foreign-source income, at times without the cooperation of the taxpayer generating the income or the foreign country where income is generated.[65] Information exchange is therefore crucial for countries that exercise worldwide tax regimes, such as the United States and, now, Israel. Information exchange is also particularly instrumental in circumstances where a lower tax rate is levied abroad compared to the domestic country, but less vital for territorial income tax systems that exempt foreign-source income altogether.[66]

Information exchange is not limited to sharing data about the identity of suspicious transactions and taxpayers. It can also include information about similar "arm's length" commerce, which can be useful in verifying the adequacy of pricing or enforcement procedures, and in expanding international cooperation by means of bilateral and multilateral agreements.[67]

International Tax Information-Sharing Alternatives

For income tax purposes, Israel and most of its treaty partners practice information sharing in line with the information-sharing articles detailed in the respective bilateral tax treaty.[68] Israel has 53 bilateral tax treaties in effect, 42 of which were negotiated and signed over the last two decades.[69] Most of these treaties adopt the OECD Model Tax Convention, but the wording and scope of each information-exchange article varies from treaty to treaty.[70] One of the key questions arising in this respect is the extent to which Israel's Tax Authority is willing and able to share information; in other words, what type of information it collects and is thus available for exchange.

There are several commonly used methods of international information sharing. The most widely used mechanism is information sharing upon request. Most bilateral tax treaties incorporate an article that offers contracting countries the authority to demand information about transactions that either involve a resident of the country

---

[64] *Ibid.*

[65] *Ibid.*

[66] *Ibid.*

[67] Diane M. Ring, *On the Frontier of Procedural Innovation*: *Advanced Pricing Agreement and The Struggle to allocate Income for Cross Border Taxation* 21 Mich J. Int'l L. 143 (2000).

[68] *See*, e.g., Article 29 of the Israeli-U.S. Income Tax Treaty, available at http://ozar.mof.gov.il/hachnasot/usa.pdf (in Hebrew), accessed 24.08.2015; http://www.irs.gov/Businesses/International-Businesses/Israel – Tax-Treaty-Documents (in English), accessed 24.08.2015.

[69] OECD, Exchange of Information Portal, Israel, available at http://www.eoi-tax.org/jurisdictions/IL#agreements, accessed 20.6.2015.

[70] Eight of Israel's 53 bilateral tax treaties do not include an information exchange article (treaties signed with Germany, Jamaica, Luxembourg, the Netherlands, Singapore, South Africa, Switzerland, and the United Kingdom). Additionally, none of Israel's treaties signed before September 2009 incorporate wording akin to Article 26(5) of the OECD Model Tax Convention.

that requests the information or income that was generated in that country.[71] Under this option, one tax authority approaches the other with a request to retrieve information on the relevant transaction. One key shortcoming of exercising this information-sharing alternative, and the reason why many tax authorities do not avail themselves of this option, is that countries are generally oblivious (either fully or partially) of relevant transactions regarding which they should request information.[72]

A second type of international information sharing is an automatic exchange of information, where the tax authority of the source country reports relevant consensual information to the residence nation on a regular basis. Here, the residence country is not expected to inquire about unidentified information, as in the case of "exchange upon request," but is instead provided with an ongoing information flow. Importantly, until recently, Israel has been restricted from signing Tax Information Exchange Agreements (TIEAs) devised strictly for the purpose of information sharing,[73] as opposed to writing information-sharing articles into more inclusive bilateral or multilateral treaties.[74] The Israeli Tax Authority, however, is currently working on amending the Income Tax Ordinance to allow and to facilitate the ratification of international information-sharing agreements, regardless of whether a bilateral or multilateral treaty exists.[75]

A third, most intriguing and possibly promising, type of international information sharing involves spontaneous information exchange. With this last option, the tax authority of the residence country provides the source nation with information about transactions that may be of interest to it.[76] One recent example of spontaneous information sharing is the unveiling of the identity of Israeli taxpayers who own corporations in the British Virgin Islands by the U.K. tax authorities.[77] Unfortunately, this type of international information sharing is currently underutilized and unpredictable, so it cannot be relied upon for a thorough and reliable exchange of information as internationally required.

---

[71] Tsilly Dagan, *The Tax Treaties Myth*, 32 N.Y.U. J. OF INT'L LAW and POL. 939 (2000).

[72] Tonny Schenk-Geers, *supra* note 63.

[73] For Israel's restriction to enter into international agreements exclusively devised for administrative tax assistance purposes, see GF Report, *supra* note 59, p. 68.

[74] *Id.*, p.62.

[75] Amendment 200, 2014, available at http://knesset.gov.il/Laws/Data/BillGoverment/838/838.pdf (in Hebrew), accessed 20.06.2015. More recently, the Israeli Parliament circulated a bill proposal expanding tax information sharing and increasing criminal liability for income tax offences. *See* http://www.tazkirim.gov.il/Tazkirim_Attachments/42355_x_AttachFile.docx (in Hebrew), accessed 20.06.2015. *See also* Israel's signing into the OECD Multilateral Convention on Mutual Administrative Assistance in Tax Matters in 2015 and for assuming commitment for Common Reporting Standard (CRS) and Country by Country Reporting (CBC) in 2016. *See* https://taxes.gov.il/About/SpokesmanAnnouncements/Pages/Ann_150516_1.aspx (in Hebrew).

[76] With spontaneous information-sharing, the source country is not expected to actively request information, while the information provided remains tax-relevant so as not to overflow the recipient country with useless and time-consuming data.

[77] http://www.theguardian.com/uk/2013/apr/03/offshore-secrets-offshore-tax-haven, accessed 20.06.2015.

Tax Information Collection

Reporting Obligations

Provision §131 of the Income Tax Ordinance requires foreign residents who generate Israeli-source income, and Israeli residents over the age of 18, to file personal income tax returns in Israel, unless they are otherwise exempt.[78] In practice, most Israeli residents are exempt from the obligation to file because they earn income on which tax is already withheld by employers or financial institutions (i.e., by means of employment, interest, dividends, or capital gains).[79] In contrast, high-income earners (making above approximately USD 200,000 per year), the self-employed, and 10 % stockholders of Israeli corporations are normally required to file annual income tax returns as well as periodic capital statements.[80] Even within these groups of taxpayers, however, numerous waivers are granted.[81] Additionally, because Israel provides various exemptions for income arising from the disposition of real estate, and because it taxes neither gifts nor inheritances, tax data collection becomes a daunting challenge.

To some extent, deficiencies in Israel's tax data collection may explain the significant magnitude of the nation's black (or shadow) economy, which amounted to an estimated NIS 185 billion in 2013 (approximately USD 53 billion).[82] This is equal to 20–25 % of Israel's GDP that year.[83] But, despite the substantial size and repercussions of Israel's shadow economy, the Income Tax Commissioner and Minister of Finance are united in opposing further mandatory tax filing and report-

---

[78] §131. Income Tax Regulations (Income Tax Return Filing Exemption), 1988; Income Tax Authority Circular 25/2004, (Individual Income Tax Return Filing Exemption), 2003, available at https://taxes.gov.il/incometax/documents/hozrim/hoz25-2004.pdf   (in   Hebrew),   accessed 20.08.2015.

[79] §134A (authorizing income tax filing wavers); Income Tax Authority Circular 25/2004 (Individual Income Tax Return Filing Exemption) 2–3, 2003, available at https://taxes.gov.il/incometax/documents/hozrim/hoz25-2004.pdf (in Hebrew), accessed 20.08.2015.

[80] *Ibid*, pp. 4–5.

[81] *Ibid*, pp. 5–6.

[82] Unreported or shadow economy generally refers to economic activity carried out beyond the reach of the regulator and without paying taxes. For useful discussions of this issue *see*, e.g., Friedrich Schneider and Dominik H. Enste, The Shadow Economy (2014); Friedrich Schneider and Dominik H. Enste, *Hiding in the Shadows: the Growth of the Underground Economy*, Economic Issues #30 (IMF, 2002), available at http://www.imf.org/external/pubs/ft/issues/issues30/, accessed 20.08.2015.

[83] A World Bank 2010 report indicates that in 2007, Israel's shadow economy amounted to 23 % of its GDP, placing Israel in 38th place out of 151 countries (following Belgium and Kuwait, and preceding India and Spain). Friedrich Schneider et al., Shadow Economies All over the World: New Estimates for 162 Countries from 1999 to 2007 (The World Bank, Policy Research Paper 5356, July 2010), available at https://openknowledge.worldbank.org/bitstream/handle/10986/3928/WPS5356.pdf?sequence=1.

ing obligations.[84] One of the most significant filing exemptions currently under scrutiny is the exemption for "new immigrants" and "veteran returning residents."

Income Tax Exemptions for "New Immigrants" and "Veteran Returning Residents"

Pursuant to provisions §134B and §135 of the Income Tax Ordinance, both "new immigrants" and "veteran returning residents" are exempt from Israeli income tax on their foreign-source income and gains.[85] The Tax Ordinance defines new immigrants as persons who became Israeli residents for the first time, and veteran returning residents as Israeli citizens who resided abroad for at least 10 consecutive years before returning to Israel and reestablishing residence there.[86] Both exemptions can be claimed for a 10-year period, starting with the first year in which the taxpayer became an Israeli resident or returned to Israel after spending time abroad.[87] The Tax Ordinance also offers new immigrants and veteran returning residents[88] a 10-year exemption from the obligation to file an income tax return and capital statements.[89] To further attract wealthy individuals with significant capital holdings overseas, the Tax Ordinance was yet again amended in 2009 to offer an additional 10-year tax holiday and reporting waiver, up to 20 years altogether, to individual taxpayers making substantial financial investments in Israel within 2 years of their immigration.[90]

Recent Legislative Changes

Under the Bill for Changes in National Priorities (legislative amendments implementing budgetary goals for fiscal years 2013 and 2014), the tax holidays and waivers available for new immigrants and veteran returning residents remain largely intact.[91] But international pressures posed by Israel's trading partners, particularly OECD member countries, gave rise to a proposal to repeal the filing exemption for

---

[84] *See*, e.g., http://www.globes.co.il/news/article.aspx?did=1000005594, accessed 20.06.2015.

[85] §134B and §135.

[86] §14.

[87] Tsilly Dagan, International Taxation 243–268 (2004) (In Hebrew).

[88] Amendment 168, 2008, available at https://taxes.gov.il/about/reforms/documents/hakalot2008/2184_08.pdf (in Hebrew), accessed 24.08.2015.

[89] The window for claiming the exemption from the obligation to file starts from the first year in which the new immigrant or veteran returning immigrant establishes residence in Israel. §14.

[90] §165(4) of the Economic Arrangement Law, enacted in 2009. To our knowledge, however, such a benefit has yet to be awarded.

[91] Changes in National Priorities Bill (budgetary legislative amendments for fiscal years 2013 and 2014), 2013. Final version (in Hebrew): http://www.prisha.co.il/UserFiles/File/pdf/hoz/tax20132014.pdf, accessed 20.06.2015.

new immigrants and veteran returning residents. The Israeli parliament, however, has yet to approve the proposal, and the filing exemption is currently intact.[92] The Bill for Changes in National Priorities was more successful in altering Israel's trust regime in order to deter abusive tax planning and increase the integrity of trusts.[93] The Bill repealed several key tax benefits that had been in place, allowing taxpayers to exploit overseas accounts to form a trust for their benefit.[94] Among other changes, trusts created abroad, where the trustee has no legitimate family relation to the beneficiary, are now subject to regular tax and filling obligations.

Finally, the Ministry of Justice and the Income Tax Authority have proposed to amend Israel's Money Laundering Law to classify aggressive tax planning as an offence.[95] If the amendment is enacted into law, the Financial Intelligence Unit responsible for the Money Laundering Law enforcement and for receiving real-time reports on suspicious money transfers from banks and other financial institutions, would be able to share such information with the Income Tax Authority.[96] This would greatly enhance Israel's tax data collection capabilities, enabling the Tax Authority, in turn, to share this information internationally.

Bilateral and Multilateral Cooperation

Israel joined the OECD in May 2010.[97] By that time, it was already a member of several leading international organizations, such as the World Trade Organization, the International Monetary Fund, and the United Nations.[98] Adopting the OECD Model Tax Convention in many of its bilateral tax treaties,[99] Israel was able to form a bilateral treaty network with most of its trading partners, including all EU member countries, 16 of the G20 members, and almost all OECD member countries. All of these treaties incorporate information-exchange articles, five of them with the exact

---

[92] *Ibid. See also* explanatory legislative comments at http://www.nevo.co.il/Law_word/law15/memshala-768.pdf *p. 687* (in Hebrew), accessed 20.06.2015. Arguably, the proposal was removed from the final bill due to political pressures within the Israeli Parliament. For media discussions on global financial disclosure, see, for example, http://www.themarker.com/news/1.2185603 (in Hebrew), accessed 20.06.2015.

[93] Increasing Tax Collection and Enhancing Tax Enforcement Bill (legislative amendments and temporary orders), 2012, available at http://www.knesset.gov.il/Laws/Data/BillGoverment/740/740.pdf (in Hebrew), accessed 20.06.2015.

[94] *Supra* note 92.

[95] GF Report, *supra* note 59 (discussing the legislative proposal).

[96] *Ibid.*

[97] OECD, Israel's Accession to the OECD, available at http://www.oecd.org/israel/israelsaccessiontotheoecd.htm, accessed 20.06.2015.

[98] GF Report, *supra* note 59.

[99] Article 26 of the OECD Model Tax Convention (information exchange) is a good example of the broad implementation of the OECD model tax convention in Israeli treaties. For additional information, *see supra* note 71.

wording of Article 26 of the OECD Model Treaty.[100] Furthermore, of the 53 bilateral tax treaties, 47 include provisions that require the exchange of information deemed necessary for the administration of these treaties.[101] Sharing tax information internationally, however, relies profoundly on the collection of relevant and reliable data and on the ability to share that data internationally.[102]

> The information should cover the type of information that other countries might legitimately expect to receive in response to a request. Information should be available on all persons that come within the territorial jurisdiction of a given country. Countries should ensure that such information is either maintained or obtainable by the authorities and can be exchanged [...].[103]

In view of the sizeable number of filing exemptions currently in place in the Tax Ordinance, recent national and international criticisms have voiced doubts regarding Israel's sincerity in internationally cooperating and sharing useful and reliable tax information.[104] The critics are calling for a drastic change in that area.[105]

In sum, despite significant increases in the use of information-sharing mechanisms in recent years, given the existing waivers and exemptions in the Israeli tax law, foreign- source countries tend to be mistrustful of Israel's intentions and, therefore, reluctant to cooperate and share tax information. One recent example of this

---

[100] See GF Report, *supra* note 59, p. 60 (listing the eight countries with which the information-exchange provision does not conform to the standard: Germany, Jamaica, Luxembourg, the Netherlands, Singapore, South Africa, Switzerland, and the United Kingdom).

[101] *Supra* note 71. For the full list of treaties see http://ozar.mof.gov.il/hachnasot/agreements-h.asp (in Hebrew), accessed 24.08.2015.

[102] Foreign source income is not easily traceable because relevant transactions generally take place abroad, either fully or partially. Therefore, international information sharing becomes a prerequisite for taxation to take place.

[103] OECD, Behind the Corporate Veil: Using Corporate Entities for Illicit Purposes (2001), available at http://www.oecd.org/daf/ca/behindthecorporateveilusingcorporateentitiesforillicitpurposes.htm.

[104] Under Amendment 168, only new immigrants and veteran returning residents arriving in Israel after 2007 are eligible for the new immigrants' and veteran returning residents' tax breaks. Since the implementation of this Amendment, approximately 92,500 new immigrants have settled in Israel, and from 2010 to 2012 approximately 20,000 veteran returning residents arrived. Discussing the State of Israel, the OECD report concludes: "The tax authorities' powers to obtain information from new immigrants, veteran returning residents and the trustees of foreign resident settler trusts, in respect of foreign source income, are inadequate." The OECD report further indicates that after May 19, 2013, Israel "has taken a decision to eliminate the exemption from filing tax returns by new immigrants and veteran returning residents." Id., p. 16. However, because the Israeli parliament never enacted this decision, the extent to which the government stands behind it remains unclear. *Supra* note 92 and accompanying text.

[105] The existing waivers and exemptions in the Tax Ordinance undercut the capacity of the Israeli Tax Authority to collect complete and accurate information despite the fact that, in some cases, valuable tax information is readily available. For example, information concerning passive income of Israeli residents generated in Israel is already being collected by banks and other financial institutions, which withhold 15–30 % of the income and remit these sums to the Tax Authority. This information is underutilized for information sharing purposes. Income Tax Regulations (withholding from Interest), 2002.

caution is, in a sense, underlying the FATCA agreement signed between the Israeli Tax Authority and the Internal Revenue Service (IRS) in 2014. According to this agreement, Israel is committed to sharing tax information of U.S. citizens with the IRS, and, in return, the IRS will consider reciprocating with the Israeli tax authority in the future.[106]

Attracting Inbound Capital Investments

Introduction

Over the past few decades, the enactment of legislative incentives devised to attract foreign investments and redirect them to further regional development, increase exports, and raise employment rates has become a common worldwide practice.[107] In an effort to boost its economy, the young State of Israel adopted similar inducements soon after its establishment.[108] The most significant vehicle introduced in Israel, primarily to attract inbound investment, is the Law for the Encouragement of Capital Investments, 1959 (hereinafter, the "Investment Law" or the "Law"). Another vehicle, adopted by the Israeli legislature in 2006, is the participation exemption. This section explores each of these arrangements and illuminates the metamorphosis the Israeli legislation has undergone over the last decade in an effort to attract foreign investments.

The Investment Law and Its Preferential Tax Incentives for Foreign Investors

Seeking to address acute problems of unemployment in the Israeli periphery, a human capital deficit, and a general need for foreign investments, the Israeli Parliament enacted the Investment Law in 1959.[109] Initially, the key objectives of the Law included boosting the productivity of the Israeli economy, increasing exports, and absorbing immigration. These were to be accomplished by introducing specifi-

---

[106] The imbalanced FAC TA agreement also represents a broader discrepancy of powers between Israel and the United States. For an announcement of this agreement, see https://taxes.gov.il/About/SpokesmanAnnouncements/Pages/Ann_020714_4.aspx (in Hebrew), accessed 20.08.2015.

[107] DAFNA SCHWARTZ, INVESTMENT ENCOURAGEMENT LAW AND INCENTIVES LOCATION, REVIEW OF THE LITERATURE – DIRECT INCENTIVES TO ENCOURAGE INVESTMENTS INDUSTRY – INTERNATIONAL EXPERIENCE, p. 3 (working paper #20; Negev Center for Regional Development Ben-Gurion, 2002).

[108] For example, see §20A (granting an accelerated depreciation for investments in research and development).

[109] ISRAEL MINISTRY OF FINANCE, THE PUBLIC COMMITTEE FOR TAX REFORM, p.143 (Jerusalem, 2000), available at http://ozar.mof.gov.il/reform/pdf/avi09.pdf (in Hebrew), accessed 20.6.2015 (hereinafter, "the 2000 Report").

cally tailored economic initiatives designed to attract local and foreign investments.[110]

Up until 2012, the Investment Law offered two groups of incentives: government grants (hereinafter, "the Grant Program") and tax benefits (hereinafter, "the Tax Benefits Program").[111] Corporations applying for incentives under the Investment Law were required to show proof of a designated capital investment to qualify for the status of "Approved Enterprise," and to choose between the Grant Program and the Tax Benefits Program.[112] One popular benefit that was built into the Tax Benefits Program offered a deferral of corporate income tax liability for up to 10 years, depending on certain geographic criteria and the size of the capital investment made.[113] The 10-year deferral was fully reversible once untaxed income created during the deferral period was distributed to shareholders.[114] Because of the extensive complexity embedded in the pre-2012 Investment Law, however, only a handful of corporations and investors were able to benefit from it,[115] and the Law spawned countless legal disputes requiring constant rulings and clarifications.

In January 2010, the Israeli government appointed a committee to study the effectiveness of the Investment Law (hereinafter, "the Committee").[116] The Committee published its conclusions and recommendations nine months later, in October 2010.[117] It found that the Investment Law's objectives, as originally drafted, failed to match the economic challenges to Israel's economy and that both the Grant Program and the Tax Benefits Program were insufficiently effective in cultivating the Israeli periphery.[118]

Regarding the Tax Benefits Program, the Committee determined that the distribution of incentives was inefficient, for the following key reasons: (a) 90 % of the

---

[110] §1 of the Investment Law, prior to the Amendment 68 version of the Investment Law (detailing the objectives of the Investment Law).

[111] Investment Law, chapters 6 and 7.

[112] ITA Circular 2/2006 Amendment 60 to the Investment Law, available at http://taxes.gov.il/IncomeTax/Documents/Hozrim/hozer2_2006.pdf (in Hebrew), accessed 20.06.2015.

[113] See §51A of the Investment Law in its prior to Amendment 68 version.

[114] Once corporations distributed dividends from the untaxed income, they were required to pay the standard statutory corporate tax rate, as if they were never granted a deferral or a reduced rate, as well as a 15 % tax on the dividend distribution. See §47 of the Investment Law, in its version prior to Amendment 68 of the Investment Law.

[115] CONCLUSIONS OF THE INTER-MINISTERIAL COMMITTEE EXAMINING THE INVESTMENT LAW, p. 53 (October 2010), available at http://mof.gov.il/releases/documents/2010-41294.pdf (in Hebrew), accessed 5.07.2015 (hereinafter, "the 2010 Report").

[116] For press release of the committee's appointment, see http://www.moital.gov.il/NR/exeres/3817290D-1D10-44C7-A07D-3E3656443B8F.htm (in Hebrew), accessed 20.06.2015.

[117] The 2010 Report, *supra* note 115.

[118] The committee concluded that the periphery had not been advanced from the point of view of either employment or growth. The 2010 Report, *supra* note 115, pp. 45–57. The report also indicated that the Grant Program required a disproportionate use of capital investment relative to human capital, and that it was chosen mainly by large low-tech corporations. *Id.*, p. 140.

Investment Law benefits eventually went to a limited number of corporations, including one company that obtained more than USD 250 million worth of benefits, far exceeding the actual size of its tax liability.[119] Similarly, under the Law, four of the largest corporations in Israel in 2010 (Teva, ICL, Intel, and Check Point)[120] received approximately USD 1.2 billion worth of tax incentives overall, while their tax payments amounted to only USD 350 million.[121] The total effective tax rate these four corporations paid that year was only 3.3 %,[122] while the tax benefits they enjoyed constituted 70 % of incentives granted under the Investment Law[123]; (b) most of the incentives distributed pursuant to the Investment Law were granted to approved enterprises located in the hub of the country, rather than in its periphery[124]; (c) the Tax Benefits Program failed to attract foreign investors yet led to a significant decline in tax revenue[125]; and (d) a significant portion of incentives were granted to government-owned and mineral companies, even though these entities are disinclined to make their investment or location decisions based on such incentives, rendering these incentives ineffective.[126] The Committee also concluded that the Investment Law was too complex and that it produced significant uncertainty regarding the prospective tax rates to be levied under the Law. Due to this uncertainty, to counter the risk of potentially high applicable tax rates, corporations applying for the Investment Law benefits were prone to artificially report lower annual profits.[127]

The Investment Law was further unsuccessful in motivating corporations to distribute exempted profits created during the 10-year tax deferral period of the Tax Benefits Program. For this reason, a large number of eligible corporations made no

---

[119] The 2010 Report, *supra* note 115, p. 53.

[120] The four companies' full names are Teva Pharmaceutical Industries Ltd., Israel Chemical Ltd., Intel Israel Ltd., and Check Point Software Technologies Ltd. For additional details and analysis see ISRAEL CENSUS BUREAU ANNUAL REPORT, 2009–2010, ch.9, available at http://ozar.mof.gov.il/hachnasot/doch09-10/docs/perek9.pdf (in Hebrew), accessed 20.08.2015.

[121] STATE COMPTROLLER OF ISRAEL, ANNUAL REPORT 64A, published on 15.10.2013, available at http://www.mevaker.gov.il/he/Reports/Pages/113.aspx# (in Hebrew). The relevant chapter is available at http://www.mevaker.gov.il/he/Reports/Report_113/f869aee3-ca0a-482d-b596-0c791a1acb15/107-hatavot.pdf (in Hebrew), accessed 20.06.2015 (hereinafter, "State Comptroller's Report").

[122] *Id.*, p. 176.

[123] *Ibid*; ISRAEL CENSUS BUREAU ANNUAL REPORT, 2009–2010, ch. 9, available at http://ozar.mof.gov.il/hachnasot/doch09-10/docs/perek9.pdf (in Hebrew), accessed 20.08.2015.

[124] The 2010 Report, *supra* note 115, p. 53.

[125] *Id.*, pp. 57–58.

[126] *Id.*, p. 57.

[127] *Id.*, pp. 57–58. The committee noted two main reasons for the uncertainty over the applicable tax rates: (a) corporations are unable to accurately predict the extent of foreign investments they will receive; (b) corporations are unable to accurately predict whether and to what extent the Tax Authority considers future investments as dividend distributions.

distributions and, instead, accumulated their profits tax-free.[128] According to the Tax Authority, between 1988 and 2010, the untaxed and undistributed corporate profits produced by the Investment Law amounted to approximately USD 35 billion.[129] This controversial practice resulted in heated legal and regulatory disputes, including, for example, over what constitutes a distribution under the Investment Law.[130] In November 2012, Amendment 69 to the Investment Law for one year enabled eligible companies to release what came to be known as the "trapped profits" at a significantly reduced tax rate.[131] This amendment was roundly criticized by Israel's State Comptroller,[132] as well as by Israeli politicians and nonprofit organizations across the board.[133]

Based on the recommendations of the Committee, the Investment Law was radically amended in 2010 to revoke the tax benefits and grants to industrial enterprises whose main activity was mining, quarrying, oil and gas exploration, or production in Israel.[134] Corporations and partnerships fully owned by the government also became ineligible for the Investment Law programs.[135] These changes reflect a legislative understanding that such entities cannot easily migrate overseas, so that incentivizing them to invest in Israel is unjustified, inefficient, and distortive.[136] Following the Committee's recommendations,[137] Amendment 68[138] also altered the tax benefits available under the Law so as to place foreign and local shareholders on an equal footing in terms of benefits eligibility, at both the corporate and the shareholder level.

---

[128] State Comptroller's Report, *supra* note 121, p. 183.

[129] *Ibid.*

[130] *Id.*, pp. 186–187.

[131] Amendment 69 of the Investment law, available at http://www.lionorl.co.il/WEB/8888/NSF/Web/5415/klooaim.pdf (in Hebrew), accessed 20.08.2015.

[132] State Comptroller's Report, *supra* note 121, pp. 183–190.

[133] For media coverage see http://www.themarker.com/misc/1.2161513 (in Hebrew), accessed 20.08.2015; http://www.calcalist.co.il/local/articles/0,7340,L-3616897,00.html (in Hebrew), accessed 20.08.2015.

[134] §51 of the Investment Law.

[135] *Ibid.*

[136] Israel Census Bureau Annual Report, 2009–2010, ch. 9, available at http://ozar.mof.gov.il/hachnasot/doch09-10/docs/perek9.pdf (in Hebrew), accessed 20.08.2015.

[137] The 2010 Report, *supra* note 115, p. 64.

[138] *See* ITA Circular 3/2012 Amendment 68 to the Investments Law, available at https://taxes.gov.il/IncomeTax/Documents/Hozrim/hoz03-2012.pdf (in Hebrew), accessed 5.07.2015 (hereinafter, "Amendment 68 Circular"). Before the Amendment, an approved enterprise that invested in an "area A" was eligible for a 2-year tax exemption and for reduced tax rates of 25 % for the subsequent 5 years; an approved enterprise owned by foreign investors, in otherwise similar circumstances, was entitled to reduced tax rates of 10–20 %, depending on the size of foreign investment, for a 10-year period.

Improving the Competitiveness of Industrial Enterprises

Before 2005, the Investment Law defined an approved enterprise[139] based on several criteria, including the ability to compete in international markets, the use of new technology, and meeting a threshold of capital investment.[140] Amendment 60 of the Investment Law, which came into effect in 2005, altered the definition of an approved enterprise, placing the emphasis on export.[141] As a result, only competitive facilities that contribute to Israel's overall GDP are now eligible for an approved enterprise status.[142] Additionally, with some exceptions, the Law now requires that to be an approved enterprise at least 25 % of the income produced by the enterprise must be from exports to a market of at least 14 million residents.[143] It is unclear, however, whether the 25 % export criterion could in some cases be at odds with Israel's undertaking not to subsidize local goods, which is part of its obligations under existing international trade and economic cooperation agreements with countries throughout North America, Europe, and Asia.[144]

Amendment 68 to the Investment Law materially changed the tax benefit regime of the Law, replacing the 10-year corporate tax deferral with a unified tax rate structure levied on all approved enterprises.[145] However, because of a shortfall in tax revenue, and critical media reports debating the depleted proceeds collected from multinational corporations by the Tax Authority, an additional Amendment, number 71, was enacted in August 2013, slightly increasing the applicable rates.[146] Consequently, as of 2014, an approved enterprise enjoys a 16 % corporate tax rate for investments made in the center of the country and a 9 % rate for investments in its periphery.[147] Only a "Special Approved Enterprise," defined in §51 T of the

---

[139] ITA Circular 2/2006 Amendment 60 to the Investments Law http://taxes.gov.il/IncomeTax/Documents/Hozrim/hozer2_2006.pdf (in Hebrew), accessed 20.06.2015.

[140] ISRAEL MINISTRY OF ECONOMY, INVEST IN ISRAEL, available at http://www.investinisrael.gov.il/NR/exeres/08348DA2-83D3-47B1-B043-ED418D9AA846.htm, accessed 20.06.2015.

[141] *Supra* note 139.

[142] Amendment 68 Circular, *supra* note 138.

[143] The original Amendment required a market of at least 12 (compared to 14) million residents. §18A of the pre-Amendment 68 version of the Investment Law. *Ibid.*

[144] TEL AVIV and CENTRAL ISRAEL CHAMBER OF COMMERCE, available at http://www.chamber.org.il/content.aspx?code=932 (in Hebrew), accessed 20.01.14. An argument to this effect was raised and overruled by Judge Abraham in Nazareth District Court, Tax Appeal (Nazareth District Court) 1028/07 *D.C. Paper and Plastic Industries v. Afula Assessment Officer*, Missim (28.03.2010) (in Hebrew).

[145] For a list of changes implemented by Amendment 68 to the Investment Law, see Amendment 68 Circular, *supra* note 138.

[146] §51 of the Investment Law, in its post-Amendment 71 version, is available at http://www.nevo.co.il/Law_word/law14/law-2405.pdf (in Hebrew) pp. 171–172, accessed 20.06.2015.

[147] §51P of the Investment Law.

Investments Law,[148] is eligible for lower 8 % and 5 % rates, respectively.[149] These last changes have further modified the Investment Law's objectives to emphasize innovation and rapid development of Israel's production capacity, competitiveness in international markets, and cultivating infrastructures for new and sustainable workplaces.

It is too early to determine the cumulative effect of Amendments 68–71. It is clear, however, that corporate tax rates under the Investment Law remain considerably low compared to the Israeli standard statutory corporate tax rate (26.5 % in 2015 and 25 % in 2016) and far below standard statutory corporate tax rates in other industrial countries.[150] According to Israel's State Comptroller's report, despite a drastic corporate tax rate cut from 36 % to 25 % between 2003 and 2010, corporate tax benefits under the Investment Law increased, rising from NIS 2.3 billion in 2003 to NIS 5.6 billion during fiscal year 2010.[151] In November 2013, following yet another public outcry over the Investment Law, Israel's Minister of Finance appointed a new committee to reexamine the scope of tax benefits granted under the Law.[152] Although three years have passed since its appointment, the committee has yet to officially issue its recommendations. According to media reports, one key quandary the committee faces is whether, and if so to what extent, tax incentives under the Investment Law should now be capped.[153]

---

[148] According to §51T of the Investment Law, the status of Special Approved Enterprise is granted to particularly large corporations that exceed a threshold of annual income and are likely to significantly contribute to the Israeli economy.

[149] The corporate tax schedule under the Investment Law exhibited a gradual decrease until 2015: 10 % in the periphery and 15 % in the center of Israel for 2011–2012; 7 % in the periphery and 12.5 % in the center for 2013–2014.

[150] For useful comparative corporate tax rate data, see the OECD TAX DATABASE, available at http://www.oecd.org/tax/tax-policy/tax-database.htm and http://www.oecd.org/tax/tax-policy/tax-database.htm#C_CorporateCaptial, accessed 24.08.2015. *See also* the REVENUE STATISTICS – COMPARATIVE TABLES, available at https://stats.oecd.org/Index.aspx?DataSetCode=REV, accessed 24.08.2015.

[151] State Comptroller's Report, *supra* not 121, pp. 172, 176. The increase in the total amount of benefits stems mainly from a sharp rise in the scope of benefits awarded under the Investment Law to the four largest companies in Israel, representing 70 % of total benefits in 2010, compared to 32 % of benefits in 2003.

[152] *See* http://www.calcalist.co.il/articles/0,7340,L-3616945,00.html (in Hebrew), accessed 6.07.2015.

[153] For relevant media reports see, for example, http://www.calcalist.co.il/Ext/Comp/ArticleLayout/CdaArticlePrintPreview/1,2506,L-3662908,00.html (in Hebrew), accessed 6.07.2015; http://www.calcalist.co.il/local/articles/0,7340,L-3662804,00.html (in Hebrew), accessed 6.07.2015; http://www.themarker.com/opinion/1.2676760 (in Hebrew), accessed 6.07.2015.

Participation Exemption

In the last few decades, a growing number of European countries have been introducing a participation exemption arrangement to attract foreign-based holding companies of multinational enterprises.[154] The participation exemption generally grants a reduced or zero corporate tax rate on dividend, interest, and capital gains earnings that these holding companies receive from their subsidiaries.[155] The exemption also offers beneficial tax treatment to shareholders of these companies.[156]

In an attempt to attract inbound investment, Amendments 132, 147, and 169 to the Income Tax Ordinance introduced a specifically tailored exemption from capital gains taxation to foreign residents.[157] According to provisions §97(b2) and §97(b3) of the Income Tax Ordinance, foreign residents are generally exempt from tax on the sale of stock holdings when the stocks are either of an Israeli corporation or of a foreign corporation whose assets are located in Israel (either directly or indirectly).[158] The exemption is provided when the gain arising from these sales is not attributable to a permanent establishment of the foreign resident, and if the relevant stocks were purchased by a person unrelated to the seller.[159] The exemption extends only to capital gains and corporate distributions (mainly dividends).[160] Otherwise, tax applies to capital gains, interest, and dividend income at a fixed rate of 25 or 30 % on individuals and of 25 % on corporate shareholders.[161] Consequently, foreign investors can be taxed on corporate distributions in Israel, yet be exempt upon disposition of their investments there.[162] Recently, foreign investors of the Israeli startup company, Waze Ltd., notoriously claimed the capital gains exemption upon the company's acquisition by Google in June 2013 for over USD 1 billion.[163]

---

[154] The Israeli version of the participation exemption relief is based on the Kapota Maza Committee recommendations. *See* http://ozar.mof.gov.il/hachnasot/v2005-06-D.pdf (in Hebrew), accessed 20.06.2015.

[155] *Ibid. See also* https://www.kpmg.com/LU/en/IssuesAndInsights/Articlespublications/Documents/Luxembourg-participation-exemption-regime-13.pdf, accessed 5.07.2015.

[156] *Ibid.*

[157] Specifically, Amendment 132 introduced the capital gains exemption for foreign shareholders upon disposal of their shares in Israeli companies; Amendment 147 introduced the participation exemption from corporate tax for certain capital gains, dividends, and interest income, and reduced the tax rate for foreign shareholders upon corporate distributions of such incomes. Amendment 169 further broadened the tax benefits granted to foreign investors who invest in Israeli corporations.

[158] §97(b2) and §97(b3) (referring to the majority of assets of foreign corporations).

[159] *Ibid.*

[160] *Ibid.*

[161] §91, §126. The exact tax rate for individuals depends on the ownership percentage of shareholders and a reduced tax rate applies to corporate shareholders if the foreign investor is a resident of a country with which Israel has an income tax treaty. *See* §203.

[162] *Ibid.*

[163] http://www.ynetnews.com/articles/0,7340,L-4391116,00.html (in Hebrew), accessed 20.06.2015.

Because Waze was held mainly by foreign shareholders, once the exemption was claimed the Israeli Tax Authority was able to collect only a fraction of the tax liability arising from the buyout.[164]

In 2006, Amendment 147 to the Income Tax Ordinance expanded the Israeli participation exemption regime. Following the enactment of provisions §§67B-67K of the Income Tax Ordinance, some Israeli holding companies are now eligible for an income tax exemption at the corporate level.[165] This includes companies whose capital consists of at least USD 14.5 million and companies that invest mainly in foreign corporations or financial enterprises.[166] Foreign shareholders further enjoy a reduced tax rate of 5 % on corporate distributions from gains derived from the sale of subsidiaries, and on interest income derived from investments in the Israeli financial market.[167] These new benefits come on top of the gains tax exemption on the disposition of stocks in Israeli holding companies.[168]

Notably, the uncapped capital gains exemption granted to foreign investors under provision §97 of the Income Tax Ordinance appears wasteful and unjustified, especially when compared to tax rates of 25–30 % normally levied on Israeli residents. A reduced rate of no more than 10 %, for example, instead of an unlimited exemption, could maintain Israel's economic competitiveness, while increasing tax revenues, market efficiency and equity. Likewise, for Israeli holding companies, the participation exemption regime under provisions §§67B–67K is practically ineffective and should be either repealed or amended in line with the European Directive and comparable standards in countries such as Belgium and the Netherlands.[169]

Summary and Conclusions

In the past two decades Israel's income tax regime underwent a significant transformation, from what may best be described as a quasi-territorially-based income tax system to a mixed regime with a stronger emphasis on residency: the Income Tax Ordinance now levies taxes on Israeli residents on their worldwide income, while foreign residents are still territorially taxed on income earned or produced in Israel. In the course of this metamorphosis, provisions that limit the benefits derived from

---

[164] For more information about the acquisition of Waze and the estimated tax payments, see http://www.globes.co.il/news/article.aspx?did=1000873089 (in Hebrew), accessed 20.06.2015, and at http://www.globes.co.il/news/article.aspx?did=1000851320 (in Hebrew), accessed 20.06.2015.

[165] §§67B-67K.

[166] The exemption is unobtainable for holding companies that invest in Israeli (as compared to foreign) corporations. *Ibid.*

[167] *Supra* note 156.

[168] §97(b)(2).

[169] STATE OF ISRAEL, MINISTRY OF ECONOMY, INVEST IN ISRAEL – CONDITIONAL GRANTS OBJECTIVES, available at http://ec.europa.eu/taxation_customs/taxation/company_tax/parents-subsidiary_directive/index_en.htm, accessed 20.08.2015.

aggressive tax planning of foreign corporations, controlled foreign corporations, and foreign trusts were written into the Tax Ordinance. New rules were also included to better address circumstances of transfer pricing and offer exemptions to holding companies of multinational enterprises. During this time, Israel signed 42 out of its 53 bilateral income tax treaties and enhanced many of its information-exchange mechanisms with key trading partners.

On closer inspection, however, data collection by the Israeli Tax Authority remains inadequate, largely because of extensive reporting exemptions for taxpayers who are, for example, new immigrants, veteran returning residents, and salary and low-income earners. The Tax Ordinance also casts a relatively narrow tax net, further contributing to the inadequacy of data collection: there is no inheritance or gift tax, as well as no capital gains taxation on foreign shareholders selling their stock holdings in Israeli corporations. Such data collection deficiencies, in turn, play a crucial role in the size and repercussions of Israel's shadow economy.[170]

To improve tax data collection, Israel must amend its tax rules to narrow existing reporting exemptions and, particularly, end reporting holidays for new immigrants and veteran returning residents. Because Israel regards itself as a capital importing country and seeks to draw investments without out of pocket funding, the Israeli legislature is often inclined to incorporate tax incentives into the Tax Ordinance, instead of directly subsidizing goods and services. Unfortunately, while such incentives offer substantial benefits to a limited number of individuals and corporate entities that at times remain virtually untaxed, other taxpayers are taxed to the hilt, leading to a discriminatory and inefficient tax practice. Extending tax benefits to additional groups of taxpayers while narrowing the scope of benefits each group receives and strengthening the administration of benefits would constitute an important step in the right direction, and the Law for the Encouragement of Capital Investments is probably a good place to start.

Finally, before the enactment of Amendment 68, the Investment Law gave rise to a corporate environment in which, to minimize their tax liability, corporations kept large quantities of capital undistributed. Aggressive tax planning was then utilized to transfer all or part of these undistributed and untaxed dollars abroad, instead of reinvesting them in the Israeli economy. One of the intended consequences of Amendment 68 is that corporations are now subject to a generally unified tax rate structure, with no deferrals, while shareholders are also offered reduced rates but only upon corporate distributions. It is, however, unclear whether the Investment Law currently in place nonetheless contradicts Israel's undertaking not to subsidize local goods and, by so doing, undermines international cooperation and the work accomplished in that area.

---

[170] *Supra* note 83 and accompanying text.

Chapter 10
How Italian Tax Policy Provides Incentives for Investment in Developing, Emerging, or Low-Income Countries

Claudio Sacchetto

Abstract Italy has designed its international tax system to avoid distortion of investment decisions of its residents. This prevents the use of tax incentives to encourage investment in developing or low-tax countries. Italy has, instead, chosen to employ non-tax strategies to assist these nations in fighting poverty and to otherwise to develop viable economies. Although Italy once included tax sparing clauses in treaties with developing countries, it has in recent years not allowed them, hoping to direct investment into poor regions in Italy rather than those abroad. In lieu of tax sparing, Italy has entered into many agreements with developing countries to promote and protect investment. It has also provided relief in the area of customs duties through the Cotonou Agreement. In addition, a special regime for non-profit organizations dedicated to the pursuit of certain social goals may be used to assist low-income countries by providing tax benefits for donors.

Synopsis Having adopted the tax policy principle of neutrality, Italy has designed its international tax system so as not to distort the investment decisions of its constituents. This translates into a decision not to encourage investment in developing countries through the use of Italian tax incentives. Instead, Italy has employed non-tax strategies believed to assist these nations to fight poverty and to otherwise thrive.

Italian residents, both individuals and corporations, are taxed on their worldwide income. This represents a shift from the prior territorial regime which was eliminated in 1973. Double taxation of income under the worldwide taxation regime is alleviated by use of the foreign tax credit contained in Italian legislation or via a double taxation treaty. Adoption of the worldwide tax system may represent a prevailing view in Italy that the territorial system may not advantageous to poor countries that sacrifice revenue needed for development by engaging in tax competition. Use of the worldwide system with a foreign tax credit disrupts the ability of developing countries to attract foreign investment by offering lower tax rates.

C. Sacchetto (✉)
University of Turin, Turin, Italy
e-mail: sacchetto.c@tin.it

© Springer International Publishing Switzerland 2017   189
K.B. Brown (ed.), *Taxation and Development - A Comparative Study*,
Ius Comparatum - Global Studies in Comparative Law 21,
DOI 10.1007/978-3-319-42157-5_10

Italy has a participation exemption that applies to dividends received from foreign subsidiaries as well as to capital gains resulting from the sale of shares held in these companies. If requirements are met, 95 % of the dividend received is exempt from corporate income tax. Capital gain on the sale of shares is also exempted from tax. The exemption is not allowed if the subsidiary is a "black-listed" company.

Controlled foreign corporation (CFC) rules treat the profits of a controlled (or connected) subsidiary as those of the parent. The rules cover only companies organized in a jurisdiction that has an effective tax rate significantly lower than Italy's and does not have an adequate exchange of information agreement with Italy. The CFC rules do not apply if the parent corporation can demonstrate that the subsidiary conducts real business activity in the listed jurisdiction or establish that the subsidiary is not used exclusively to shift profits. The CFC rules also extend to deductibility of costs relating to transactions with companies located in specified low-tax jurisdictions. These provisions remove any advantage an Italian corporation would hope to gain by investing in a developing country with low tax rates.

While in the 1970s Italy negotiated a number of treaty containing tax sparing clauses, with the advent of OECD's disapproval of these clauses in the 1990s, it has moved to eliminate them as it renegotiates treaties. Tax sparing was not included in treaties with Eastern Europe because these have been negotiated only recently. In addition, these types of treaties are lacking because Italy hoped to direct its residents to investments in poor regions in Italy rather than those abroad. In lieu of tax sparing, Italy has entered into numerous agreements with developing countries for the promotion and protection of investments.

Because of the EU prohibitions on State Aid, among other reasons relating to difficulty in targeting the appropriate companies, Italy has refrained from enacting tax legislation that would provide direct incentives for investment in developing countries. Instead it has taken initiatives in the area of customs duties through the "Cotonou Agreement" with African, Caribbean, and Pacific states arranged through the EU. This has led to assistance in structural reforms, maritime accords, and free trade zones. Italy has aligned itself with current recent developments, including the Base Erosion and Profit Shifting initiative of the OECD, that suggest that the appropriate strategy is to assist developing nations create a stable market economy rather than offer tax incentives, aid, or unilateral investments.

A special regime for non-profit entities working for social good, the ONLUS (Non-profit Organization for Social Utility) regime, may be used to assist developing countries. Eligible entities, dedicated to pursuit of certain social and solidarity goals, benefit from exemptions for direct taxes and VAT. Donors to an ONLUS may deduct specified percentages of their annual income.

Tax exemptions provided the Roman Catholic Church may also indirectly benefit poor nations. Possibly because it is expected to support the poorest populations both in Italy and abroad, the Church enjoys tax exemptions and its contributors are allowed tax deductions for amounts paid to it and other religious organizations.

In order to avoid unintended effects, Italy does not employ tax incentives to encourage investments in developing countries. Instead it makes monetary donations, subsidizes loans and cancellation and conversion of debts, and funds cooperative projects.

Introduction

This chapter analyses Italian tax policy towards developing countries. After deep analysis of the situation from many perspectives, it is evident that Italy is building a tax system *as neutral as possible* in respect of both domestic and international situations. The exercise demonstrates that Italy is not aiding developing countries through tax tools. Nevertheless, being active in a large number of international organizations, Italy contributes to fighting poverty around the world in different ways not involving use of tax law incentives.

The Italian tax system does not provide any specific tax incentive for investments in emerging or developing countries. Also because of its membership in various international organizations, such as the European Union and the World Trade Organization, Italy is shaping its tax system on the principles of neutrality and reciprocity, and with the purpose not to distort the investment decisions of its resident taxpayers.[1]

This contribution is divided in three main parts. The first, entitled *Internal Neutrality*, is aimed at analyzing *'pure'* domestic legislation that can affect poor countries. It demonstrates that Italy is not specifically encouraging taxpayers to invest in developing countries through tax tools. The second, entitled *External Neutrality*, analyzes aspects of Italian foreign tax policy that can affect poor countries. It demonstrates that Italy is contributing to the general tendency not to use *distortive* tax tools in the transnational context, but rather to create "big tax-neutral business environments" (e.g. free-trade zones), in which the private sector can work profitably for the benefit of both rich and poor countries. The third part presents two peculiar pieces of Italian tax legislation: the ONLUS regime and preferential treatment for religious entities. These are not investment incentives, but rather incentives to private charity: they do not specifically target non-profit activities carried out abroad or in developing countries, but, as a factual matter, they often benefit entities carrying out such activities. Brief reflections are provided at the end of this contribution.

---

[1] For an in-depth analysis of the topic see also: Sacchetto, C., *Política de tratados em matéria tributária para países emergentes vis-à-vis países desenvolvidos e em via de desenvolvimento*, in *Revista Dereito Tributario Atual N° 23*, 2010, p. 528 ff.

Internal Neutrality: Features of the Italian Tax System That May Affect Developing Economies

The Italian Tax System: From Territoriality to Worldwide Taxation

In 1973, Italy switched from a *territorial* to a *worldwide-income-taxation* regime. This is one of the key-points of the Italian Tax Code (hereinafter TC),[2] and is clearly related in Articles 1–3 and 72–83 TC. "Connection of the taxable income with the country" is the main prerequisite for the assertion of Italian taxation rights. This is true both for natural and juridical persons and requires a preliminary evaluation based on the taxpayer residence. The first outcome of this system is that "resident subjects" bear Italian taxation on all worldwide-earned income, while non-residents bear it only on income produced in Italy.

Many of the provisions dealing with the treatment of foreign income are included in Articles 165–169 of the TC. Under Italian tax legislation, resident subjects can solve the problem of international juridical double taxation, either *unilaterally*, by using some specific provisions included in the TC, or *internationally*, by taking advantage of provisions included in international treaties against double taxation. Paragraph 1 of Article 165 TC, sets the general rule that allows Italian-resident taxpayers to credit taxes paid abroad on foreign incomes. This foreign tax credit regime is integrated by the provision of Article 169 TC, under which the taxpayer may opt for the most-favorable treatment – either one provided *unilaterally* by Italy or another possibly provided by an international treaty.

In the academic community, the debate about the efficiency of these two systems remains open and many questions have not yet been answered. From the perspective of developing countries, two different points can be considered: some scholars argue that, by adopting worldwide taxation systems, wealthy nations seriously harm the developing opportunities of poorer countries, because they neutralize their only practical way to get investments, which is to engage in tax competition. On the other hand, even the adoption of territorial systems does not guarantee a positive result, because there is a high risk that poor countries, by engaging in tax competitions, sacrifice the revenue needed for development.[3]

---

[2] The Italiam Code refers to: *Testo Unico delle Imposte sui Redditi – Decreto del Presidente della Repubblica 22 Dicembre* 1986, n. 917, and its subsequent modifications.

[3] See also Fleming C./Peroni R./Shay S., *Perspectives on the Worldwide* vs. *Territorial Taxation Debate*, in *Tax Notes*, 2009, pp. 1079–1106.

Dividends, Participation Exemption and CFC Rules

In general, there is no difference of treatment of domestic- and foreign-source dividends. This is due to a new tax regime introduced in 2004.[4] It provides a partial exemption for qualified corporate owners that meet certain ownership requirements. More precisely, according to Article 89 TC, as much as 95 % of the dividends paid[5] to Italian-resident companies by wholly or partly owned foreign subsidiaries, are exempted from corporate income tax.[6]

Article 87 of the TC provides a participation exemption regime for the disposal of shares or other participation forms. It allows the exemption from corporate income tax of 95 % of capital gains resulting from sale of share ownership or other forms of participation. In order to be eligible for this exemption regime, the taxpayer must meet four requirements: establish that it has held the participation from the first day of the 12th month prior to the disposal, book the participation in the first balance sheet closed during the ownership period as a *long-term investment*, establish that the participated entity has not been a resident of a *black-listed country*, and establish that it has carried out an effective business activity during the preceding 3 fiscal years.[7]

While these domestic measures are not specifically an expression of a policy in favor of investment in countries in the developing world, they may result in benefitting investment in those states.

On the other side, like many other OECD (Organisation for Economic Cooperation and Development) countries, Italy adopted remedies aimed at countering the shifting of taxable profits to low-tax jurisdictions which may include developing countries. The pillar of this policy is the Controlled Foreign Company Legislation (hereinafter CFC) introduced on November of year 2000. It is now contained in Articles from 167 to 168-bis TC. Unlike the OECD report on Harmful Tax Competition,[8] Italian legislation combating shift of profits abroad does not distinguish either from the theoretical or the practical point of view between *tax havens* and *harmful tax regimes*.[9]

Italian CFC legislation allows tax authorities to treat a controlled foreign company meeting specified requirements as a sort of permanent establishment of the

---

[4] The law introducing this new regime is the Decreto Legislativo 344/2003, that came into force on 1 January 2004.

[5] See also, Galli C., *Italy Corporate Taxation – IBFD Country Analysis*, Amsterdam, March 2013, pp. 55–59.

[6] The term *"corporate income tax"* refers to the 'Imposta Generale sul Reddito delle Società' (IRES).

[7] See also, Zanotti E./Bono B., *New Guidance on Italian Participation Exemption*, in *European Taxation*, 2013, pp. 406–408.

[8] See also, OECD, Report on Harmful Tax Competition – An Emerging Global Issue (Paris 1998), Chapter II, pp. 19–35; available on the OECD official website 'www.oecd.org'

[9] See also, Paganuzzi M., *La CFC legislation*, in Sacchetto C., *Principi di diritto tributario europeo e internazionale*, Torino 2011, pp. 343–361; Caumont Caimi, C., – Franzè R., *Participation Exemption for Inbound Dividends and Anti-Tax-Havens Rules*, in *European Taxation*, 2001, pp. 187–193;

holding company. As a consequence, CFC income is treated as that of the parent company, with a credit for taxes paid abroad. Unlike other CFC legislation, the Italian rules are quite broad in scope and applicable not only to *controlled* companies, but also to *connected* ones. In fact, Article 168 TC extends the rules to taxpayers that earn, either directly or indirectly (e.g. through trusts or interposed persons/companies), more than 20 % of total company profits (more than the 10 % in case of listed companies).[10] These measures to fight tax evasion or avoidance may in fact result in a disincentive to invest in poor countries.

Italian CFC rules are based on the jurisdictional principle, under which all profits realized by a company in a listed jurisdiction are either covered by CFC rules, or not at all. Article 168-bis TC empowers the Ministry of Economy to issue a Decree listing all countries that provide an adequate exchange of tax information and in which the effective tax rate is not significantly inferior to the Italian one (the so-called "white list"). As a final list is not yet enacted, a provisional listing system[11] which has been in force has been modified several times over the last years.[12]

Political pressure has not caused the Italian government to exclude developing countries from the "black list."

Paragraph 5 of Article 165 TC lists all the situations in which a company does not fall within the scope of the CFC legislation scope, even if it is located in a listed country. The CFC rules do not apply if either the 'controlled' company carries out an effective economic activity as a core business in the listed jurisdiction,[13] or the parent or holding company is able to demonstrate to tax authorities that the outcome of the involved ownership arrangement is not exclusively the localization of profits in such low-tax jurisdiction.[14]

Finally, it is worth mentioning that in addition to the CFC legislation, Italy has adopted a number of other measures aimed at countering the shifting of taxable items to low-tax jurisdictions.[15] Other important legislation is provided by paragraphs 10 and 11 of Article 110 TC, which deals with the (non)deductibility of costs

---

[10] See also, Maisto, G., *Italian Anti-Avoidance Rules and Tax Treaties*, in *Bulletin for International Taxation*, 2010, pp. 441–444, and Valente P.- Magenta, M., *Analysis of Certain Anti-Abuse Clauses in the Tax Treaties Concluded by Italy*, in *Bulletin for International Taxation*, 2000, pp. 41–46.

[11] The basic listing is provided by a Ministerial Decree issued on 21 November 2001, published on the Italian Public Gazette n. 273 of November 2001. It has been modified several times over the last few years, and the actual version is available on the official website of the Italian Tax Administration, "www.agenzia delleentrate.gov.it." Technically speaking, this transitory list is a "black list" because it names all countries not meeting the abovementioned requirements, while the final one is expected to list compliant countries.

[12] See also Garufi, S., *Amendments to the Italian Controlled Foreign Company Rules: A Witch-Hunt,?* in *European Taxation*, 2009, pp. 504–507.

[13] Special standards are provided by paragraph 5-bis for Banks, Insurances and Financial Institutions.

[14] See also, Campolo, G., *New Regulation Provides clarification regarding the tightened CFC and Anti-Tax-Havens Rules*, in *European Taxation*, 2011, pp. 42–48.

[15] See also, Galli, C., *Transfer Pricing Rules for Transactions Involving Low-Tax Countries*, in *International Transfer Pricing Journal*, 2008, pp. 44–49.

originated from operations carried out with companies located in certain low-tax jurisdictions. These jurisdictions are listed in a Decree issued by the Ministry of Economy and Finances on 23 January 2002, and published on the Italian Public Gazette n. 29 of 4 February 2002, the so-called "black list Decree." Unlike the CFC legislation, these provisions are applicable regardless of an ownership connection between the involved companies. As in the case of the CFC legislation, these rules do not apply if the company either carries out an effective business activity or has a "real" economic interest.[16] This measure can seriously hinder investment in a developing country with low taxation particularly because these activities typically involve higher costs than in developed economies.

As the above review indicates, it is evident that the Italian tax system is extensively based on the capital export neutrality principle. In fact, since switching from a territorial to a worldwide taxation system, Italian tax policy has been aimed at eliminating tax disparities for investors choosing between domestic and foreign investment opportunities. Nevertheless, departures from a "pure" export neutrality system, such as the CFC legislation, are necessary to prevent manipulation of tax results through cross-border arbitrage. Generally speaking, the capital export neutrality does not place any barrier to investment abroad, but the strict limitations provided by CFC and similar legislation prevent developing countries from engaging in tax competition. As a consequence, in normal situations, investors do not enjoy any advantage in investing in developing countries, because they bear a similar tax burden while possibly facing a less-developed infrastructure and lower quality of public services.

External Neutrality: Aspects of Italian Tax Policy That May Affect Developing Economies

Tax Treaties

As in the case of the majority of European countries,[17] Italy does not tend to actively promote developing countries through international tax tools. For example, in the last decade, Italy has either avoided or, where possible, reversed the inclusion of tax-sparing and matching credit clauses in its treaties.[18] Although there are differ-

---

[16] See also Banfi, I. Brambilla, A., *The Deductibility of Costs Arising from Transactions with Residents of Tax Havens*, in *European Taxation*, 2011, pp. 67–73; GALLI, C., *Commissionaire Held Accountable for Justifying its Relationship with its Principal Established in a Tax Haven*, in *International Transfer Pricing Journal*, 2005, pp. 145–149.

[17] See also, Meirelles, M., *Tax Sparing Credits in Tax Treaties: the Future and the Effect on EC Law*, in *European Taxation*, May 2009, pp. 263–273.

[18] See also, Lombardo, M., *Italy*, in Lang M., *Recent Tax Treaties Developments around the Globe*, Vienna 2009, p. 249. In order to have a general outline of the topic, see the following scientific article, in which the situation of Italy is also quoted: BRUGGEN. E., *Tax Treaty Renegotiations by*

ences, this chapter treats these two types of clauses as similar from a policy perspective, treating both as "tax-sparing."[19]

The Italian approach to treaties with developing countries has changed in recent years.[20] Beginning in 1971, Italy signed approximately 20 tax treaties which included tax sparing clauses. These covered all or, in some cases, specified types of income or covering all of them.[21] In the 1990s, Italy began to avoid, and when possible, to remove tax-sparing clauses in its Treaties. The tax-sparing clauses allowed by Italy over the years can be classified as follows:

- Tax Sparing Clauses covering all types of income (*Clausola senza limiti di applicazione* – which can be literally translated as *"clause without limits to application"*). This kind of clause was present in ten treaties in 2004. Currently, it is present in the treaties with the following countries: Algeria (art. 24, par. 4), Ivory Coast (art. 22, par. 4), Trinidad and Tobago (art. 22. Par. 4), and Venezuela (art. 23, per. 4).
- Tax Sparing Clauses covering only specified types of income (*Clausola ad applicazione limitata* – which can be literally translated as *'clause with application limits'*). Negotiation of even this limited type of tax sparing has been avoided, or, where possible, re-negotiated. Currently, this kind of clause is present, for example, in the Treaties signed by Italy with: Argentina (art. 24, par. 4), Bangladesh (art. 23, par. 4), China (art. 23, par. 4), Tunisia (art. 22, par. 4), Sri Lanka (art. 24, par. 4), and others.[22]

Tax sparing clauses have been included in tax treaties for decades, with the first ones dating back to the 1950s. Tax policy changed in the 1990s, because it became evident that these tools were more useful to avoid domestic taxation, than to help developing economies.[23] Italian tax policy in this area has generally been in line with OECD recommendations. In the same period in which the OECD changed its tax-sparing policy, Italy started to remove those clauses. The U. S., however, has resisted the tax-sparing clause.[24]

Developing Countries: A Case Study Using Comparative Analysis to Assess the Feasibility of Achieving Policy Objectives, in *Asian-Pacific Bulletin*, 2002, pp. 255–272.

[19] See also, Mayr, S., *Il 'matching credit' all' italiana*, in *Corriere Tributario*, 1990, pp. 343–354, and Ferreira, V. A. Marinho A. T., *Tax sparing and Matching Credit: from an Unclear Concept to an Uncertain Regime*, in *Bulletin for International Taxation*, 2013, pp. 397–413.

[20] See also, Nanetti F., *I profili fiscali del matching credit secondo la Cassazione*, in *Rubrica di Diritto Tributario e Comparato*, Part V, 2013, pp. 10–29.

[21] See also, Pau, F., *Il Matching Credit*, in *Diritto e Pratica Tributaria Internazionale*, 2003/ III, pp. 199–226.

[22] See also the official website of the Italian Department of finances 'www.finanze.it', which is updated on a regular basis.

[23] See also, OECD, Tax Sparing: A Reconsideration (Paris 1998), Chapter I, pp. 12–13.

[24] See also, Fleming, C. Peroni R., Shay, S. *Perspectives on the Worldwide* vs. *Territorial Taxation Debate*, in *Tax Notes*, 2009, p. 1103.

As noted by scholars,[25] in the list of Italian treaties containing tax-sparing clauses, Eastern European countries are missing. As those countries are capital importers, and Italian companies are big investors in many of them, some policy reasons may explain this phenomenon. The lack of tax-sparing clauses in treaties with Eastern European countries may be partially explained by Italy's desire to attract national investors to poor Italian regions, rather than to encourage them to "go abroad." This can also be explained when one considers the political situation: for much of the period in which Italy included tax sparing clauses in its treaties, Eastern European countries were economically tied to the Soviet Union. It is reasonable to conclude that *tax sparing* was not on the political agenda of either party. Because the OECD reconsidered advisability of tax sparing just a few years after the radical change of the economic system in East Europe, it is reasonable to conclude that tax sparing clauses were never included in treaties with those countries due to the afore-mentioned timing reasons.[26]

Economic Agreements

Italian policy towards poor countries is also reflected in the many *Agreements for the Promotion and the Protection of Investments*[27] signed by Italy. These agreements were all signed with developing countries (or with countries considered poor at the time), but they all included provisions based on the principle of reciprocity, and therefore were not exclusively aimed at helping the poor counterpart. For example, Article 2 of an agreement signed in 1991 with Albania[28] provided that, at least theoretically, both contracting parties equally undertake to promote, in their own territory, investments coming from the other contracting State.[29]

---

[25] See also, Pau F., *Il Matching Credit*, in *Diritto e Pratica Tributaria Internazionale*, 2003/III, pp. 199–226.

[26] See also, Sacchetto, C., *Política de tratados em matéria tributária para países emergentes vis-à-vis países desenvolvidos e em via de desenvolvimento*, in *Revista Dereito Tributario Atual N° 23*, year 2010, p. 528.

[27] This is the literal translation of: *"Accordi per la promozione e la protezione degli investimenti."*

[28] Entered into force with Law 709/1994.

[29] See also the official website of the Italian Department of finances 'www.finanze.it', and of the Ministry for Economic Development 'www.sviluppoeconomico.it'

Italy and International Organizations

The Italian Constitution[30] makes many references to "external" and "international" legal orders,[31] and the desire to establish "cooperation among nations" as one of its main principles.[32] Italy has a long general tradition of international cooperation and an extensive network of treaties and agreements with many countries. This is true also in the field of taxation.[33] Italy is a member of the European Union (EU),[34] the Council of Europe, the OECD, the World Trade Organization, and the OECD Global Tax Forum. As an EU Member State, it is subject to European legislation (e.g., in the field of State aid), as well as the decisions of the European Court of Justice.[35]

Italy has always adapted its domestic legislation and national policy to the inputs coming from the organizations of which is member. This is equally true for all tax measures that potentially affect developing countries. The best example is the state aid policy: a tax tool aimed at helping developing economies should be targeted to companies that are able to invest in poor countries. In fact, access to these markets is not easy, and specific know-how is necessary, including understanding specialized personnel, finding management aware of specific problems, managing high transport costs, and developing an ability to cope with political and other instability. Any help to poor countries realized with tax tools should be provided only to companies having the above-mentioned knowhow. Because there is a scarce supply of such companies, it would be very difficult for such a measure to pass the "selectivity test" provided by Article 87 of the EC Treaty. Moreover, even if in some specific circumstances "aid having social character" is allowed, the tax incentives helping developing countries would be subject to challenge under the non-discrimination principle because it is likely to constitute an "unfair tax competition affecting trade between Member States."

Nevertheless, even if it is almost impossible to find any trace of an Italian tax policy aimed at either encouraging or discouraging economic behaviours with regard to poor countries, many of the international organizations, of which Italy is a

---

[30] It was adopted on 27 December 1947, and entered into force on 1 January 1948. It is the outcome of new values and principles adopted by Italy after World War II and 20 years of fascist regime.

[31] For example: Article 7, which set forth the reciprocal independence of the State legal order and the Ecclesiastical one; Article 10, which deals with the foreigner's status, etc. For more details on the tax outcomes of these provisions, see also Mastellone Pietro, *Religion and Taxation in Italy: the Principle of Laicite and Compliance with EU Law*, in *European Taxation*, August 2013, pp. 378–392.

[32] See also Articles 10 and 11 of the Italian Constitution.

[33] See also Bizioli, G., *Il processo di integrazione dei principi tributari nel rapporto fra ordinamento costituzionale comunitario e diritto internazionale*, Padova, 2008, pp. 31–62.

[34] See also Sdudoczky, M., *Vienna Conference on 'The EU and Third States: Direct Taxation'*, in *European Taxation*, February 2007, pp. 93–98.

[35] See also Pistone, P., *The Impact of the ECJ Case Law on National Taxation*, in *Bulletin for International Taxation*, 2010, pp. 412–428; and, Gallo F.-Melis, G., *The Italian Tax System: International and EU Obligations and the Realization of Fiscal Federalism*, in *Bulletin for International Taxation*, 2010, pp. 400–410.

member, actively promote development in different ways. Many such initiatives are taken in the field of custom duties.

One of these initiatives is supported by the EU through the so-called "Cotonou Agreement." This is a partnership agreement signed in 2000 by a group of African, Caribbean, and Pacific States (hereinafter "ACP"). The main provisions of the Agreement were published on 15 December 2000 in the Official Journal of the European Communities (2000/483/CE), followed by two Regulations issued in 2005 and 2010. The Cotonou Agreements contain the following relevant provisions:

(i) Paragraph 1, point a) of Article 22, deals with 'macroeconomic and structural reforms and policies.' It provides that cooperation shall support ACP, among others, in *strengthening fiscal discipline, enhancing budgetary transparency and efficiency, improving the quality, equity and composition of fiscal policy,*

(ii) Paragraph 3 of Article 42, concerning "maritime transport," which provides that *each Party shall grant, inter alia, a treatment no less favourable than that accorded to its own ships, for ships operated by nationals or companies of the other Party, and for ships registered in the territory of either party, with respect to access to ports, as well as related fees and charges, Article 44 custom facilities and the assignment of berths and facilities for loading and unloading,* and

(iii) A number of tax provisions regarding custom duties, included in Annexes I and IV, aimed at creating a *free trade zone* and at preventing tax-discrimination regarding funds entering the interested countries to finance developing projects.

One further step in the analysis of the EU tax policy toward developing countries and, therefore, also that of Italy, can be taken with the study of Regulation (CE) 980/2005 on *generalised tariff preferences* and of the Regulation (CE)N. 1528/2007 on the implementation of Cotonou Agreement. This policy is very well summarized in points (7) and (8) of the Preamble of Regulation (CE) N. 1528/2007, which indicate that a relationship with developing countries should be based on economic partnership, rather than on a special tariff system. With this in mind, it is possible to explain the Italian tax policy of the last decades as consistent with a European policy to assist underdeveloped economies through the creation of big *free trade zones* to be implemented, *inter alia*, with the abolition of customs duties, the application of non-discrimination principle to maritime trade, and the financing of specific development projects.

The intent of EU policy makers is to pattern the legal framework of relationships with developing countries on the principle of reciprocity. As a consequence, instead of providing tax incentives to taxpayers that invest in poor countries, Europeans are building a tax system *as neutral as possible* while integrating with each other and at the same time, trying to create the best conditions possible to foster development of the private sector in poor nations. The final goal is to make these countries better equipped to come out of their unfavourable situation by doing business on an equal and reciprocal basis.

Another example of this European policy can be found in the Declaration of Barcelona for the creation of a "Euro-Mediterranean Region" (which dates back to 1995, but is currently not active because of the political instability of many North African countries). One of the main long-term objectives under this Declaration is the *progressive establishment of a free-trade area* through the progressive elimination of tariff and non-tariff trade barriers for services, agricultural, and manufactured products. In the present day, however this Declaration is nothing more than a statement of purposes, but, even without binding effect, it confirms European policy toward developing countries. This policy can be clearly identified as follows:

> *To facilitate the progressive establishment of this free-trade area through the adoption of suitable measures as regards rules of origin, certification, protection of intellectual and industrial property rights and competition; to pursue and develop policies based on the principles of market economy and the integration of their economies taking into account their respective needs and levels of development; to give priority to the promotion and development of the private sector in particular by the progressive elimination of obstacles to such investment which could lead to the transfer of technology and increase production and exports; above all to encourage sustainable indigenous development and the mobilization of local economic operators.*

The intention is to create a business environment in which the private sector can develop on reciprocal basis, rather than merely encourage rich taxpayers to make donations to poor countries.

As noted above, Italy is an OECD member. Recently, this Organization took a very important step toward international tax harmonization by publishing the Report on the *Base Erosion and Profit Shifting* ("BEPS"), and a 'to do list' entitled *Action Plan on Base Erosion and Profit Shifting*. The end of the Report contains an important paragraph entitled "Tax and Development."[36] In this paragraph, OECD states that developing countries need to become able to effectively employ tools that counter the BEPS phenomena in relation to international tax issues. This would happen as a result of the support provided by developed nations on policy issues, administrative structures, regulation, guidance and building practical auditing skills, implementation of rules on the registration of the statutory accounts of unlisted companies, and other mechanisms. There is no mention of tax incentives that should be granted to private taxpayers. The OECD appears to be encouraging rich nations to create a profitable business environment, consistent with its work in the Barcelona Declaration, rather than private donations or unilateral investments in developing countries.

---

[36] See also pages 86–87 of the 2013 OECD Report '*Base Erosion and Profit Shifting*', available on the OECD official website 'www.oecd.org'

Italian Legislation on Charity: Substantial Help or Crumbs?

Two very peculiar pieces of Italian tax legislation are discussed below. As explained in 1.1, these are not investment incentives, but, rather, incentives to private charity. They provide tax incentives for non-profit activities carried out by "non-commercial bodies" (*enti non commerciali*), "non-profit organizations of social utility," "*charities,*" "voluntary organizations," and provide some preferential rules originating from the "special relationship with ecclesiastical bodies." These incentives are not specifically created to help poor countries, but, as a matter of fact, they often benefit entities that are socially active in disadvantaged regions.

The ONLUS Regime

The Legislative Decree 460/97 introduced the possibility, for some legal entities carrying out entrepreneurial activities, to opt for the so-called "ONLUS regime." This regime is relevant only for tax purposes and provides the classification of the legal entity as ONLUS, literally meaning "*Non-Profit Organization for Social Utility.*"[37] After opting for this regime, the ONLUS is registered on a special list of all entities working non-profit for social purposes: the so-called "anagrafe (registry office) ONLUS." This regime provides special limitations on powers of directors and managers. Limitations include: prohibition on profit distribution; in case of liquidation, the obligation to transfer the assets to another entity with similar objectives; and, the prohibition on selling the "membership." On the other hand, many benefits are provided for these entities, such as simplified bookkeeping, direct taxes and VAT exemptions for social activities and fund-raising.

In order to be eligible for the ONLUS regime the entity must meet the following requirements: (1) the performance of activities in one or more areas strictly listed by the law,[38] (2) the exclusive pursuit of social and solidarity goals, (3) the prohibition on carrying out activities other than those referred to in (1), above, except for those directly connected to the permitted activity, (4) the obligation to use profits for social and solidarity goals, and (5) the use of the acronym ONLUS in the name of the legal entity.[39]

---

[37] See also, Sacchetto, C. *La tassazione internazionale degli enti non commerciali: un problema aperto*, In Rassegna tributaria, 2012, p. 563 nad seq.

563 The exact meaning of ONLUS is "Organizzazione Non Lucrativa di UtilitàSociale." The literal translation is "Non-Profit Organization for Social Utility."

[38] According to Italian legislation, the areas listed are: social assistance; health care; charity; education; training; amateur sport; protection and promotion of artistic and historical heritage; protection of the environment; protection of civil rights and scientific research.

[39] See also the report produced for Italian Tax Police Academy in 2005 by di Gregorio, C., *Il controllo fiscale degli enti non profit* (of which the literal translation is "Tax Assessment of Non-Profit Entities"). Available on the official website of the Italian Tax Police – *Guardia di Finanza*, 'www. gdf.gov.it'

Italian Tax Law provides significant deductions for taxpayers that make donations to ONLUS. Individuals have the possibility to deduct their donations either up
to the 10 % of their total declared income, with a threshold of Euro 70.000, or up to
the 19 % with a threshold of Euro 2065, or up to 2 % without any threshold.
Companies may deduct their donations either up to 10 % of their total income, also
with a threshold of Euro 70.000, or up to 2 % with a threshold of Euro 2065.

Specific official data on the "ONLUS situation" is unavailable, but, on July 2013,
the National Institute of Statistics (ISTAT) published the results of the last census on
the non-profit sector.[40] It documents the constantly increasing size of the so-called
"third sector" of non-profit activities, but without any specific reference to the
ONLUS tax regime. In fact, not all of the 301,191 non-profit legal entities involved
in social activities in year 2011 opted for this preferential tax regime. Nevertheless,
as there is a significant growth, in general, of non-profit entities (28 % compared to
2001 data – when there were 235,232 of these legal entities), it is reasonable to
conclude that, in the same period, there was a significant increase of ONLUS as
well.

What is relevant for present purposes is that the model of ONLUS grants can also
be directed for assistance in foreign countries and in the case in developing
countries.

The Roman Catholic Church

Article 7 of Italian Constitution establishes the principle that the Republic of Italy
and the Roman Catholic Church are both independent and sovereign, each in its
own legal order. Their relationship is governed by the so-called Lateran Pacts, a
very peculiar type of international agreement signed with the State of Vatican City.
Moreover, Article 20 of the Constitution establishes a sort of 'non-discrimination'
principle, according to which no special tax burdens may be imposed on any institution or association on the basis of its "religious or ecclesiastical nature."

Within the above-mentioned legal framework, some economic incentives are
granted to religious entities, also through peculiar tax tools. The most important
system of incentives is established by Law 222/85, which provides the possibility
for taxpayers to donate the "eight per thousand" of reported revenue to some religious entities while submitting their annual tax report. The technical functioning of
this system is quite complex, because, from the practical point of view, it works as
follows: based on the number of taxpayers that exercised this option in their annual

---

[40] See also the report, *9° Censimento dell'industria e dei servizi e Censimento delle istituzioni non
profit* (of which the literal translation is "9th Census of industry and services sector, and Census of
non-profit sector"), available on the official website of ISTAT, the National Institute of Statistic,
'www.istat.it'

tax report, the "eight per thousand" of the total State revenue is distributed among religious entities that are included in a special list, without regard to the tax amount actually paid by each donor. As a consequence, each religious entity takes advantage from the number of persons opting for it in the annual tax report, rather than from the wealth of the single taxpayers who opt for it.[41]

In order to be eligible for a portion of this "eight per thousand fund," religious entities have to reach an agreement with the State and be included in a list. Presently, the list includes: the Roman Catholic Church, Waldensian Protestant Church, Italian Union of Seventh-day Adventist Churches, Assemblies of God in Italy, Union of Italian Jewish Communities, Evangelical Lutheran Church in Italy, Baptist Evangelical Christian Union of Italy, Italian Buddhist Union and Italian Hindu Union. While submitting their annual tax report, taxpayers may opt to contribute to the Italian State as well, or decide "not to opt." The number of people that decided "not to opt" is equally distributed among all beneficiaries.

This "eight per thousand" system is doubtless a great help to the Roman Catholic Church in Italy. It is the only 'non-neutral' provision of the Italian tax system in this area. Moreover, this incentive is accompanied by certain tax discounts on the real estate properties of religious entities. The roots of these provisions are found in the deep historical relationship between the Italian society and the Catholic Church. It is widely accepted at the level of policy-makers and justified with the argument that it complements very efficiently the Italian welfare state.

These provisions are relevant because the expectation is that a portion of the tax revenue for the institutions of worship will be used to support initiatives in favor of poor countries. Therefore, albeit indirectly through the bodies of the Catholic religious tradition, assistance is provided to the poorest populations. The objective is not pursued by the state but by the Church through use of the revenue diverted from the State to the institutions of worship.

Conclusions

The ostensible neutrality of Italian policy toward developing countries is mitigated by Italy's membership in a number of international organizations. Even though it does not explicitly use tax tools, Italy is helping developing countries through donations, subsidized loans, cancellation and conversion of debts, and by funding cooperative projects.[42]

Italy is not using directly any tax tool to help poor countries, but it is participating in different ways in their development. Obviously, there are no official statements that explain this policy, but academic analysis supports this conclusion. The

---

[41] See also, Sacchetto, C. Dagnino, A and Santagata, F, *Profili fiscali e finanziari del sovvenzionamento delle confessioni religiose in Italia*, in *Société, Droit et Religion*, 2012. p. 125.

[42] For more details, see also the dedicated section of the official website of the Italian Ministry of Foreign Affairs, 'www.cooperazioneallosviluppo.esteri.it'

rationale is most likely based in the economic interests of Italy. On the one hand, it must adapt to policies of various organizations, like the EU and WTO, of which it is a member. On the other hand, like all other industrialized countries, it does not profit from reducing its own revenue for the exclusive benefit of others. It does, however, work to create *big transnational business environments*, such as free trade zones, in which private companies can profitably work for the benefit of many parties. The two pillars of Italy's policy in this regard are the principles of neutrality and reciprocity.

Finally, it is important to make a general reflection. As policy toward developing countries appears to be switching from a territorial to a worldwide taxation system, some lessons emerge. Compared to one that allows tax incentives to investors in poor countries, a neutral tax system makes it easier to prevent unwanted effects. In fact, through direct aid (such as debt cancellation) it is possible to advance specific policies, and reward deserving countries or behaviours, such as, for example, the respect of human rights and the rights of women.[43] A system of tax incentives granted to private investors makes this task more difficult and opens up many possibilities for tax avoidance and for investments in countries that are (or might become) hostile. Moreover, direct aid made by developed nations is more democratic, because it is open to input by public opinion and mass media. On the contrary, it is almost impossible to control who benefits from tax incentives, which countries are the beneficiaries, and whether the granted tax incentive is really useful for fighting poverty and achieving other development goals.

---

[43] See also, Fleming, C., Peroni, R., Shay, S., *Perspectives on the Worldwide* vs. *Territorial Taxation Debate*, in *Tax Notes*, December 2009, pp. 1079–1106.

Chapter 11
Taxation and Development: Japan

Yoshihiro Masui

Abstract Although Japan taxes the income of its residents on a worldwide basis, one territorial feature of its regime is the participation exemption. This regime exempts from tax 95 % of dividends paid by a foreign subsidiary to a Japanese parent corporation. Japan closely monitors tax haven activities by strengthening CFC legislation, transfer pricing regulations, and thin capitalization rules. Japan has concluded tax sparing agreements in its bilateral treaties with developing countries, including those with Indonesia, Sri Lanka, Zambia, Thailand, China, Bangladesh, and Brazil. These agreements are typically of limited duration and some have already expired.

Synopsis Japan emerged as one of the leading world economies in the latter part of the twentieth century. Various income tax exemptions or rate reductions for financial income (interest, dividends, and capital gains) have provided stimulus for investment into Japan. Addressing demand, Japan ultimately exempted from taxation various forms of portfolio interest payments to non-residents. As Japan heightened enforcement of transfer pricing regulations, a number of multinational enterprises (MNEs) restructured or relocated to tax-friendlier jurisdictions. In order to prevent artificial transfer of profits outside of Japan's jurisdiction to tax, it has reformed and tightened controlled foreign corporation (CFC) rules. Japan has been actively involved in anti-tax avoidance initiatives, such as the OECD's Harmful Tax Competition and Base Erosion Profit Shifting (BEPS) projects.

The statutory corporate tax rate at the national level is 23.4 % (29.97% for 2016 when national and local taxes are combined), applicable to domestic and foreign corporations (operating a branch in Japan, for example).

Individual and corporate residents are taxed on worldwide income with a foreign tax credit (with a limitation to avoid refund of foreign tax imposed at a rate higher than in Japan) available to eliminate double taxation. A territorial feature of Japan's international tax regime is a type of participation exemption. Beginning in 2009, 95 % of dividends paid by a foreign subsidiary (at least 25 % owned, or in some cases, 10 % by treaty) to a Japanese parent are exempt from taxation. Capital gains and

Y. Masui (✉)
University of Tokyo, Tokyo, Japan
e-mail: masui@j.u-tokyo.ac.jp

© Springer International Publishing Switzerland 2017
K.B. Brown (ed.), *Taxation and Development - A Comparative Study*,
Ius Comparatum - Global Studies in Comparative Law 21,
DOI 10.1007/978-3-319-42157-5_11

losses from disposition of the shares of a subsidiary, whether foreign or domestic, are not exempt.

The CFC regime (taxing the retained profits of the subsidiary as if derived by the parent) applies if the controlled subsidiary is resident in a jurisdiction with an effective tax rate below 20 % or, if the effective rate is 20 % or higher, it does not conduct a substantive business activity in that location. The rules apply to mobile income (royalties and financial income) in all cases.

Although Japan does not have a regime specifically penalizing investment in tax haven jurisdictions, it does police such investments by strengthening transfer pricing and thin capitalization rules. In addition, it normally refuses to conclude bilateral treaties with tax havens, except regarding information exchange.

Japan participates in the Global Tax Forum, having received a rating of compliant. In this regard, Japan has worked to maintain conformity to internationally agreed standards for exchange of information. This has included expansion of investigatory powers of tax officials and exempting from confidentiality rules information provided to treaty partners. Japan has several Tax Information Exchange Agreements (TIEAs). Japan's standard information exchange provision in bilateral treaties follows the OECD Model's article 26. It exchanges information on request, spontaneously, or automatically. Adhering to the G20 Initiative on automatic exchange of information, Japan introduced the Common Reporting Standard for financial account information. It has signed an Intergovernmental Agreement (IGA Model II) with the U.S. to meet FATCA requirements.

Regarding developing countries, Japan has concluded tax sparing agreements in bilateral treaties. These have been concluded with countries, such as Indonesia, Sri Lanka, Zambia, Thailand, China, Bangladesh, and Brazil. In recent years, the tax sparing clauses have been for a limited period of time and many are either set to expire (e.g., Korea, Singapore, Malaysia, Mexico, Turkey, Bulgaria, and Vietnam) or have expired. With the phase-out of tax sparing and the existence of the worldwide tax regime, the ability of developing countries to attract investment by lowering tax rates is impaired. On the other hand, the participation exemption, eliminating 95 % of dividends paid by foreign subsidiaries from Japanese tax, might encourage investment in developing regions.

Japan has taken steps to stimulate economic activity through a number of tax incentives. Research and development, employment, and other tax credits have been expanded significantly. There has been vigorous consideration of corporate tax rate reduction as a vehicle to make operations in Japan more attractive, but this change faces a significant budgetary constraint.

Introduction

From a historical perspective, all countries were once developing countries. Japan was no exception when it started modernization in the late nineteenth century. Most tax revenue came from land taxes initially.[1] Rapid industrialization in the early twentieth century was accompanied by the rise of liquor tax and various excises. It was in the 1920s that income tax became the largest revenue raiser within Japan's tax mix. The need to finance war in the Continent transformed the nature of income tax. In 1940, income tax became a mass tax. Previously, it was paid by wealthy individuals and large businesses. After 1940, it was paid also by ordinary workers and small proprietors.

Japan's fiscal conditions deteriorated during the Second World War. After the war, in 1949, the Shoup Mission recommended a progressive income tax system with a comprehensive tax base.[2] The recommendation was legislated in 1950. It laid the foundation of Japan's post-war tax system. However, the reformist regime did not last long. As early as in 1953, Japan's policymakers preferred to modify the recommended system. Japan's income tax began to have a clear pro-growth orientation. Most capital income was exempted at an individual investor level. Corporations were granted special tax incentives.

In 1953, foreign tax credit was granted generously to business corporations with international operations.[3] During the 1960s Japan's economy took off with a spectacular growth rate. By the 1980s, Japan-based multinational enterprises (MNEs) became strong enough that they no longer needed government assistance.[4] The foreign tax credit system has been tightened gradually. Tax sparing credits in Japan's bilateral income tax treaties have been scaled down, following the reconsideration at the OECD.[5]

On the domestic front, the sweeping tax reforms in 1987–1988 widened the individual income tax base.[6] The new law repealed the exemption measures for interest income arising from bank deposits, bringing it back to the personal income tax base but at a flat rate. The new law also repealed the exemption of capital gain on the sale

---

[1] Hugh Ault and Brian Arnold ed., *COMPARATIVE INCOME TAXATION* 93 (3rd edition, 2010, Kluwer Law International).

[2] W. Elliot Brownlee, The Transfer of Tax Ideas during the 'Reverse Course' of the US Occupation in Japan, in Holger Nehring and Florian Shui ed., *GLOBAL DEBATE ABOUT TAXATION 158* (2007, Palgrave Macmillan).

[3] Yoshihiro Masui, The Influence of the 1954 Japan-United States Income Tax Treaty on the Development of Japan's International Tax Policy, Bulletin for international taxation Vol.66, No.4/5, 243 (2012).

[4] Yoshihiro Masui, International Taxation in Japan: A Historical Overview, Tax Notes International, December 18, 2000, 2813.

[5] OECD, Tax Sparing: A Reconsideration (1998).

[6] Hiroshi Kaneko, The Reform of the Japanese Tax System in the Latter Half of the Twentieth Century and into the Twenty-First Century, in Daniel H. Foote ed., *LAW IN JAPAN: A TURNING POINT* 564 (2007, University of Washington Press).

of shares. Dividends remain taxable at a flat rate, separate from other sources of income under the otherwise progressive income tax rate structure. As a result, a lower flat rate applied to financial income compared with labor and business income earned by high income earners.

At the turn of the twenty-first century, one of the key efforts of National Tax Agency was its enforcement of transfer pricing regulations. More and more MNEs conducted business restructurings. They relocated profit-making businesses out of Japan towards more tax-friendly neighboring jurisdictions. Japan had various tax incentives to stimulate the economy, but few of them had regional targets. Facing pressures from global financial markets, Japanese domestic law had gradually exempted withholding tax on outgoing interest payments incurred on portfolio debt even when such payment was sourced within Japan.[7]

At present, Japan's basic statutory corporate income tax rate is relatively high compared with neighboring countries. In order to prevent income from being artificially transferred abroad, the Japanese government reformed its Controlled Foreign Corporation (CFC) rule in 2010. Japan also has been active in the OECD initiative on countering Harmful Tax Competition, and more recently, the G20/OECD Base Erosion Profit Shifting (BEPS) Project.

For developing countries, the Japanese government has been providing technical assistance in the area of development aid as well as tax administration. Various lessons regarding development have been drawn from the experience of Japan as a non-European latecomer in modernization. These are shared with tax officials in other countries.

The balance of this chapter examines Japan's current tax law in the order of the following.

- International aspects of Japan's tax system
- Countering harmful tax competition and BEPS
- Giving tax incentives for international transactions

The developments referenced is this chapter reflect legislation and treaties as in force on October 1, 2016 (including 2016 tax reform).

International Aspects of Japan's Tax System

Tax System in General

Currently, more than 50 % of tax revenue, national and local levels combined, comes from income taxes.[8] For the fiscal year 2016, the share of individual income tax and corporate income tax is 30.9 % and 21.7 %, respectively. On the other hand,

---

[7] Yoshihiro Masui, Taxation of Cross-Border Interest Flows: Japanese Responses, Paul Kirchhof, Moris Lehner, Arndt Raupach and Michael Rodi ed., *STAATEN UND STEUERN: FESTSCHRIFT FÜR KLAUS VOGEL* 863 (C.F. Müller, 2000).

[8] Ministry of Finance, http://www.mof.go.jp/tax_policy/summary/condition/001.htm (visited March 27th 2015).

VAT generates 21.9 % of all tax revenue. The current VAT rate is 8 % and is expected to increase further to 10 % in April 2019. This would change the overall tax mix. As VAT allocates tax revenue among jurisdictions on a destination basis, rather than on an origin basis, this shift is likely to result in a larger revenue allocation in countries where consumers reside.

The basic statutory corporate tax rate is 23.4 % on the national level. For a small and medium corporation, a reduced 15 % rate applies to the first 8 million yen of corporate income. When the local level taxes are combined with this national level tax, the tax rate is just below 30 %.

The same tax rate structure applies to both domestic and foreign corporations. For example, when a foreign corporation operates a branch within Japan and earns profits through the branch, the profits are subject to the same corporate tax rate as their domestic counterparts.

Tax Rules Governing International Transactions

In taxing foreign income, Japan takes a worldwide approach and grants a foreign tax credit. Individual residents and domestic corporations are taxable on their world-wide income. The amount of foreign taxes paid abroad is creditable against domestic tax. There is an upper limit of the creditable amount for the taxable year based on an overall limitation calculation. The limitation is designed to avoid a refund of foreign tax amount imposed at a rate higher than Japan's tax rate.

Resident individuals and domestic corporations are taxable on the profits attributable to their permanent establishments located abroad. In other words, Japan does not have a pure "territorial" regime employed in a number of European countries.

However, the law now has a territorial feature in practice. An exemption for dividends repatriated from foreign subsidiaries to a domestic parent company began in 2009.[9] Ninety-five percent of the dividends is exempt from Japanese tax if the parent holds 25 % or more of the issued shares in the foreign subsidiary. The shareholding requirement is often reduced to 10 % in bilateral treaties with selected trade partners with Japan.

Inter-corporate dividends are also exempt in a purely domestic context. When a domestic parent company holds 25 % or more of the issued shares in a domestic subsidiary, the entire amount of the dividends is exempt at the parent level. The exempt amount is reduced by the pro rata amount of interest expense incurred on the debt to purchase the shares in the domestic subsidiary.

The parent-level corporate income tax base fully includes capital gains and losses arising from the disposal of shares in a subsidiary. This is true both for shares in a foreign subsidiary and for shares in a domestic subsidiary. Thus, Japan does not

---

[9] Yoshihiro Masui, Taxation of Foreign Subsidiaries: Japan's Tax Reform 2009/10, Bulletin for International Taxation Vol.64, No.4, 242 (2010).

have a wider participation exemption rule that covers both dividends and capital gains/losses.

Countering Harmful Tax Competition and BEPS

Efforts to Discourage Investment in Tax Haven Jurisdictions

Japan introduced its CFC legislation in 1978.[10] Its basic approach focuses on the attributes of the CFC and inquires whether the foreign entity conducts a substantive business activity in the low tax jurisdiction. If the entity is engaged in a substantive business activity, the CFC is exempted from the application of CFC rule. The retained earnings of the CFC generally are not subject to Japan's corporate income tax. In 2010, however, an income approach was added. Under this new approach, certain mobile income, including royalty and financial income, may be captured (and subject to tax) even when the foreign entity conducts substantive business activities locally.

Japan's CFC legislation originally had a "black list" designating a number of targeted low-tax jurisdictions. This rule was amended in 1992 because it was difficult to monitor the rapid tax developments in foreign jurisdictions. The new rule targets a CFC by looking into its local effective tax rate. The "trigger" threshold rate is currently 20 %. After the 2010 reform, an increased number of CFCs of a Japanese parent company is targeted because the new approach overrides the substantive business exemption.

Discourage Investment in Harmful Tax Regimes

Other than the CFC rule, Japan's domestic tax law does not have a regime that is specifically designed to discourage investment in tax haven jurisdictions. However, legislative measures of a more general nature, including transfer pricing regulations and thin capitalization rules, are often employed in the context of cross-border transactions involving offshore financial centers. Moreover, Japan traditionally had refused to conclude a bilateral income treaty with tax haven jurisdictions. The policy has been somewhat relaxed, but the treaties with offshore financial centers are still strictly limited to information exchange.

---

[10] Kotaro Okamoto, Japan, in IFA, The taxation of foreign passive income for groups of companies, Cahier de droit fiscal international Vol.98a, 423 (Sdu, 2013).

Regional/International Agreements

Japan is a party to the WTO agreements and is bound by them. WTO/GATT rules are mostly binding on indirect taxes and are specifically made inapplicable to direct taxes including individual and corporate income tax. Negotiations for Trans-Pacific Partnership (TPP) are under way. It is not clear at the stage if they would contain clauses affecting corporate income tax in a significant manner.

Japan's bilateral income tax treaties contain non-discrimination provisions. So far their impact has been almost negligible as there are still very few cases where such provisions were applied.

Global Tax Forum and Information Exchange

Japan participates in the OECD's Global Tax Forum. After going through Phase 1 and Phase 2 of the peer review process, Japan obtained an overall rating as compliant.[11]

Japan's domestic law has been amended to keep up with the internationally agreed standard for exchange of information. In order to meet requests from treaty partners, the National Tax Agency has been given more powers. In 2003, tax officials were given the power to investigate. In 2006, a statutory basis was established for tax criminal investigation. In 2010, the exemption from confidentiality requirement was created for cases where the National Tax Agency hands over taxpayer information to Japan's treaty partners. The 2010 amendment in the domestic law also gave legal grounds for the Japanese Government to conclude information exchange (only) agreement without obtaining consent of the Diet.

The first example of a Tax Information Exchange Agreement (TIEA) with an offshore jurisdiction for Japan was its TIEA with Bermuda, which was signed in February 2010 approved by the Parliament, and became effective in August 2010. The number of TIEA is increasing. Japan also signed the multilateral Convention on Mutual Administrative Assistance in Tax Matters without reservation in November 2011.

The exchange of information clause in the standard bilateral income tax treaties has also been amended to meet the internationally agreed standard. Japan's treaty practice closely follows Article 26 of the 2012 OECD Model Tax Convention on Income and on Capital. Thus, information may be exchanged on request, spontaneously, or automatically. Requested state may be able to decline to provide information in a limited circumstance described in each treaty provision.

Japan also responded to the United States FATCA regime by concluding an Inter-Governmental Agreement (IGA Model II). In March 2015, following the G20 ini-

---

[11] Global Forum on Transparency and Information Exchange for Tax Purposes, PEER REVIEW REPORT COMBINED: PHASE 1 + PHASE 2, INCORPORATING PHASE 2 RATINGS JAPAN (2013).

tiative on automatic exchange of information, Japan introduced the Common Reporting Standard (CRS) for financial account information in its domestic law. There will be a dual regime for the time being: the IGA with the US on the one hand, and the Competent Authority Agreement with a number of other countries committed to automatic exchange of information on the other hand. The two need to converge.

Tax Incentives for International Transactions

Tax Incentives Provided for Investment in Developing countries

Japan's bilateral income tax treaties with developing countries often contain a tax sparing clause. Examples include treaties with: Indonesia, Zambia, Sri Lanka, Thailand, China, Bangladesh and Brazil. Recent treaties tend to apply a sunset clause phasing out these arrangements. A five year period is set for Korea and Singapore, 7 years for Malaysia, 9 years for Mexico, 10 years for Turkey and Bulgaria, and 15 years for Vietnam. As a result, many have expired.

Because Japan's basic approach is worldwide taxation, without the treaty-based sparing credit, reduction in the amount of taxes paid to a foreign jurisdiction, including developing countries, automatically reduces the amount of creditable taxes, leaving a residual tax to be paid to Japan. However, after the 2009 introduction of exemption for a repatriated foreign dividend, the situation changed. Foreign subsidiaries may be able to enjoy the local tax incentives provided by developing countries. When they make a dividend distribution to the Japanese parent company, 95 % of the dividend amount will go tax free.

In helping people living in countries in extreme poverty, tax incentives have a limited role to play. Japan's overseas development assistance (ODA) was the largest in the world in the 1990s. It remains ranked among the five largest donor counties. Its contribution to IMF and Asian Development Bank is also significant. The National Tax Agency, in collaboration with National Tax College and Japan International Cooperation Agency (JICA), continues to assist tax officials in the developing world by providing technical advice.

No special tax regimes exist for former colonies.

Attracting Economic Activity to Japan

Stimulating economic activity has been a top priority for the Japanese government for years. After the Liberal Democratic Party took office, 2013 tax reform significantly expanded R&D, employment, and other credits. The number of tax incentives which have a clear regional target is limited. In connection with the amendment of Okinawa Development Special Measure Law, existing tax preferential measures for employee stock options was extended in the 2014 tax reform. There was a heated policy discussion in the middle of 2014 as the Cabinet pushed for an across-the-board corporate income tax reduction with its agenda under "Abenomics" under the current Abe Administration.

Amnesty

Japan does not seem to be keen on granting tax amnesties. Voluntary disclosure of a tax position may be exempt from the otherwise automatic levy of 10 % civil penalty if the taxpayer can establish a "legitimate reason" for taking the position. The Supreme Court interprets this requirement rather narrowly.[12]

---

[12] Supreme Court Decision of 20 April 2006, *Minshu* Vol.60 No.4 Page1611.

Chapter 12
The Maldives: A Fledgling International Tax Jurisdiction

Kevin Holmes

Abstract Individual residents of the Maldives are taxed on business profits on a territorial basis. Resident partnerships and corporations are taxed on worldwide income, but the tax rate is quite modest (a flat rate of 15 % or 0 % in some cases). A special regime for Maldivian offshore financial services centers (deriving all income outside the Maldives) taxes income at a flat rate of 5 % (or 0 % in some cases). In order to attract economic activity to the Maldives, the country permits an investor to enter into an agreement that confers exemption from the business profits tax.

Synopsis In the Maldives, resident individuals are taxed on a territorial basis, while resident partnerships and corporations are taxed on a worldwide basis. Individuals are taxed only on business profits arising from carrying on business in the Maldives. Corporations and partnerships are taxed on all income wherever it is derived and allowed a credit against Maldivian income tax liability for foreign taxes paid. The Business Profit Tax (BPT) is imposed at a flat rate of 15 % (or 0 % on low amounts of profits). Under a special regime, Maldivian offshore financial services centers (which derive income from business outside the Maldives or from certain financial instruments, loans, royalties, or real property outside the Maldives) are taxed a flat rate of 5 % (or 0 % on low amounts of profits).

A company not resident in the Maldives is subject to BPT (at the above rates) on profits attributable to any business carried on in the Maldives that are attributable to a permanent establishment located there. Non-corporate nonresidents are taxable on profits derived from carrying on a business in the Maldives, whether or not though a permanent establishment (e.g., a non-resident auditor that visits a client in the Maldives to perform work), on rents from buildings leased in the Maldives, and on royalties and management fees paid by a resident of the Maldives or through a permanent establishment in the Maldives.

Maldives has no participation exemption. Dividends paid by resident companies to non-residents are not generally subject to BPT. Where the recipient is subject to BPT, the BPT is deducted in computing taxable profits.

K. Holmes (✉)
International Tax Consultant, Wellington, New Zealand
e-mail: drkevinholmes@gmail.com

© Springer International Publishing Switzerland 2017   215
K.B. Brown (ed.), *Taxation and Development - A Comparative Study*,
Ius Comparatum - Global Studies in Comparative Law 21,
DOI 10.1007/978-3-319-42157-5_12

Although the Maldives, formerly a tax haven, does not participate in the OECD's Global Tax Forum, its regime has emerged as one that conforms to internationally accepted standards of taxation.

The Maldives is party to the South Asian Association for Regional Cooperation (SAARC) Limited Multilateral Agreement on Avoidance of Double Taxation and Mutual Administrative Assistance in Tax Matters. This agreement permits information exchange, including exchange of information relating to tax havens or harmful tax regimes if it does not violate internal law or exceed normal administrative mechanisms. The Maldives has concluded its first Tax Information Exchange Agreement (TIEA with India) and expects to conclude future agreements.

In order to attract economic activity to the Maldives, an investor may enter into an agreement under the Law on Foreign Investments that confers an exemption from BPT. These agreements are intended to support investments of importance to the economy, whether to support tourism or non-tourism. Agreements are concluded with foreign governments to facilitate economic and social development. In addition, investment in Special Economic Zones offers tax concessions providing exemptions from BPT as well as temporary exemptions from goods and services tax (GST) and withholding tax.

The Madives is a party to a number of trade and investment agreements.

International Tax System of the Maldives

Until 2011, the Maldives was a tax haven. The Business Profit Tax (BPT) Act (Law No. 5/2011) was enacted on 18 January 2011 and took effect 6 months later, on 18 July 2011. Subject to a *de minimis* threshold, BPT is imposed only on business profits derived in a tax year,[1] whether or not those profits are derived by an individual, company, partnership, association or any other legal person. BPT is levied at a flat rate of 15 %.[2]

Insofar as residents of the Maldives are concerned, the BPT Act is a hybrid of residence jurisdiction taxation and territorial taxation, depending on whether or not a taxable person is a company or a partnership on one hand, or an individual or other taxable person on the other. For non-residents, the BPT Act adopts the principle of source based taxation.

A company is a resident of the Maldives if it is incorporated in the Maldives or, if not incorporated in the Maldives, it has its place of central management and control of its business in the Maldives.[3] Unusually by international norms, a partner-

---

[1] A tax year is the period from 1 January to 31 December (sec. 43(a) BPT Act), although a company must generally calculate its taxable profits on the basis of its accounting period (sec. 8(a)(1) BPT Act).

[2] Sec. 7(b)(2) BPT Act. The first MVR 500,000 (approximately USD 32,500) of taxable profits is subject to tax at 0 %: sec. 7(b)(1) BPT Act.

[3] Sec. 46(d) and (e) BPT Act.

ship, trust or other body of persons is a resident of the Maldives if it carries on any business in the Maldives.[4]

Broadly, an individual is a resident of the Maldives if he or she:

(a) Is actually in the Maldives for 183 days or more in a tax year; or
(b) Arrives in the Maldives in a tax year with the intention of establishing his or her residence in the Maldives; or
(c) Is ordinarily resident in the Maldives in a tax year but leaves before the end of that year.[5]

Taxation of Residents

A company that is a resident of the Maldives is taxed on the "full amount" of the profits which it derives in a tax year, "wherever the profits arise and whether or not they are received in or transmitted to [the] Maldives …"[6] Thus, the Maldives taxes companies on their worldwide profits, including capital gains. This principle is extended to partnerships because the taxable profits of a partnership are to be calculated as if the partnership were a company.[7]

Where double taxation arises, a foreign tax credit is allowed for tax paid in another country subject to a maximum credit of the amount of Maldives tax applicable to the foreign sourced income.[8]

However, individuals and other taxpayers,[9] which are not companies or partnerships,[10] are subject to a territorial system of taxation. They are assessed BPT on taxable profits derived from carrying on any business "in the Maldives."[11] This rule applies to both residents of the Maldives and non-residents.

The difference in tax treatment between resident companies and individuals is a clear breach of the principle of tax neutrality, in that it creates a tax bias in favour of offshore investments and trade carried out by Maldives resident individuals, rather than by Maldives resident companies. No clear policy objective has been enunciated to substantiate this position.

---

[4] Sec. 46(c) BPT Act.

[5] An individual is "ordinarily resident in the Maldives" if he or she is habitually resident in the Maldives except for absences of a temporary nature: sec. 46(b) BPT Act.

[6] Sec. 3(b) BPT Act.

[7] Sec. 5(a)(1) BPT Act. In fact, sec. 5(a)(1) states that the taxable profits of a partnership are to be taxed as if the partnership were a "body corporate". Sec. 43(a) defines a company to mean any body corporate.

[8] Secs. 52 and 53 Tax Administration Act (Law No. 3/2010).

[9] For ease of reading, the remainder of this report shall refer to this group as individuals.

[10] For ease of reading, the remainder of this report shall refer to this group as companies.

[11] Sec. 4(a) BPT Act.

Taxation of Non-residents

Subject to specific rules for rent derived from the lease of immovable property, royalties and management fees,[12] a company that is not a resident of the Maldives is liable to BPT only on its taxable profits that are attributable to any business carried on by the company through a permanent establishment in the Maldives.[13] A "permanent establishment" is defined along the lines of (but not exactly duplicating) the definition of permanent establishment in Article 5(2), (3)(a) and (5) of the United Nations model double tax convention.[14]

However, as observed under section "Taxation of Residents", section 4(a) of the BPT Act imposes BPT simply on taxable profits derived from the Maldives by a non-corporate, non-resident who carries on any business in the Maldives. This test brings greater amounts of Maldives sourced income within the BPT net because business income can be derived in the absence of a permanent establishment, e.g., a non-resident auditor who visits his client's Maldives branch to perform an audit and charges his client for that work, derives business income from the Maldives without having a permanent establishment there. Again, there is no obvious policy reason why corporate non-residents are subject to a more generous liability-to-tax test than non-corporate non-residents.

Concession for Offshore Investment Businesses

In what is apparently an attempt to establish an offshore financial services centre in the Maldives, a concessionary tax rate of 5 % of taxable profits[15] derived from sources outside the Maldives is offered to companies that[16]:

(a) Are registered under the Companies Act of the Republic of Maldives (Law No. 10/96); and
(b) Are not resident of another country; and
(c) Derive income from:

    (i) A business carried on wholly outside the Maldives; or
    (ii) Bonds, shares, debentures, loans or other financial instruments issued by a person that is:

        1. Not a resident of the Maldives; or

---

[12] See under *Foreign corporations* below.

[13] Sec. 3(c)(2) BPT Act.

[14] See secs. 43(e) and (f) BPT Act.

[15] Sec. 7(a)(2) BPT Act. The first MVR 500,000 (approximately USD 32,500) of taxable profits is subject to tax at 0 %: sec. 7(a)(1) BPT Act.

[16] Sec. 2(b) BPT Act.

> 2. A resident of the Maldives, but for the purpose of a capital project car-
>   ried on outside the Maldives; or

(iii) Loans of any nature; or

(iv) Royalties payable by a person that is not a resident of the Maldives; or

 (v) Immovable property that is situated outside the Maldives; and

(d) Do not carry on any business or have any other source of income.

Taxation of Dividends

There is no exemption from BPT for dividends paid to a resident company by wholly or partly owned foreign subsidiary companies. There is no participation exemption for dividends paid from one company to another (foreign or domestic) company. However, Tax Ruling TR-2012/B17 *Business Profit Tax: Treatment of dividend income* allows dividends paid by a resident company and derived by a person (whether a company or individual) that is subject to BPT on the dividend income to be deducted in the calculation of that person's taxable profits.

Tax Havens and Harmful Tax Regimes

The Maldives does not have tax laws designed to discourage investment in tax haven jurisdictions.

Nor does it have tax laws designed to discourage investment in harmful tax regimes. The Maldives is not a party to any agreements to sanction harmful tax regimes nor does it impose penalties against such regimes. Harmful tax regimes are not defined in Maldives law.

International Agreements

The Maldives is a party to only one international tax agreement, the SAARC [South Asian Association for Regional Cooperation] Limited Multilateral Agreement on Avoidance of Double Taxation and Mutual Administrative Assistance in Tax Matters. That agreement does not address unfair competition for capital or discrimination against, or favoring, certain types of investment.

OECD Global Tax Forum

The Maldives participates in the OECD's Global Tax Forum. Its tax regime was transformed in 2011 from a tax haven to one that broadly conforms to internationally acceptable standards of taxation of business profits. As noted in section "Information Exchange Agreements", below, the Maldives has entered into a bilateral tax information exchange agreement with India.

Information Exchange Agreements

As noted in section "International Agreements", above, the Maldives is party to the SAARC Limited Multilateral Agreement on Avoidance of Double Taxation and Mutual Administrative Assistance in Tax Matters, which took effect on 19 May 2010. Article 5 of that agreement provides for the exchange of information between the eight SAARC member states.[17] Article 5(1) provides that information that is approved for exchange under the agreement is:

> such information, including documents and public documents or certified copies thereof, as is necessary for carrying out the provisions of this Agreement or of the domestic laws of the Member States concerning taxes covered by this agreement insofar as the taxation thereunder is not contrary to the Agreement.

Art. 5(2) imposes a limitation on the information to be exchanged under Article 5(1). Article 5(2) states that a member state is not obliged:

(a) To carry out administrative measures at variance with the laws and administrative practices of that or of the other Member State;
(b) To supply information, including documents and public documents or certified copies thereof, which are not obtainable under the laws or in the normal course of the administration of that or of the other Member State;
(c) To supply information which would disclose any trade, business, industrial, commercial or professional secret or trade process, or information, the disclosure of which would be contrary to public policy (ordre public).

The SAARC Agreement empowers a member state to seek information relating to transactions in tax haven jurisdictions or in countries considered to have a harmful tax regime to the extent that the information is held in the other member state, and that the request does not contravene Article 5(2).

The Maldives signed a tax information exchange agreement with India on 11 April 2016.

The above agreements, and future tax information exchange agreements with other countries, are intended to be concluded by treaty.

---

[17] The member states are Afghanistan, Bangladesh, Bhutan, India, the Maldives, Nepal, Pakistan and Sri Lanka.

Tax Incentives for Investment in Emerging and Developing Countries or High-Poverty, High-Income Inequality Countries

The Maldives offers no tax incentives to encourage investment in emerging or developing countries.

It offers no tax incentives to encourage investment in countries with low incomes, high poverty rates or high rates of economic inequality. It is worth noting that the Maldives itself is a country with a high level of economic inequality.[18]

Measures to Attract Economic Activity

Business profits of a person that is a party to an agreement approved under the Law on Foreign Investments in the Republic of Maldives (Law No. 25/79) made after 18 July 2011 are exempt from BPT to the extent that the agreement confers the exemption.[19] That law is intended to facilitate foreign investments of significant value in both the tourism and non-tourism sectors of the Maldives economy, whether or not in collaboration with the Maldives Government, Maldives companies or Maldives nationals.

In addition, from time to time, the Government (or its agencies) enters into agreements with foreign governments (or their agencies) and international organizations to facilitate investment in the Maldives with the aim of enhancing economic and social development. Those agreements often contain tax exemption provisions. If such an agreement imposes obligations on citizens of the Maldives, the agreement does not have legal force in the Maldives until it is approved by the Maldives Parliament.[20]

In 2014, Parliament passed the Special Economic Zones (SEZ) Act (Law No. 24/2014), which gave broad powers to the SEZ Investment Board to permit developers and investors to establish and operate SEZs. A wide range of generous tax concessions offered by the SEZ Act, which overrides the taxing acts, includes:

- Guaranteed incentives to developers of SEZs by way of an unlimited exemption from BPT, and 10-year exemptions from goods and services tax (GST) and withholding tax (WHT)

---

[18] Based on the latest available data, the Gini coefficient for the Maldives is 0.448 and for Male', the capital city (which accounts for approximately one-third of the country's total population), it is 0.636. See Department of National Planning, Ministry of Finance and Treasury, *Household Income & Expenditure Survey – Findings 2009/2010*, at http://planning.gov.mv/hies/HIES2012/FINAL%20HIES%20REPORT%20april%202012.pdf, p. 61.

[19] Sec. 15(b) BPT Act.

[20] Article 115(k)(2) Constitution of the Republic of Maldives 2008.

- Negotiable incentives to developers of SEZs by way of potentially unlimited exemptions from GST, WHT and taxes imposed in connection with the purchase or ownership of land
- Industry based guaranteed tax incentives available to investors, investments and businesses in a SEZ by way of various exemptions from BPT, GST and WHT ranging from 2 to 20 years
- The President granting exemptions from BPT, GST, WHT and taxes related to the purchase of land for potentially unlimited periods to a hotel or tourism project in a SEZ, which assists in regional development.

Tax Amnesties and Tax Holidays

The Maldives has not provided nor is expected to provide a tax amnesty or tax holiday for income from specific types of investments, except for profits from investments that qualify for a BPT exemption by virtue of the Law on Foreign Investments in the Republic of Maldives, any specific agreement between the Maldives Government and a foreign government or international organization which contains a tax exemption article, and tax exemptions provided for under the SEZ regime (each referred to under section "Measures to Attract Economic Activity", above).

Corporate Tax Structure

Domestic Corporations

As noted under section "International Tax System of the Maldives", above, a company that is a resident of the Maldives is subject to BPT at the rate of 15 % on its worldwide annual taxable profits. The first MVR (Maldivian Rufiyaa) 500,000 of taxable profits is taxed at a rate of 0 %.[21] Taxable profits are calculated in the normal way of subtracting deductions allowable under the BPT Act from the company's gross income, which includes capital gains.

Foreign Corporations

Also as noted under section "Taxation of Non-residents", above, a non-resident company is subject to BPT on:

---

[21] Sec. 7(b)(1) BPT Act.

(a) Rent received from the lease of land and buildings in the Maldives[22];
(b) Taxable profits that are attributable to any business carried on by the company through a permanent establishment in the Maldives[23]; and
(c) Royalties and management fees payable by a person who is a resident of the Maldives or by a non-resident person with a permanent establishment in the Maldives, which are not taken into account under (b) above.[24]

The tax rates and calculation of taxable profits are the same as those for a Maldives-resident company.

All commercial banks are exempt from BPT, and are instead subject to a 25 % Bank Profit Tax under the Bank Profit Tax Act (Law No. 9/85).

The following payments made to a non-resident are subject to a final WHT at source at the rate of 10 % of the gross amount of the payment[25]:

(a) Rent, royalties and any other such consideration for the use of plant, machinery, equipment or other property for the purposes of a business;
(b) Payments made for carrying out research and development;
(c) Payments made for the use of computer software;
(d) Payment of fees for management, personal or technical services and any other commission or fee not constituting income from employment;
(e) Payments made in respect of performances by public entertainers;
(f) Rent in respect of the viewing in Maldives of cinematographic films.

Trade and Investment Agreements

Multilateral Trade and Investment Agreements

The Maldives is a party to the South Asian Free Trade Area (SAFTA) Agreement, which came into force on 1 January 2006 (and was a party to its forerunner, the SAARC Preferential Trading Arrangement Agreement (SAPTA)). The objective of the SAFTA Agreement is to reduce tariffs on goods traded in the SAFTA to 0 % by 2016.[26]

As a member of SAARC, the Maldives is also party to the SAARC Agreement on Trade in Services (SATIS), which entered into force on 29 November 2012. The

---

[22] Sec. 3(c)(1) BPT Act.

[23] Sec. 3(c)(2) BPT Act.

[24] Sec. 3(c)(3) BPT Act.

[25] Sec. 6(a) BPT Act.

[26] Least developed countries in the SAFTA (viz. Afghanistan, Bangladesh, Bhutan, the Maldives and Nepal) are permitted to reduce their tariffs at a slower rate than the developing member states (viz. India, Pakistan and Sri Lanka). Four rounds of trade negotiations have been concluded, which have resulted in tariff concessions on a product-by-product basis for more than 5000 commodities.

SATIS is intended to promote and enhance trade in services, and to establish a framework to liberalize, on a "request-and-offer" basis, trade in services between the eight member states.

As a member of the WTO, the Maldives is also party to the General Agreement on Tariffs and Trade (GATT).

Bilateral Trade and Investment Agreements

The Maldives has entered into bilateral trade and investment agreements with China, India and the United States. It has signed an agreement with Qatar and is in negotiations with Sri Lanka.

The trade agreement with India took effect on 31 March 1981. Subject to a number of exceptions, it, in essence, provides for most favoured nation status for each country. This agreement is pending revision.

The Zero Tariff Agreement with China took effect on 1 February 2009. It provides for preferential tariff relief with respect to 278 products.

The Maldives and the United States entered into a Trade and Investment Framework Agreement with effect from 17 October 2009 to monitor trade and investment relations and to identify trading opportunities. The Maldives has also entered into an Investment Incentive Agreement with the United States, with effect from 15 March 2010, under which the United States government agency which supports private sector investment in developing countries (OPIC)[27] provides United States investors in the Maldives with financing, guarantees, political risk insurance and private equity investment fund support.

An agreement on economic, trade and technical cooperation was signed between the Maldives and Qatar on 15 April 2013, and negotiations are currently taking place between the Maldives and Sri Lanka on a cooperation agreement on, *inter alia*, trade, and banking and finance.

---

[27] Overseas Private Investment Corporation.

Chapter 13
Extensive Treaty Network and Unilateral Credits Support Foreign Investment: The Dutch Approach

Raymond H.C. Luja

Abstract Although the Netherlands has a worldwide system of taxation for residents, certain foreign profits are excluded from the tax base by treaty or internal law. The internal law exemption applies to active business income as well as certain passive income subject to a threshold tax rate of at least 10 %. The existing participation exemption removes from the Dutch income tax base certain dividends received from a 5 %-or-more owned foreign or domestic corporation. This participation exemption also encompasses certain gains realized on the sale of stock as well as on the liquidation of the corporation. There is a unilateral credit, available for Dutch recipients of dividends, royalties and interest payments from entities resident in developing counties. The Dutch participation exemption, the unilateral credit for specified investments, and the extensive treaty network provide considerable incentives for investment in developing countries.

Synopsis Although the Netherlands has a worldwide system of international taxation for resident companies, since 2012 foreign business profits and losses are excluded from the tax base either by treaty or under internal law. The exemption relates to profits and losses attributable to a permanent establishment in another state, profits and losses from real estate in the other state, and income from shares held other than as a portfolio investment. The exemption is not allowed where the income derives from ownership in a foreign passive financing company or ownership in a foreign company engaged in portfolio investments which is not subject to an effective rate of tax of at least 10 %. When the exemption does not apply because of the effective-rate-of-tax rule, a limited foreign tax credit may be available to offset Netherlands tax on the income.

A previous version of this chapter was published in Van Vliet, C.S., Netherlands Reports to the 19th International Congress of Comparative Law, Intersentia 2015. The text has been updated until July 2015.

R.H.C. Luja (✉)
Maastricht University, Maastricht, The Netherlands
e-mail: Raymond.Luja@maastrichtuniversity.nl

© Springer International Publishing Switzerland 2017   225
K.B. Brown (ed.), *Taxation and Development - A Comparative Study*,
Ius Comparatum - Global Studies in Comparative Law 21,
DOI 10.1007/978-3-319-42157-5_13

Under a longstanding participation exemption (its predecessors dating back to 1893), resident corporations may exempt from the income tax base any dividends received from a 5 %-or-more owned foreign corporation. Gains and losses on the sale of shares held are also exempt. Profits realized upon liquidation of a subsidiary are covered as well, but losses from such a transaction are allowed in certain circumstances. The participation exemption does not apply if the foreign subsidiary is primarily engaged in passive investments or passive group financing or leasing and is not subject to a minimum level of taxation (an effective tax rate of at least 10 %).

Dutch recipients of dividends, royalties, and interest paid by developing county residents are eligible for a unilateral credit (subject to certain limitations) against Dutch income tax for taxes paid (either a withholding tax or corporate income tax) to entities in these jurisdictions on the income. This credit is available whether or not the payer is resident in a country with a treaty with the Netherlands and amount allowed may be higher than the actual developing country rate. The Dutch corporate tax provides for an "innovation box," subjecting specified income from patents and other research and development to an effective tax burden of 5 %. When the 5 % burden applies, the credit is correspondingly limited.

Regarding exchange of information, Dutch tax administration must spontaneously provide information to treaty partners concerning Dutch entities which are international group financing and licensing companies if they do not meet requirements entitling them to treaty benefits. As a member of the EU, the Netherlands must comply with Directives and Conventions on administrative cooperation, including exchange of information. In addition, it is bound by the EU Code of Conduct and other prohibitions, including the one on provision of state aid, that may limit its ability to offer special tax incentives to invest in developing countries.

The Netherlands is party to approximately 100 bilateral investment and protection agreements.

Because of its participation exemption, the Dutch tax regime offers opportunities to developing countries to attract active business operations (portfolio and passive financial income does not benefit from the regime if not subject to an effective rate of tax of at least 10 %). Additionally, investors may be attracted to the Dutch system because of the approachability of the Dutch tax officials and the ability to obtain legally certain guidance relating to transfer pricing and other transactions in advance. Because of these features, so-called special purpose entities (SPEs) are organized in the Netherlands in order to direct investment into developing countries. It is estimated that developing countries lose substantial revenue in the form of source taxes on dividends and interest because the income is routed through the Netherlands and passed on to parents in third countries lacking an advantageous treaty. This disadvantage is believed to be outweighed by the substantially larger inflow of investment through Dutch SPEs in developing countries that are parties to a treaty with the Netherlands. Partly to remedy any unintended disadvantage to developing countries through treaty-shopping, the Dutch authorities have proposed to negotiate inclusion of limitations of benefits provisions in existing tax treaties with 23 developing countries.

The Dutch Corporate Income Tax System: Relevant Items

Worldwide Income Taxation as a Starting Point

The Dutch corporate income tax has a general tax rate of 25 %.[1] The first €200,000 in taxable profits are subject to a lower rate of 20 %. These rates apply to both foreign and domestic corporations. There are no regional corporate tax rates. No tax holidays are provided.

The Dutch CIT in essence provides for a system of worldwide income taxation of resident companies. However, as of 2012, foreign profits and losses by resident companies are excluded from the corporate income tax base if certain conditions are met. The exclusions apply on the following basis[2]:

– In case of a tax treaty with another state (or an agreement reached with the Caribbean countries that are part of the Kingdom of the Netherlands: Aruba, Curaçao and Sint Maarten)[3]: an exclusion of any profits and losses attributable to a permanent establishment in that other state, an exclusion of any profits and losses from real estate in that other state and an exclusion of other profits and related losses attributed to the other state in the treaty (or agreement). These exclusions are granted only if a full tax exemption has been agreed upon regarding these sources of income.
– In the absence of a treaty (or agreement): an exclusion of any profits and losses attributable to a permanent establishment in that other state, an exclusion of any profits and losses from real estate in that other state and an exclusion of income from shares in companies whose place of effective management is based in the other state, except for portfolio investments.

As a result of these exclusions for profits derived in another state, that state determines the tax base and tax rate applicable to those profits within the limits of its tax sovereignty. Unless otherwise provided by a tax treaty, the aforementioned exemptions are not allowed in situations of a 5 % or greater participation in a foreign company engaged in portfolio investments or a passive group financing company if they are not subject to an effective tax burden of at least 10 %. The effective rate is

---

[1] The relevant taxes are the "Wet inkomstenbelasting 2001" (hereinafter: the personal income tax or PIT) and the "Wet op de vennootschapsbelasting 1969" (hereinafter: the corporate income tax or CIT). As this contribution is primarily concerned with the inflow of income from developing countries, the dividend withholding tax will not be addressed.

[2] Article 15e CIT.

[3] Until 2010 the Kingdom of the Netherlands consisted of three countries: the Netherlands, the Netherlands Antilles and Aruba (which got a status apart in 1986). As of 10 October 2010 the Netherlands Antilles have been dissolved. Now Curaçao and Sint Maarten are considered to be separate countries within the Kingdom as well. The remaining Caribbean islands (Bonaire, Saba and Sint Eustatius) have become 'special' (oversees) municipalities of the Netherlands (the so-called BES-islands), albeit with a somewhat different tax regime. The tax system discussed in this contribution will be that of the Netherlands mainland.

determined using Dutch tax base principles, although minor differences are disre-
garded. In case the foreign tax base and the Dutch tax base have serious disparities,
such as the possibility to deduct profit distributions in the other country or the
absence of anti-abuse provisions in respect of interest deductions, a calculation
must be made or other proof must be provided to show that the effective tax burden
would still be at a minimum of 10 %. A nominal tax rate of less than 10 % would
not necessarily disqualify the foreign regime if the tax base is broader.

If the effective tax burden is less than 10 % there is no exclusion from the tax
base.[4] However, a tax credit would be allowed for the lowest of (a) 5 % of the non-
excluded income, or, alternatively, the amount of foreign tax actually paid, (b) a pro
rata part of the corporate income tax due, or (c) total corporate income tax due after
avoidance of double taxation and the participation credit (see section "The
Participation Exemption", below).[5]

The Participation Exemption

The Dutch have known some sort of participation exemption since 1893. The current participation exemption ('Deelnemingsvrijstelling') provides for a full exemption of profits and losses resulting from a 5 % or greater participation in both foreign
and domestic subsidiaries.[6] This exemption covers both dividends (and other forms
of distribution of profits) as well as any gains and losses upon the sale of shares.[7] It
does not cover any other profits from business activities carried out in relation to a
subsidiary (such as income from sales, interest, royalties and the like).

While profits realized upon liquidation of a foreign subsidiary would be exempt
as well, losses could be deductible subject to a number of restrictions.[8] For instance,
an adjustment to the loss will be made for any dividend or informal profit distribution to the shareholders prior to liquidation in the previous 5–10 years.[9] Furthermore,
any such loss deduction is postponed in case the business activity of the liquidated
subsidiary is continued by another related company. ("Related," in this context,
means a parent company either holding a direct or indirect share amounting to one
third of the total, a subsidiary in which one third of the shares is held, or a sister

---

[4] Articles 15e, para. 7, 15g and 15h CIT.

[5] Article 23d CIT.

[6] Article 13 CIT.

[7] By excluding capital gains and losses from qualifying participations, the Dutch exemption goes
beyond what is required by the EU's Parent-Subsidiary Directive (Council Directive 2011/96/EU
of 30 November 2011, Official Journal of the European Union (OJ) L 345/8 of 29 December
2011).

[8] Article 13d CIT.

[9] As an anti-abuse rule, any losses at the level of the subsidiary being liquidated resulting from
changes in the value of a sub-subsidiary will not be deductible in case the participation in the latter
is being transferred to the parent upon liquidation.

company that has a common parent that directly or indirectly holds one third of shares in both.)

The participation exemption may also extend to income from certain profit participating loans that are treated as equity for Dutch tax purposes, in case a related company holds a qualifying participation in a debtor. Upon request, profits and losses resulting from exchange rate hedges of the value of the subsidiary can be brought within the scope of the exemption as well. If a participation drops below 5 % there is a phase-out period of 3 years and any later profits and losses from an earn-out arrangement would be covered by the participation exemption as well.

By and large, the participation exemption will not apply to subsidiaries that are themselves primarily engaged in portfolio investments or passive group financing and/or leasing activities when they are not subject to effective taxation abroad (see section "Worldwide Income Taxation as a Starting Point" above). If the effective tax burden is less than 10 % there will be a switch-over at the time of the actual income distribution and the aforementioned foreign income will not be excluded from the tax base, but rather grossed-up by a factor 100/95.[10] However, a tax credit would then be possible in the amount of (a) 5 % of the non-excluded income, (b) a pro rata part of the corporate income tax due, or (c) total corporate income tax due after avoidance of double taxation, whichever is less.[11]

The participation exemption is part of the Dutch corporate income tax. It does not apply to any participation held by a natural person as part of his business activity. The income from participating in a subsidiary by a (self-employed) entrepreneur or by a partner in a business partnership is taxed in the personal income tax (see section "Spontaneous Exchange of Information").

Unilateral Tax Credit Scheme for Developing Country Dividends, Royalties and Interest

The Dutch have an extensive tax treaty network covering nearly 90 countries (excluding treaties limited to information exchange, better known as TIEAs and treaties limited to airlines). Furthermore, a unilateral regulation is in place to avoid double taxation in the absence of a treaty. As income attributable to foreign permanent establishments has already been excluded from the corporate income tax base as of 2012, this regulation is only relevant as far as dividends, interest and royalties that are included in the Dutch corporate income tax base are concerned.

If the distributor of the dividend or the obligor for the interest or royalty is based in a developing country, a tax credit will be allowed against Dutch corporate income

---

[10] Article 13aa CIT.

[11] Article 23c CIT. For EU subsidiaries and subsidiaries from certain EEA countries factor (a) can be replaced by the tax actually paid abroad, in case the EU's Parent-Subsidiary directive applies.

tax.[12] The following countries have been designated as developing countries for the purpose of this credit:

> Afghanistan, Algeria, Angola, Belize, Benin, Bhutan, Bolivia, Botswana, Burkina Faso, Burundi, Cambodia, the Republic of Cameroon, Cape Verde, the Central African Republic, Chad, Colombia, the Comoros, the Republic of the Congo, the Democratic Republic of the Congo, Costa Rica, the Republic of Côte d'Ivoire, Cuba, Djibouti, Dominica, the Dominican Republic, Ecuador, El Salvador, Equatorial Guinea, Eritrea, Ethiopia, Fiji, Gambia, Grenada, Guatemala, Guinea, Guinea-Bissau, Guyana, Haiti, Honduras, Iraq, Iran, Jamaica, Kenya, Kiribati, Laos, Lesotho, Lebanon, Liberia, Madagascar, Malawi, the Maldives, Mali, the Marshall Islands, Mauritania, Micronesia, Mongolia, Mozambique, Myanmar, Namibia, Nepal, Nicaragua, Niger, North Korea, the Palau Islands, the territories governed by the Palestinian Authority, Papua New Guinea, Paraguay, Peru, Ruanda, St. Vincent and the Grenadines, the Solomon Islands, São Tomé and Príncipe, Senegal, Sierra Leone, Sudan, Somalia, Swaziland, Syria, Tanzania, Togo, Tonga, Tuvalu, Vanuatu, West Samoa, South Sudan, Yemen.[13]

The maximum credit is the lowest of (a) the tax levied in the developing country, with a maximum of 15 % in case of dividends, (b) the dividends/interest/royalties received minus related costs, multiplied by 25 % (the current Dutch maximum corporate income tax rate), or (c) the total corporate income tax due in the Netherlands in a given year.[14] The qualifying foreign tax may either be a classical source tax or any other tax on corporate income/profit actually including the dividends, interests and/or royalties in the tax base. No credit is given if the recipient of the relevant income is not the beneficial owner.

The Dutch corporate income tax provides for an innovation box, which allows certain income from patents and other research and development (R&D) activities to be taxed effectively at 5 %.[15] Any royalties received from developing countries will, therefore, only be credited at 5 % if included in the innovation box (and not at 25 % as described in (b) of the preceding paragraph).[16]

If, as a result of either (b) or (c) the foreign tax levied cannot be fully credited, the residual amount can be carried forward and considered under (a) in the second preceding paragraph in the next year.[17] A Dutch tax payer could opt out of the unilateral credit and be allowed to deduct its foreign tax as costs from its Dutch tax base.

---

[12] For developing countries only, any compensation for the rendering of technical services in-country will be considered to be a royalty for the purpose of this credit.

[13] Article 6 Besluit voorkoming dubbele belasting 2001 (the "Double Tax Avoidance Decree of 2001").

[14] Article 36 para. 6 Besluit voorkoming dubbele belasting.

[15] Article 12b CIT. Only 5/25th of qualifying income will be included in the tax base and taxed at a maximum of 25 %. As costs of R&D will first be fully deductible at 25 % qualifying income will first be taxed regularly at 25 % to recapture these costs before the reduced tax base kicks in.

[16] Article 36a para. 2 Besluit voorkoming dubbele belasting.

[17] Article 37 Besluit voorkoming dubbele belasting.

Apart from the special unilateral tax credit mentioned above, no other specific tax incentives are offered for investment in developing countries or in low income countries.

Spontaneous Exchange of Information

The Dutch tax authorities are required to engage in spontaneous exchange of information to treaty partners if Dutch entities whose main activity is to receive interest, rent, royalties and lease income from foreign group companies (i.e. international group financing and licensing companies) do not meet minimum substance requirements entitling them to treaty benefits. This is done in order to enable the treaty partner to determine whether, for instance, a reduction of withholding tax should be awarded. The (cumulative) substance requirements have been revised as of 1 January 2014 and are as follows[18]:

– At least half of the statutory board members who are allowed to vote must reside in the Netherlands or be actually established there.
– These board members must have the necessary professional knowledge to perform their duties. These duties include the power to decide on transactions and the handling thereof.
– The entity has qualified personnel to implement and register the aforementioned transactions.
– Management decisions are being taken in the Netherlands.
– The principal bank accounts must be in the Netherlands and the company's books must be kept there.
– The business address of the entity must be in the Netherlands.
– To the best of its knowledge, the entity must not be considered to be a resident for tax purposes in another country.
– The taxpayer must run actual risks in relation to its financing and contracts in respect to interest, royalties, rents and lease terms payable and receivable and have at least an amount of equity necessary to perform those activities that is appropriate in light of those real risks.

---

[18] See Article 3a Uitvoeringsbesluit internationale bijstandsverlening. (Translation provided by the author may not necessarily be accurate in every detail.) This rule also applies in relation to EU Member States in cases in which the EU's Interest and Royalty Directive is to be applied (Council Directive 2003/49/EC of 3 June 2003, OJ L 157/49 of 26 June 2003).

The Dutch Personal Income Tax System

The Dutch personal income tax system is schedular in nature.[19] Investment in businesses abroad by natural persons, such as acquiring shares in foreign entities, will be taxable in one of three boxes. The PIT is also based on the world wide income tax principle.

Box 1: Income from Business, Employment, Pensions and Primary Dwellings

"Box I" includes income from business, employment, pensions, and imputed income from primary dwellings, which is subject to rates ranging from 36.25 % to 52 %. Any income from business investment by a natural person as an entrepreneur or as a partner in a business partnership, such as the establishment of a (non-incorporated) company or partnership abroad (or a permanent establishment thereof) or by participating in a foreign subsidiary, will fall in this box. Any profits and losses attributable to the foreign company or a permanent establishment are included in box I, as are any distributed profits and realized capital gains and losses from foreign participations, subject to a maximum effective tax burden of 44.72 %.[20]

Under box I, in the case of a tax treaty, there is normally a pro rata exemption of foreign business/PE-income after it has first been included in the tax base to determine the applicable tax rate (unless the treaty specifically prohibits the latter). In the absence of a treaty, a unilateral tax exemption nonetheless may apply.[21]

Box 2: Income from Substantial Participations

For natural persons who, not being entrepreneurs themselves, hold a 5 % or greater participation, any distributed profits or realized capital gains and losses are subject to a tax rate of 25 % in "box II." In case of a participation in a foreign company (or in a domestic tax-exempt investment company) it is assumed that a dividend has been paid of at least 4 % of the value of the shares at the beginning of the taxable year.[22] The latter, however, does not apply to listed banks, insurance companies, to companies not primarily engaged in portfolio investments, or to companies subject to effective taxation abroad.

---

[19] Generally available tax credits are not considered in this paragraph.

[20] While the maximum tax rate is set at 52 %, the maximum effective tax burden will be 44.72 % due to a 14 % deduction allowed for entrepreneurial profits by (near) full-time entrepreneurs.

[21] Article 9 para. 1(a) Besluit voorkoming dubbele belasting 2001.

[22] Article 4.14 PIT.

Box 3: Income from Savings and (Portfolio) Investments

Any income from private investment in businesses abroad and any non-entrepreneurial shareholdings of less than 5 % will be taxed in box III at the rate of 30 %. This box covers income from savings, real estate (other than primary dwellings) and any (non-substantial) investments. The tax base consists of an assumed income of 4 % of the value of asset at the beginning of the taxable year. Actual distributions or realized capital gains are not taken into account for the latter determination.[23] This 'box III' tax effectively results in a 1.2 % tax (30 % of 4 %) on the value of assets, such as shares, but for Dutch tax (treaty) purposes it is treated as an income tax instead of a tax on capital.

Until 2013 an exemption of up to €56,420 per adult taxpayer was available for 'social-ethical' portfolio investments into developing countries, meaning that this amount would not be included in the tax base and hence not be subject to the 1.2 % tax. Qualifying investments were those aimed at improving food safety and food production, stimulating social and cultural development and/or improving economic development, employment, and regional development in those countries. In addition to this exemption from box III, a 0.7 % tax credit was available related to the value of qualifying investments (not actual income) until 2013 as well.[24]

Unilateral Tax Credit Scheme for Developing Country Dividends, Royalties and Interest

In the absence of a tax treaty, a unilateral tax credit is provided to individuals subject to the personal income tax, if they receive qualifying income from dividends, interest and/or royalties from developing countries.[25] Their maximum credit is the lowest of (a) the tax levied in the developing country, with a maximum of 15 % in case of dividends and – in case of portfolio income in box III – interest and royalties as well, (b) a pro rata part of the Dutch income tax due in respect of dividends/interest/royalties received minus related costs, or (c) the total personal income tax due in the Netherlands in a given year in respect of the box concerned.[26]

---

[23] The first €21,139 of capital will not be included in this calculation (Article 5.5 PIT).

[24] The combined total tax benefit of the exemption and the credit would have amounted to a maximum of €1072 per person per year.

[25] For a list of qualifying developing countries, see section "Unilateral Tax Credit Scheme for Developing Country Dividends, Royalties and Interest" above.

[26] Articles 15, 19 and 25 Besluit voorkoming dubbele belasting.

Tax Havens

No specific tax provisions have been put in place to discourage investments in tax haven jurisdictions or in harmful tax regimes apart from the limitations described in section "Spontaneous Exchange of Information" above. For corporate income tax purposes no CFC legislation is in force. The idea is that as far as local activities are concerned it is for the relevant country to determine an appropriate level of domestic taxation.[27] While the Netherlands has an extensive tax treaty network, it has not, for obvious reasons, concluded treaties with tax havens, except TIEAs.

Non-tax Agreements

The Netherlands is one of the founding members of the European Union. As such, it is fully subject to the EU's restrictions on (fiscal) state aid and it is bound by the Code of Conduct on Business Taxation. Within the EU, the freedom of capital (Article 63 TFEU) would effectively not allow for the introduction of new restrictions on investments into or payments made to other Member States of the EU or third countries. While there may be a difference in treatment of resident and non-resident taxpayers and of domestic and foreign investment, that difference should not be a means of arbitrary discrimination or a covert restriction on foreign investment.[28]

Because it is an EU Member, the EU's Directive on administrative cooperation in the field of taxation is applicable.[29] The latter provides for an exchange of information upon request among EU Member States and spontaneous exchange of information in particular circumstances in addition to automatic exchange of information (as of 2014) for certain sources of income to the extent the information is available to domestic tax authorities. Within the EU the Netherlands also exchanges information on private savings based on the EU's Savings Directive.[30]

Tax incentives that would be targeted at multinationals only – requiring activities in multiple countries or continents – would likely violate the EU's state aid prohibition. In theory special tax incentives offered to stimulate investment in particular developing countries could come within the scope of this prohibition and there is

---

[27] If there were investment from or via a tax haven into the Netherlands, such as the provisions of loans, extensive anti-abuse provisions would apply to protect the Dutch tax base from excessive debt financing. As this report concerns outgoing investments, these issues will not be touched upon.

[28] In respect of dealings with developing countries, financial sanctions and national security issues could construe an exemption to the freedom of capital, albeit that it is unlikely that those would be put into effect through the tax system.

[29] Council Directive 2011/16/EU of 15 February 2011, OJ L 64/1 of 11 March 2011 (as amended).

[30] Council Directive 2003/48/EC of 3 June 2003, OJ L 157/38 of 26 June 2003 (as amended). This Directive will be withdrawn as of 2016 and be replaced by automatic exchange of information obligations to be included in the aforementioned administrative corporation directive.

very little leeway under current rules to get special permission from the European Commission.

As an OECD Member, the Netherlands also participates in the Global Tax Forum. The Netherlands has signed about 30 TIEAs (Tax Information Exchange Agreements) in addition to its full tax treaties. It is also a signatory to the Multilateral Convention on Mutual Administrative Assistance in Tax Matters (as amended by the 2010 Protocol). By law a regulation was enacted to avoid double taxation among the four countries of the Kingdom of the Netherlands, as no treaty can be signed amongst them.[31]

The Netherlands has signed nearly 100 bilateral investment (protection) agreements, and it is a Member of the World Trade Organization. As an EU Member it is also bound to any trade agreements signed on behalf of the EU. The Dutch model agreement contains the following most favoured nation (MFN) provision:

Article 4

With respect to taxes, fees, charges and to fiscal deductions and exemptions, each Contracting Party shall accord to nationals of the other Contracting Party who are engaged in any economic activity in its territory, treatment not less favourable than that accorded to its own nationals or to those of any third State who are in the same circumstances, whichever is more favourable to the nationals concerned. For this purpose, however, any special fiscal advantages accorded by that Party, shall not be taken into account:

(a) *under an agreement for the avoidance of double taxation; or*
(b) *by virtue of its participation in a customs union, economic union or similar institution; or*
(c) *on the basis of reciprocity with a third State.*

Bilateral investment (protection) agreements have been signed with the following countries[32]:

Albania, Algeria, Argentina, Armenia, Bahrain, Bangladesh, Belarus, Belize, Benin, Bolivia (terminated), Bosnia-Herzegovina, Brazil (not yet ratified by Brazil), Bulgaria, Burkina Faso, Burundi, Cambodia, Cameroon, Cape Verde, Chile (not yet ratified by Chile), (People's Republic of) China, Costa Rica, Côte d'Ivoire, Croatia, Cuba, Czechia, Dominican Republic, Ecuador, Egypt, El Salvador, Eritrea (not yet ratified by Eritrea), Estonia, Ethiopia, Gambia, Georgia, Ghana, Guatemala, Honduras, Hong Kong, Hungary, India, Indonesia, Jamaica, Jordan, Kazakhstan, Kenya, (South) Korea, Kuwait, Laos, Latvia, Lebanon, Lithuania, Macau, (Former Yugoslav Republic of) Macedonia, Malawi, Malaysia, Mali, Malta, Mexico, Moldova, Mongolia, Montenegro, Morocco, Mozambique, Namibia, Nicaragua, Nigeria, Oman, Pakistan, Panama, Paraguay, Peru, Philippines, Poland, Romania, Russian Federation, Senegal, Serbia, Singapore, Slovakia, Slovenia, South Africa (terminated), Sri Lanka, Sudan, Suriname, Tajikistan, Tanzania, Thailand, Tunisia, Turkey, Uganda, Ukraine, Uruguay, Uzbekistan, Venezuela (terminated), Vietnam, Yemen, Zambia, Zimbabwe.

---

[31] This "Belastingregeling voor het Koninkrijk" (Tax regulation for the Kingdom) will gradually be replaced by "bilateral" agreements between the different countries of the Kingdom.

[32] Translation of a list provided for by the Dutch Government at:
http://www.rijksoverheid.nl/onderwerpen/internationaal-ondernemen/documenten-en-publicaties/rapporten/2010/02/22/ibo-landenlijst.html. The agreements terminated by Bolivia, Venezuela and South Africa will still apply for a period of 15 years to grandfathered investments done prior to 1 November 2009, 1 November 2008 and 1 May 2014 respectively.

Conclusion and Ongoing Developments

In essence the Dutch tax system would not hinder developing countries from creating an attractive tax regime aimed at substantial foreign direct investment by or via Dutch companies as long as active companies are concerned. In the case of portfolio investments and passive financing activities not meeting the effective taxation-test (requiring a tax burden of at least 10 % under Dutch standards), the Dutch regime does impose limits. Apart from its extensive tax treaty network and the broad participation exemption, the Dutch tax regime is also attractive because of the approachability of the Dutch tax authorities and its extensive APA/ATR practice, providing legal certainty in advance, within the limits of the law, essentially in accordance with the OECD transfer pricing guidelines.[33]

Given the attractiveness of the Dutch tax climate, the Netherlands is frequently used to locate special purpose entities (SPEs) to reroute investments into developing countries because of treaty entitlement to lower source taxes. According to a 2013 estimate from a study commissioned by the Policy and Operations Evaluation Department of the Dutch Ministry of Foreign Affairs developing countries, as a group, lose about €0.5 billion a year in source taxes on dividends and interest due to income that is routed through the Netherlands and passed on to third countries parents (which did not have an advantageous treaty entitlement in their own right).[34] This amount should be put into perspective, however. One report estimates the total inward FDI into developing countries via Dutch SPE's to amount to €72 billion (2007), of which €53 billion goes to developing countries that concluded a tax treaty with the Netherlands. Of this latter amount, only €1 billion was found to be of direct Dutch origin according to this report.[35] This raises the question whether similar levels of direct FDI would have been realized without the interposing of Dutch SPEs, which is open to speculation.

Partially in response to this, in 2014 the Dutch government approached 23 developing countries to include anti-avoidance provisions like limitation of benefits (LOB) provisions in existing tax treaties. As of mid-2015, agreements have been reached with Ethiopia, Ghana, Malawi, Kenia and Zambia and negotiations have been or will shortly be initiated with Bangladesh, Egypt, Kyrgyzstan, Pakistan and Morocco.[36] Next to this, ongoing efforts to help develop tax administrations in

[33] While individual details of advanced pricing agreements and advanced tax rulings cannot be made public by the tax authorities due to tax secrecy provisions, the addressee of such agreement or ruling is at liberty to do so.

[34] See F. Weyzig, IOB Study 386, Evaluation issues in financing for development: Analyzing the effects on Dutch corporate tax policy on developing countries, 2013, available at http://www.iob-evaluatie.nl/belastingbeleid_studie. This report uses an average of four reports issued in the Netherlands on this topic in 2013.

[35] In comparison, total FDI worldwide through Dutch SPE's is estimated to be about €1.533 billion (2007), of which €96 Billion in capital directly originates from the Netherlands. For all data referred to, see F. Weyzig, Tax treaty shopping: structural determinants of Foreign Direct Investment routed through the Netherlands, *International Tax and Public Finance*, vol. 20 (2013), no. 6, pp. 910–937, para. 3.

[36] Letter to parliament by the Secretary of Finance of 20 April 2015, IZV/2015/292. It should be noted that for the purpose of the unilateral tax credit Bangladesh, Egypt, Ghana, Kirghizia,

selected developing countries have been intensified and the Dutch tax authorities will participate in the OECD's Tax Inspectors without Borders Initiative that was announced in July 2015; it previously ran a pilot with Ghana in 2014.[37]

It should be noted that the Dutch tax system is likely to change as a result of EU initiatives introducing anti-tax-avoidance rules in several of its Directives, including the Parent-Subsidiary Directive covering the participation exemption and the Interest and Royalty Directive. There are also plans to introduce somewhat harmonised anti-tax-avoidance rules in national corporate tax codes across the EU. All of these may affect the Dutch tax system in the years to come once adopted.

Pakistan, Morocco and Zambia have not been designated as developing countries, although they are treated as such for the purpose of this government effort (see section "Unilateral Tax Credit Scheme for Developing Country Dividends, Royalties and Interest").

[37] See http://www.oecd.org/tax/taxinspectors.htm and a letter to parliament by the Minister of Foreign Trade and Development and the Secretary of Finance of 19 September 2014, ENV-2014.8052.

Chapter 14
Tax Incentives in the System of Direct Taxes in Poland

Włodzimierz Nykiel and Michał Wilk

Abstract As a member of the EU and the OECD Global Forum, Poland has moved to bring its tax system in line with internationally accepted standards. This has caused it to abolish tax sparing provisions in tax treaties, update exchange of information provisions, and draft new anti-tax avoidance rules. It is party to a robust network of information exchange agreements with tax administrations, including those viewed as tax havens. These developments raise the question whether Poland's attractiveness as an investment destination will diminish. As it transitioned to a free market system, Poland adopted a number of tax incentives designed to attract foreign investment. These relate primarily to the areas of research and development, accelerated depreciation allowances and support for new businesses.

Synopsis Following the majority, Poland taxes its resident companies on their worldwide income. Companies are resident if their effective place of management is in Poland. A credit for foreign taxes paid helps to alleviate the potential for double taxation when another country also subjects the income to taxation. The credit may not exceed the Polish tax liability on the foreign source income. Nonresidents are taxed on only income from Polish sources.

Dividends from foreign sources are taxed at the regular corporate tax rate of 19 % that applies to other income. Where a subsidiary is at least 75 %-owned, the Polish company may receive a credit for any taxes paid by the subsidiary on the profits distributed. A 19 % withholding tax applies to dividends paid by Polish companies unless a tax treaty provides otherwise.

Poland has entered into more than 90 tax treaties which follow either the OECD or UN Model treaties. The treaties contain both the exemption and tax credit methods. In the case of dividends received by Polish residents, for example, treaties either exempt the foreign source payment (e.g., Malaysia and Ireland) or provide for a reduced withholding tax rate. Poland is in the process of renegotiating treaties that provided a tax-sparing credit, believing that these were used improperly for tax avoidance purposes.

W. Nykiel (✉) • M. Wilk
University of Łódź, Łódź, Poland
e-mail: wnykiel@uni.lodz.pl; mwilk@uni.lodz.pl

© Springer International Publishing Switzerland 2017
K.B. Brown (ed.), *Taxation and Development - A Comparative Study*,
Ius Comparatum - Global Studies in Comparative Law 21,
DOI 10.1007/978-3-319-42157-5_14

239

In legislation following the EU's Parent-Subsidiary Directive, dividends received from companies resident in the EU, EEA, or Switzerland are exempt from Polish tax, if a minimum level of shareholding is met. To qualify for the exemption, shares must be held for at least 2 years before the distribution and the subsidiary must be subject to tax in the relevant jurisdiction on a worldwide basis.

There is a special regime for transactions with resident of countries deemed to be engaged in harmful tax competition. Under these rules, special documentation is required concerning transfer pricing. The Minister of Finance determines which tax regimes are "harmful," a term not defined in the legislation, and publishes that list. Thirty-seven countries, many of which are developing countries, appear on the list.

As a member of the EU and of the OECD Global Form, Poland has moved to bring its tax system in line with accepted standards. This has caused it to pursue new tax policy initiatives, including renegotiating tax treaties to abolish tax sparing, updating exchange of information provisions, attempting to close loopholes in its tax system, and drafting new anti-tax avoidance rules (in the form of a General Anti-Abuse Rule or GAAR) and Controlled Foreign Corporation (CFC) legislation. These developments raise the question whether these changes will have the effect of reducing Poland's attractiveness as an investment location. Addition of complexity into Poland tax regime and administration may make doing business in Poland less desirable. Introduction of CFC rules may decrease a competitive advantage now held by Polish investors.

Poland is a party to a robust network of information exchange on bilateral and multilateral fronts. It is also engaged in a campaign to expand information exchange with countries viewed as tax havens, having concluded information exchange agreements with Bahamas, Liberia, Isle of Man, Jersey, Guernsey, Belize, Andorra, Dominica, and others. Legislation has opened the door to exchange of information normally protected by bank secrecy laws.

As it transitioned from a socialist to a free market system, Poland adopted a number of tax incentives designed to attract foreign investment. These include special deductions for research and development centers, tax exemptions for investment in special underdeveloped economic zones, accelerated depreciation deductions for investments in certain assets, and temporary tax holiday for new businesses. While these measures are important tools to enable Poland to attract investment, they are viable only so long as they do not violate EU restrictions on State Aid.

Poland is a party to more than 60 bilateral trade and investment agreements.

Introduction

Concerning the impact of taxes on economic development, tax policy supports two alternative models of the construction of tax systems. One approach favors state intervention, which may serve different objectives, among others – the development of the economy. The other model assumes indifference of the state towards non-fiscal objectives of tax law. Leaving aside that dispute, which seems to be of a rather political and ideological nature concerning mainly the conflict between opposing values and political doctrines, one may observe that in contemporary tax law systems, when the state is faced with aggressive competition from other economies, implementation of certain measures to increase investment attractiveness is commonly accepted.

An intensity of state intervention in the area of investment incentives may lead to harmful tax competition and tax havens on the edge which distort fair competition between economies and disturb fair allocation of income. On the other hand, a certain degree of state aid and investment incentives should be acceptable, especially when practiced by developing countries and countries in transition. In this chapter we assess the tax system in Poland as a whole and offer details concerning tax incentives in the light of an acceptable level of state intervention. This chapter covers only income taxation. Indirect taxes are not considered.

Polish Income Tax System: Overview

Co-existence of Source and Residence Principles

Polish income tax system is based on a general distinction between corporate and personal income taxation. Therefore, there are two separate legal acts that cover income taxation in Poland: the Corporate Income Tax Act (CIT)[1] and the Personal Income Tax Act (PIT).[2] Both systems are built on parallel application of residence and source principles.

Basically companies that meet residence test are subject to unlimited taxation on their worldwide income (residence principle). By contrast, non-resident taxpayers are taxable only with regard to income derived from Polish sources (source principle). Residence criteria in Polish domestic CIT regulations are set forth in Art. 3 of the CIT. Under that provision the key determinants of resident status of a company are seat or place of management. While is there is no legal definition of those terms, it is helpful to determine the seat of a company by reference to the provisions of the Commercial Companies Code.[3] Place of management of the company is to be construed similarly to the place of effective management concept laid down by the OECD Model Tax Convention. Thus, it is a place from which the day-to-day management of the company is carried out.

The same principles apply to individual taxation, but the PIT applies different criteria for residence. A person is deemed a Polish resident when his or her centre of personal or economic interests (centre of vital interests) is in Poland or he or she stays in the territory of Poland for over 183 days in a given tax year.

---

[1] Journal of Laws 2011, no. 74, item 397, as amended, hereinafter: the CIT Act.

[2] Journal of Laws 2012, item 361, as amended, hereinafter: the PIT Act.

[3] Journal of Laws 2013, item 1030.

Above-mentioned principles apply unless a tax treaty provides otherwise (which may be the case in particular when there is a dual residence conflict and tie-breaker rules from the treaty must be applied).

In principle when a non-resident taxpayer carries out business activity in Poland through a branch it is subject to tax in the same manner as a Polish resident. Where there is a treaty concluded between Poland and a residence state of that taxpayer, normally Art. 7 of the treaty allocates business profits derived by that taxpayer to Poland.

Parallel application of residence principle in Poland and source principle in the country where Polish resident derives income may cause juridical double taxation. Hence there is a need for implementing regulations aimed at avoidance of that detrimental phenomenon. In Poland such mechanisms are applied at three levels: domestic, international and EU.

Taxation of Inbound Dividends

Dividends derived by Polish companies from foreign sources, in principle, are combined with other worldwide income and subject to 19 % tax. Global income is then declared in a yearly tax return and payable at the end of the third month following the end of a given fiscal year.

As mentioned above there are three different layers of instruments for avoiding double taxation of dividends: unilateral, bilateral and EU. Under the general rule, Polish residents deriving income from inbound dividends are allowed to subtract tax withheld at source from tax on their worldwide income, but the amount of the reduction may not exceed that part of tax calculated which is proportionally associated with foreign income (ordinary tax credit). A similar principle applies to individuals deriving foreign income.

Under CIT, there is also a specific regulation which aims at avoiding economic double taxation. Under Art. 20(2) of the CIT, a Polish resident company deriving dividend income from a subsidiary (75 % threshold of shareholding level is required) subject to tax on its worldwide income in the territory of a state bound by a tax treaty with Poland which is not an EU, EEA Member State, or Switzerland may also reduce the amount of tax on profits out of which the dividends were paid. The amount of that reduction depends on the level of share ownership by the parent company in the profits of its subsidiary.

Apart from unilateral measures for double taxation avoidance an international tax law regime should be considered. Poland has entered into 91 tax treaties that generally follow either the OECD or UN Model Tax Convention or contain a mixture of provisions. As for tax relief, Polish tax policy does not prefer any specific method for avoidance of double taxation. In Polish treaties, both exemption (mainly with progression) and credit (ordinary) methods are applied. Some treaties use the tax sparing credit for income derived by Polish residents from foreign sources, however, current tax policy tends to favor renegotiating such treaties in order to abolish that method of avoiding double taxation.[4] Such treaties, in the view of the Ministry of Finance, were improperly used for tax avoidance.

The regulation concerning allocation of dividend income in Polish tax treaties in general follows Art. 10 of the OECD Model Convention (MC). There are, however, certain differences in dividend taxation when compared to that provision which pertain to tax rates (one uniform rate instead of two rates, except an exemption at source in tax treaties with Malaysia and Ireland under certain conditions),[5] reliance on voting rights rather than holding of shares (treaties with Ireland and the USA – the "old" treaty of 1974),[6] and the absence of a beneficial ownership clause (e.g., treaties with Russia, Spain, Pakistan, Sri Lanka and the "old" treaty with the USA). In the treaty with Singapore dividends are exempt from tax at source if paid to the government of other contracting state.

Being a Member of EU, Poland was required to implement the Parent-Subsidiary Directive which affects the system of dividend taxation to a great extent. Dividends paid out by companies based in one of the EU or EEA Member States or Switzerland to a Polish company are exempt from tax in Poland if the shareholding level exceeds 10% (25% for dividends from an entity resident in Switzerland) and the subsidiary paying out dividends does not enjoy any general exemption from tax on worldwide income. Shares in the foreign company must be held for an uninterrupted period of at least 2 years after the dividend is paid.

Outbound Dividends

Dividends paid out by Polish companies to non-resident shareholders are subject to 19% withholding tax (both CIT and PIT) unless a double tax treaty otherwise provides, which is most often the case. Double taxation treaties concluded by Poland follow the OECD MC by limiting source taxation (usually 5% or 10%). Being a Member State of EU, Poland exempts dividends paid out to shareholders (both domestic, EU and EEA based) when the shareholding exceeds 10%. That exemption applies also to dividend payments to residents of Switzerland, but the shareholding threshold is higher – 25%. The recipient of the dividend must hold the stock directly for an uninterrupted period of 2 years after the dividend is paid.

---

[4] See recently renegotiated treaty with Cyprus.

[5] J. Banach, *Polskie umowy o unikaniu podwójnego opodatkowania*, C.H. Beck, Warsaw 2002, p. 221.

[6] *ibidem*, p. 221.

Certificate of Residence

For outbound passive income payments, exemptions or rate reductions in double taxation treaties apply in the Polish withholding tax system only if an additional requirement is met. Residence of foreign recipient of such income (that is dividends, interest and royalties) must be evidenced by a "certificate of residence," which is an official document issued by the competent tax authority of the residence state confirming the residence of that taxpayer. Polish debtor paying out passive income to a non-resident taxpayer may not apply benefits set forth by the treaty unless a certificate of residence is provided by the recipient of the payment. Otherwise withholding income tax at lower tax rate or applying the exemption may be questioned by tax authorities. If the documentation is not provided, the entity making the payment is liable for tax arrears in such case.

Polish tax regulations do not specify the form of the certificate of residence due to richness of various types of such documents all over the world. Generally, Polish tax authorities accept certificates in any form as long as they are normally issued in that form by a foreign competent authority. There is a question whether the person who pays out passive income must hold a certificate of residence of the taxpayer at the moment of payment. Although the tax authorities and administrative courts take such a position, that interpretation of the requirements does not have a ground in either CIT or PIT Acts. Basically it should be sufficient for the withholding agent to be able to prove the residence of the taxpayer with an official certificate at the moment of tax audit or tax proceedings. It is advisable, however, for the payer to request a certificate of residence prior to making the payment (no matter how burdensome the task).

Anti-tax Havens and Anti-harmful Tax Regimes

There is no distinction between tax havens and harmful tax regimes in Polish tax law. In fact, tax havens are treated as harmful tax regimes. Under Art. 25a of the PIT Act and Art. 9a of the CIT Act taxpayers carrying out transactions with residents of countries engaged in harmful tax competition are bound to draft a transfer pricing documentation of such a transaction. That documentation must include information concerning:

- Functions of each party to the transaction (including assets used and assumed risk),
- All anticipated expenses related to the transaction, their payment form, and term,
- Methods for profits calculation and determination of the price of the transaction,
- Business strategy and other factors – if that strategy or other factors influenced the transaction value,

– Expected benefits for the taxpayer related to the transaction – applicable to transactions for intangible services.

The documentation obligation applies if the total amount resulting from the agreement or total amount actually paid in a given fiscal year exceeds 20,000 EUR. Tax documentation must be submitted by taxpayers upon request of tax authorities within 7 days from the delivery of that request.

As the CIT Act explicitly refers to "states and territories using harmful tax competition," there was a question concerning the definition and criteria to use to so characterize a given state or territory. Polish legislators chose the most efficient solution – the Minister of Finance published an official list of such states and territories.[7] It is clear that, as mentioned above, that list refers not only to harmful tax regimes, but also (or perhaps primarily) to tax havens.

The list currently includes 37 countries and territories: Andorra, Anguilla, Antigua and Barbuda, Aruba/Saint Maarten/Curacao, the Bahamas, Bahrain, Barbados, Belize, Bermuda, British Virgin Islands, Cook Islands, Dominica, Gibraltar, Grenada, Sark, Hong Kong, Cayman Islands, Liberia, Liechtenstein, Macau, the Maldives, the Marshall Islands, Mauritius, Monaco, Montserrat, Nauru, Niue, Panama, Samoa, Seychelles, Saint Kitts and Nevis, St. Lucia, Saint Vincent and the Grenadines, Tonga, Turks and Caicos Islands, Virgin Islands, Vanuatu.

Poland was not party to the Code of Conduct for Business Taxation adopted in 1997, nonetheless as a Member State (since 2004) of EU, it must and it does abide by those recommendations. Although this measure is of a non-binding character, it does have an impact on EU Member States' tax policy. Poland also participates in the OECD Global Forum on Transparency and Exchange of Information for Tax Purposes. The Ministry of Finance, following OECD BEPS recommendations, has recently pursued a new tax policy embracing:

1. Renegotiating tax treaties in order to abolish tax sparing credit mechanisms, implementing specific anti-avoidance rules (e.g., main purpose test), and enhancing exchange of information clauses,
2. Concluding new tax treaties including exchange of information treaties,
3. Amending income tax system in order to close numerous tax planning opportunities,
4. Drafting new anti-avoidance rules, in particular a General Anti-Abuse Rule[8] (which is treated by the Ministry of Finance (MF) as an implementation of European Commission recommendations of 6 December 2012 on aggressive tax planning)[9] and CFC regulations – there is also discussion of implementing exit taxes and limiting accessibility of advance tax rulings for tax avoidance schemes,

---

[7] Currently, Regulation of the Minister of Finance of 9 April 2013 concerning territories and countries applying harmful tax competition in corporate income tax (Journal of Laws 2013, item 494).

[8] GAAR, implemented in 2003, was abolished by the Constitutional Court in 2004, which found it in violation of the rule of law as well as of the requirement of statutory imposition of taxes and, thus, unconstitutional.

[9] C(2012)8806.

Those ideas are either being implemented or discussed for the time. Because of extensiveness of tax law system amendments in this regard, it remains to be seen whether MF's attempts to tightening up tax law system will have, as a side effect, a lowering of the attractiveness of Poland as an investment destination, because this would complicate the system, introducing new burdensome administrative obligations and increasing compliance costs.[10] At the same time, introducing CFC rules may decrease competitiveness of Polish investors abroad.

Exchange of Information

Poland has a well developed system of exchange of information provisions, including regulations on EU, international (both bilateral and multilateral) and domestic levels. Being a Member State of EU Poland is bound by the 2011/16/EU Directive (repealing Directive 77/799/EEC) on administrative cooperation in the field of taxation. These provisions were already required to be implemented by in their domestic legal systems by Member States, except for certain specific regulations (e.g., automatic exchange of information) which were to be implemented by 1 January 2015.

Polish tax authorities base exchange of tax information on an international level on two foundations: the Strasbourg Convention on Mutual Administrative Assistance in Tax Matters of 25 January 1988,[11] as amended by the Protocol of 2010 (which has been already ratified by Poland and entered into force on 1 October 2011), and a network of bilateral international agreements: double taxation treaties and specific treaties on exchange of information (11 agreements). One observes a clear tendency to expand the network of exchange of information agreements with countries treated as tax havens. Recently Poland has concluded such treaties with: the Isle of Man, Jersey, Guernsey, San Marino, Andorra, Dominica, Grenada, Gibraltar, Belize, the Bahamas, Liberia (only first four already ratified). It is expected that in the near future such agreements are to be concluded also with: Monaco, Cayman Islands, British Virgin Islands, Bermuda, Turks and Caicos Islands, Montserrat and Anguilla.[12] The above indicates that, in general, Polish tax policy aims at building exchange of information instruments network in order to facilitate tax audits of taxpayers involved in carrying out investments in tax havens or harmful tax regimes.

The scope of exchange of information varies and depends on the available legal basis. Tax treaties, in general, contain only a narrow exchange of information clause, specific exchange of information treaties may cover income taxes and also Value

---

[10] Poland's rank in Paying Taxes 2014 PwC and World Bank Group report is relatively very low (113 rank out of 189 economies), see: http://www.pwc.com/gx/paying-taxes/assets/pwc-paying-taxes-2014.pdf (access: 27.11.2013).

[11] Journal of Laws 1998, no. 141, item 913, as amended.

[12] Response of the Ministry of Finance to the parliamentary request no. 680 concerning foreign tax reliefs, http://www.sejm.gov.pl/sejm7.nsf/InterpelacjaTresc.xsp?key=3FFF765A (access: 16.11.2013).

Added Tax (see the treaty with Guernsey). However, since both the 2011/16 Directive and the Strasbourg Convention of 1988 provide a broad base for exchange of information it may be concluded that the type of information which may be exchanged by Polish tax authorities is rather wide. A key concept which limits the scope of information subject to exchange is the "foreseeable relevance" clause found in numerous sources of exchange of information regulations[13] The Polish tax administration engages in s spontaneous or automatic exchange of information as well as exchange upon request. Domestic exchange of information provisions serve primarily to an implement both EU law and international tax law obligations of Poland.

Despite that fact that information obtained by tax authorities is subject to tax secrecy protection, such information may be made available for a number of public bodies.[14] Principally, exchange of information and the access of tax authorities to tax information is not impeded by bank secrecy. On one hand the protection of bank secrecy is relatively high. On the other hand Polish legislator has implemented effective measures which enable tax authorities to obtain requested information.[15]

Tax Incentives

In General

Poland in the time of transition from a centralized, socialist system to a free market economy has developed a number of incentives to attract foreign direct investments. Tax incentives play an important role in the system. For now the choices include:

1. Relief for Research and Development (R&D) Centers,
2. Special Economic Zones regulations,
3. Investment relief,
4. Technological relief, and
5. Tax credit,

The Polish tax law system does not provide any explicit tax incentives for investment in emerging, developing and low income/high poverty countries. It should be noted, however, that a number of Polish tax treaties are based on UN Model Tax Convention, which may, in effect have some indirect impact in facilitating investments in developing countries. An example of such regulations would be the tax sparing credit which may make an investment in some countries or territories more favorable (when the source state decides to exempt e.g., dividend income, the state

---

[13] For a thorough analysis, see H. Filipczyk, Ł. Pikus, D. Wasylkowski, *Exchange of information and cross-border cooperation between tax authorities*, *National Report for Poland*, Cahiers de droit fiscal international, IFA 2013, p. 624.

[14] *ibidem*, p. 618.

[15] *ibidem*, p. 618.

of residence nonetheless allows a credit). It should be stressed that grant of a tax sparing credit to Polish residents is treated by the MF, in general, as support of tax avoidance. Accordingly, current tax policy seeks its abolition.

Research and Development Centers

Relief for R&D Centers is an element of the system of promoting innovation in Poland. Creating a R&D Center garners a number of benefits, including those of a purely tax character. An R&D Center may create an innovation fund formed from a monthly contribution (not exceeding 20 % of gross income derived by the Center in a given month), which is treated as deductible expense. Resources accumulated in the fund may be allocated for covering R&D costs. In addition, R&D Centers enjoy tax exemption from property local taxes (real estate tax, agricultural tax and forestry tax).

Special Economic Zones

The Special Economic Zones (hereinafter "SEZ") mechanism is an example of a territorial and temporary exemption provided by Polish tax law regulations. SEZs were created by the Special Economic Zone Act of 20 October 1994.[16] A Special Economic Zone forms a geographically separate and uninhabited part of the territory of Poland. There are presently fourteen1 SEZs located throughout Poland.

Under the SEZ Act, the zones are established upon a regulation of the Council of Ministers which determines the name, the area (territory), the management (a majority state or municipality owned company) and the period for which it has been established. Business activity may be carried out in the SEZ only upon a special permit issued in the form of an administrative decision by an Minister of Economy or the company managing the respective Zone.

Tax incentives provided by the SEZ Act involve:

1. Corporate and personal income tax exemption,[17]
2. Real estate tax exemption,

Those incentives are dependent on maintaining the validity of the SEZ permit. Therefore, it is vital to determine fundamental requirements imposed on the investors. SEZ permits encompass several different requirements which must be met by the investors in order to enjoy tax exemptions[18]:

---

[16] Journal of Laws 2007, no. 42, item 274 as amended, hereinafter: the SEZ Act.

[17] Art. 17(1)(34) of the CIT Act and Art. 21(1)(63a) of the PIT Act.

[18] K. Grabowska-Klimczak [in:] A. Tałasiewicz (ed.), *Prawne i podatkowe aspekty prowadzenia działalności w Specjalnych Strefach Ekonomicznych*, Wolters Kluwer, Warsaw 2010, p. 38.

1. Minimum level of investment expenses,
2. Creation of new jobs,
3. Time-frame for the investment (project deadline),
4. Maximum value of eligible costs,
5. Abiding by the SEZ regulation,
6. Maintaining the ownership of the assets,
7. Maintaining the investment for a certain period.

The tax exemption for SEZ is limited. A maximum level of tax exemption is calculated separately for each taxpayer and is dependent on two principal criteria:

– Maximum amount of regional state aid determined for a given territory (30–50 % of eligible costs depending on a region)[19] and
– Incurred investment costs which may be covered by the state aid.

In addition to the tax exemption, entrepreneurs carrying out business activity under a SEZ permit on the territory of the Zone may also enjoy exemptions in local real estate tax. There are two legal bases for such exemption: the Act of 2003 amending the SEZ Act[20] and municipal council resolutions. Art. 10 of the Act of 2003 amending the SEZ Act exempts from tax buildings, structures and land used in business activity on the territory of the SEZ under a SEZ permit. The amount of the real estate tax exemption is included in the calculation of the general maximum amount of tax exemption in SEZ (as described above). Moreover designated municipalities are entitled to establish additional real estate tax exemptions (limited, however, by specific regulations).

Incentives granted by Poland in a form of tax exemption for a business operating in SEZ form constitutes regional state aid compatible with the common market under TFEU.[21]

Introducing the SEZ regime in Poland has turned out to be a great success. As of June, 2013 the total value of realized investments was close to 89 billion PLN (approximately 21 billion EUR). SEZs have generated 188,042 new jobs – 1,602 permits have been granted.[22]

Investment Relief

Investment relief in both corporate and personal income tax reduces the income tax base for entrepreneurs by accelerating depreciation of certain categories of capital assets. Taxpayers may exploit two alternative opportunities: accelerated depreciation in a strict sense (which is based on increasing the depreciation rates) and

---

[19] For small and medium enterprises that limit is increased by 20 % (small enterprises) and 10 % (medium enterprises).

[20] Journal of Laws 2003, no. 188, item 1849, as amended.

[21] K. Grabowska-Klimczak, *op. cit.*, p. 17.

[22] See: http://www.mg.gov.pl/files/upload/7809/Tabela%20za%20II%20kw.%202013%20r.pdf (access: 14.11.2013).

one-off depreciation. One-off depreciation is accessible for small taxpayers and other taxpayers opening business and may cover capital assets for which the book value does not exceed 50,000 EUR.

Eligible assets include, in general, machines and technical appliances as well as means of transportation (excluding cars).

Technological Relief

Technologies under certain conditions are eligible for depreciation. That rule pertains to intangibles acquired by the taxpayer with business application (copyrights, licenses, industrial property rights, and know-how) where the expected period of use exceeds 1 year. Within the depreciation period the whole amount of incurred acquisition expenses is deducted.

In addition, under Art. 18b of the CIT Act corporate taxpayers are entitled to deduct an additional 50 % of costs incurred for acquisition of new technologies defined as technological knowledge in the form of intangibles. This includes in particular results of research and development which allow the production of new goods or services or improves existing production. That knowledge may not be applied anywhere else in the world for a period of at least 5 years.

The innovative character of the technological knowledge must be confirmed by an opinion of an independent scientific institute as described by the Science Financing Principles Act.

Tax Credit Relief for New Businesses

Under Art. 44(7a) of the PIT Act, individuals opening businesses for the first time may apply for a so-called "tax credit."[23] That relief involves an exemption in the first year following the year in which the business was started (if it was carried out for at least 10 months, otherwise the beneficial regime is applicable for the next 2 years). However, that regime is not a "tax holiday" in a strict sense, because the amount of "saved" tax must be paid in the 5 succeeding years (20 % of the tax each year). It is a kind of deferred tax payment." A similar regime is accessible to CIT taxpayers – Art. 25(11) of the CIT Act.

---

[23] This should not be confused with the tax credit used for avoiding double taxation.

State Aid

State aid, in its broad meaning, is an instrument for state support of private entrepreneurs (and thus the economy).[24] Such activities carried out by the state should be limited, however, in the market economy since they may lead to the distortion of competition. Poland, as a member of the EU, is subject to EU law regulations on state aid. As a general rule set forth by Art. 107(1) of the TFEU *"any aid granted by a Member State or through State resources in any form whatsoever which distorts or threatens to distort competition by favouring certain undertakings or the production of certain goods shall, in so far as it affects trade between Member States, be incompatible with the internal market."* As an exception certain categories of state aid are treated as compatible with the internal market[25] and some may be so qualified.[26]

From the jurisprudence of the European Court of Justice (ECJ) one may infer the following features of the state aid:

1. Benefit or advantage,
2. Granted by the state,
3. Selectivity.[27]

Corporate Tax Rates in Poland

Income tax rates vary depending on the category of tax (PIT or CIT), income, and taxpayer (residents, non-residents). While personal income taxation is of progressive character, general CIT tax rate is flat and amounts to 19%. It applies both to resident and non-resident taxpayers carrying out a business activity in the territory of Poland. In general 19% tax rate is applied to net income. As an exception exists when a non-resident taxpayer (either directly or through a PE) derives business income from Polish sources and does not maintain proper books and records. Because it is not possible to determine taxable income in this case, under Art. 9(2a) of the CIT Act an estimated net income is determined using the following ratios:

1. Five percent of gross income from wholesale or retail sale activities,
2. Ten percent of gross income from construction, assembly and transport activities,

---

[24] A. Nykiel-Mateo, *Pomoc państwa a ogólne środki interwencji w europejskim prawie wspólnotowym*, Wolters Kluwer, Warsaw 2009, p. 11–12.

[25] See: Art. 107(2) Treaty on the Functioning of the European Union (hereinafter: TFEU).

[26] Art. 107(3) TFEU.

[27] A. Nykiel-Mateo, *op. cit.*, p. 44, J. Kociubiński, *Selectivity Criterion in State Aid Control*, Wroclaw Review of Law, Administration and Economics 2012, no. 1, p. 2.

3. Sixty percent of gross income for agency activities (only if agency fees are calculated on a commission basis),
4. Eighty percent of gross income for legal and expertise services,
5. Twenty percent of gross income for all other income sources.

Certain categories of income are subject, however, to special regimes and special tax rates. Dividends paid out to resident shareholders are included in the shareholders income tax base by way of self-assessment. Income derived from dividends is combined with other worldwide income and subject to the 19 % rate under general rules. Dividends paid out to non-residents are subject to a special withholding regime under which a Polish subsidiary, acting as a paying agent, is obliged to calculate and withhold tax and pay it to the competent tax authority. The 19 % tax rate is applied to gross income – no expenses may be deducted.

The same system applies to taxation of interest and royalties. When those categories of income are paid to Polish residents, they are subject to 19 % tax under general rules by way of self-assessment. On the other hand, if such income is paid out to a non-resident, the paying agent is bound to withhold due tax which for interest and royalties amounts to 20 %. Under domestic law 20 % withholding tax applies also to other categories of income (which under a tax treaty normally would be treated as business profits – art. 7 of the OECD MC), including fees for the following services: advisory, legal, advertising, accounting, market research, management and control, data processing, recruitment of personnel, guarantees and other items of similar character for sports, artistic and entertainment activities. As an exception, a 10 % tax rate applies to fees paid out to non-residents for transport of cargo and passengers by foreign commercial sea transport enterprises (excluding transit cargo and passengers) and income derived in Poland by foreign air transport companies.

Statutory tax rates apply unless an applicable tax treaty or secondary EU regulations (in particular the Parent-Subsidiary and Interest and Royalties Directive) otherwise provide.

Trade and Investment Agreements

Poland is a party to 62 bilateral investment agreements (BITs) which form one of the instruments for commercial policy of Poland. These are the agreements with: Albania, Argentina, Australia, Austria, Azerbaijan, Bangladesh, Belgium and Luxembourg, Belarus, Bulgaria, Canada, Chile, China, Croatia, Cyprus, Czech Republic, Denmark, Egypt, Estonia, Finland, France, Germany, Greece, Hungary, India, Indonesia, Iran, Israel, Italy, Jordan, Kazakhstan, South Korea, Kuwait, Latvia, Lithuania, Macedonia, Malaysia, Moldova, Mongolia, Morocco, the Netherlands, Norway, Portugal, Romania, Serbia, Singapore, Slovakia, Slovenia, Spain, Sweden, Switzerland, Thailand, Tunisia, Turkey, Ukraine, United Arab Emirates, USA, Uruguay, Uzbekistan, United Kingdom and Vietnam. These agreements typically contain non-discrimination provisions which preclude less favorable treatment of foreign investments and capital flows.

Poland as a member of European Union and World Trade Organization is also bound by the system of, among other things, non-discrimination provisions set forth by EU law and the Agreement establishing the World Trade Organization.

Conclusions

Tax measures aimed at providing investment incentives in Poland are highly selective. They are either specifically designed to attract new businesses to particular regions (Special Economic Zones) for particular purposes (creating new jobs etc.) or have more general impact (relatively low, flat CIT tax rate, permissibility of accelerated depreciation and investment relief). One also observes an intention to make the economy more innovative and efficient which is implemented by granting certain benefits to R&D Centers and to entrepreneurs implementing new technologies.

As a Member of EU and WTO Polish tax policy is constrained by regulations and principles which preclude discriminatory treatment. In addition, there are state aid limitations set forth by the primary EU law which restricts tax policy of EU Member States in the area of tax incentives.

Assessing the legal system in Poland and taking into account the need to further support development and the drive for innovation, we are of the opinion, in general, that the Polish system's of encouragement of investment is justified and desirable.

Chapter 15
Overview of Income and Investment Taxation in Portugal

Fernando Rocha Andrade

Abstract Portugal taxes its resident companies on worldwide income and, in order to prevent double taxation, allows a credit for foreign taxes paid to another jurisdiction. An exemption from Portuguese tax (participation exemption) is provided for dividends paid by a foreign subsidiary resident in the EU or EEA. This participation exemption has been extended to companies resident in former Portuguese colonies in Africa. Portugal has enacted a number of provisions designed to discourage investment in tax havens or similar regimes. It is party to a number of multilateral and bilateral exchange of information agreements which are designed to promote administrative cooperation. Until the end of 2020, there are special tax incentives for investment in certain industrial sectors, including manufacturing and mining, tourism, information technology, research and development, energy and telecommunications.

Synopsis Portugal taxes its resident companies on worldwide income, allowing a credit for foreign taxes paid to another jurisdiction (on a country-by-country basis). The credit is limited to the Portuguese tax on the foreign income in question.

Nonresidents are taxed on income either from Portuguese sources or arising out of activities through a Portuguese permanent establishment.

There is a participation exemption for dividends paid to a company resident in Portugal by a foreign subsidiary if the entity is resident in the EU or EEA. In this case, both the payer of the dividend and the recipient must qualify under the EU Parent-Subsidiary Directive.

Portugal has enacted a number of provisions designed to discourage investment in tax havens or other "clearly more favorable tax regimes." Tax havens are either countries listed by the Ministry of Finance or countries in which income is exempted from tax or subject to a tax liability less than 60 % of what the liability would have been in Portugal. The investment disincentives include: controlled foreign corporation (CFC) rules taxing profits of tax havens to Portuguese shareholders, a special transfer pricing regime, non-deductibility of payments (and a higher rate of

F.R. Andrade (✉)
University of Coimbra, Coimbra, Portugal
e-mail: fra@fd.uc.pt

© Springer International Publishing Switzerland 2017
K.B. Brown (ed.), *Taxation and Development - A Comparative Study*,
Ius Comparatum - Global Studies in Comparative Law 21,
DOI 10.1007/978-3-319-42157-5_15

255

taxation on payments) made to persons or companies in tax havens, and denial of contractual investment incentives.

After a phase two review by the OECD's Global Tax Forum found Portugal mostly compliant with transparency and exchange of information guidelines, changes to two special tax regimes were made. One regime, the Free Zones of Santa Maria, Azores, was abolished. The other in Madeira is scheduled to terminate.

Portugal is party to a number of multilateral and bilateral exchange of information agreements, either contained in tax treaties or in simplified form. The simplified agreements (involving only procedures for automatic and spontaneous exchange) have been signed with Span, Brazil, Cape Verde, and Mozambique and involved strengthened procedures for administrative cooperation. It has adopted the OECD's Common Reporting Standard and it is a party to a FATCA agreement with the U.S., signed in August, 2015, which is under implementation.

A special tax regime for former Portuguese colonies in Africa applies. Companies resident in these countries are treated as domestic for the purpose of the participation exemption available only for dividends between domestic corporations (unless they are EU or EEA member states). This exempts dividends paid by these companies to Portuguese residents from Portuguese tax.

In order to attract investment in Portugal (both domestic and foreign), a special regime allowing for "tax-incentive" contracts is in place. These contracts apply to specified investments before the end of 2020 (manufacturing and mining, tourism, computers and related services, agriculture, research and development, information technology, environment, energy and telecommunications). They may grant a tax credit for a specified level of investment in Portugal, a participation exemption for dividends received from foreign corporations, exemption from stamp duties and property taxes, and extra R & D deductions.

The corporate tax rate in Portugal is 25 %, with a surtax for corporations with taxable income in excess of specified levels. Corporations not involved in commercial, industrial, or agricultural activity are taxed at the rate of 21.5 %.

Withholding tax on Portuguese source income paid to nonresidents is 21 %, but this may elevate to 35 % if the payment is to entities located in tax havens.

Portugal is a party to numerous bilateral and multilateral trade or investment agreements.

Portugal's International Tax System

Income in Portugal is subject to two direct taxes: personal income is taxed under *Imposto sobre o Rendimento das Pessoas Singulares* (IRS), a progressive comprehensive income tax. Corporate income (and income of other legal persons) is taxed under *Imposto sobre o Rendimento das Pessoas Colectivas* (IRC).

Under IRS, residents are taxed on worldwide income. Under IRC, corporations with headquarters or effective management in Portugal are also taxed on their worldwide income. In both cases, a credit for taxes paid to foreign countries is allowed. In the absence of a tax treaty, the tax credit is limited, as a proportion of tax liability, to the proportion of foreign taxable income in total taxable income. The tax credit limit is calculated separately for each foreign country in which the taxpayer has taxable income.

Portuguese-source income of non-resident persons or corporations is also taxed. Non-residents that carry out their activity through a permanent establishment in Portugal are taxed on the profit allocated to the permanent establishment. The definition of permanent establishment generally conforms to the OECD model convention rules. Non-residents without a permanent establishment are subject to withholding tax on income from Portuguese sources.

IRC law recognizes a participation exemption for dividends paid from one domestic corporation to another. A resident company subject to IRC may deduct 100 % of dividends received from another resident company (subject to and not exempt from IRC) if all of the following conditions apply:

- The recipient company owns directly at least 5 % of the capital of the payer.
- The recipient company holds that position for an uninterrupted period of at least 24 months.

The participation exemption is not granted for dividends paid to resident entities by foreign subsidiaries, except in the following case:

A 100 % dividends-received deduction is granted for dividends paid by entities from EU or EEA member countries to Portuguese entities if both the payer and recipient of the dividends qualify under the EU Parent-Subsidiary Directive (Council Directive 2011/96/EU).

Anti-tax Haven Provisions

Several provisions of the income tax code (and other tax codes) are meant to discourage investment in tax havens, or other "clearly more favorable tax regimes." Tax havens are either (1) countries or territories listed as such by the Ministry of Finance or (2) for some purposes, countries or territories where income is exempt from taxation or taxes paid are below 60 % of what would be the tax liability in Portugal. Eighty-one countries or territories are presently listed as tax havens.

Provisions in the tax laws meant to discourage investment in tax havens include:

- CFC rules: profits of corporations in tax havens accruing to shareholders resident in Portugal may be taxed at the shareholder level, if that shareholder holds at least 25 % of the capital or voting rights (if at least 50 % of the shares of the corporation are held, directly or indirectly, by entities subject to Portuguese income tax, shareholders are taxed if they hold 10 % of the corporation);
- Special relationships for the purpose of the transfer pricing regime are considered to exist when payments are made to an entity in a tax haven;

- Payments to persons or corporations in tax havens are, in principle, non-deductible (burden of proof is reversed) and subject to separate taxation at a higher tax rate (35 %);
- Portuguese citizens moving to tax havens, continue to be treated as residents in Portugal, for tax purposes, for a period of 5 years;
- Investment in territories listed as tax havens is not eligible for contractual tax incentives to investment.

Investments in Harmful Tax Regimes

Portuguese tax law does not distinguish harmful tax regimes from tax havens and other "clearly more favorable tax regimes" (see section above entitled "Anti-tax Haven Provisions"). Presently, no harmful tax regimes are listed, other than territories listed as tax havens (Luxembourg was removed from the list following the abolition of the 1929 holding company regime), or, for some purposes, countries or territories where income is exempt from taxation or taxes paid are below 60 % of what would be the tax liability in Portugal.

Global Tax Forum

Portugal participates in the OECD's Global Tax Forum. The tax regime has been found mostly compliant with OECD transparency and exchange of information guidelines in phase two: *Implementation of the Standard in Practice*. Two special tax regimes (the "Free Zones of Madeira and Santa Maria, Azores") were identified as tax havens. The Santa Maria Free Zone was abolished in 2011. The International Business Center of Madeira has had its regime modified and scheduled to phase out.

Information Exchange Agreements

Tax information exchange is carried out both through multilateral and bilateral treaties and within the framework of EU Directives on cooperation and information exchange for tax purposes (namely Council Directive 2008/55/CE of 26 May 2008 on mutual assistance for the recovery of claims relating to certain levies, duties, taxes and other measures, Council Directive 2011/16/EU of 15 February 2011 on administrative cooperation in the field of taxation; and most recently Council Directive 2014/107/EU, on mandatory automatic exchange of information in the field of taxation).

Portugal has signed the Convention on Mutual Administrative Assistance in Tax Matters. Bilateral exchange of information relationships exist in sixty-seven Double Tax Conventions ("DTCs") and 16 Tax Information Exchange Agreements.

Within the framework of existing DTCs, simplified agreements for information exchange have been signed with a few countries (Spain, Brazil, Cape Verde and Mozambique) providing reinforced administrative cooperation (with the presence of tax administration officials in the foreign country) and procedures for "automatic" and "spontaneous" information exchange.

Portugal was also one of the "early adopters" of the Common Reporting Standard (OECD), and signed the Agreement to Improve International Tax Compliance and to implement Foreign Account Tax Compliance Act (FATCA) with USA in 6 August 2015, and is currently implementing the necessary internal regulatory measures and procedures for entry into force of that Agreement.

Tax Incentives for Investment in Emerging, Low-Income or Developing Countries

Portuguese tax law does not provide tax incentives specifically for investment in emerging or developing countries.

Portuguese tax law does not provide tax incentives specifically for investment in countries with low incomes, high poverty rates or high rates of economic inequality.

Special Tax Regimes for Former Colonies

A special tax provision exists for corporations resident in the former Portuguese colonies in Africa – Angola, Cape Verde, Guinea-Bissau, Mozambique and São Tomé and Príncipe – and for Timor Leste (East Timor). They are treated as domestic corporations for the purpose of elimination of double taxation of dividends. Corporations subject to Portuguese income tax are granted a participation exemption on dividends paid by corporations resident in those countries under the same terms that apply to dividends paid by Portuguese corporations (profits previously subject to income tax are deductible from taxable income).

Measures to Attract Economic Activity to Its Own Jurisdiction

Portuguese tax benefits for economic activity are not restricted to foreign corporations (benefits are also available to resident entities). However, some of them are obviously aimed at attracting foreign investment. The most important is the

Investment Tax Code, approved in 2009. The Code made it possible to grant tax benefits, on a contractual basis, for productive-investment projects above €3.000.000 initiated before December 31, 2020. These benefits are subject to a tax-incentive contract with a duration of up to 10 years from the start date of an investment project.

Tax incentive contracts may grant the following:

- A tax credit of up to 25 % of the value of the investment made in Portugal. The credit is deducted on the amount due under the Corporate Income Tax (*IRC*);
- A participation exemption on dividends received from abroad;
- Exemption or reduction of stamp duties (*Imposto de Selo*), and municipal taxes on real property (*IMI*) and on the transfer of real property (*IMT*).

These tax incentives are only available to investments in specific economic activities, but these are rather broadly defined: (1) Manufacturing and mining industry (2) Tourism and the tourism-related activities (3) Computers and related services and activities (4) Agriculture, fisheries, forestry and livestock (5) Research and development of high-tech activities (6) Information technology and audiovisual and multimedia production and (7) Environment, energy and telecommunications.

Tax law also provides for extra deductions for expenses in research and development (R&D) investments, and new jobs creation. These are not especially targeted to foreign corporations, but they are available for these entities.

Also in 2009, a special regime of the personal income tax was created for people moving to Portugal, especially aimed at professionals in activities "of high value-added, with a scientific, artistic or technical nature." Tax benefits include exemption from taxation of work income earned abroad (if it is taxed abroad, regardless of DTC) and a reduced income tax rate (20 %) for work income earned in Portugal.

In the past, Portugal created two special enterprise zones that could be classified as tax havens: the International Business Centers of Madeira and of Santa Maria (Azores). The latter was terminated in 2011 and the former is being phased out, with special tax benefits ceasing in 2020.

Tax Amnesties

Portugal has had several tax amnesties for income from financial assets held abroad.

The last amnesty, called "Exceptional Regime for Tax Settlement" (*Regime Excepcional de Regularização Tributária, or RERT, III*) applied to income from deposits, equity, securities and other financial assets not located in Portugal at the end of 2010. All tax liability for non-declared income from such assets was relieved if those assets were declared, and a tax of 7.5 % of the assets' total value was paid, by June 2012. The amnesty cleared any tax liability for non- reported income prior to 2010, as well as any penalties or criminal responsibility arising from the failure to report that income.

Tax Rate Structure

Resident Entities and Permanent Establishments

The general tax rate on income of resident corporations and Portuguese permanent establishments of foreign corporations is 25 %.

The general tax rates on income earned in the Madeira and Azores Autonomous Regions are set by the regional authorities and may differ.

The general tax rate is, however, subject to several special modifications:

A surtax is levied on corporations with taxable income above €1,500,000. The surtax carries a rate of 3 % for taxable incomes between € 1,500,000 and €7,500,000, 5 % for incomes between €7,500,000 and €35,000,000 and 7 % for incomes above € 35,000,000.

Entities that do not carry out a commercial, industrial or agricultural activity as their main activity face a tax rate of 21.5 %, not subject to surtax.

Municipalities may apply a surtax (*"Derrama Municipal"*), at a maximum rate of 1.5 %, to the taxable profit before the deduction of tax losses.

Non-resident Entities Without Permanent Establishments

The general tax rates for withholding taxes on Portuguese source income of non-resident corporations without permanent establishments is 21 %. The withholding tax rate for payments made to entities in tax havens is 35 %.

Prohibitions on Providing Tax Incentives for Investment in Developing Countries

Portugal, as a member of the EU, is a party to the 1997 EU Code of Conduct for business taxation and is subject to the EU rules prohibiting unsanctioned State Aid. Portugal is not prohibited from providing tax incentives for investment abroad, except when such incentives are in violation of EU law (including the state aid limitations).

Bilateral or Multilateral Investment Agreements

Portugal is party to multiple bilateral or multilateral trade or investment agreements and to international treaties affecting trade and investment.

The primary multilateral engagements arise from participation in international organizations:

- Portugal is a member of the European Union, and, as such, a party to the large body of EU law and treaties on trade and investment,
- Portugal has signed the World Trade Organization Agreement and is a founding member of WTO,
- Portugal has signed the Convention on the Settlement of Investment Disputes between States and Nationals of Other States and is a member of the International Center for the Settlement of Investment Disputes,
- Portugal is a member of CPLP (Community of Portuguese Language Countries) and, within that framework, a party to agreements with minor trade and investment aspects (namely the Convention for Technical Cooperation Between Customs Administrations).

Portugal has signed bilateral Agreements on Promotion and Reciprocal Protection of Investments with 50 countries (and with the autonomous territory of Macao). These agreements do not typically contain any tax provisions or concessions.

The countries with which such agreements have been concluded are: Albania, Algeria, Angola, Argentina, Bosnia-Herzegovina, Brazil, Bulgaria, Cape Verde, Chile, China, Croatia, Cuba, Czech Republic, Egypt, Gabon, Germany, Guinea-Bissau, Hungary, India, Kuwait, Latvia, Libya, Lithuania, Macao, Mauritius, Mexico, Morocco, Mozambique, Pakistan, Paraguay, Peru, Philippines, Poland, Qatar, Republic of the Congo, Romania, Russia, São Tomé and Príncipe, Senegal, Serbia, Slovakia, Slovenia, South Korea, Timor-Leste, Tunisia, Turkey, Ukraine, United Arab Emirates, Uruguay, Uzbekistan, and Venezuela.

Chapter 16
Taxation and Development: The South African Position

Craig West and Jennifer Roeleveld

Abstract South Africa has a modified worldwide system of taxation. In order to alleviate double taxation, a credit is allowed for foreign taxes paid. Certain income, like foreign services income remunerated by entities resident in other African nations, may be eligible for a unilateral credit that operates as an exemption of tax on this income. Dividends received by a South African company from a 10 %-owned foreign company may be eligible for a full or partial exemption from tax. South Africa addresses harmful tax competition through transfer pricing, controlled foreign corporation provisions, and tax information exchange agreements. It has instituted tax measures to attract economic development, primarily in the areas of manufacturing, research and development, foreign film and television, and industrial innovation.

Synopsis South Africa has a modified worldwide system of taxation. Although residents are taxed on worldwide income, limited types of income arising from foreign sources may be exempt from tax. To alleviate double taxation, a credit is allowed against South African tax liability for foreign taxes paid. The credit is limited to the amount of the South African tax that would have been paid absent the credit. A credit is also available in certain circumstances for foreign taxes paid on South African source income. This is a unilateral credit allowed South African residents in the special case in which the foreign country (in particular, other African nations) imposes a tax on services provided from South Africa when paid by the foreign country's resident.

Foreign dividends received by a South African company may be eligible for a full or partial participation exemption. To qualify for the exemption, the recipient must hold at least 10 % of the equity interest and voting rights in the distributing company. If a foreign dividend is paid in cash on a share listed in the Johannesburg Securities Exchange (JSE), the dividend is exempt from corporate tax, but generally subject to a South African tax on dividends.

This contribution was finalized in January 2014 and is current through that date.

C. West (✉) • J. Roeleveld
University of Cape Town, Cape Town, South Africa
e-mail: Craig.West@uct.ac.za; Jennifer.Roeleveld@uct.ac.za

© Springer International Publishing Switzerland 2017   263
K.B. Brown (ed.), *Taxation and Development - A Comparative Study*,
Ius Comparatum - Global Studies in Comparative Law 21,
DOI 10.1007/978-3-319-42157-5_16

While there are no express anti-harmful tax competition rules, tax avoidance is addressed through transfer pricing and controlled foreign corporation provisions. These rules discourage investment in harmful tax regimes. In addition, there are no anti-tax haven rules. The absence of double tax agreements with these regimes has eliminated bilateral relief. This has been addressed by recent negotiation of tax information exchange agreements. Although it is typically viewed as a tax haven, Mauritius has had a favourable double tax agreement with South Africa. It has been updated, but the revised version has not yet entered into force.

The Southern African Development Community (SADC), of which South Africa is a member, has acted to cooperate in tax matters and to harmonize the disparate tax regimes. A Memorandum of Understanding (MOU) to effect these changes, issued in 2002, encourages a common approach to tax incentives. It also has identified factors, similar to those described by the OECD, that indicate the presence of harmful tax competition and recommends avoidance of those types of regimes.

South Africa participates in the OECD Global Forum. As a result it has taken action to align its tax system with international trends and norms.

South Africa is party to more than 70 double tax agreements and 7 Tax Information Exchange Agreements (TIEAs). Exchange of information is by request or, occasionally, spontaneous. It has positioned itself to engage in automatic exchange, having joined a pilot program. It has also entered into an Inter-Governmental Agreement (Model 1 IGA) with the U.S. under FATCA.

South Africa's Department of Trade and Industry (DTI) is involved in supporting African regional economic integration and development. It works with regional organizations to develop the free trade area and to extend African integration.

South Africa has instituted measures to attract economic development. Film production and post-production (primarily foreign film and television, manufacturing, and research and development) are activities which benefit from special allowances that reduce the effective tax rate. Other special regimes are provided for industrial innovation. Some of these regimes are provided by legislation and managed by the South African Revenue Service. Most are managed by grant by the DTI under a process that is not transparent.

South African companies and branches of foreign companies are taxed at a flat rate of 28 %. Small businesses are taxed at reduced rates.

South Africa has entered into a substantial number of bilateral and multilateral trade and investment agreements.

South African Tax System and Treatment of Cross Border Income

"The residence basis of taxation adopted in South Africa may be referred to as the 'residence minus' system, which means that receipts and accruals of income derived by 'residents' from worldwide sources are subject to tax, but certain limited categories of income arising from activities undertaken outside the Republic are exempt from tax."[1] Residence of individuals is determined in terms of either a subjective legal test of residence (the "ordinarily resident" test) or the objective test ("physical presence" test). For corporate entities, incorporation, formation, establishment or place of effective management may trigger residence. Note that the residence test contains a general override for tax treaties in that residence determined by a treaty overrides the domestic definition. There are some additional exclusions from the residence definition for certain companies.

Foreign taxes levied on foreign source income subject to South African income tax for residents are permitted as a credit against the South African tax liability but limited to the South African tax that would have been levied on the foreign taxable income. In addition a credit is provided for foreign taxes levied on South African sourced income of residents. This arose from practical difficulties within Africa as described in the Explanatory Memorandum to Act 24 of 2011 as: "A number of African jurisdictions impose withholding taxes in respect of services (especially management services) rendered abroad if funded by payments from their home jurisdictions."[2]

"These withholding taxes are sometimes imposed even when tax treaties suggest that the practice should be otherwise. African imposition of these withholding taxes in respect of South African sourced services is no exception."[3] As a result of this particular problem, the unilateral relief offered in terms of the South African Income Tax Act 58 of 1962 did not include relief for South African source income. As South African companies were subject to double tax, and the deduction for such foreign taxes did not equate to the effect of a credit, the additional credit relief provision was inserted.

In certain selected circumstances amounts not qualifying as credits under the unilateral relief provisions may yet qualify for deduction.

South Africa does not overtly have a territorial regime from which it exempts certain foreign source income, but legacy items remain after the change to residence-based taxation in 2000. For example, exempt from taxation for a resident is all remuneration for service as crew on a ship provided the employee was outside of the Republic for more than 183 days for any 12-month period starting or ending in a year of assessment. Similarly foreign source pensions are exempt from South African tax.

With respect to foreign dividends received by South African companies, full or partial exemption applies depending on the circumstances. Four different exemptions may apply before a general partial exemption is applied, namely:

(a) The participation exemption

To qualify, the shareholder must hold at least 10 % of the equity shares and voting rights in the declaring company. In the event the shareholder is a

---

[1] De Koker, A. and Williams, R. (eds). 2013. *Silke on South African Income Tax*. Service Issue 50. Durban: LexisNexis at paragraph 14.1

[2] South Africa. South African Revenue Service. 2011. *Explanatory Memorandum on the Taxation Laws Amendment Bill, 2011*. Pretoria: Government Printers at 100–101. Available at: http://www.sars.gov.za/AllDocs/LegalDoclib/ExplMemo/LAPD-LPrep-EM-2011-02%20-%20Explanatory%20Memorandum%20Taxation%20Laws%20Amendment%20Bill%202011.pdf

[3] Ibid.

company, the shareholding in the declaring company can be held jointly with fellow group[4] companies.[5]

(b) The country-to-country exemption

Should the foreign dividend be paid to a foreign company resident in the same jurisdiction as the declaring company, such dividend is exempt. This exemption applies with no reference to the size of the shareholding.[6]

(c) Exemption for dividends from controlled foreign companies

As a result of the attribution of income from a controlled foreign company (CFC), the subsequent dividend declared by that company is exempt to the extent of up to the amounts previously attributed net of foreign tax on such proportional inclusion. This prevents domestic double tax on both the attribution and the dividend received.[7]

(d) Exemption for dividends from JSE listed foreign companies

Where a cash foreign dividend is paid in respect of a listed share (generally a share listed on both the Johannesburg Securities Exchange (JSE) and another exchange, the dividend is exempt. As dividends in such a case are subject to dividends tax, this exemption was necessary to prevent the instance of domestic double taxation.[8]

Both (a) and (b) above are subject to certain exclusions. These are mostly to prevent the exemption of dividends treated as a deduction in the other foreign State (i.e. deduction and no income as contemplated in the BEPS Action Plan for Hybrid Instruments). Secondly, foreign dividends paid to collective investment schemes do not receive such exemption. The reason being, for example, the conduit nature of the collective investment scheme such that the individual holding the participatory interest does not hold the required percentage.

For any balance of foreign dividends that remain taxable after applying the above exemptions, a general exemption is applied (largely to ensure that the normal tax applied to such dividends will be applied at a rate that will not exceed the 15 % withholdings tax on dividends.[9]

---

[4] This reference is to "group company" as defined in the Income Tax Act 58 of 1962, which is different from the financial accounting definition.

[5] De Koker, A. and Williams, R. (eds). 2013. *Silke on South African Income Tax.* Service Issue 50. Durban: LexisNexis at paragraph 9.27.

[6] Ibid.

[7] Ibid.

[8] Ibid.

[9] South Africa. South African Revenue Service. 2011. *Explanatory Memorandum on the Taxation Laws Amendment Bill, 2011.* Pretoria: Government Printers at 40. Available at: http://www.sars. gov.za/AllDocs/LegalDoclib/ExplMemo/LAPD-LPrep-EM-2011-02%20-%20Explanatory%20 Memorandum%20Taxation%20Laws%20Amendment%20Bill%202011.pdf

Treatment of Tax Havens

There are no specific tax laws in place to discourage investment into tax havens. There are also no sanctions per se but as residents of South Africa are taxed on worldwide income these interests and any income arising would have to be declared on the annual tax return. As there are usually no Double Taxation Agreements (DTAs) with tax haven States, no bilateral relief is on offer. Recently tax information exchange agreements (TIEAs) have been negotiated with tax haven countries. An exception to the rule has been Mauritius which was always regarded as a low tax jurisdiction and which was supported by a favourable DTA. The DTA however was recently renegotiated but has not yet entered into force. This new treaty is largely based on the OECD model, but dual residence of corporate entities will be resolved by mutual agreement procedures.

TIEAs have been signed and come into force with the following tax haven countries: Argentina, Bahamas, Belize, Barbados, Bermuda, Cayman Islands, Cook Islands, Gibraltar, Guernsey, Jersey, Liberia, Liechtenstein and San Marino. Further TIEAs are in the negotiation process.

Prevention of Harmful Tax Competition

Exchange Control regulation limits the outflow of capital from South Africa. Within the tax law, General Anti-Avoidance Rules (GAAR) prevent certain arrangements. Other standard anti-avoidance provisions, such as transfer pricing and controlled foreign company rules, partly prevent engagement in harmful tax regimes and competition. There are no express anti-harmful tax competition rules.

Regional and International Agreements Preventing Unfair Competition

The Southern African Development Community (SADC) consists of 15 member states. In an effort to co-operate in tax matters and to harmonise tax regimes (partly to prevent harmful tax competition between the members States), a Memorandum of Understanding on Co-Operation in Taxation and Related Matters (MoU) was issued in 2002. In the context of tax incentives,[10] Article 4 encourages member states to achieve a common approach to tax incentives.[11] It further identifies six

---

[10] Defined for the SADC MoU as meaning: "a fiscal measure that is used to attract local or foreign investment capital to certain economic activities or particular areas in a country" (Article 1).

[11] Article 4(2) of the MoU provides examples of tax incentives in broad terms.

factors[12] to identify harmful tax competition (arising presumably from tax incentive regimes) and specifies that member states should attempt to avoid such regimes. The six factors identified by the SADC MoU are similar to those identified in the OECD Report of 1998 for Harmful Tax Competition.[13]

OECD Global Forum

South Africa participates in the Global Forum. One of its revenue authority officials was appointed as the "Chair of the Global Forum on Transparency and Exchange of Information for Tax Purposes for the period commencing January 2013 to December 2014."[14] He was re-elected for a further 2 year term at the meeting held in October 2014. South Africa has been subject to a combined Phase 1 and Phase 2 Report with the findings released in October 2012.[15]

Whether in response to or aside from the Global Forum, South Africa has in recent years made significant changes to the tax system aligning with international trends and norms from the change to the residence basis of taxation in 2000, to the change from Secondary Tax on Companies (STC), to a dividend withholding tax system in 2012. In the STC system the company bore the tax on any dividends declared. This was problematic as it was seen as a tax on profits paid by the company and if double tax occurred the shareholder therefore could not claim tax relief nor the company as this type of tax was not a tax covered in many treaties. In the new regime of dividends tax the company withholds the dividends tax from the dividend payment to the shareholder whether resident or non resident and pays this over to the tax authorities on behalf of the shareholder. Non residents may be subject to lower rates of dividends tax in terms of a DTA.

---

[12] These are: zero or low effective rates of tax; lack of transparency; lack of effective exchange of information; restricting tax incentives to particular taxpayers (usually non-residents); promotion of tax incentives as vehicles for tax minimisation; or, the absence of substantial activity in the jurisdiction to qualify for a tax incentive.

[13] Van Wijk, A.J. 2011. *Whether Tax Incentives to stimulate Foreign Direct Investment for manufacturing in the SADC region as an indicator of Harmful Tax Competition.* Cape Town: University of Cape Town. (MCom (Taxation)) at 65.

[14] http://www.oecd.org/tax/transparency/biographykosielouwchairoftheglobalforum.htm

[15] OECD (2012), Global Forum on Transparency and Exchange of Information for Tax Purposes Peer Reviews: South Africa 2012: Combined: Phase 1 + Phase 2, OECD Publishing. http://dx.doi.org/10.1787/9789264182134-en

Exchange of Information

South Africa has a substantial treaty network of DTAs (21 in Africa and 52 with the rest of the world in force) and an increasing number of Tax Information Exchange Agreements (seven in force and many more under negotiation or signed but not ratified). In addition, two multilateral treaties on exchange of information have been signed and another is under negotiation. An Inter-Government Agreement (IGA) relating to withholding and other obligations under the U.S.'s Foreign Account Tax Compliance Act (FATCA) has been negotiated with the United States and entered into force on the 28 October 2014. There seems to be an unofficial policy to conclude Double Tax Agreements with trading partners and Tax Information Exchange Agreements with other countries, particularly the former so-called tax havens.

For Double Tax Agreements, the form of Article 26 of the OECD Model is generally followed with some treaties carrying some additional text from the UN Model article. The TIEAs are generally modelled on the 2002 OECD Tax Information Exchange Agreement model with few variations.

As indicated in the OECD Global Forum Report, South Africa mainly enters into exchange of information by request, but has had a few instances of spontaneous exchange. South Africa has also been a recipient of automatic information exchange, but has not provided information on this basis. South Africa has not yet supplied information on an automatic basis cross-border, despite authority to do so arising from the Double Tax Conventions (DTCs).[16] South Africa currently lacks the mechanisms to engage in automatic exchange of information.[17] With respect to FATCA, South Africa has entered into an Inter-Governmental Agreement (IGA) to facilitate the exchange of information with the USA. It is the reciprocal Model 1 IGA.

South Africa is engaged in a pilot programme, with respect to the Southern African Customs Union (SACU) for the Assessment of a sub regional IT-automated Customs connectivity Pilot Programme. The pilot programme governs information exchange between South Africa and Swaziland. "As part of this Programme and with support of the Swedish International Development Cooperation Agency, the IT connectivity pilot between South Africa and Swaziland looks into Customs-to-Customs interoperability between the South African TATIS systems and the Swaziland ASYCUDA++ system".[18] The outcomes of this pilot programme are not yet known. These pilots are in pursuance of the annexures to the SACU Agreement, which provides in Annexure E Article 7 that the Member States may by mutual

---

[16] OECD (2012), Global Forum on Transparency and Exchange of Information for Tax Purposes Peer Reviews: South Africa 2012: Combined: Phase 1 + Phase 2, OECD Publishing. http://dx.doi.org/10.1787/9789264182134-en at 61 (paragraphs 188–189).

[17] Supra footnote 16.

[18] World Customs Organisation (2013), WCO SACU Customs Development Programme: Assessment of two sub regional IT-automated Customs connectivity Pilot Programmes in the Southern African region. http://www.wcoomd.org/en/about-us/~/media/WCO/Public/Global/PDF/About%20us/Vacancies/SACU%20ITC%20Vacany%20announcement.ashx at 3 [Accessed 16 September 2013].

agreement exchange any of the information contemplated within the Annexure on an automatic basis.[19] Launching of the pilot programmes is the precursor to automatic exchange, which has not yet taken place. The existence of such pilot programmes does, however, demonstrate the enormous work to still be undertaken with respect to planning for automatic exchange of information.

On 12 October 2013, it was announced by National Treasury that: "South Africa will join the pilot scheme for the automatic exchange of tax information launched by the United Kingdom, along with France, Germany, Italy and Spain. This initiative has received growing support worldwide, demonstrating the growing number of jurisdictions committed to quickly implementing the new standard in the automatic exchange of tax information being developed by the OECD".[20]

International exchanges of information only take place via tax treaties. Although the domestic tax legislation refers to exchange of information by request,[21] such exchange is only facilitated via the tax treaty network.

None of the tax treaties specify the nature of the information that is intended to be exchanged.

Investment Tax Incentives

There are no particular tax incentives for investment in emerging or developing countries however part of the Department of Trade and Industry's (DTI) international engagement is to support African regional economic integration and development. This is in support of the objectives and strategies of the African Union (AU), the New Partnership for Africa's Development (NEPAD) the Southern African Customs Union (SACU) and the Southern African Development Community (SADC). The DTI seeks, through SADC to "consolidate[e] the achievement of the free trade area, and work[] to extend the African integration through pursuit of the Tripartite SADC-EAC-COMESA FTA.[22] The Department[] continue[s] to engage with the EU to ensure Economic Partnership Agreements support and not disrupt-Integration in Southern Africa".[23]

---

[19] The Annexures to the SACU 2002 Agreement can be found at: http://www.sacu.int/publications/annexures.pdf

[20] SOUTH AFRICA. Ministry of Finance. 2013. *Statement of Auto Exchange Tax Info.* Available at: http://www.treasury.gov.za/comm_media/press/2013/2013101202%20-%20Statement%20on%20Auto%20Exchange%20Tax%20info.pdf

[21] See section "Prevention of Harmful Tax Competition" of the Tax Administration Act 28 of 2011. Available at: http://www.acts.co.za/tax-administration-act-2011/index.html

[22] Forum on Tax Administration (FTA), is the pre-eminent international body concerned with tax administration, comprising heads of tax administrations from the OECD, G20 and large emerging economies.

[23] The dti Department of Trade and Industry Republic of South Africa- African Regional Intergration. http://www.dti.gov.za/trade_investment/ited_ari.jsp (2013/12/05).

South Africa is between a developing and developed country and although it does provide assistance to other counties in some respects there are no particular tax incentives for investments in countries with low incomes, high poverty rates or high rates of economic inequality.

South Africa does treat former colonies and neighbouring countries more favourably in certain instances. SACU was established in 1910 as a Customs Union Agreement between the Union of South Africa and certain High Commission territories. SACU now includes five members (Botswana, Lesotho, Swaziland, South Africa and Namibia). SADC includes 15 member States. The priority of the SADC treaty is to consolidate the SADC free trade agreement.

South Africa has many measures in place to attract economic activity into the country. These measures vary depending on the type of industry or project.

South Africa does offer tax allowances (section 12I tax allowance Supported Projects) for specific projects (whether conducted by residents or non residents) within its own borders. The objectives of these incentives are to improve the productivity of the South African manufacturing sector, to support the training of personnel, to improve labour productivity and the skills profile of the labour force.[24]

A package of incentives is available for the film industry (whether resident or not). This consists mainly of the Foreign Film and Television production and post-production incentive and the South African Film and Television Production and Co-Production incentive. The objective of these incentives is to attract large film and television productions and post-production work that will contribute towards employment creation, enhancement of international profile, and increase the country's creative and technical base.[25]

Film production (in addition to other incentives), manufacturing and research and development activities all enjoy particular tax allowances. These tax allowances lead to a reduction in the effective tax rate.

Qualifying small businesses are taxed at reduced actual tax rates up to a certain threshold.

Mining companies are taxed differently than other companies due to the nature of the industry.

Numerous additional incentive schemes are provided for industrial innovation. Not all such schemes are provided by tax legislation or even managed by National Treasury. The majority of such schemes are in the form of grants. Such grant schemes are usually managed by rules issued in terms of the scheme rather than legislation. A multitude of schemes to attract foreign investment also exist in a variety of forms (some obvious and others less so). Co-ordination of such schemes is not evident.[26]

---

[24] The dti Department trade and Industry Republic of South Africa- Trade, Export and Incentive Financial Assistance (incentives) http://www.thedti.gov.za/financial_assistance/financial_incentive.jsp?id=45&sub (2013/12/05).

[25] http://www.dti.gov.za/trade_investment/export_incentive.jsp?id=7&subthemeid...=2013/12/05.

[26] J. Hattingh, *South Africa – Business and Investment* sec. 5., Country Surveys IBFD (accessed 23 Jan. 2014) at http://online.ibfd.org/document/gthc_za_s_5

Many of the grant schemes (termed "Financial Assistance") are managed by the Department of Trade and Industry (DTI).[27] A full guide to the incentive schemes is provided on the DTI site.[28] Most are geared toward South African companies (not necessarily tax resident). The guide lists the following incentives:

A. Industrial Development Incentives

- Automotive Investment Scheme (AIS)
- Capital Projects Feasibility Programme (CPFP)
- Clothing and Textile Competitiveness Improvement Programme (CTCIP)
- Production Incentive (PI)
- Critical Infrastructure Programme (CIP)
- Manufacturing Competitiveness Enhancement Programme (MCEP) People-Carrier Automotive Incentive Scheme (P-AIS)
- Section 12I Tax Allowance Incentive (12I)
- Support Programme for Industrial Innovation (SPII)
- Aquaculture Development Enhancement Programme (ADEP)

Broadening Participation Incentives

- Black Business Supplier Development Programme (BBSDP)
- Co-operative Incentive Scheme (CIS)
- Technology and Human Resources for Industry Programme (THRIP)
- Incubation Support Programme (ISP)

Trade, Export and Investment Incentives

- Business Process Services (BPS)
- Export Marketing and Investment Assistance (EMIA)
- Film and Television Incentive
- Foreign Film and Television Production and Post-Production Incentive.
- South African Film and Television Production and Co-Production Incentive
- The South African Emerging Black Filmmakers Incentive
- Sector-Specific Assistance Scheme (SSAS)

There are currently no tax holiday regimes but tax amnesties have been on offer over time and, from 2012, an ongoing amnesty is in place. The amnesty generally applies to undeclared foreign income and is called the Voluntary Disclosure Programme. This relief is in respect of penalties (excluding late submission), additional tax and criminal prosecution but is not available in respect of the original tax due, interest and foreign exchange contraventions.

Previous amnesties involved certain foreign exchange contraventions.

---

[27] Full details available at: http://www.thedti.gov.za/financial_assistance/financial_assistance.jsp
[28] http://www.thedti.gov.za/financial_assistance/docs/thedti_Incentive_Guide2014_2015.pdf

South African companies are taxed at a flat rate of 28 %. Branches of foreign companies are also taxed at 28 % from 1 April 2012 (previously at a higher rate of 33 % when a secondary tax on companies (STC)[29] was in place). Controlled foreign company (CFC) legislation is in place whereby South African resident shareholders of CFC's have to include the profits of the CFC in their income. There are certain exceptions such as the participation exemption which will exclude all distributed profits of the CFC.

Small business corporations are taxed at rates ranging from nil to 28 %.

The legal framework of exchange control is therefore one of a total prohibition to deal in foreign exchange except with the permission of and on the conditions set by the Treasury. The economic policy underlying exchange control is, however, not totally prohibitive, since such an approach would not be conducive to the conduct of normal international trade and payments.

The main purpose of exchange control is to:

- Ensure the timely repatriation into the South African banking system of certain foreign currency acquired by residents of South Africa, whether through transactions of a current or of a capital nature; and
- Prevent the loss of foreign currency resources through the transfer abroad of real or financial capital assets held in South Africa.[30]

South Africa maintains foreign currency reserves which are primarily earned by means of foreign borrowings as well as the export of goods (including gold) and services abroad.

These reserves are mainly utilised for the payment of goods and services imported into the country and for the servicing of the country's foreign debt.

Bilateral or Multilateral Investment Agreements

South Africa has entered into a number of trade and investment agreements, most of which are bilateral in nature but include some multilateral agreements. Certain of these agreements, particularly those pertaining to customs, contain tax provisions.

Since the proposal of the Promotion and Protection of Investment Bill, many of the bilateral investment treaties (BITs) may be terminated. In a written response to a question from a Member of Parliament, the Minister of Trade and Industry (R. Davies) provided: "South Africa entered into bilateral investment treaties (BITs) with some Member States of the European Union (EU) and not the EU itself. Investors from all countries, including EU countries, are granted strong protection for their investment through the legal framework governing investment in South Africa that is also guaranteed by the property protection clauses in the Constitution.

---

[29] STC was a dividend tax payable by the company which was replaced by a withholding tax payable by the shareholder on 1 April 2012. Branches of foreign companies were not subject to STC hence the higher tax rate.

[30] http://www.resbank.co.za/RegulationAndSupervision/FinancialSurveillanceAndExchangeControl/EXCMan/Section%20E/Section%20E.pdf

When South Africa notifies its intention to terminate a BIT, termination is effected between 6 and 12 months thereafter. It should be noted that protection under terminated BIT's can extend for between 10 and 20 years".[31]

> The Protection and Promotion of Investment Bill was published for public comment on 1 November 2013. The period for comment ends at the end of January 2014. We expect the Bill could become an Act of Parliament in the course of 2014. The Bill reconfirms all the protections currently granted to investors in South Africa under the existing legal framework and clarifies how provisions ordinarily found in BITs are interpreted in South African law. The Bill specifies the strong standards of protection granted to all investors in South Africa in a non-discriminatory manner and is not limited to countries with previously maintained BITs.[32]

South Africa has concluded a number of trade agreements.[33] Some are bilateral and others regional or multilateral. In summary, the main agreements are as follows:

Customs Unions

Southern African Customs Union (SACU)
Member states include: South Africa, Botswana, Lesotho, Namibia and Swaziland. The union aims to provide for the duty free movement of goods with a common external tariff on goods entering any of the countries from outside the SACU.

Free Trade Agreements (FTAs)

1. Southern African Development Community (SADC) Free Trade Agreement between 12 of the members states. Aim is duty free trade between these states on most products.
2. Trade, Development and Cooperation Agreement (TDCA) Free Trade Agreement between South Africa and the European Union (EU). There is currently a review of the agreement underway, which is aimed at broadening the scope of product coverage. This is taking place under the auspices of the Economic Partnership Agreement (EPA) negotiations between SADC and the EU.
3. EFTA-SACU Free Trade Agreement between SACU and the European Free Trade Association (EFTA) represented by Iceland, Liechtenstein, Norway and Switzerland. Only applies to selected goods.

---

[31] Available at https://pmg.org.za/question_reply/426/ (question 3029).

[32] Available at https://pmg.org.za/question_reply/426/ (question 3029).

[33] These are listed on the website of the Department of Trade and Industry at: http://www.thedti.gov.za/trade_investment/ited_trade_agreement.jsp

Preferential Trade Agreements (PTAs)

1. SACU-Southern Common Market (Mercosur) Preferential Trade Agreement between SACU and Mercosur (represented by Argentina, Brazil, Paraguay and Uruguay). Only applies to selected goods.
2. Zimbabwe/South Africa bilateral trade agreement for selected goods.

Non-reciprocal Trade Arrangements

1. Generalised System of Preferences (GSP), being the non-reciprocal systems of tariff preferences are offered by some developed countries to some developing countries without prior negotiations and agreements, is offered to South Africa as developing country by Japan, Kazakhstan, Norway, Russia, Turkey, and the US. It applies to selected products for preferential market access.
2. Africa Growth and Opportunity Act (AGOA) is a unilateral assistance measure granted by the US to 39 Sub-Saharan African (SSA) countries. It provides for preferential access to the US market through lower tariffs or no tariffs on some products.

Other Agreements

1. Trade, Investment and Development Cooperation Agreement (TIDCA) which is a cooperative framework agreement between SACU and the US. Makes provision for the parties to negotiate and sign agreements relating to sanitary and phytosanitary measures (SPS), customs cooperation and technical barriers to trade (TBT). It also establishes a forum of engagement of any matters of mutual interest, including capacity-building and trade and investment promotion.
2. Trade and Investment Framework Agreement (TIFA) between South Africa and the US. Provides a bilateral forum for the two countries to address issues of interest, including AGOA, TIDCA, trade and investment promotion, non-tariff barriers, SPS, infrastructure and others.

Current Trade Negotiations

1. SACU-India Preferential Trade Agreement for tariff reductions on selected goods.
2. SADC-EAC-COMESA Tripartite Free Trade Agreement. The Tripartite Framework derives its basis from the Lagos Plan of Action and the Abuja Treaty establishing the African Economic Community (AEC), which requires rationalisation of the continent's regional economic communities. The FTA will be

negotiated over the next 3 years, with the possibility of an additional 2 years for completion.

The Tripartite initiative comprises three pillars that will be pursued concurrently, in order to ensure an equitable spread of the benefits of regional integration: market integration, infrastructure development and industrial development. The FTA will, as a first phase, cover only trade in goods; services and other trade-related areas will be covered in a second phase.

The South African Revenue Service also administer a number of trade agreements or protocols or other parts or provisions thereof, and other international instruments mainly relating to customs.[34]

---

[34] Detail of these agreements can be found at: http://www.sars.gov.za/Legal/International-Treaties-Agreements/Trade-Agreements/Pages/default.aspx and include the following:

- Agreement on Trade, Development and Co-operation between the European Community and their Member States and the Republic of South Africa (TDCA)
- Treaty of the Southern African Development Community and Protocols concluded under the provisions of Article 22 of the Treaty (SADC Treaty and Protocols)
- Agreement between the Government of the Republic of South Africa and the Government of the United States of America regarding Mutual Assistance between their Customs Administrations (AGOA)
- Southern African Customs Agreement between the Governments of the Republic of Botswana, the Kingdom of Lesotho, the Republic of Namibia, the Republic of South Africa and the Kingdom of Swaziland (SACU)
- Memorandum of Understanding between the Government of the Republic of South Africa and the Government of the People's Republic of China on promoting Bilateral Trade and Economic Co-operation (MOU with People's Republic of China)
- Free Trade Agreement between the EFTA States and the SACU States (EFTA)
- SA-EU TDCA: SA cheese imports from the EU under TRQ

Chapter 17
International Taxation: The Case of Uganda

Jalia Kangave

Abstract In general, the worldwide tax system in place in Uganda removes any advantage resulting from investment in a low-tax country because it will collect tax at Ugandan rates after allowance of a credit for foreign taxes paid. Uganda has moved to gain conformity with internationally accepted tax practices, in particular by assisting in drafting or ratifying multilateral tax administrative assistance conventions. Although the number is small, all of Uganda's double taxation agreements contain exchange of information provisions. Additional treaties are under negotiation. In order to attract investment, Uganda has eliminated barriers to foreign ownership of private investments. It provides tax incentives to local and foreign investors that offer special allowances for research and development, workforce training, and asset depreciation. Certain industries, including farming, aircraft operations, and consumer goods exporting, benefit from certain tax exemptions. The practice of issuing incentive certificates that provided 3–6 year tax exemptions has ended. The government may, however, continue to provide tax holidays on an ad hoc basis in certain special circumstances.

Synopsis Uganda taxes its residents on their worldwide income. A dividend paid by one Ugandan company to another (owning at least 25 % of the voting power) is exempt from Ugandan tax. Dividends paid by a Ugandan company to a nonresident company are taxed at the rate of 15 % if the recipient owns at least 10 % of the voting power of the payer.

While there are no specific provisions targeting investments in tax haven jurisdictions, the worldwide tax system in place in Uganda removes any advantage of investing in a low-tax country because Uganda will collect tax at Ugandan rates after allowance of a tax credit for the foreign taxes paid. Regarding transactions between associated companies, the Uganda Revenue Administration (URA) has the authority to re-allocate income from a lower-taxed to a higher-taxed party in order to reflect arm's-length dealings. Thin capitalization rules prevent stripping out of

J. Kangave (✉)
International Centre for Tax and Development (ICTD) at the Institute of Development
Studies, UK
e-mail: jaliak@yahoo.com

© Springer International Publishing Switzerland 2017
K.B. Brown (ed.), *Taxation and Development - A Comparative Study*,
Ius Comparatum - Global Studies in Comparative Law 21,
DOI 10.1007/978-3-319-42157-5_17

earnings as interest payments where a corporation's debt to equity ratio is high (currently in excess of 1–1). The URA Commissioner has authority to re-characterize or disregard a transaction without economic substance and entered into in pursuance of a tax avoidance scheme. In addition, Uganda has adopted limitation-of-benefits type provisions that eliminate treaty benefits, such as a rate reduction or exemption, where the treaty beneficiary organized in a treaty country is in reality owned 50 % or more by nonresidents.

Uganda is moving toward conformity with internationally accepted tax practices. In this connection, transfer pricing guidelines have been issued. All of Uganda's double taxation agreements (DTAs) contain an exchange of information clause. In connection with the OECD's Global Forum, it has assisted in drafting an Agreement on Mutual Assistance in Tax Matters along with the African Tax Administration Forum (ATAF), which is not yet in force. Approval of the ratified OECD Convention on Mutual Administrative Assistance in Tax Matters is pending. Because Uganda does not enter into free-standing Tax Information Exchange Agreements (TIEAs), which are frequently very comprehensive, its exchange of information agreements in the DTAs have not in the past provided adequate guidance on standards, scope of coverage, and procedures. The selection of the URA's Tax Investigative Department as the Competent Authority for treaty purposes has allowed for the issuance of standards and expedited procedures.

Uganda's treaty network is quite small. Only the following nine DTAs are in force: Zambia, UK, Norway, South Africa, Denmark, India, Mauritius, Italy, and the Netherlands. Other treaties under negotiation are those with Egypt, China, Belgium, United Arab Emirates, Seychelles, and the East African Community.

Uganda has made efforts to attract investment. The non-tax measures include elimination of barriers to foreign ownership of private investments (100 % ownership is permitted) and investment in infrastructure (chiefly roads and hydropower). It has a large qualified workforce and is relatively politically stable.

Tax incentives (available to local and foreign investors) include special allowances for research and development, workforce training, and depreciation. In addition, there are exemptions from income tax for specified activities or industries, including interest earned by financial institutions on loans granted for purposes of various type of farming, and income from aircraft operation, exporting of finished consumer goods (10-year period), and agro-processing. Interest paid by Ugandan residents on certain debentures issued outside of Uganda for the purpose of raising funds outside of Uganda for use by a company carrying on business in Uganda or interest paid to a bank or a public financial institution is exempt from income tax. In the absence of an exemption, Uganda imposes a tax of 15 % of the gross amount of interest paid by Ugandan residents.

A now-repealed provision allowed issuance of incentive certificates that allowed exemption from income tax for 3–6 years depending upon the level of investment in Uganda. Although there is no legal framework, the government may continue to provide tax holidays on an ad hoc basis.

The corporate tax rate is generally 30 %. Nonresident companies are taxed on dividends received from Ugandan companies at the rate of 15 %. The rates may vary depending on the type of income derived.

Uganda is party to 15 bilateral investment treaties (BITs), with 7 in force. These agreements contain a type of non-discrimination clause (such as that contained in the BIT between Uganda and that Netherlands) that requires the contacting parties to treat residents of the other state as favorably as their own residents or residents of third party states in the same circumstances and accorded favorable treatment. These types of agreements may have a bearing on taxation rights, unless the particular BIT provides otherwise.

Uganda's International Tax System

Uganda taxes its residents on their worldwide income and gives a tax credit for income tax paid on foreign source income.

With the exception of transactions relating to petroleum operations, the Income Tax Act[1] (the ITA) does not distinguish between classes of dividends. As far as petroleum operations are concerned, a participation dividend is defined as "... a dividend paid by [a resident] contractor to a non-resident company that has a 10 % or greater voting interest in the voting power of the contractor." Participation dividends are taxed at 15 %. This is the same rate applicable to other dividend payments (whether to resident or non-resident companies), with one exception.

A dividend is exempt from tax where it is paid by one resident company to another resident company where the company receiving the dividend controls (directly or indirectly) at least 25 % of the voting power in the company paying the dividend.

Anti-tax Haven Provisions

There are no laws designed specifically to discourage investment in tax haven jurisdictions. There are, however, some aspects of the ITA that have a bearing on those who choose to invest in these jurisdictions. First, taxing residents on worldwide income ensures that tax not paid on foreign source income is paid in Uganda. Whether this has been achieved in practice as far as tax administration is concerned is of course a different matter.

The ITA also contains anti-avoidance provisions. First, for transactions between associates, the Commissioner General of the URA (Uganda Revenue Administration) is empowered to adjust income, deductions or credits between taxpayers to reflect

---

[1] Chap 340 Laws of Uganda.

the chargeable income that would have been realized in an arm's length transaction. Second, in determining tax liability under the Act, the Commissioner may re-characterize transactions that are entered into as part of tax avoidance schemes, disregard transactions which have no substantial economic effect, and re-characterize transactions whose form does not reflect the substance.

In 2004, the thin capitalization rules were amended to provide that where a foreign-controlled resident company has a foreign debt to foreign equity ratio in excess of 1 to 1, no deduction would be allowed on interest paid on the part of the debt exceeding that ratio. Before this, the ratio was 2 to 1. In June 2015, the Minister of Finance proposed that this ratio be revised to 1.5 to 1 but this proposal is yet to be reflected in the ITA.

Lastly, to protect against the abuse of double taxation agreements and other international agreements, the ITA provides that those benefiting from these agreements should have underlying ownership. Specifically, it provides that where an international agreement exempts or reduces tax payable in Uganda, the taxpayer will not benefit from the exemption or reduction if 50 % or more of the taxpayer's underlying ownership is held by an individual or individuals who are not residents of the other contracting state for purposes of the agreement.

There are no sanctions specific to investment in tax haven jurisdictions but the general provisions on interest and penalties for the late payment of taxes and making false or misleading statements may apply. There is no formal publically available record of the countries considered to be tax havens. However, given Uganda's deference to OECD guidelines in documents, such as its Transfer Pricing Regulations, it is safe to argue that Uganda considers as tax havens those countries considered to be tax havens by the OECD.

Coordination with Other Countries to Combat Unfair Tax Competition

As a member of the East African Community, Uganda is working toward agreement to coordinate action against countries that unfairly compete.

In addition, Uganda is a member of the OECD Global Forum.

Conformity with Internationally Accepted Tax Practices

Uganda is in the process of taking steps to conform with internationally accepted tax practices. In June 2011, the Minister of Finance issued The Income Tax (Transfer Pricing) Regulations. These Regulations are largely modeled after and applied in accordance with the OECD Transfer Pricing Guidelines.

Tax Information Exchange Agreements

Uganda does not have any separate agreements in force that are specific to information exchange. However, all the double taxation agreements (DTAs) in force in the country have a clause on exchange of information. In addition, Uganda is a member of the African Tax Administration Forum (ATAF), which, with the help of the OECD Global Forum, has drafted a multilateral *Agreement on Mutual Assistance in Tax Matters*. This agreement is, however, not yet in force. The country signed the OECD's Multilateral Convention on Mutual Administrative Assistance in Tax Matters in November, 2015.

In general, all information exchange provisions in DTAs are to the effect that the contracting states should exchange all information that is necessary for carrying out the provisions of the treaty or the domestic laws of the contracting states as long as taxation under the latter is not contrary to the provisions of the DTA. Agreements in force apply to income taxes.

The DTAs also provide that the contracting states shall be under no obligation to:

(a) Carry out administrative measures that vary with the laws and administrative practice of the contracting state;
(b) Obtain information which is not obtainable under the laws or in the normal course of administration of matters in the contracting states;
(c) Supply information which would disclose trade, business, industrial, commercial or professional secret or trade processes; or
(d) Supply information, the disclosure of which would be contrary to public policy.

These agreements only cover exchange of information in income tax matters.

In addition, while the DTAs have a clause on exchange of information, they lack the comprehensiveness that is characteristic of independent tax information exchange agreements (TIEAs). As such, there has been a lack of adequate information on issues such as procedures, standards and scope of usage of information exchanged. The 2014 adoption of the URA's Tax Investigation Department as the Competent Authority, however, has enabled more expedited processes. Moreover, since it became Competent Authority, the URA has designed a standard to be used for information exchange.

Finally, there is a small treaty network consisting of only nine DTAs in force with a few others at different stages of negotiation. Uganda has DTAs with Zambia, United Kingdom, Norway, South Africa, Denmark, India, Mauritius, Italy and the Netherlands. Treaties at different stages of negotiation include the ones with the East African Community, Egypt, China, Belgium, United Arab Emirates and Seychelles.

The ITA requires that exchange of information take place only where Uganda has either entered into a double taxation agreement or an agreement for the exchange of information.

Measures to Attract Investment

Uganda has taken various measures to attract economic activities to its jurisdiction. As just a few examples, it allows full repatriation of profits after payment of taxes and 100 % foreign ownership of private investments. There are also efforts towards investing extensively in infrastructure (particularly roads and hydropower), the country is relatively stable politically, has a large pool of qualified human resources, enters into DTAs and Bilateral Investment Treaties (BITs) and exempts and excludes from Value Added Tax the supply of various goods and services.

As far as international agreements are concerned, where there is inconsistency between an agreement and the ITA or any other law of Uganda dealing with matters covered by the agreement, the agreement prevails. The ITA defines an international agreement to mean an agreement signed with a foreign government to provide relief against double taxation and prevent fiscal evasion or an agreement signed with a foreign government or foreign organization providing for administrative assistance in tax matters.

There are a number of incentives and concessions provided in the ITA, some of which are outlined below. It should be underlined, however, that while these incentives appear largely geared towards attracting investments into the country, they can also be enjoyed by local investors who meet the relevant requirements.

Generally, the ITA allows deductions for a number of expenditures or losses including:

  (i) Expenditures and losses incurred in the production of income included in gross income;
 (ii) Yearly allowances for the depreciation of assets;
(iii) Unlimited carry forward losses;
(iv) Deductions for start-up costs;
 (v) Industrial building allowances;
(vi) Deductions for bad debts;
(vii) Deductions for scientific research expenditure; and
(viii) Deductions for training or tertiary education expenditure.

Some of the more specific concessions include:

  (i) Exemption from income tax for certain types of income, including income of an investor compensation fund; interest earned by financial institutions on loans granted to persons for purposes of farming, forestry, fish farming, bee keeping, animal and poultry husbandry; income derived from the operation of aircraft in domestic and international traffic or from leasing of aircraft; income derived from the exportation of finished consumer and capital goods for a period of 10 years; and income derived from agro-processing;
 (ii) Deductions for expenditures incurred by persons carrying on mining operations for expenditures of a capital nature connected with searching for, discovering, and testing or winning access to deposits of minerals in Uganda;

(iii) Special provisions relating to deductions allowed for contract expenditures in petroleum operations; and

(iv) Exemption from tax for interest paid by a resident company in respect of debentures as long as the debentures were issued by the company outside Uganda for the purpose of raising loans outside the country, the interest is paid outside Uganda and the debentures are widely issued for purposes of raising funds for use in a company carried on in Uganda or the interest is paid to a bank or a financial institution of a public character.

Tax Holidays

Uganda has offered no tax amnesty or publicized future amnesty for specific types of investments. It has previously given amnesties more generally in which it has waived interest and penalties on unpaid taxes.

Until 1997, the Investment Code provided that holders of certificates of incentive would be exempted from income tax for periods ranging between 3 and 6 years. To qualify for the 3 year income tax holiday, investors had to invest between USD 50,000 and USD 300,000. Five to 6 year holidays were given to investors making investments in excess of USD 300,000. Expatriate staff of those investors with incentive certificates were also exempt from import duty on their vehicles and personal effects. The 1997 ITA repealed the relevant section of the Investment Code that granted these certificates, allowing those investors who held certificates to continue to benefit from them until the exemption expired. All such certificates have since expired.

While there is no legal framework backing tax holidays, the government continues to provide them on an ad hoc basis.

Corporate Tax Rate Structure

Type of income	Resident company	Non-resident company
Corporate tax	30 % of chargeable income (gross income minus allowable deductions)	30 % of chargeable income plus 15 % of repatriated profits. The Act provides a formula for the calculation of repatriated income
Mining companies	Between 25 % and 45 % of chargeable income	Same as resident mining companies with the additional 15 % for repatriated profits
Ship operator, charterer or air transport operator		2 % of gross income
Telecommunication services	30 % of chargeable income	5 % of gross income

(continued)

Type of income	Resident company	Non-resident company
Petroleum operations	Contractors: 30 %	Contractors: 30 %
		Participation dividend: 15 %
		Subcontractor: 15 %
Withholding tax on interest	15 % of gross interest	15 % of gross interest. This tax is a final tax. It is not included in the gross income of the non-resident and no deductions are allowed for expenditures incurred in earning the income
	20 % on interest payments on government securities. This is a final tax	
Withholding tax on dividends	15 % of gross dividends	15 % of gross dividends. This tax is a final tax. It is not included in the gross income of the non-resident and no deductions are allowed for expenditures incurred in earning the income

Investment Treaties

Publicly available information indicates that as of 2003, Uganda had signed bilateral investment treaties (BITs) with 15 countries. However, only seven of these treaties are in force.

Some of the agreements contain tax provisions. For example, Article 4 of the BIT between Uganda and Netherlands provides:

> With respect to taxes, fees and charges and to fiscal deductions and exemptions, each Contracting Party shall accord to investors of the other Contracting Party who are engaged in any economic activity in its territory, treatment not less favorable than that accorded to its own investors or to those of any third State who are in the same circumstances, whichever is more favourable to the investors concerned. For this purpose, however, there shall not be taken into account any special fiscal advantages accorded by that Party:
>
> (a) Under an agreement for the avoidance of double taxation; or
> (b) By virtue of its participation in a customs union, economic union or similar institution; or
> (c) On the basis of reciprocity with a third State.

Arguably, even those agreements that do not contain tax-specific provisions can have a bearing on taxing rights through the provisions pertaining to the national treatment standard, the most favoured nation standard, and the protection against expropriation, as some cases before arbitral tribunals in other jurisdictions have revealed. There are, however, some cases where such an interpretation is expressly excluded. For example, in the BIT between Uganda and the United Kingdom, it is expressly stated that the national treatment standard or treatment given to third states shall not be construed as imposing an obligation on a contracting party to extend to the nationals or companies of the other contracting state the benefit of any treatment, preference or privilege resulting from an international tax agreement or domestic tax legislation.

There are BITs in force are with: Denmark, France, Germany, Italy, Netherlands, Switzerland and United Kingdom.

Chapter 18
Britain Open for Business

Rita Cunha

Abstract The UK Government has recently declared its commitment to creating the most competitive tax regime in the G20 for holding companies and business hubs. In pursuing this goal, it has reduced corporate tax rates and introduced a branch profits exemption. It has also created a new patent box regime and extended business deductions and investment exemptions. Investment in emerging countries is promoted through tax sparing provisions and an extensive network of bilateral investment treaties. It is not yet clear how Brexit will impact the UK tax system, but the Government has already announced its intention to privilege trade with emerging economies.

Synopsis The UK Government has expressly asserted that the UK tax system aims to promote foreign investment. Several measures have been introduced for this purpose. The corporate tax rate has been gradually reduced from 28 to 20 % and further reduction to 18 % is contemplated. Another strategy has been to move towards a more territorial corporate tax regime. Despite the general rule being taxation on a worldwide basis, the recent branch profits exemption justifies the claim that territorial principles now dominate the UK corporate tax regime. Generous exemptions for inbound and outbound dividends have been created over the years. In the absence of an exemption, a credit for foreign taxes paid is allowed against the UK tax liability (either under domestic law or a treaty). For attracting

R. Cunha (✉)
University of London, London, UK
e-mail: rcd250@nyu.edu

© Springer International Publishing Switzerland 2017
K.B. Brown (ed.), *Taxation and Development - A Comparative Study*,
Ius Comparatum - Global Studies in Comparative Law 21,
DOI 10.1007/978-3-319-42157-5_18

specific types of investment, a new patent box regime was created (featuring a 10 % tax rate for profits from the development and exploitation of patents), along with generous research and development (R & D) deductions. Special deductions for film, television, theater and video game development have been introduced over the past few years.

Investment in emerging countries is promoted via tax sparing provisions in tax treaties and an extensive network of bilateral investment treaties. Tax sparing provisions are contained in the following tax treaties: Bangladesh, Belize, Bosnia and Herzegovina, Botswana, Bulgaria, Croatia, Cyprus, Egypt, Ethiopia, Fiji, The Gambia, Guyana, India, Indonesia, Israel, Ivory Coast, Jamaica, Kenya, Kiribati, Malaysia, Mauritius, Montenegro, Morocco, Nigeria, Pakistan, Papua New Guinea, Portugal, Serbia, Spain, Sri Lanka, Sudan, Thailand, Trinidad and Tobago, Tunisia, Turkey, Tuvalu, Uganda, and Zambia.

While promoting inward and outward investment, the UK has also adopted a number of strategies to protect its tax base from abusive practices. It introduced a GAAR (General Anti-Avoidance Rule) in 2013 and continues to introduced SAARs (specific anti-avoidance rules) every financial year. The deterrent effect of the GAAR was reinforced in 2014 when the HMRC was attributed the power to require taxpayers to pay the tax upfront, regardless of the tax liability being litigated (Advanced Payment Notice). Other important anti-avoidance regimes include CFC legislation, transfer pricing rules, worldwide debt caps and the unique Diverted Profits Tax (the so-called "Google Tax"). The latter may determine a charge of 25 % of the profits diverted through (i) the exploitation (by foreign enterprises) of the permanent establishment regime; and (ii) transactions or entities lacking economic substance.

The UK has introduced disclosure regimes to deter avoidance schemes and promote transparency in the tax regime. Taxpayers and promoters are required to provide prescribed information to HMRC, under the Disclosure of Tax Avoidance Schemes (DOTAS) regime.

The Promoters of Tax Avoidance Schemes (POTAS) regime reinforces the disclosure obligations under DOTAS. Failure to comply with these regimes may result in serious penalties. At the international level, the UK has entered into a number of FATCA agreements and TIEAs (Tax Information Exchange Agreements). It collaborates with the OECD regarding the implementation of international standards for exchanging information. The OECD's Global Tax Forum has considered the UK to be largely compliant, despite suggesting the renegotiation of several of its older treaties.

United Kingdom's International Tax System

Individuals[1] and corporations[2] resident in the UK are taxed on their worldwide income.[3] Significant exemptions are provided for foreign income (see section "Territorial features of UK's international tax system: individuals", below). When such exemptions do not apply, a tax credit for foreign taxes paid (or deemed to be paid) may be granted under a tax treaty or domestic law.[4] Alternatively, foreign taxes may be deducted in calculating the income or capital gain.[5]

Individuals who are resident and domiciled[6] in the UK are liable to UK income tax on their worldwide income and UK capital gains tax (CGT) on their worldwide gains in the tax year in which that income or gains arise. Individuals who are resident but not domiciled in the UK have the possibility to be taxed on a remittance basis instead.[7] In such case, individuals will only be subject to UK tax on their foreign source income and gains, if and when such income and gains are remitted to

---

[1] In 2013, a statutory residency test for individuals was enacted to replace the residency rules previously developed by courts and the HM Revenue & Customs (HMRC) (Section 218 and Schedule 45 of the Finance Act 2013, FA 2013). According to the new statutory test, residency is established according the following alternative tests (applicable in order of priority): (1) Individual meets the first automatic UK test: Individual spends 183 days or more in the UK in the relevant tax year; (2) Individual does not meet one of the three automatic overseas tests: (a) Individual is resident in the UK for more than 1 year in the 3 preceding tax years but spends less than 16 days in the UK in the relevant tax year; (b) Individual is not resident in the UK in any of the 3 preceding years and spends less than 46 days in the UK in the relevant tax year; (c) Individual works full-time overseas and spends less than 91 days in the UK in the relevant tax year; (3) Individual meets the second automatic UK test: Individual has a home in the UK during the relevant tax year and spends sufficient amount of time in that home; (4) Individual meets the third automatic UK test: Individual works full-time in the UK, with no significant break; (5) Individual meets the sufficient ties test (for details and examples, see "Guidance Note: Statutory Residence Test" (RDR3), December 2013).

[2] A company is resident in the United Kingdom if: (1) it is incorporated in any one of its three company jurisdictions, i.e. England and Wales, Scotland and Northern Ireland (section 14 of CTA 2009), or (2) its business is centrally managed and controlled in the United Kingdom (*De Beers Consolidated Mines v. Howe*, HL 1906 5 TC 198).

[3] Income tax and corporations tax legislation is contained in the Income and Corporation Taxes Act 1988 (ICTA), the Taxation of Chargeable Gains Act 1992 (TCGA), the Capital Allowances Act 2001 (CAA), Income Tax (Earnings and Pensions) Act 2003 (ITEPA), Income Tax (Trading and Other Income) Act 2005 (ITTOIA), Income Tax Act 2007 (ITA), Corporation Tax Act 2009 (CTA 2009), Corporation Tax Act 2009 (CTA 2010) and Taxation (International and Other Provisions) Act 2010 (TIOPA).

[4] Section 9 of TIOPA. Domestic law provisions granting unilateral relief from double taxation are contained in TIOPA.

[5] Section 112–115 of TIOPA.

[6] Domicile is decided under general law, i.e., determined according to court rulings of the courts. In general terms, an individual has his domicile in the country that is his real or permanent home to which, if he has left, he intends to return.

[7] Prior to 6 April 2013, an individual could also choose to be taxed on the remittance basis if they had foreign income and were resident but not ordinarily resident in the UK. The concept of ordinary residence has been abolished for tax purposes from 6 April 2013. For the taxable year 2013–2014, this possibility is only available to individuals that are not domiciled in the UK.

the UK (see section "Territorial features of UK's international tax system: individuals" below).

In 2015, the Chancellor of the Exchequer announced that the non-domicile status will be abolished for all tax purposes from 6 April 2017 onwards. Non-domiciled individuals who have been resident in the UK for more than 15 or 20 years will be deemed UK domiciled for all tax purposes.

Companies resident in the UK are also subject to corporation tax on their worldwide profits, whether or not the profits are distributed, and whether or not they are remitted to the United Kingdom. This general rule is subject to one significant exception, the branch exemption rules (see section "Territorial features of UK's international tax system: corporations" below), which justify the claim that territorial principles now predominate in the UK.

When double taxation occurs, relief by way of credit can be granted under tax treaty or domestic law. If a tax credit for the foreign tax may be allowed under a tax treaty, it will not be allowed under domestic law.[8] When a treaty is not available, UK domestic legislation provides for unilateral relief from double taxation by means of an ordinary foreign tax credit.[9]

Territorial Features of UK's International Tax System: Individuals

Specified types of foreign income and capital gains derived by individuals and corporations resident in the UK can be exempted from taxation in the UK. For individuals, the main exemption is available only to non-domiciled individuals, who can choose to be taxed on a remittance basis. For corporations, the main exemption is the branch profit exemption. Both regimes are voluntary.

Individuals who are resident but not domiciled in the UK can elect to pay tax on a remittance basis, in which case foreign income and capital gains are exempted from UK tax only until remitted to the UK.[10] The statutory definition of "remittance" is wide and covers situations in which a remittance is deemed to occur even if income or gains are not physically brought to the UK.[11]

The remittance basis of taxation applies to the following specified income[12]:

1. *Foreign earnings*, i.e., *employment income when services are provided outside the UK – Sections 22 and 26 of ITEPA ("Overseas Workday Relief").* When not domiciled in the UK, resident individuals are eligible to be taxed on a remittance basis with respect to their offshore employment income, if (i) paid by a foreign

---

[8] Section 11 of TIOPA.

[9] Part 2 of TIOPA.

[10] Sections 809B, 809D and 809E of ITA 2007.

[11] Section 809L of ITA deals with alienation, conversion and exporting debts.

[12] Section 809F of ITA.

employer, and (ii) the duties are performed wholly outside the United Kingdom.[13] The employee is not eligible if he was a UK resident in any of the 3 years previous to the relevant tax year.[14] Employment-related securities income can be also exempted from charge if not remitted to the UK.[15]

2. *Relevant foreign income charged on the remittance basis – Section 830 of ITTOIA.* "Relevant foreign income" is income arising from a source outside the United Kingdom falling in one the following categories: trade profits, profits of property business, interest, dividends from non-UK companies, purchased life annuity payments, profits from deeply discounted securities, sales of foreign dividend coupons, royalties and other income from intellectual property, non-trade income from films and sound recordings, non-trade income in respect of certain telecommunication rights, state income, annual payments not otherwise charged to tax and any income not otherwise charged, partner's share of the profits of the trade arising outside the United Kingdom, and foreign pensions.

3. *Foreign chargeable gains charged on the remittance basis – Section 12 of Taxation of Chargeable Gains Act (TCGA).* "Foreign chargeable gains" are chargeable gains accruing from the disposal of an asset which is situated outside the United Kingdom.

In order for the remittance basis to apply, the individual has to make a claim. In such a case, he is not entitled to any personal allowance, married couples' tax reduction, or capital gains tax annual exemption for the year she claims the exemption.[16] For long-term UK residents, the claim for remittance basis is accompanied by a charge (remittance basis charge), as following: once the individual has been resident in the UK for more than 7 out of the 9 years before the relevant tax year, a charge of £30,000 applies (7-year residence test). The amount rises to £50,000 after 12 out of 14 years of UK residence (12-year residence test).[17] Long-term residents are required to nominate the income and capital gains which will be subject to charge.[18] When the identified income and gains are remitted to the UK, they will not be taxed again. Individuals with less than £2,000 unremitted foreign income and gains are exempt from the remittance basis charge, and keep their entitlement to the personal allowances and capital gains tax annual exemption (*de minimis* exception).[19]

FA 2012 introduced a "business investment relief,"[20] allowing remittance basis users to remit foreign income and gains to the UK without these being treated as taxable remittances. This benefit applies to qualifying investments, i.e., where the remitted income and gains are used to obtain newly issued shares in a target company

---

[13] Section 26 of ITEPA.

[14] Section 26A of ITEPA.

[15] Section 41A and *seq.* of ITEPA.

[16] Section 809 of ITA.

[17] Section 809C(1) of ITA.

[18] Sub-sections 809C(2) and (3) of ITA.

[19] Under section 809D of ITA, the individual is not required to make the claim.

[20] Sections 809VA and seq. of ITA.

or to grant a loan to such a company (the target company should be a trading company or the holding company of a trading group). The qualifying investment must be made within 45 days of remittance of the foreign income or gains to the United Kingdom.

Territorial Features of UK's International Tax System: Corporations

FA 2011 granted UK corporations the possibility to elect an exemption of foreign permanent establishment (PE) profits and losses.[21] The exemption also applies to capital gains or losses arising on the disposal of an asset (including immovable property) where that property has been used for carrying on the foreign PE's business. The election is irrevocable. With this regime, the UK has moved from a system of worldwide taxation for UK companies to a broadly territorial tax system where the focus is on taxing profits earned in the UK.

Exemption for Dividends from Foreign Subsidiaries

Most dividends received after 1 July 2009 by UK companies from foreign subsidiaries are fully exempted from tax.[22] Where the exemption does not apply, or the company makes an election for the exemption not to apply, double tax relief by way of a tax credit is available (direct and indirect tax credit).

Dividend Exemption for Medium or Large Companies

FA 2009 provides for the exemption of most dividends and other distributions (including capital distributions) received by medium or large companies, irrespective of source (i.e., whether domestic or foreign).[23] For the exemption to be available, the distribution must fall within one of several "exempt classes:"

(a) *Distributions from controlled companies (section 931E of CTA 2009)*
    A distribution falls into this class if either of two conditions is met.

    1. The recipient company controls the paying company, or
    2. The recipient is one of two persons who, taken together, control the payer, and the recipient must be a person who has interests, rights and powers represent-

---

[21] Sections 18A to 18S of CTA 2009.

[22] The relevant provisions are set out in Pt. 9A of CTA 2009.

[23] Part 9ᴬ CTA 2009.

ing at least 40 % of the holdings, rights and powers in respect of which the recipient and the other person are taken as controlling the company; the second person must have interests, rights and powers representing at least 40 %, but not more than 55 %, of the holdings, rights and powers in respect of which the two persons are taken as controlling the company.

(b) *Distributions in respect of non-redeemable ordinary shares (section 931F of CTA 2009)*[24]

(c) *Distributions in respect of portfolio holdings (section 931G of CTA 2009)*
    This exemption applies if the recipient:

   – Holds less than 10 % of the issued share capital of the payer;
   – Is entitled to less than 10 % of the profits available for distribution to holders of the issued share capital; AND
   – Is entitled, on a winding up, to less than 10 % of the assets available for distribution to holders of the issued share capital.

(d) *Dividends derived from transactions not designed to reduce tax (section 931H of CTA 2009)*
    The dividend must be paid out of "relevant profits," i.e., profits available for distribution at the time the dividend is paid, which are not the result of a transactions aimed at reducing UK tax.

(e) *Dividends in respect of shares accounted for as liabilities (section 931I of CTA 2009)*
    A share that is accounted for as a liability is treated as a loan relationship if it is held for an "unallowable purpose." The distribution exemption applies in respect of shares accounted for as liabilities, if they are not treated as a loan relationship.

In addition to the specific anti-avoidance rules which apply in respect of each of the exempt classes, there are several exceptions to the dividend exemption: (a) *schemes in the nature of loan relationships (section 931M of CTA 2009)*, (b) *schemes involving distributions for which deductions are given (section 931N of CTA 2009)*, (c) *schemes involving payments for distributions (section 931O of CTA 2009)*, (d) *schemes involving payments not on arm's length terms (section 931P of CTA 2009)*, and (e) *schemes involving diversion of trade income (section 931Q of CTA 2009)*.

---

[24] "Ordinary share" is defined in section 931U of CTA 2009 as a share that does not carry any present or future preferential right to dividends or to a company's assets on its winding up. For the purposes of the legislation, a share is "redeemable" only if it is redeemable as a result of its terms of issue (or any collateral arrangements) (i) requiring redemption, (ii) entitling the holder to require redemption or (iii) entitling the issuing company to redeem.

Small Companies

Small companies[25] may qualify for the exemption in respect of distributions paid to them, if certain conditions are met:

1. The paying company must be resident in the United Kingdom, or in a "qualifying territory" (i.e., a territory with which the United Kingdom has a double taxation arrangement with a non-discrimination clause) and must not be a dual resident company; AND
2. The distribution should not be part of a scheme to gain a tax advantage.

Imputation Credit

Resident companies receiving an exempt "qualifying distribution" are entitled to a tax credit equal to one-ninth of the distribution, whether the distribution is made by a resident or non-resident company. The tax credit of one-ninth attaching to the dividend is not repayable, except under a tax treaty providing for repayment. This rule is effective for distributions paid on or after 1 July 2009. Before this date, the tax credit was available only in respect of distributions paid by UK resident companies.

Double Tax Relief via Credit

When foreign-source dividends do not qualify for the exemption or an election has been made not to apply the exemption, relief is available from double taxation under the ordinary credit method.

Where a company has 10 % or more voting power in a non-resident company, credit relief is also given in respect of tax paid on the profits out of which the dividend payment is made, known as underlying tax (indirect tax credit). This relief follows through any number of companies in a chain, irrespective of their country of residence, so long as there is a 10 % voting power relationship between dividend recipient and payer at every link of the chain.

The tax credit may be carried backwards for 3 years or carried forward indefinitely. It may only be set against the UK tax payable on dividends of the permitted type. The unrelieved foreign tax may also be surrendered to another company in the same group.

---

[25] As defined in the Annex to Commission Recommendation 2003/361.

General Anti-abuse Rule (GAAR)[26]

In addition to the promotion of exchange of information at international forums (as the G20), which makes offshore investment more transparent and discourages investment in tax havens, the UK has adopted domestic legislation to tackle offshore tax evasion and tax avoidance. Regarding tax avoidance, some of the measures are of general application (GAAR, DOTAS, POTAS), while other measures specifically discourage the shifting of profits to lower tax jurisdictions (Transfer Pricing, CFC legislation, Diverted Profits Tax).

FA 2013 introduced a GAAR to counter arrangements that "*cannot reasonably be regarded as a reasonable course of action.*" The GAAR applies to income tax, corporation tax, capital gains tax, petroleum revenue tax, inheritance tax, stamp duty land tax, the annual tax on enveloped dwellings, National Insurance Contributions (since 2014), and diverted profits tax.

Since 17 July 2014, the HMRC has the power to issue an Advanced Payment Notice to require taxpayers to pay the tax upfront, even if the liability for that tax is the subject of a dispute or litigation. It suffices that (i) a tax arrangement has been subject to a counteraction notice under the GAAR, and (ii) the opinion of two members of a GAAR panel concludes that entering into the arrangements was not a reasonable course of action.

The government is currently considering the introduction of a GAAR Penalty of 60 %.[27] The GAAR penalty would not apply to taxpayers who correctly self-assess for the GAAR, and/or settle with HMRC before the arrangements are referred to the GAAR panel.

The Government has also confirmed its intention to introduce a surcharge and special reporting requirements for serial avoiders (Serial Avoiders' Regime).

Disclosure of Tax Avoidance Schemes (DOTAS)[28]

DOTAS requires a tax arrangement to be disclosed where it will, or might be expected to, enable any person to obtain a tax advantage, or when it is a hallmarked scheme. The duty to disclose normally falls on the scheme promoter[29] (within 5

---

[26] Part 5 of FA 2013, with effect from 1 April 2013.

[27] In 2015, the Government has conducted two consultations on the GAAR Penalty: 30 January–12 March 2015 and 22 July–14 October 2015.

[28] Part 7 of FA 2004.

[29] A person is a promoter if, in the course of a relevant business they are responsible for the design of a scheme, make a firm approach to another person with a view to making a scheme available for implementation by that person or other, make a scheme available for implementation by others, or organise or manage the implementation of a scheme. Both UK and non-UK based promoters are subject to the disclosure rules but they only apply to the extent that the scheme enables or is expected to enable a UK tax advantage to be obtained.

days of the trigger event), or the user of the scheme when (i) a non-UK based promoter does not disclose a scheme, (ii) the promoter is a lawyer and legal professional privilege prevents him from providing the prescribed information to the
HMRC; (iii) there is no promoter (i.e., the scheme is devised 'in-house' for use
within that entity or a corporate group to which it belongs).

Once a scheme has been disclosed, the HMRC issues a scheme reference number. If the scheme promoter made the disclosure, he must send the reference number
on to his clients. The scheme user must including the number on his tax return. The
promoter must also provide the HMRC with periodic lists of persons to whom they
issued a scheme reference number.

The objective of DOTAS is to obtain early information about tax arrangements,
how they work, and who has used them. The disclosure of a tax arrangement has no
effect on the tax position of the taxpayer, except if it is rendered ineffective by
Parliament with retrospective effect.

Penalties may be imposed on promoters and users of schemes if they don't comply with DOTAS obligations.[30]

In 2015, Government conducted a consultation on measures to improve large
business tax compliance (22 July–14 October 2015), including a statutory obligation for businesses to publish their tax strategy and a voluntary Code of Practice on
Taxation for Large Business.

Promoters of Tax Avoidance Schemes (POTAS)[31]

The objective of POTAS is to deter the development and use of avoidance schemes
by influencing the behaviour of promoters, their intermediaries and clients. It reinforces the disclosure obligations under DOTAS. For the purposes of POTAS, a
monitored promoter is a promoter subject to a monitoring notice issued by the
HMRC (i) after he breached a conduct notice (imposing conditions about how a
promoter must behave), and (ii) after the First-tier Tribunal approved the monitoring
notice.

The monitoring notice may impose several obligations on the promoter (subsequent penalties may apply for failure to comply with such obligations): (i) the publication by the promoter of its monitored promoter status on the internet and in
publications and correspondence (£1,000,000); (ii) a duty on the promoter to tell
clients that it is a monitored promoter and to provide them with a promoter reference number (PRN) (£5,000); (iii) a duty on clients to put the PRN on their returns;
(iv) duty of monitored promoter or intermediary to provide information and documents (£1,000,000); (v) ongoing duty of monitored promoter to provide information and documents (£1,000,000); (vi) duty of monitored promoter or intermediary
to provide information about persons who have taken part in avoidance schemes

---

[30] Section 98C of Taxes Management Act 1970.

[31] Part 5 and schedules 34–36 of FA 2014 (from April 2015).

(£10,000); (vii) ongoing duty of monitored promoter to provide information about clients (£5,000).

This regime applies to the following taxes: Income Tax, Capital Gains Tax (CGT), Corporation Tax (CT), Petroleum Revenue Tax (PRT), Inheritance Tax (IHT), Stamp Duty Land Tax (SDLT), Stamp Duty Reserve Tax (SDRT), Annual Tax on Enveloped Dwellings (ATED).

Diverted Profits Tax (Google Tax)[32]

The Google Tax is aimed at catching profits being diverted away from the United Kingdom, typically by multinational enterprises. The rules target two main types of transaction: (i) where UK profits are diverted away by the exploitation (by foreign enterprises) of the permanent establishment rules; and (ii) where tax advantages are created by means of transactions or entities lacking economic substance. Several exemptions from the diverted profit tax apply, including for small and medium-sized companies, companies with limited UK sales or expenses, and where arrangements give rise to loan relationships only. The diverted profits tax charge is 25 % of the diverted profits relating to UK activity.

Transfer Pricing and CFC Legislation

To reduce and prevent base erosion by profit shifting to low tax jurisdictions, the UK has in place transfer pricing rules[33] and Controlled Foreign Company (CFC) legislation.[34] A foreign company is a CFC if it is controlled by UK persons and if the foreign tax paid in its territory of residence is less than 75 % of the corresponding UK tax on its profits.

Debt Cap Provisions

Finance Act 2009 introduced debt cap provisions for companies which are members of large groups (i.e., a group in which no member falls within the categories of micro, small, and medium-sized enterprises for the purposes of Commission Recommendation 2003/361).[35] The worldwide debt cap (WWDC) limits the corporation tax deduction for interest and other finance expenses of the UK members of large groups of companies that have net finance expenses.

---

[32] Part 3 of FA 2015 (for profits arising on or after 1 April 2015).

[33] Part IV of TIOPA.

[34] Part 9A of TIOPA.

[35] Part 7 of TIOPA.

Penalties for Offshore Tax Evasion

HMRC charges penalties in cases where income and capital gains are not declared
or notified to HMRC (either deliberately or through a failure to take reasonable
care) in addition to the tax that has been lost and interest thereon. Penalties correspond to a percentage of the amount of tax that has been lost. The level of penalty is
based on the behavior that leads to the understatement of tax. For example, where
income in omitted from a return, a maximum penalty of 30 % may be charged if the
error is due to a failure to take reasonable care. The percentage increases to 70 %,
where the understatement is deliberate, and to 100 %, where a deliberate understatement is aggravated by concealment. These percentages vary according to the
Treasury's classification of the territories in which the income or gain arises. FA
2015 set that for 2016, the following categories apply:

- For territories in 'category 0', the penalty rates referred above (standard penalty)
  apply. Category 0 applies to most transparent countries, which have accepted the
  global Common Reporting Standard set out by the OECD.
- For territories in 'category 1,' the penalty rate is 1.25 times the standard penalty.
  Category 1 includes a list of territories with automatic exchange of information
  on savings income with the UK such as Cayman Islands, Cyprus, Guernsey,
  Ireland, Isle of Man, Lichtenstein, Malta, Netherlands, Switzerland, and the US.
- For territories in 'category 2,' the penalty rate is 1.5 times the standard penalty.
  Category 2 includes all territories that are not listed in category 1 or 3.
- For territories in 'category 3,' the penalty rate is double the standard penalty.
  Category 3 includes a list of territories that do not exchange information with the
  UK or whose agreements do not follow the international standard for exchange
  of information such as Albania, Andorra, Brazil, Colombia, Macau, Monaco,
  Panama, Paraguay, United Arab Emirates.

These penalties can be increased by 50 % (aggravated penalty) when the taxpayer moves the proceeds of tax evasion (after 27 March 2015) in order to escape
tax transparency.

New Measures to Tackle Offshore Tax Evasion

In 2015, the UK Government announced new measures to clampdown on offshore
tax evasion, including:

- A new strict liability criminal offence for failing to declare untaxed offshore
  assets. The HMRC would no longer need to prove that individuals who have
  undeclared income offshore intended to evade tax in order for a criminal convic-
  tion to be handed down. Demonstrating that the income was taxable and undeclared would be enough for criminal sanctions to be imposed, including unlimited
  penalties and imprisonment,

- A new corporate criminal offence of failure to prevent the facilitation of evasion,
- Civil sanctions for enablers of offshore evasion (i.e., individual or corporation providing services which assist a UK taxpayer to evade UK tax),
- Increasing civil penalties for offshore evaders, including an additional asset based penalty equivalent to a portion of the value of the asset linked to the evasion,
- Naming and shaming offshore evaders.

Tax Laws Designed to Discourage Investment in Harmful Tax Regimes

The UK has entered into a FATCA agreement with the United States. It has also adopted its own FATCA according to which financial institutions in Jersey, Guernsey and the Isle of Man (the Crown Dependencies) and the Overseas Territories of Anguilla, Bermuda, the British Virgin Islands, the Cayman Islands, Gibraltar, Montserrat and the Turks and Caicos Islands (the Overseas Territories) are required to automatically provide information relating to the financial affairs of UK resident clients.

To persuade UK residents to repatriate funds from tax havens, currently there are two disclosure facilities for offshore investments. One instrument is the Liechtenstein Disclosure Facility (2009), under which a taxpayer with undisclosed assets may regularize his tax situation by paying the tax and interest due and all capped penalties (10 % for 2008/2009, 20 %/30 % thereafter). The Liechtenstein Disclosure Facility expired on 31 December 2015. The other mechanism is the Crown Dependencies Disclosure Facility (2013). Jersey, Guernsey and the Isle of Man signed parallel agreements with the UK introducing broadly similar voluntary disclosure facilities. These agreements also expired at the end of 2015.

In 2015, the UK Government announced a new disclosure facility for 2016/2017 for unpaid taxes connected with overseas bank accounts.

Codes of Conduct and Other Agreements Limiting Unfair Competition for Capital

As an EU Member-State, the UK is expected to follow the Code of Conduct for Business Taxation (1997), i.e., to refrain from introducing tax measures that constitute harmful tax competition.

As an OECD Member, the UK participates in the OECD Forum on Harmful Tax Practices and on the OECD BEPS project, which have ongoing work on this area.

Global Tax Forum

The UK is a member of the OECD's Global Tax Forum and has been subject to a combined peer review encompassing phase 1 (assessment of the legal and regulatory framework) and phase 2 (practical implementation of that framework). According to the combined report (September 2011), the UK is *largely compliant*. The supplementary report (April 2013) assessed the improvements made in the UK legal framework and practical mechanisms since the adoption of the previous report in September 2011.

Regarding the availability of information, the UK was deemed to comply with the standards set for accounting records and banking information. However, both 2011 and 2013 reports highlight that the name of the owners of bearer shares were not recorded in the company's register and could be sold without the company being notified. As the information concerning the bearer shares owners was not available, the UK would need to ensure that the owners are identified or the bearer shares eliminated.

The Small Business, Enterprise and Employment Act 2015 has prohibited companies from issuing new bearer shares and established a mechanism to abolish the existing bearer shares (surrender of bearer shares for conversion into registered shares).

With respect to information access, the notification requirements and rights and safeguards were deemed compliant. The combined report of 2011 highlighted that the tax authorities were not allowed to gather information where the name of taxpayer was not known. The report recommended a statutory change allowing the access to third party information where the name of taxpayer was not known. In this regard, the United Kingdom has introduced new legal provisions and procedures empowering the HMRC to obtain information where the name of the taxpayer is not provided by the requesting jurisdiction (section 5A of Schedule 36 of FA 2012).

Both 2011 and 2013 reports underscore that the formal process to obtain information is complex and slow, causing undue delay to exchange of information (it was noted that on average it takes 12 months for the information to be provided to the requesting jurisdiction). Both reports recommend that the procedure for accessing information needs to be improved.

Several UK tax treaties were deemed not to comply with the international standards (e.g. Barbados, Egypt, Fiji, Gambia, Israel, Jamaica, Kenya, Liechtenstein, Namibia, Nigeria, Oman, Papua New Guinea, Sri Lanka, Swaziland, Switzerland, Tunisia, Zambia and Zimbabwe). The suggestion is that the UK renegotiate its older treaties that do not meet the standard as well as continue to develop its treaty network.

Another area of concern is the timeliness of responses to request for information. It was noted in both the 2011 and 2013 reports that when the requested information was not provided within 90 days after a request, the UK did not provide status updates. It was recommended that new processes be put in place to allow such status updates. The UK informed that it developed a new database in March 2012 to improve administrative practices.

BEPS Project

Following the reports published by the OECD in the context of the BEPS Project, the HM Treasury has opened public consultations on the implementation of country-by-country reporting, with effect for accounting periods commencing on or after 1 January 2016 (5 October 2015–16 November 2015); the UK Patent Box (22 October 2015–4 December 2015) and the deductibility of corporate interest expenses (22 October 2015–14 January 2016). These and other legislative changes are expected to take place soon.

Exchange of Information Agreements

The UK has one of the largest networks of treaties in the world with more than 120 tax treaties and almost 30 tax information exchange agreements (TIEAs). These instruments allow exchange of information on request, spontaneous exchange of information, and automatic exchange of information. The UK is also a member of the new voluntary automatic exchange of information group, which is currently working toward the development and implementation of a Common Reporting Standard allowing automatic exchange of information.

The majority of UK tax treaties follow the international standard of exchange of information on request of foreseeably relevant information for the administration or enforcement of the treaty and domestic legislation of the contracting states. The UK is updating its older agreements in order to comply with the international standard. The UK follows the OECD Model Convention as well as the accompanying guidelines regarding the situations in which a contracting state may refuse to provide the requested information.

TIEAs are negotiated when there is no need to negotiate taxation rights. Several of these agreements are with states deemed to be tax havens – for instance, Anguilla (signed in July 20, 2009), Antigua and Barbuda (January 18, 2010), Aruba (November 5, 2010), Bahamas (October 29, 2009), British Virgin Islands (October 29, 2009), Guernsey (January 1, 2009), Isle of Man (September 29, 2008), Jersey (March 10, 2009).

The UK also exchanges information under the joint Council of Europe/OECD Multilateral Convention on Mutual Administrative Assistance in Tax Matters; the new EU Council Directive 2011/16/EU on administrative co-operation in the field of taxation and the EU Council Directive 2003/48/EC on taxation of savings income in the form of interest payments.

Another agreement allowing exchange of information is the UK-Swiss Tax Cooperation Agreement, signed on 6 October 2011 (in force since 1 January 2013). According to this agreement, taxpayers may authorise their bank (or paying agent) to provide details of their Swiss assets to the HMRC. If taxpayers opt not to provide such information, they will be subject to (1) a one-off payment on 31 May 2013 to clear past unpaid tax liabilities, and/or (2) a withholding tax on income and gains arising after 1 January 2013.

Tax Incentives for Investment in Emerging or Developing Countries

While the UK adopts defensive measures against harmful tax competition and the erosion of the tax base by shifting profits to low tax jurisdictions (tax avoidance and tax evasion), it also promotes investment in emerging countries by negotiating tax sparing provisions in its tax treaties. Such provisions contribute to the effectiveness of local tax incentives for foreign direct investment.

Sections 4 and 20 of TIOPA enable UK residents to obtain credit for the tax which would have been payable under the law of a foreign territory, but for a relief given under the law of that territory, with a view to promoting industrial, commercial, scientific, educational or other development in the territory ("tax spared") as established in the tax treaties. The UK offers tax sparing credits under the tax treaties with the following countries: Bangladesh, Belize, Bosnia and Herzegovina, Botswana, Bulgaria, Croatia, Cyprus, Egypt, Ethiopia, Fiji, The Gambia, Guyana, India, Indonesia, Israel, Ivory Coast, Jamaica, Kenya, Kiribati, Malaysia, Mauritius, Montenegro, Morocco, Nigeria, Pakistan, Papua New Guinea, Portugal, Serbia, Spain, Sri Lanka, Sudan, Thailand, Trinidad and Tobago, Tunisia, Turkey, Tuvalu, Uganda, and Zambia.

UK's tax sparing clauses identify the specific domestic legislation under which the tax incentive is provided and whether they apply to other provisions of a similar nature which are subsequently enacted. Per HMRC's International Manual at INTM161270, credit for "tax spared" is limited to the amount of tax which would otherwise have been paid under the terms of the tax treaty. For example, if a UK resident receives a royalty which, under the foreign country's specific legislation, is exempted from its domestic withholding tax of 25 %, but the royalties article in the tax treaty limits the rate of tax to 10 %, the credit for the "tax spared" is 10 %, and not 25 %.

Most treaties limit tax sparing credits to a period of 10 years after the exemption or reduction was first granted to the investor. Exceptions are the treaties with Belize, Cyprus, Israel and Sudan (without time limit); Botswana and Ethiopia (with fixed expiring dates).

Section 17 of TIOPA extends unilaterally the scope of situations to which tax sparing provisions contained in tax treaties apply. Under this provision, a tax sparing credit is allowed where a UK company would have such tax credit under a tax treaty if it had invested directly in the foreign company benefiting from the tax incentive, instead of investing in a holding company (one that owns the foreign company benefiting from the tax incentive) in the same country. For section 17 to apply, the following conditions must be met:

(a) The tax spared would have been payable, but for the relief, by a company resident in a foreign country;
(b) This company pays a dividend to another company resident in the same contracting state;
(c) The company receiving the dividend pays a dividend to a company resident in the UK;
(d) If the foreign company paying the dividend to the UK company were a UK company, it would have been entitled to a credit for the tax spared.

Measures to Attract Economic Activity

The UK Government has adopted several measures to create an attractive tax jurisdiction for foreign investment: *"We are committed to creating the most competitive tax regime in the G20."*[36] In order to achieve this goal, it reduced general corporation tax rates (see section "UK corporate tax rates" below) and adopted a more territorial approach to corporate taxation (branch profits exemption). Also, the UK government provided exemptions for certain types of investments, granted generous deductions for certain types of expenses, and created a very competitive Patent Box regime for international standards. The purpose seems clear: *"making the UK an attractive location for headquarters, regional holding companies and global or regional business hubs."*[37] On 25th May 2015, Her Majesty the Queen announced no tax increases for 5 years before both Houses of Parliament (income tax, VAT and National Insurance Contributions).

Exemptions

– *Outbound dividends*: In addition to the exemptions referred in section "Exemption for dividends from foreign subsidiaries" above (inbound dividends), there is no dividend withholding tax in the UK, irrespective of the location of the recipient (outbound dividends). The exception is dividends from tax-exempt Real Estate Investment Trusts (REITs), essentially property investment businesses, which are subject to a 20 % withholding tax (or 15 % under recent tax treaties).
– *Capital gains*: Exemption from capital gains on the disposal of a 10 % or greater shareholding in a trading company, so long as the selling company must be a member of the trading group and the shareholding held for at least a year.

---

[36] UK Government, "A guide to UK taxation" (March 2013) 1.

[37] UK Government, "A guide to UK taxation" (March 2013), p.3.

Deductions

- *Relief for R&D expenditures for large companies*: Qualifying companies may claim a deduction of 130 % of qualifying R&D expenditures. Finance Act 2013 contains measures that enable large companies to obtain tax relief for their qualifying R&D expenditure by means of a taxable above-the-line (ATL) tax credit (i.e., the relief is given in the tax computation before the "profit before tax" line). The ATL credit will be 11 % of qualifying R&D spent and payable to companies with no tax liability.[38] Currently, companies have a choice between claiming the enhanced deduction of 130 %, described above, and claiming an ATL tax credit. However, the ATL tax credit will become mandatory by April 2016.
- *Relief for R&D expenditure for SMEs*[39]: SMEs may qualify for an additional deduction of 125 % of relevant expenditure. This increases the general 100 % relief for R&D spending to 230 %. SMEs making a loss may surrender such loss in return for a tax credit. SMEs may claim the relief available to large companies, for example, where the SME undertakes certain R&D as a subcontractor, or where the SME has a subsidised expenditure (as this is not eligible for relief under the rules applicable to SMEs). An SME may also claim relief under the large company rules where the total "R&D aid" for the project exceeds EUR 7.5 million.[40]

  - *Vaccine research relief (VRR)*: This benefit is available for large companies incurring expenditure on the R&D of vaccines against tuberculosis, malaria, HIV and AIDS. The relief amounts to an additional deduction of 40 % of the qualifying expenditure.[41]
  - *Film tax relief*[42]: Film production companies may be granted a benefit corresponding to (i) an additional tax deduction of 100 %[43] of enhanceable expenditure, or (ii) a tax credit in case of loss. Enhanceable expenditure is the lesser of (i) 80 % of the total core expenditure; or (ii) actual UK core expenditure incurred. If a loss is surrendered, the tax credit corresponds to the lesser of (i) 25 % of the loss surrendered, or (ii) amount of enhanceable expenditure. In order to be eligible for tax relief, a film needs to be certified as a "British

---

[38] Corporation Tax Act 2009 (CTA 2009) Part 3 Chapter 6A.

[39] A SME, for the purposes of the UK R&D tax relief, is a company which, together with certain related companies, has fewer than 500 employees and either a turnover not exceeding €100 m or total assets not exceeding €86 m.

[40] CTA 2009 Part 13 Chapter 2.

[41] Section 1088 of CTA 2009.

[42] The new Film Tax Relief was introduced by chapter 3 of FA 2006, together with schedules 4 and 5 (replacing previous reliefs relating to film-making). It has been amended over the years.

[43] For this purpose, limited-budget films are those with a total core expenditure of £20 million or less. "Core expenditure" corresponds to expenditure on pre-production, principal photography and post-production (and excludes expenditure incurred on development, distribution or other non-production activities). "UK expenditure" is expenditure on goods or services that are used or consumed in the United Kingdom.

Film" by passing a cultural test (administered by the British Film Institute (BFI) on behalf of the Department for Culture, Media and Sport). In addition, at least 10 % of the total core expenditure must be UK expenditure (irrespective of the nationality of the persons carrying out the activity).

- *Television Production Tax Relief*[44]: Television production companies producing a television programme (drama, documentary or animation) may be granted a benefit corresponding to (i) an additional tax deduction of 100 % of the enhanceable expenditure, or (ii) a tax credit in case of loss. Enhanceable expenditure is the lesser of (i) 80 % of the total core expenditure; or (ii) actual UK core expenditure incurred.[45] If a loss is surrendered, the tax credit corresponds to the lesser of (i) 25 % of the loss surrendered, or (ii) amount of enhanceable expenditure. Excluded programmes (e.g., promotional programme, game show, panel show, variety show) do not qualify for the relief. In order to be eligible for tax relief, the television programme needs to be certified as a "British Programme" by passing a cultural test (administered by BFI), In addition, at least (i) 10 % of the total core expenditure must be UK expenditure. Eligible drama and documentaries have two additional requirements not applicable to animation: (i) the average qualifying production costs per hour of production length is not less than £1 million per hour, and (ii) the slot length in relation to the programme must be greater than 30 min. For the programme to be qualified as animation, 51 % of the total core expenditure must be on animation

  - *Video Games Development Tax Relief*[46]: Video games development companies may be granted a benefit corresponding to (i) an additional tax deduction of 100 % of the enhanceable expenditure, or (ii) a tax credit in case of loss. Enhanceable expenditure is the lesser of (i) 80 % of the total core expenditure; or (ii) actual UK/EEA core expenditure incurred. If a loss is surrendered, the tax credit corresponds to the lesser of (i) 25 % of the loss surrendered, or (ii) amount of enhanceable expenditure.[47] In order to be eligible for tax relief, the video game needs to be certified as a "British Video Game" by passing a cultural test (administered on behalf of the Secretary of State), and at least (i) 25 % of the total core expenditure must be UK/EEA expenditure.

---

[44] Schedule 16 of FA 2013 introduced Part 15A of CTA 2009.

[45] For this purpose, "core expenditure," in relation to a relevant programme, means production expenditure on pre-production, principal photography and post-production of the programme. "UK expenditure", in relation to a relevant programme, means expenditure on goods or services that are used or consumed in the United Kingdom.

[46] Schedule 16 of FA 2013 introduced Part 15B of CTA 2009.
This benefit is available from 1 April 2014.

[47] For this purposes, "core expenditure" means expenditure on designing, producing and testing a video game. It does not include expenditure incurred in designing the initial concept for a video game, or in debugging a completed video game or carrying out maintenance in connection with such a video game. "UK/EEA expenditure" means expenditure on goods or services that are used or consumed in the United Kingdom or other member of the European Economic Area.

- *Theatre Tax Relief*[48]: Theatrical production companies may be granted a benefit corresponding to an additional tax deduction corresponding to the lesser of (i) 80 % of the total core expenditure; or (ii) actual UK/EEA core expenditure incurred.[49] If a loss is surrendered, the tax credit corresponds to the lesser of (i) 25 % (touring productions) or 20 % (non-touring productions) of the amount of loss surrendered, or (ii) the amount of the additional tax deduction. In order to be eligible for tax relief, there is no need for cultural test. Theatrical productions include plays, operas, musicals, and ballet. For the relief to apply, 10 % of the total core expenditure must be UK/EEA expenditure.

The UK Government continues to show interest in developing creative industry tax reliefs. After announcing a new orchestra tax relief in September 2014 and conducting a formal consultation (23 January and 5 March 2015), in 2015 the Chancellor of the Exchequer has formally announced that orchestras will get tax relief of 25 % on qualifying expenditure from 1 April 2016.

Patent Box Rules[50]

A corporation tax rate of 10 % applies to profits from the development and exploitation of patents and equivalent forms of intellectual property in the UK. The relief applies to worldwide profits from IP patented by the UK Intellectual Property Office, the European Patent Office and certain other patent offices. The range of qualifying income is broad – it is not only royalties and income from the sale of patents that qualify for this regime. Profits from the sales of products that incorporate a patented innovation are also eligible.

A company qualifies if it owns (or licenses on exclusive terms) qualifying patents and has either created or developed the patented innovation or a product incorporating it. If another group or company has carried out this development, the firm must have responsibility for and be actively involved in the ongoing decision-making concerning the further development and exploitation of the patent.

Currently, this regime is the object of public consultation (22 October 2015–4 December 2015) in view of the new internationally harmonized framework for preferential IP regimes that resulted from the BEPS Project (Action 5). The objective of the consultation is to seek input on the design of the UK Patent Box and anticipates that the later will be amended in 2016 so that it operates within the new international framework.

---

[48] Schedule 4 of FA 2014 introduced Part 15C of CTA 2009. This benefit is available from 1 April 2014.

[49] For this purpose, "core expenditure" expenditure on the activities involved in producing the production, and closing the production.

[50] Part 8A of CTA 2010.

UK Corporate Tax Rates

UK Corporations

In 2015, the general tax rate was merged with the small profits tax rate.[51] This change followed the gradual decrease of the general rate over the past 5 years (from 28 to 20 %)[52] that resulted in the general rate matching the small profits rate set at 20 % since 2011.

For the financial year 2015/2016, the general tax rate is 20 %.[53] The Government has recently announced that the general tax rate will be further reduced to 19 % in 2017 and 18 % in 2020.

Foreign Corporations

Dividends: As a general rule, outbound dividends are exempt.

Interest and royalties: 20 % withholding tax, unless (i) reduced or exempted by tax treaty, or (ii) exempt under EU Interest and Royalties Directive.

Capital gains: As a general rule, exempt unless asset held through a UK PE (subject to certain anti-avoidance rules).

Bilateral or Multilateral Trade or Investment Agreements

The UK is a Member of the WTO and a party to WTO agreements. Therefore, the UK is subject to the common limitation that such instruments represent when legislating tax matters.

The UK bilateral investment treaties protect various investments against expropriation without fair compensation (including certain unfair harmful regulations), and provide foreign investors with fair and equitable treatment in the host state, full protection and security, national treatment, most-favored-nation treatment, and the right to repatriate investment and returns. Generally, investment treaties apply to tax matters, unless they contain express exceptions and reservations for tax measures.

---

[51] Prior to 2015, the main rate of corporation tax applied to profits above £1.5 million. Resident companies whose taxable profits (including chargeable gains) do not exceed £300,000 were taxed at a "small profits rate" on their profits. For 2014, the rate was 20 %. If profits fell between £300,000 and 1.5 million, "marginal relief" applied, with an effective rate of 23.75 % applying to profits falling within the bracket.

[52] In 2010, the general rate of corporation tax was 28 %. It was reduced to 26 % in 2011, to 24 % in 2012, to 23 % in 2013, to 21 % in 2014.

[53] Different rates apply for companies with ring fence profits (i.e., deriving profit from oil and gas activities), to whom the distinction between general and small profits rates continues to apply.

They can provide for a broad express exception for all matters of taxation or specific express exceptions such as the exception to Most-Favored-Nation treatment for obligations under international tax conventions. The majority of UK investment treaties only have the exception for most-favored-nation treatment, which means they apply generally to tax matters.

The UK has signed Bilateral Investment Treaties with 108 states:

Country	Signature date	Entry into force
Albania	30.3.1994	30.8.1995
Angola	4.7.2000	–
Antigua and Barbuda	12.6.1987	12.6.1987
Argentine	11.12.1990	19.2.1993
Armenia	27.5.1993	11.7.1996
Azerbaijan	4.1.1996	11.12.1996
Bahrain	30.10.1991	30.10.1991
Bahrain	2.5.2006	3.7.2006
Bangladesh	19.6.1980	19.6.1980
Barbados	7.4.1993	7.4.1993
Belarus	1.3.1994	28.12.1994
Belize	30.4.1982	30.4.1982
Benin	27.11.1987	27.11.1987
Bolivia	24.5.1988	16.2.1990
Bosnia and Herzegovina	2.10.2002	25.7.2003
Brazil	19.7.1994	–
Bulgaria	11.12.1995	24.6.1997
Burundi	13.9.1990	13.9.1990
Cameroon	4.6.1982	7.6.1985
Chile	8.1.1996	21.4.1997
China	15.5.1986	15.5.1986
Colombia	17.3.2010	–
Congo (Republic of)	25.5.1989	9.11.1990
Costa Rica	7.9.1982	–
Côte d'Ivoire	11.3.1997	16.4.1998
Croatia	11.3.1997	16.4.1998
Cuba	30.1.1995	11.5.1995
Czech Republic	10.7.1990	26.10.1992
Dominica	23.1.1987	23.1.1987
Dominican Republic	11.7.2002	–
Ecuador	10.5.1994	24.8.1995
Egypt (Arab Republic of)	11.6.1975	24.2.1976
El Salvador	14.11.1999	1.12.2001
Estonia	12.5.1994	16.12.1994
Ethiopia	19.11.2009	–
Gambia	2.7.2002	
Georgia	15.2.1995	15.2.1995

(continued)

Country	Signature date	Entry into force
Ghana	22.3.1989	25.10.1991
Grenada	25.2.1988	25.2.1988
Guyana	27.10.1989	11.4.1990
Haiti	18.3.1985	27.3.1995
Honduras	7.12.1993	8.3.1995
Hong Kong	30.7.1998	12.4.1999
Hungary	9.3.1987	28.8.1987
India	14.3.1994	6.1.1995
Indonesia	27.4.1976	24.3.1977
Jamaica	20.1.1987	14.5.1987
Jordan	10.10.1979	24.4.1980
Kazakhstan	23.11.1995	23.11.1995
Kenya	13.9.1999	–
Korea, Republic of	4.3.1976	4.3.1976
Kuwait	8.10.2009	–
Kyrgyz Republic	8.12.1994	18.6.1998
Lao People's Democratic Republic	1.6.1995	1.6.1995
Latvia	24.1.1994	15.2.1995
Latvia	13.3.2000	13.3.2000
Lebanon	16.2.1999	16.9.2011
Lesotho	18.2.1981	18.2.1981
Libya	23.12.2009	–
Lithuania	17.5.1993	21.9.1993
Malaysia	21.5.1981	21.10.1988
Malta	4.10.1986	4.10.1986
Mauritius	20.5.1986	13.10.1986
Mexico	12.5.2006	–
Moldova	19.3.1996	30.7.1998
Mongolia	4.10.1991	4.10.1991
Morocco	30.10.1990	–
Mozambique	18.3.2004	–
Nepal	2.3.1993	2.3.1993
Nicaragua	4.12.1996	21.12.2001
Nigeria	11.12.1990	11.12.1990
Oman	25.11.1995	21.5.1996
Pakistan	30.11.1994	30.11.1994
Panama	7.10.1983	7.11.1983
Papua New Guinea	14.5.1981	22.12.1981
Paraguay	4.6.1981	23.4.1992
Peru	4.10.1993	21.4.1994
Philippines	3.12.1980	2.1.1981
Poland	8.12.1987	14.4.1988
Qatar	18.9.2009	–
Romania	13.7.1995	10.1.1996

(continued)

Country	Signature date	Entry into force
Russian Federation	6.4.1989	3.7.1991
Saint Lucia	18.1.1993	18.1.1993
Senegal	7.5.1980	9.2.1984
Serbia	6.11.2002	14.5.2004
Sierra Leone	8.12.1981	–
Sierra Leone	13.1.2000	20.11.2001
Singapore	22.7.1975	22.7.1975
Slovak Republic	10.7.1990	26.10.1992
Slovenia	3.7.1996	27.3.1999
South Africa	20.9.1994	27.5.1998
Sri Lanka	13.2.1980	18.12.1980
Swaziland	5.5.1995	5.5.1995
Tanzania	7.1.1994	2.8.1994
Thailand	28.11.1978	11.8.1979
Tonga	22.10.1997	22.10.1997
Trinidad and Tobago	23.7.1993	8.10.1993
Tunisia	14.3.1989	4.1.1990
Turkey	15.3.1991	22.10.1996
Turkmenistan	9.2.1995	9.2.1995
Uganda	24.4.1998	24.4.1998
Ukraine	10.2.1993	10.2.1993
United Arab Emirates	8.12.1992	13.12.1993
Uruguay	21.10.1991	1.8.1997
Uzbekistan	24.11.1993	24.11.1993
Vanuatu	22.12.2003	–
Venezuela	15.3.1995	1.8.1996
Vietnam	1.8.2002	1.8.2002
Yemen (Republic of)	25.2.1982	11.11.1983
Zambia	17.11.2009	–
Zimbabwe	1.3.1995	–

Chapter 19
Taxation and Development: The U.S. Perspective

Tracy Kaye

Abstract The big exception to the U.S. regime of worldwide taxation for residents (with a foreign tax credit to avoid double taxation) is the rule of non-taxation of the foreign source active business income (as opposed to passive or tax-avoidance type income) of foreign subsidiaries of U.S. parents. This system operates as a disincentive, rather than as an incentive, for investment in developing countries by U.S. companies, in part because repatriated profits of the subsidiary are subject to U.S. tax. More importantly, however, with the advent of tax-rate competition by developed countries, such as Ireland, U.S. companies are able to achieve lower rates without moving to developing countries and can rely on a well-developed treaty network (with countries such as the Netherlands) to further reduce the ultimate tax on earnings by stripping them out to entities in countries that do not tax certain types of income, such as royalties. The combination of low rates, potential tax base erosion, and the stable, sophisticated infrastructure and labor force offered by low-tax developed countries virtually eliminates a foreign investment role for developing countries unless they possess natural resources or other unique on site advantages.

Synopsis The United States taxes all U.S. persons, including domestic corporations, on worldwide income, but provides a credit against U.S. tax liability for taxes paid on foreign source income. A corporation is domestic if organized under the laws of the United States or one of the states. As a result, a domestic corporation hoping to shelter income from U.S. taxation may simply organize a subsidiary under the laws of a foreign jurisdiction. The income of the foreign subsidiary is free of U.S. tax unless under controlled foreign corporation (CFC) provisions it earns certain tax-avoidance income (generally passive income, certain sales and services income derived on behalf of the parent, insurance income and foreign oil and gas

T. Kaye (✉)
Seton Hall University School of Law, Newark, NJ, USA

University of Illinois, Champaign, IL, USA

DePaul University, Chicago, IL, USA

Georgetown University Law Center, Washington, DC, USA
e-mail: tracy.kaye@shu.edu

© Springer International Publishing Switzerland 2017   309
K.B. Brown (ed.), *Taxation and Development - A Comparative Study*,
Ius Comparatum - Global Studies in Comparative Law 21,
DOI 10.1007/978-3-319-42157-5_19

income). This income, known as subpart F income, results from transactions suggesting that the parent is using a foreign subsidiary to shift income offshore and is deemed distributed to the domestic corporation even if no amount is actually received.

While non-subpart F income may be safely shifted outside of the U.S. taxing jurisdiction through use of a foreign affiliate, the tax deferral ends when profits are returned to the U.S. parent in the form of dividends, interest, or royalties, etc., because, unlike many of the other countries featured in this volume, the U.S. has no participation exemption or other similar relief for repatriated profits. Thus, in order to minimize tax, U.S. companies have organized subsidiaries in low-tax regimes and kept the profits offshore to the extent possible. In recent years, some have expatriated, becoming domestic subsidiaries of a foreign parent in what has become known as "inversion" transactions. These inversions insulate most of the affiliated groups' profits from U.S. taxation and, in some cases, allow the new foreign parent to strip earnings from the new U.S. subsidiary through transfer pricing and other tax-minimizing strategies.

Counterintuitively, this system operates as a disincentive, rather than as an incentive, for U.S. companies to invest in developing countries. With the advent of tax-rate competition by developed countries, such as Ireland, U.S. companies can achieve lower rates without moving to developing countries and can rely on a well-developed treaty network (with countries such as the Netherlands) to further reduce the amount ultimately subject to tax by stripping out earnings to subsidiaries organized in countries that do not tax certain types of income, such as royalties. The combination of low rates, potential tax base erosion, and the stable, sophisticated infrastructure and labor force offered by low-tax developed countries virtually eliminates a foreign investment role for developing countries unless they possess unique attractions, such as natural resources, that must be exploited on site. Moreover, the promise of an additional tax holiday like the one enacted by the U.S. Congress in 2004, enabling U.S. parents to bring home as much as $500 million in offshore profits at a 5.25 % tax rate, provides a strong incentive for multinationals to maintain the status quo.

The United States provides no tax incentives for investment in developing countries. Although some countries offer (or offered) tax sparing provisions in treaties that allow their multinationals to benefit from tax incentives offered by developing countries, the United States has never done so. Tax sparing provisions were negotiated with certain countries, including India, Israel, Pakistan, and the United Arab Republic, however, the U.S. Senate has never ratified them.

No incentives are currently offered for investment in countries with low incomes or high poverty rates. A provision that afforded relief from the subpart F rules for investment in "less developed" countries was repealed in 1975.

The United States does provide some tax advantages for its territories. In general, corporations organized under the laws of the territories are treated as foreign corporations, subject to tax only on U.S. source income and income effectively connected to a U.S. trade or business and not on worldwide income. Dividends received from U.S. sources by specified corporations organized under the laws of one of the territories are either exempt or subject to a reduced withholding tax. An important tax break, exempting from U.S. taxation as foreign source income profits derived by domestic corporations operating (and generating employment) in Puerto Rico, was repealed in 1996. While the U.S. continues to look for ways to support economic development in Puerto Rico, the repealed regime was found not to generate benefits commensurate with the cost of the incentive to the U.S. Treasury.

The U.S. has taken measures to encourage economic activity within its own jurisdiction. The Foreign Sales Corporation (FSC) rules, exempting a portion of a U.S. exporter's profits from sales through a U.S. subsidiary, were repealed after a successful challenge by the EU caused the WTO to declare the regime an illegal export subsidy. A replacement regime, the extraterritorial income exclusion (ETI), was also repealed after the WTO found it provided the same prohibited subsidy. In order to compensate for the loss of ETI and stimulate domestic manufacturers to create jobs, Congress enacted the deduction for domestic production activities. It provides for a deduction equal to 9 % of specified domestic production activities which effectively amounts to a tax rate reduction.

While the federal government provides a limited array of tax incentives to attract economic activity, the various state governments rely heavily on them to attract investment. Economic studies indicate that the U.S. state and local subsidies outweigh those provided by the EU states. While nearly every state has offered some type of investment incentive, there is concern that the costs in the form of foregone revenue may outweigh the benefits to the locality.

The U.S. corporate tax system is partially integrated. The domestic corporation is separately taxed on its profits and the shareholders who are individuals are taxed on dividend distributions but at a preferential rate. For dividends received by domestic corporations (and some foreign corporations with U.S. trade or business income) there is a deduction ranging from 70 to 100 %. The taxable income of a corporation is taxed at the rates of 15 %, 25 %, and 35 %. A corporation with taxable income in excess of $18,333,333 pays tax at a flat 35 % rate. States may also impose tax on corporate income.

The United States is a party to numerous bilateral and multilateral trade and investment treaties.

International Tax System of the U.S.: Corporations

The United States taxes all U.S. persons, including domestic corporations, on their worldwide income, regardless of geographic origin.[1] The U.S. uses a place of incorporation test such that a domestic corporation is one that is created or orga-

---

[1] STAFF OF J. COMM. ON TAX'N, 112TH CONG., BACKGROUND AND SELECTED ISSUES RELATED TO THE U.S. INTERNATIONAL TAX SYSTEM AND SYSTEMS THAT EXEMPT FOREIGN BUSINESS INCOME 2(Comm. Print 2011), *available at* https://www.jct.gov/publications.html?func=startdown&id=3793

nized under the laws of the United States or one of the states.[2] The domestic corporation's foreign business income is currently taxed if earned through branch operations in the foreign jurisdiction rather than through a separate foreign corporation.[3] If the foreign business income is earned indirectly through a foreign corporate subsidiary, the income is generally not subject to U.S. tax until repatriated, most often as a dividend distribution to its parent corporation.[4] The U.S. only asserts taxing jurisdiction over foreign corporations with respect to income that has a sufficient nexus to the United States.[5] However, this deferral of U.S. tax is limited by the anti-deferral rules of Subpart F.[6] This combination of worldwide taxation of U.S. persons, limited deferral for the foreign income of foreign subsidiaries of U.S. companies, and territorial taxation of U.S.-source income of foreign persons is known as the U.S. hybrid international tax system.[7]

The Subpart F rules impose current U.S. taxation on the domestic parent corporation for certain types of income earned by certain foreign corporations known as controlled foreign corporations ("CFCs").[8] A CFC is defined as a foreign corporation where U.S. shareholders own more than 50 % of the combined voting power or total value of the stock of the corporation.[9] For the purpose of this test, a U.S. shareholder is any person with a 10 % or greater interest.[10] Under the Subpart F rules, these U.S. shareholders of a CFC are subject to U.S. tax currently on their pro rata

---

[hereinafter BACKGROUND]. The current maximum U.S. corporate tax rate is 35 %. *See infra* 7.1 for a discussion of the U.S. corporate tax rate structure.

[2] Most enacted tax legislation is codified as part of the Internal Revenue Code (I.R.C.), which is Title 26 of the United States Code. The current Code is entitled the "Internal Revenue Code of 1986." Unless otherwise indicated, all section references are to the Internal Revenue Code of 1986, as amended. I.R.C. § 7701(a)(4) (2014). U.S. persons include domestic corporations. I.R.C. § 7701(a)(30) (2014).

[3] BACKGROUND, *supra* note 1, at 2.

[4] *Id.*

[5] STAFF OF J. COMM. ON TAX'N, 111TH CONG., PRESENT LAW AND BACKGROUND RELATED TO POSSIBLE INCOME SHIFTING AND TRANSFER PRICING 29 (Comm. Print 2010), *available at* https://www.jct.gov/publications.html?func=startdown&id=3692 [hereinafter INCOME SHIFTING]. Under international law, each sovereign nation has the right to regulate based on a nexus to the territory or to a person (commonly known as source or residence jurisdiction). RESTATEMENT (THIRD) OF FOREIGN RELATIONS LAW OF THE U.S. §§ 402, 403 (1987).

[6] I.R.C. §§ 951–964 (2014); STAFF OF J. COMM. ON TAX'N, 109TH CONG., THE IMPACT OF INTERNATIONAL TAX REFORM: BACKGROUND AND SELECTED ISSUES RELATING TO U.S. INTERNATIONAL TAX RULES AND THE COMPETITIVENESS OF U.S BUSINESSES 13, 15 (Comm. Print 2006), *available at* https://www.jct.gov/publications.html?func=startdown&id=1498 [hereinafter IMPACT OF INTERNATIONAL TAX REFORM].

[7] STAFF OF J. COMM. ON TAX'N, 113TH CONG., PRESENT LAW AND BACKGROUND RELATED TO PROPOSALS TO REFORM THE TAXATION OF INCOME OF MULTINATIONAL ENTERPRISES 3–4 (Comm. Print 2014) *available at* https://www.jct.gov/publications.html?func=startdown&id=4656 [hereinafter TAX REFORM PROPOSALS].

[8] BACKGROUND, *supra* note 1, at 2.

[9] I.R.C. § 957(a) (2014).

[10] I.R.C. § 951(b) (2014).

shares of certain income earned by the CFC, whether or not the income is distributed to the shareholders.[11] This anti-deferral regime is "intended to prevent taxpayers from avoiding U.S. tax by shifting passive or other highly mobile income into low-tax jurisdictions."[12] On the other hand, deferral of U.S. tax for most types of active business income earned abroad is accepted.[13] The transfer pricing rules [14] of section 482 and the accompanying Treasury regulations also preserve the U.S. tax base "by ensuring that income properly attributable to the United States is not shifted to a related foreign company through aggressive transfer pricing that does not reflect an arm's-length result."[15]

U.S. multinationals may claim a credit for income taxes paid to foreign governments on income earned abroad, but not in excess of their U.S. tax liability on that income.[16] A foreign tax credit is available "whether the income is earned directly by the domestic corporation, repatriated as an actual dividend, or included in the domestic parent corporation's income under one of the anti-deferral regimes."[17] In general, the foreign tax credit is limited to the U.S. income tax liability on foreign-source income in order to ensure that the credit mitigates the double taxation of foreign-source income without offsetting the U.S. tax on U.S.-source income.[18] Any excess credits are allowed to be carried back to the immediately preceding taxable year and carried forward 10 taxable years but only to the extent that there is excess foreign tax credit limitation in the carryback or carryforward year.[19] Credits not utilized within the carryback and carryforward period expire.[20] U.S. multinationals may, however, take advantage of cross-crediting, using excess credits from income

---

[11] I.R.C. §§ 951–964.

[12] IMPACT OF INTERNATIONAL TAX REFORM, *supra* note 6, at 15.

[13] *Id.*

[14] The term "transfer price" refers to the "price at which one company sells goods or services to a related affiliate in its supply chain." Thus, "transfer pricing" is the "system of laws and practices used by countries to ensure that goods and services transferred between related companies are appropriately priced, based on market conditions, such that profits are correctly reflected in each jurisdiction." The principal tax policy concern is that profits may be "artificially inflated in low-tax countries and depressed in high-tax countries" through aggressive transfer pricing that does not reflect an arm's-length result from a related-party transaction. INCOME SHIFTING, *supra* note 5, at 132.

[15] *Id.* at 18.

[16] CONG. BUDGET OFFICE, PUB. NO. 4150, OPTIONS FOR TAXING U.S. MULTINATIONAL CORPORATIONS 5 (2013), *available at* http://www.cbo.gov/sites/default/files/cbofiles/attachments/43764_MultinationalTaxes_rev02-28-2013.pdf [hereinafter CBO, OPTIONS].

[17] IMPACT OF INTERNATIONAL TAX REFORM, *supra* note 6, at 13 (citing I.R.C. §§ 901, 902, 960, 1291(g) (2014)).

[18] *Id.* (citing I.R.C. §§ 901, 904 (2014)).

[19] IMPACT OF INTERNATIONAL TAX REFORM, *supra* note 6, at 14–15.

[20] *Id.* at 15.

earned in high-tax countries to offset the U.S. tax due on income earned in low-tax countries.[21]

U.S. multinationals generally pay tax on the income of their foreign subsidiaries only when they repatriate the income, a delay of taxation known as deferral.[22] Deferral, the foreign tax credit limitation, and cross-crediting of foreign taxes all provide strong incentives for firms to shift income from the United States and other high-tax countries to low-tax countries.[23] By choosing when to repatriate income, U.S. multinationals "can arrange realizations to maximize the benefits of the overall limit on the foreign tax credit" and use the excess tax credits from high-tax jurisdictions to offset U.S. tax due on income from low-tax jurisdictions.[24] Studies have found that U.S. multinationals typically pay little U.S. tax on foreign source income because of the use of the tax avoidance techniques of deferral and cross-crediting.[25] Despite its relatively high statutory corporate tax rate, the United States has lower taxes on corporate income as a share of GDP than other countries in the Organization for Economic Cooperation and Development ("OECD").[26]

The U.S. only taxes foreign persons (nonresident alien individuals and foreign corporations) on income that has a sufficient nexus to the United States, their U.S.-source income.[27] Foreign persons are taxed on income that is "effectively connected" with the conduct of a U.S. trade or business [28] in the same manner (allowing for appropriate deductions) and at the same tax rates as the income of a U.S. person.[29] Foreign persons are taxed on U.S.-source non-business income on a gross basis, usually by withholding at source at a statutory rate of 30 %.[30] There are exemptions from this withholding tax.[31] Furthermore, bilateral income tax treaties limit the amount of income tax that is imposed on the foreign income of U.S. persons by a U.S. treaty partner and on the U.S. income of foreign persons resident in the treaty partner's jurisdiction by the United States.[32]

---

[21] JANE G. GRAVELLE, CONG. RESEARCH SERV., R40623, TAX HAVENS: INTERNATIONAL TAX AVOIDANCE AND EVASION 12 (2013), *available at* http://www.fas.org/sgp/crs/misc/R40623.pdf.

[22] *Id.* at Summary.

[23] *Id.* at 12–13.

[24] *Id.* at 12; *see also* Jennifer Gravelle, *Who Will Benefit from a Territorial Tax?: Characteristics of Multinational Firms* 124, 132, *in* TERRITORIAL TAXATION: CHALLENGES AND ALTERNATIVES National Tax Association, *Proceedings of the Annual Conference* (2012), *available at* http://www.ntanet.org/images/stories/pdf/proceedings/12/15_gravelle.pdf.

[25] *See,* e.g., Melissa Costa & Jennifer Gravelle, *Taxing Multinational Corporations: Average Tax Rates*, 65 TAX L. REV. 391, 404–7, 409–10 (2012).

[26] Bruce Bartlett, *Are Taxes in the U.S. High or Low?*, N.Y. TIMES, May 31, 2011, 6:00 AM, *available at* http://economix.blogs.nytimes.com/2011/05/31/are-taxes-in-the-u-s-high-or-low/.

[27] IMPACT OF INTERNATIONAL TAX REFORM, *supra* note 6, at 29.

[28] *Id.*

[29] I.R.C. §§ 871(b), 882 (2014).

[30] I.R.C. §§ 871(a), 881 (2014).

[31] *See,* e.g., I.R.C. § 871(h) (2014) (the portfolio interest exception).

[32] IMPACT OF INTERNATIONAL TAX REFORM, *supra* note 6, at 31.

Tax treaties often reduce the withholding taxes on dividends, interest, and royalties paid to residents of the other treaty country as well as define when the business activities of a resident of the other treaty country rise to the level of a permanent establishment, thus taxable by the host treaty country.[33] These treaties also determine which of the taxes imposed by the treaty country in which income is earned, are creditable for the purpose of computing the amount of tax owed to the other country with respect to that income.[34] The United States has a network of bilateral income tax treaties covering more than 65 countries.[35] This network includes all of the OECD member countries as well as the majority of other countries attracting the foreign trade and investment of U.S. businesses.[36]

U.S. International Tax System: Individuals

Similar to the tax treatment of U.S. multinational firms, the U.S. taxes its citizens and residents on worldwide income such that all amounts, whatever their nature or source, are included in income.[37] U.S. persons are therefore taxed on both U.S. and foreign-source income on the basis of the citizenship or residence of the taxpayer.[38] Foreign persons are generally taxed on U.S.-source income but foreign-source income is not subject to U.S. taxation because there is no source or residence jurisdiction.[39]

Individuals and corporations can be subject to double taxation because of the overlap between source and residence jurisdiction in that "both the jurisdiction in which income is generated (the country of source) and the jurisdiction in which the income earner is resident or organized as a matter of law (the country of residence) claim jurisdiction to tax."[40] In order to give relief to these individuals and corporations, the U.S. offers a foreign tax credit in certain situations by allowing "a dollar-for-dollar credit for foreign [income] taxes paid against the [U.S.] taxes imposed on foreign-source income."[41] If a foreign country collects income taxes on income

---

[33] *Id.*

[34] *Id.* Treaties also outline the procedures by which the two treaty countries may mutually resolve inconsistent positions taken by the countries on a single item of income or deduction. *Id.*

[35] *United States Income Tax Treaties – A to Z*, IRS, *available at* http://www.irs.gov/Businesses/International-Businesses/United-States-Income-Tax-TreatiesDOUBLEHYPHEN-A-to-Z   (last updated February 25, 2015) [hereinafter *U.S. Income Tax Treaties*]. *See infra* 3.1 for a discussion of the U.S. tax treaty network.

[36] IMPACT OF INTERNATIONAL TAX REFORM, *supra* note 6, at 31.

[37] I.R.C. § 61 (2014). "Gross income means all income *from whatever source derived…*" *Id.* (emphasis added).

[38] ALLISON CHRISTIANS, SAMUEL A. DONALDSON, & PHILLIP F. POSTLEWAITE, UNITED STATES INTERNATIONAL TAXATION 5 (2nd ed. 2011).

[39] *Id.*

[40] *Id.* at 64.

[41] *Id.*; I.R.C. §§ 901(a), 901(b) (2014).

earned within its jurisdiction by a U.S. resident, that person applies the foreign tax credit to reduce the U.S. tax on that income. However, if the foreign country does not collect any taxes, the U.S. residence-based tax is preserved.[42]

Territorial Regime Features

By mitigating double taxation through the use of a foreign tax credit regime, the U.S. preserves its residence-based taxation to the extent that the foreign-source income of its citizens and residents is taxed at a lower rate than the U.S.-source income. This differs from the approach of some other countries that use a territorial regime, which allow for as much as total exemption of active foreign-source income whether or not the foreign country imposed taxation.[43] For the most part, the United States does not have a territorial regime. However, the U.S. does not tax the active foreign business profits of a foreign subsidiary until the U.S. parent corporation "repatriates" them — that is, brings them back to the United States.[44] There is also a limited exemption for certain foreign earned income received by individual taxpayers.[45]

The debate over the merits of a territorial regime is spirited in the United States. There were rumors that President Obama was at one time considering endorsing a territorial system[46] but he did not include this idea in his latest budget proposal.[47] There is a variety of legislative proposals in Congress to reform the U.S. international tax system including transitioning to a territorial regime but no legislative action has been taken.[48] Some policymakers are recommending a move from a worldwide to a territorial system of taxation, for example, by excluding dividend income from investments abroad from the U.S. tax base.[49] One of the most developed

---

[42] CHRISTIANS, DONALDSON, & POSTLEWAITE, *supra* note 38, at 64.

[43] *Id.* at 64–65. As of 2014, 28 out of 34 countries in the OECD have some type of hybrid territorial regime. TAX REFORM PROPOSALS, *supra* note 7, at 36–37.

[44] Chye-Ching Huang, et al., *The Fiscal and Economic Risks of Territorial Taxation*, CENTER ON BUDGET AND POLICY 1, Jan. 31, 2013, *available at* http://www.cbpp.org/files/1-31-13tax.pdf.

[45] I.R.C. § 911 (2014).

[46] *See generally* Kim Dixon, *Obama Might Back Territorial Tax System*: *Business Chief*, Jan. 31, 2013, *available at*
http://www.reuters.com/article/2013/01/31/us-usa-tax-territorial-idUSBRE90U15J20130131.

[47] *See generally* DEP'T OF THE TREASURY, GENERAL EXPLANATIONS OF THE ADMINISTRATION'S FISCAL YEAR 2017 REVENUE PROPOSALS (2016), *available at* http://www.treasury.gov/resource-center/tax-policy/Documents/General-Explanations-FY2017.pdf [hereinafter ADMINISTRATION'S FY 2017 REVENUE PROPOSALS].

[48] TAX REFORM PROPOSALS, *supra* note 7, at 59–85; *see*, e.g., Press Release, Representative Dave Camp, Camp Releases International Tax Reform Discussion Draft (Oct. 26, 2011), *available at* waysandmeans.house.gov/news/documentsingle.aspx?DocumentID=266168.

[49] *See*, e.g., NAT'L COMM'N ON FISCAL RESPONSIBILITY AND REFORM, THE MOMENT OF TRUTH (2010), *available at* http://www.fiscalcommission.gov/sites/fiscalcommission.gov/files/documents/

of these proposals is the discussion draft proposal of former House Ways and Means Committee Chair David Camp.[50] This proposal allows domestic C corporations that qualify as 10 % U.S. shareholders to deduct 95% of the dividends received from CFCs that are attributable to foreign-source income (also known as a participation exemption).[51] The Final Report of the Senate Finance Committee's International Tax Reform Working Group includes a proposal to adopt a dividend exemption regime along with appropriate base erosion rules.[52]

Corporation-to-Corporation Dividends

Section 243 allows a dividends-received deduction ranging from 70 % to 100 % of dividends received from a domestic subsidiary, based on the percentage of ownership of the distributing corporation's stock by the recipient corporation.[53] Ownership of 20 % to less than 80 % of the subsidiary corporation permits an 80 % deduction and ownership of 80 % or more permits a 100 % deduction.[54] A corporation with less than 20 % ownership of the subsidiary is entitled to a 70 % deduction.[55] The dividends-received deduction is denied unless a holding period test is satisfied.[56]

This dividends-received deduction is not allowed with respect to dividends received from a foreign subsidiary "except to the extent that the foreign subsidiary

---

TheMomentofTruth12_1_2010.pdf; *see also* Roseanne Altshuler & Harry Grubert, *Corporate Taxes in a World Economy: Reforming the Taxation of Cross-Border Income, in* FUNDAMENTAL TAX REFORM: ISSUES, CHOICES AND IMPLICATIONS (John W. Diamond & George Zodrow eds., 2008) (comparing various options).

[50] *See* Stephen E. Shay, J. Clifton Fleming Jr., & Robert J. Peroni, *Territoriality in Search of Principles and Revenues: Camp and Enzi,* 72 TAX NOTES INT'L 155 (October 13, 2013) for a thorough examination of the Camp proposal as well as S. 2091 that was introduced by Senator Enzi in February 2012. *See generally* STAFF OF J. COMM. ON TAX'N, 113TH CONG., TECHNICAL EXPLANATION OF THE TAX REFORM ACT OF 2014, A DISCUSSION DRAFT OF THE CHAIRMAN OF THE HOUSE COMMITTEE ON WAYS AND MEANS TO REFORM THE INTERNATIONAL REVENUE CODE: TITLE IV- PARTICIPATION EXEMPTION SYSTEM FOR THE TAXATION OF FOREIGN INCOME (Comm. Print 2014) *available at* https://www.jct.gov/publications.html?func=showdown&id=4557 [hereinafter TAX REFORM ACT OF 2014].

[51] TAX REFORM ACT OF 2014, *supra* note 50, at 24. The 10 % shareholder must also satisfy a 6-month holding requirement of the CFC's stock in order to qualify for the 95 % deduction. *Id.* at 26.

[52] SENATE FINANCE COMMITTEE, INTERNATIONAL TAX REFORM WORKING GROUP: FINAL REPORT 72, July 7, 2015 (Senator Rob Portman, Co-Chair and Senator Charles Schumer, Co-Chair).

[53] I.R.C. § 243(a) (2014).

[54] I.R.C. §§ 243(a),(c) (2014). In general, the 100 % deduction only applies if the parent and subsidiary corporation are both members of the same affiliated group pursuant to section 1504(a). I.R.C. § 243(b) (2014).

[55] I.R.C. § 243(a)(1).

[56] I.R.C. § 246(c)(1)(A) (2014). For example, "No deduction shall be allowed...in respect of any dividend on any share of stock... which is held by the taxpayer for 45 days or less during the 91-day period..." *Id.*

earns U.S. source business income."[57] Instead, the U.S. parent may be allowed an indirect tax credit for the foreign income taxes that the foreign subsidiary paid on the income from which the dividend distribution was made.[58] A domestic corporate shareholder, owning 10 % or more of the voting stock of a foreign corporation, may take a credit against domestic income tax for the taxes that have been paid by the foreign subsidiary corporation if the foreign subsidiary's earnings and profits from which the dividend is distributed, resulted from operations subject to the foreign country's income tax.[59]

Under section 78, when a domestic corporation claims a foreign tax credit, an amount equal to the taxes deemed paid by such corporation shall be treated as a dividend received by the domestic corporation from the foreign corporation and is added in the domestic corporation's gross income.[60] Thus, the amount of the dividend taxed is "grossed-up" to include the amount of the foreign tax.[61]

Anti-tax Haven Provisions

Typically, jurisdictions that are referred to as "tax havens" impose no or low tax rates on income from sources outside their jurisdiction and offer financial secrecy laws as well as the ability to incorporate easily.[62] In general, tax havens are small, affluent countries with "high-quality governance institutions."[63] Although no formal list exists in the United States,[64] there is a variety of lists developed by the OECD, academics, and the Tax Justice Network that name countries or territories considered to be tax havens.[65] The seven common locations found on every list are: Bahamas, Bermuda, Cayman Islands, Guernsey, Jersey, Malta, and Panama.[66]

One of the most important innovations in the U.S. war on offshore tax evasion is the Foreign Account Tax Compliance Act ("FATCA"), which added sections 1471

---

[57] RICHARD L. DOERNBERG, INTERNATIONAL TAXATION 244 (2012); *see also* I.R.C. §§ 243(e), 245 (2014).

[58] I.R.C. § 902 (2014).

[59] I.R.C. § 902(a) (2014).

[60] I.R.C. §§ 78, 902(a) (2014).

[61] DOERNBERG, *supra* note 57, at 249–50; *see also* I.R.C. § 78 (2014).

[62] RONEN PALAN, RICHARD MURPHY & CHRISTIAN CHAVAGNEUX, TAX HAVENS, HOW GLOBALIZATION REALLY WORKS 30–40 (Cornell Univ. Press 2010); *see also* GRAVELLE, *supra* note 21 at 3.

[63] Dhammika Dharmapala & James R. Hines Jr., *Which Countries Become Tax Havens?*, 93 J. PUB. ECON. 1058, 1065 (2009).

[64] Although there is no official list in the Code, there has been proposed legislation over the years to create one, directing the Secretary of the Treasury to "develop and publish" a list, taking factors like: "(1) tax rate in the country, (2) lack of effective exchange of information between governments, (3) lack of transparency in financial services sector" and other relevant information into consideration. H.R. 2740, 113th Cong. (2013).

[65] GRAVELLE, *supra* note 21, at 3–8.

[66] PALAN, MURPHY & CHAVAGNEUX, *supra* note 62, at 40.

through 1474 to the Internal Revenue Code in 2010.[67] FATCA requires U.S. taxpayers holding financial assets with an aggregate value exceeding $50,000 offshore to report those assets to the IRS beginning with their 2011 tax return.[68] Failure to report foreign financial assets will result in a penalty of $10,000 (and a penalty up to $50,000 for continued failure after IRS notification).[69]

The Bank Secrecy Act, pre-dating FATCA, requires U.S. taxpayers to file a Report of Foreign Bank and Financial Accounts ("FBAR") on June 30th for each year that they have ownership of a foreign financial account of more than $10,000.[70] The FBAR was intended to provide law enforcement with information primarily to combat illegal activities such as money laundering and expand protection against terrorist financing.[71] However, the new form 8938 required by FATCA is used to report the total value of all specified foreign financial assets.[72] This is a significant expansion because it includes foreign stock or securities not held in a financial account as well as investment vehicles, such as foreign hedge funds and foreign private equity funds.[73] These are not required to be reported on the FBAR.

But more importantly, FATCA imposes reporting requirements on the foreign banks where these U.S. taxpayers are holding these offshore accounts.[74] Using third parties to increase compliance with the federal income tax has been a highly successful technique in the U.S. tax system.[75] FATCA "offers foreign banks a simple choice—if you wish to access our capital markets, you have to report on U.S. account holders," said Rangel, (then Chairman of the House Ways and Means

---

[67] I.R.C. §§ 1471–1474 were enacted in the "Foreign Account Tax Compliance" title (Title V) of the HIRE Act. Hiring Incentives to Restore Employment Act, Pub. L. No. 111–147, § 501–35, 124 Stat. 71, 97–115 (2010) [hereinafter HIRE Act]. *See*, e.g., Tracy Kaye, *Innovations in the War on Tax Evasion*, 2 BYU L. Rev. 363 (2014) (detailing the FATCA requirements).

[68] I.R.C. § 6038D(a) (2014).

[69] I.R.C. § 6038D(d) (2014). Underpayments of tax attributable to non-disclosed foreign financial assets will be subject to an additional substantial understatement penalty of 40 %. *See* Instructions for Form 8938, IRS, (Nov. 2011), *available at* http://www.irs.gov/pub/irs-pdf/i8938.pdf.

[70] Bank Secrecy Act, Pub. L. No. 91–508, Title I, § 121, 84 Stat. 1114, 1114–24 (1970) (codified as amended at 12 U.S.C.S. §§ 1829b, 1951–59 (2012)); 31 U.S.C.A. §§ 5311–22 (2012); *see also Report of Foreign Bank and Financial Accounts*, IRS, *available at* http://www.irs.gov/Businesses/Small-Businesses-&-Self-Employed/Report-of-Foreign-Bank-and-Financial-Accounts-FBAR (last updated Sept. 26, 2014). In 2009, 543,043 FBARs were filed. Susan C. Morse, *Tax Compliance and Norm Formation Under High-Penalty Regimes*, 44 Conn. L. Rev. 675, 701 (2012) (citing to a 2010 TIGTA report).

[71] *See generally* 12 U.S.C. § 1951 (2012) (discussing usefulness of reports in criminal and tax proceedings as Congressional purpose); *see also* 31 U.S.C. § 5311 (2012) (concerning protection from international terrorism as purpose).

[72] Form 8938, Statement of Specified Foreign Financial Assets, IRS (Dec. 2013), *available at* http://www.irs.gov/pub/irs-pdf/f8938.pdf.

[73] This includes foreign partnership interests. *See* Instructions for Form 8938, IRS, 4 (Dec. 2011), *available at* http://www.irs.gov/pub/irs-pdf/i8938.pdf.

[74] I.R.C. § 1471(c)(1) (2014).

[75] Leandra Lederman, *Statutory Speed Bumps: The Roles Third Parties Play in Tax Compliance*, 60 Stan. L. Rev. 695, 698 (2008).

Committee's press release for FATCA).[76] Thus, as of 2015,[77] certain foreign financial institutions are required to annually file reports directly to the IRS regarding financial accounts held by U.S. taxpayers or by foreign entities in which U.S. taxpayers hold a substantial ownership interest,[78] with respect to U.S. account information for calendar year 2014.

Investment in Harmful Tax Regimes

The term "harmful tax regime" is a subjective concept. The OECD's 1998 report entitled *Harmful Tax Competition: An Emerging Global Issue* set forth its criteria for evaluating preferential tax regimes and identifying tax havens.[79] The OECD Harmful Tax Competition Report's recommendations focused on improving transparency and communication among nations and led to the establishment of the *OECD Model Agreement on Exchange of Information in Tax Matters* in 2002.[80]

Harmful tax regimes were defined as tax policies to intentionally try to attract a mobile tax base, usually in a non-transparent way or by using unusual tax regimes.[81] Such policies usually contain no or low taxation but this alone is not sufficient; other features, including non-transparency, ring-fencing of mobile activities, or other unusual features are also required. This covers, for example, regimes that are only available to headquarters of large corporate groups and that allow the application of a notional tax base defined as a fraction of specific costs instead of profit. Harmful tax practices also include tax practices that have the intention or the potential to help foreign taxpayers evade taxation in their home country, including many practices of so-called tax havens. Although the U.S. has not enacted legislation that defines

---

[76] Lee A. Sheppard, *Getting Serious About Offshore Evasion*, 56 TAX NOTES INT'L 399, 402 (2009).

[77] The final regulations phase in implementation of the reporting requirements. *See* Regulations Relating to Information Reporting by Foreign Financial Institutions and Withholding on Certain Payments to Foreign Financial Institutions and Other Foreign Entities, 78 Fed. Reg. 5874, 5877 (Jan. 28, 2013) [hereinafter FATCA Preamble]. These dates were further amended by 78 Fed. Reg. 55202–55203 (2013). There are later deadlines for those FFIs in countries that have signed a Model 1 Intergovernmental Agreement with the United States. Summary of FATCA Timelines, *available at* http://www.irs.gov/Businesses/Corporations/Summary-of-FATCA-Timelines (last updated Apr. 13, 2015).

[78] I.R.C. § 1471(b) (2014). I.R.C. § 1473(2)(A) (2014) defines a substantial U.S. owner as a person owning an interest greater than 10 % directly or indirectly.

[79] OECD, HARMFUL TAX COMPETITION: AN EMERGING GLOBAL ISSUE 19–35 (1998), *available at* http://www.oecd.org/tax/transparency/44430243.pdf [hereinafter OECD HARMFUL TAX COMPETITION REPORT]. The 1998 Report identified four main criteria for determining whether a preferential tax regime is harmful: (1) no or low taxation on the relevant income; (2) lack of transparency; (3) lack of effective exchange of information; and (4) the regime is ring-fenced from the domestic economy. *Id.*

[80] This is a non-binding agreement that sets forth two models for bilateral agreements for increasing transparency among nations. OECD, AGREEMENT ON EXCHANGE OF INFORMATION ON TAX MATTERS 4, http://www.oecd.org/ctp/exchange-of-tax-information/2082215.pdf (last visited Aug. 14, 2013).

[81] OECD HARMFUL TAX COMPETITION REPORT, *supra* note 79, at 25.

harmful tax regimes specifically, the U.S. is a founding member of OECD, which seeks to end harmful tax regimes.[82]

The OECD issued a report on base erosion and profit shifting (BEPS) in February 2013. This BEPS report reviews various data and studies, finding an increased separation between the locations of the actual business activities and the reporting of profits for tax purposes.[83] The OECD followed up this report in July 2013 with an Action Plan of 15 steps to address profit shifting by multinational corporations and move toward international coherence in corporate income taxation.[84] The OECD BEPS Action Plan once again targets harmful tax practices by establishing a working party on aggressive tax planning and by requiring disclosure of aggressive tax planning arrangements as well as "requiring substantial activity for any preferential regime."[85] The OECD released final reports on the fifteen action items in 2015.[86]

Regional/International Coordinated Action Against Tax Avoidance

In 2004, the IRS formed the Joint International Tax Shelter Information Centre ("JITSIC") with the revenue agencies of Australia, Canada, and the United Kingdom in order to identify and curb "abusive tax avoidance transactions, arrangements, and schemes."[87] JITSIC was expanded to include China, Japan, and Korea as well as the two official observer members of France and Germany.[88] At the Dublin, Ireland meeting of the Forum on Tax Administration ("FTA") on October 24, 2014, it was announced that JITSIC was being restructured into the Joint International Tax

---

[82] See generally OECD, 2000 PROGRESS REPORT: TOWARDS GLOBAL TAX CO-OPERATION: PROGRESS IN IDENTIFYING AND ELIMINATING HARMFUL TAX PRACTICES (2000), available at http://www.oecd.org/ctp/harmful/2090192.pdf; OECD's PROJECT ON HARMFUL TAX PRACTICES: 2004 PROGRESS REPORT (2004), available at http://www.oecd.org/ctp/harmful/30901115.pdf. In September 2006, the OECD Committee on Fiscal Affairs released its last progress report evaluating the preferential tax regimes in member countries. See OECD, THE OECD's PROJECT ON HARMFUL TAX PRACTICES: 2006 UPDATE ON PROGRESS IN MEMBER COUNTRIES 3 (2006), available at http://www.oecd.org/ctp/harmful/37446434.pdf.

[83] OECD, ADDRESSING BASE EROSION AND PROFIT SHIFTING 15 (2013).

[84] OECD, ACTION PLAN ON BASE EROSION AND PROFIT SHIFTING (2013) [hereinafter OECD BEPS ACTION PLAN].

[85] See id., Action 5, at 18. ("Revamp the work on harmful tax practices with a priority on improving transparency, including compulsory spontaneous exchange on rulings related to preferential regimes, and on..."); see also Actions 11–12, at 21–22.

[86] See id., at 31. OECD, BEPS 2015 FINAL REPORTS, http://www.oecd.org/ctp/beps-2015-final-reports.htm.

[87] See Joint International Tax Shelter Information Centre Memorandum of Understanding, IRS, www.irs.gov/pub/irs-utl/jitsic-finalmou.pdf (last visited Feb. 16, 2014).

[88] Joseph E. Erwin & Fred F. Murray, Exchange of Information and Cross-border Cooperation between Tax Authorities 787, 98b Cahiers de Droit Fiscal International (2013).

Shelter Information and Collaboration ("JITSIC") Network "to focus specifically on cross border tax avoidance…open to all FTA members on a voluntary basis."[89]

OECD/Global Forum on Transparency and Exchange of Information

The United States actively participates in the Global Forum on Transparency and Exchange of Information for Tax Purposes, the multilateral framework within which work on tax transparency and exchange of information has been accomplished since 2000 by over 120 OECD and non-OECD jurisdictions.[90] The Global Forum performs peer reviews of its member jurisdictions in two phases: in Phase 1 examining the quality of the "legal and regulatory framework for transparency and the exchange of information for tax purposes;" [91] and in Phase 2 evaluating the implementation in practice of the international standards reflected in the 2002 OECD *Model Agreement won Exchange of Information on Tax Matters* and its commentary as well as Article 26 of the OECD *Model Tax Convention on Income and on Capital* (*OECD Model Tax Convention*) and its commentary.[92]

As of 2011, the Global Forum had completed its combined Phase 1 and Phase 2 reviews of the U.S. tax system.[93] It examined the categories of (A) availability of information; (B) access of information; and (C) exchanging information.[94] With respect to availability of information, the U.S. was largely compliant with respect to ownership information and reliable accounting records for entities and compliant with respect to banking information.[95] For categories B and C, the U.S. was determined by the Global Forum as compliant.[96] However, recommendations were provided for each of the respective categories.[97] For example, information exchange partners had complained about the unavailability of beneficial ownership informa-

---

[89] Final Communiqué, Meeting of the Forum on Tax Administration (FTA), 24 October 2014, Dublin, Ireland, *available at* http://www.oecd.org/ctp/administration/fta-2014-communique.pdf.

[90] OECD, THE GLOBAL FORUM ON TRANSPARENCY AND EXCHANGE OF INFORMATION FOR TAX PURPOSES: INFORMATION BRIEF 2 (2013), *available at* http://www.oecd.org/tax/transparency/global_forum_background%20brief.pdf [hereinafter OECD, GLOBAL FORUM].

[91] *Id.* at 3–4.

[92] OECD, GLOBAL FORUM ON TRANSPARENCY AND EXCHANGE OF INFORMATION FOR TAX PURPOSES PEER REVIEWS: UNITED STATES 2011: COMBINED: PHASE 1+ PHASE2, 5 (2011), *available at* http://dx.doi.org/10.1787/9789264115064-en [hereinafter OECD, UNITED STATES 2011 REVIEW].

[93] *See id.* at 11–12.

[94] *Id.* at 11.

[95] OECD, GLOBAL FORUM, *supra* note 90, at 16.

[96] *Id.*

[97] OECD, UNITED STATES 2011 REVIEW, *supra* note 92, at 91, 93, 96.

tion of LLCs in several states, including Delaware.[98] Following the combined review, an overall rating of "Largely Compliant" was awarded to the United States.[99]

Information Exchange Agreements

The United States is currently party to exchange of information agreements with 84 jurisdictions.[100] These include more than 65 double taxation conventions ("DTC") with almost all of the OECD and G20 countries as well as all major trading partners (Canada, China, Mexico, Japan, Germany, and the United Kingdom).[101] The U.S. treaty with the former U.S.S.R. did not include an exchange of information agreement and is still in effect for Armenia, Azerbaijan, Belarus, Georgia, Kyrgyzstan, Moldova, Tajikistan, and Uzbekistan.[102] According to IRS Publication 901,[103] as of March 31, 2013, the United States has tax treaties with the following countries:

Country	General effective date
Armenia	January 1, 1976
Australia	December 1, 1983
Austria	January 1, 1999
Azerbaijan	January 1, 1976
Bangladesh	January 1, 2007
Barbados	January 1, 1984
Belarus	January 1, 1976
Belgium	January 1, 2008
Bulgaria	January 1, 2009
Canada	January 1, 1985
China	January 1, 1987
Cyprus	January 1, 1986
Czech Republic	January 1, 1993
Denmark	January 1, 2001
Egypt	January 1, 1982
Estonia	January 1, 2000
Finland	January 1, 1991
France	January 6, 1996

(continued)

---

[98] *Id.* at 38–39, 87.

[99] OECD, Global Forum, *supra* note 90, at 16.

[100] OECD, Exchange of Information Portal-United States, *available at* eoi-tax.org (last visited August 12, 2015) [hereinafter OECD, Exchange of Information]; *see also* OECD, United States 2011 Review, *supra* note 92, at 74.

[101] *U.S. Income Tax Treaties*, *supra* note 35; *see also* OECD, United States 2011 Review, *supra* note 92, at 79.

[102] U.S. Gov't Accountability Office, GAO-11-730, IRS's Information Exchanges with Other Countries Could Be Improved through Better Performance Information 4 n. 7 (2011).

[103] IRS Publication 901, Table 3 (List of Tax Treaties) (2013), *available at* http://www.irs.gov/pub/irs-pdf/901.pdf.

Country	General effective date
Georgia	January 1, 1976
Germany	January 1, 1990
Greece	January 1, 1953
Hungary	January 1, 1980
Iceland	January 1, 2009
India	January 1, 1991
Indonesia	January 1, 1990
Ireland	January 1, 1998
Israel	January 1, 1995
Italy	January 1, 2010
Jamaica	January 1, 1982
Japan	January 1, 2005
Kazakhstan	January 1, 1996
Korea	January 1, 1980
Kyrgyzstan	January 1, 1976
Latvia	January 1, 2000
Lithuania	January 1, 2000
Luxembourg	January 1, 2001
Malta	January 1, 2011
Mexico	January 1, 1994
Moldova	January 1, 1976
Morocco	January 1, 1981
Netherlands	January 1, 1994
New Zealand	November 2, 1983
Norway	January 1, 1971
Pakistan	January 1, 1959
Philippines	January 1, 1983
Poland	January 1, 1974
Portugal	January 1, 1996
Romania	January 1, 1974
Russia	January 1, 1994
Slovak Republic	January 1, 1993
Slovenia	January 1, 2002
South Africa	January 1, 1998
Spain	January 1, 1991
Sri Lanka	January 1, 2004
Sweden	January 1, 1996
Switzerland	January 1, 1998
Tajikistan	January 1, 1976
Thailand	January 1, 1998
Trinidad	January 1, 1970
Tunisia	January 1, 1990
Turkey	January 1, 1998
Turkmenistan	January 1, 1976

(continued)

Country	General effective date
Ukraine	January 1, 2001
Union of Soviet Socialist Republic	January 1, 1976
United Kingdom	January 1, 2004
Uzbekistan	January 1, 1976
Venezuela	January 1, 2000

The date that is listed is that for the original treaty and does not take into account any protocols that were subsequently negotiated.

The U.S. negotiates its DTCs based on the *U.S. Model Income Tax Convention* (*U.S. Model*); however, its information exchange provision is virtually identical to that found in Article 26 of the *OECD Model Tax Convention*.[104] Although the *U.S. Model* refers to information that "may be relevant," all of the U.S. agreements allow for exchange of information that meets the "foreseeably relevant" standard of the OECD.[105] The language "shall exchange" in Article 26 of the *U.S. Model* includes specific, automatic, and spontaneous exchanges of tax information, which can be used for criminal or civil investigations.[106] "On average, the United States replies to approximately 1,000 cases (each generally constituting multiple requests for information) per year, and automatically exchanges approximately 2.5 million items of information per year."[107] However, the U.S. income tax treaties generally exclude information from its territories.[108]

The Global Forum has determined that the treaties with Austria, Luxembourg, and Switzerland do not meet the international standard.[109] The U.S. signed protocols with Luxembourg and Switzerland in 2009 that would update the information exchange provisions of these treaties.[110] In 2010, the U.S. signed income tax treaties with Hungary and Chile[111] and in 2013 with Poland as well as protocols with Spain, and Japan. Unfortunately, none of these agreements has been approved by the

---

[104] OECD, UNITED STATES 2011 REVIEW, *supra* note 92, at 75–6. *See* United States Model Income Tax Convention of November 15, 2006, Article 26, *available at* www.irs.gov/pub/irs-trty/model006.pdf.

[105] OECD, UNITED STATES 2011 REVIEW, *supra* note 92, at 75–6.

[106] U.S. DEP'T OF THE TREASURY, UNITED STATES MODEL TECHNICAL EXPLANATION ACCOMPANYING THE UNITED STATES MODEL INCOME TAX CONVENTION OF NOVEMBER 15, 2006 86–87 (2006).

[107] OECD, UNITED STATES 2011 REVIEW, *supra* note 92, at 86.

[108] *See generally* Joseph Erwin, *Business Operations in the Territories and Possessions of the United States (except Puerto Rico)*, 995-2nd TAX MGMT. (BNA) (2012) [hereinafter *Business Operations in the Territories*].

[109] OECD, EXCHANGE OF INFORMATION, *supra* note 100.

[110] STAFF OF J. COMM. ON TAX'N, 113TH CONG., TESTIMONY OF THE STAFF OF THE JOINT COMMITTEE ON TAXATION BEFORE THE SENATE COMMITTEE ON FOREIGN RELATIONS HEARING ON THE PROPOSED TAX TREATIES WITH CHILE AND HUNGARY, THE PROPOSED TAX PROTOCOLS WITH LUXEMBOURG AND SWITZERLAND, AND THE PROPOSED TAX PROTOCOLS AMENDING THE MULTILATERAL CONVENTION ON MUTUAL ADMINISTRATIVE ASSISTANCE IN TAX MATTERS 10-12 (Comm. Print 2014), *available at* https://www.jct.gov [hereinafter JCT TESTIMONY].

[111] *See id.* at 2–3.

U.S. Senate.[112] In the United States, ratification of a treaty requires the advice and consent of the U.S. Senate. Senator Rand Paul has blocked Senate action on these treaties citing privacy concerns about the tax data of American taxpayers.[113]

The U.S. also exchanges information through tax information exchange agreements ("TIEAs"), executive agreements not requiring the advice and consent of the U.S. Senate that is necessary for treaties.[114] The U.S. has signed TIEAs with over 20 countries including Costa Rica,[115] Bermuda,[116] Panama, Monaco, Gibraltar, Liechtenstein, Aruba, Jersey, the Isle of Man, Guernsey, Netherlands Antilles, British Virgin Islands, Bahamas, Cayman Islands, and Antigua & Barbuda.[117] Many of these TIEAs were negotiated prior to the development of the 2002 OECD *Model Agreement on Exchange of Information on Tax Matters* but, except for Costa Rica, "provide for exchange of information in accordance with the standards."[118] The goal of the United States in these TIEAs is to obligate the cooperation of the treaty partners in civil and criminal tax investigations.[119]

Exchange of information articles within DTCs and TIEAs typically consist of three provisions: (1) a general agreement that the "parties shall provide assistance through exchange of information that is foreseeably relevant to the administration and enforcement of the domestic laws of the parties concerning the taxes covered … including information concerning the determination, assessment, enforcement or collection of tax … or the investigation or prosecution of criminal tax matters;"[120] (2) a restriction on the use and disclosure of information received, generally requiring that information received be treated as secret and permitting disclosure of such information only to persons specified by the treaty [121]; and (3) relief for the competent authorities of any obligation to provide information that is not obtainable (either by the requesting competent authority under its own laws or the receiving compe-

---

[112] *See* U.S. Dep't of St.,Treaties Pending in the Senate (updated as of April 27, 2015) *available at* www.state.gov.

[113] Patrick Temple-West, *U.S. Treasury official urges Senate action on tax treaties*, *Reuters News* Dec. 12, 2013 *available at* www.townhall.com/news/politics/2013/12/12/us-treasury-official-urges-senate-action-on-tax-treaties-n1762191.

[114] *See* U.S. Const., Art II, Section 2, cl. 2.

[115] OECD, United States 2011 Review, *supra* note 92, at 77.

[116] *See id.*, at 76.

[117] OECD, *Tax Information Exchange Agreements (TIEAs): United States*, Global Forum on Transparency and Exchange of Information for Tax Purposes, http://www.oecd.org/tax/transparency/taxinformationexchangeagreementstieasunitedstates.htm (last visited Aug.13, 2015).

[118] OECD, United States 2011 Review, *supra* note 92, at 75–76.

[119] Bruce Zagaris, *The Procedural Aspects of U.S. Tax Policy Towards Developing Countries: Too Many Sticks and No Carrots*, 35 Geo. Wash. Int'l L. Rev. 331, 333 (2003).

[120] *See*, e.g., Agreement between the Government of the United States of America and the Government of the Principality of Liechtenstein on Tax Cooperation and the Exchange of Information Relating to Taxes, U.S.-Liech., art. i, Dec.8, 2008, HP-1320; *see also* OECD, Progress Towards a Level Playing Field: Outcomes of the OECD Global Forum on Taxation 10 (2014), *available at* http://www.oecd.org/tax/transparency/44430286.pdf.

[121] *Id.*

tent authority), would require the receiving competent authority to carry out administrative procedures at variance with its laws or those of the requesting country, or would disclose trade secrets or other information contrary to public policy.[122]

The United States is also a founding signatory of the *Convention on Mutual Administrative Assistance in Tax Matters*.[123] The parties of the Convention provide administrative assistance to each other in tax matters such as exchange of information, assistance in recovery, and service of documents.[124] The United States signed the Original Convention in 1989, provided the deposit of instrument of ratification in 1991, and entered it into force on April 1, 1995 subject to certain reservations.[125] Pursuant to these reservations, the U.S. will not provide or receive assistance (1) for taxes imposed by local authorities; (2) in the recovery of any tax claim; or (3) in serving documents.[126] On May 27, 2010, the Deputy Secretary of State signed, on behalf of the United States, a Protocol to the *Convention on Mutual Administrative Assistance* at the OECD in Paris, France.[127] However, as of June 30, 2016, the United States had yet to deposit the instrument of ratification so the Protocol has not yet entered into force.[128]

Tax Incentives for Investment in Emerging or Developing Countries

The United States is not explicitly forbidden or prohibited from providing tax incentives for investment overseas except to the extent prohibited by the World Trade Organization. However, the United States does not currently employ tax incentives, by statute or treaty, to encourage investment in emerging or developing countries. Some countries with foreign tax credit regimes allow tax sparing provisions in their bilateral income tax treaties in order to solve the inability of the multinational to benefit from a tax holiday or other tax incentive offered by the developing

---

[122] *Id.*

[123] *See generally* OECD, STATUS OF THE CONVENTION ON MUTUAL ADMINISTRATIVE ASSISTANCE IN TAX MATTERS AND AMENDING PROTOCOLS (2014), *available at* http://www.oecd.org/ctp/exchange-of-tax-information/Status_of_convention.pdf [hereinafter OECD, STATUS OF THE CONVENTION].

[124] *See generally* OECD, CONVENTION ON MUTUAL ADMINISTRATIVE ASSISTANCE IN TAX MATTERS AND AMENDING PROTOCOLS (1988).

[125] OECD, STATUS OF THE CONVENTION, *supra* note 124.

[126] STAFF OF J. COMM. ON TAX'N, 101ST CONG., EXPLANATION OF PROPOSED CONVENTION ON MUTUAL ADMINISTRATIVE ASSISTANCE IN TAX MATTERS 3 (Comm. Print 1990) *available at* https://www.jct.gov/publications.html?func=startdown&id=3160.

[127] U.S. DEP'T OF TREASURY, UNITED STATES SIGNS PROTOCOL TO MULTILATERAL TREATY ON MUTUAL ADMINISTRATIVE ASSISTANCE IN TAX MATTERS (2010), *available at* http://www.treasury.gov/press-center/press-releases/Pages/tg726.aspx.

[128] OECD, STATUS OF THE CONVENTION, *supra* note 124.

country.[129] Tax sparing involves granting a foreign tax credit for the taxes spared, those income taxes that the corporation would have paid in the absence of the tax incentives or tax holiday provided by the developing country.[130] Although some countries encourage investment in these types of markets through tax sparing provisions in their tax or investment treaties, the United States has refrained from including tax sparing provisions in its treaties with other countries.[131]

In the 1950s, the United States negotiated various income tax treaties with countries such as India, Israel, Pakistan, and the United Arab Republic that included a tax sparing provision. The U.S. Senate refused to ratify these tax sparing provisions, and since that time the United States has not included tax sparing articles in its tax treaties.[132] Professor Surrey's testimony at the Foreign Relations Committee Hearing on the Pakistan treaty probably convinced the Senate not to accept the tax sparing provision. Surrey argued, *inter alia*, that tax sparing provisions were a distortion of the tax credit mechanism, contrary to Congressional intent to favor capital export neutrality, and not necessary in light of the fact that taxes were deferred by foreign operations conducted by a foreign subsidiary corporation.[133] The OECD also does not encourage its members to engage in tax sparing provisions because of the long-term negative effects of tax sparing.[134] The only incentive that currently exists for such investment is the allowance of deferral of taxes on income earned by foreign subsidiaries of U.S. companies as long as the income remains outside the United States. This income is taxed once it is remitted in the form of dividends, royalties, interest, etc., to the U.S. parent company.[135]

---

[129] *See generally* Kim Brooks, *Tax Sparing: A Needed Incentive for Foreign Investment in Low-Income Countries or an Unnecessary Revenue Sacrifice*, 34 QUEEN's L. J. 505 (2009), *available at* http://www.s4tp.org/wp-content/uploads/2011/09/Tax-Sparing.pdf.

[130] OECD, TAX SPARING: A RECONSIDERATION 11 (1998).

[131] *See generally* James R. Hines, Jr., *"Tax Sparing" and Direct Investment in Developing Countries* (Nat'l Bureau of Econ. Research, Working Paper No. 6728, 1998), *available at* http://www.nber.org/papers/w6728.pdf. *See* DANIEL M. BERMAN & VICTORIA J. HANEMAN, MAKING TAX LAW 248–49 (2014) for a discussion of treaty negotiations with Brazil. *See also* Jason R. Connery et al., *Current Status of U.S. Tax Treaties and International Tax Agreements*, 42 TAX MGMT. INT'L J. 485, 488 (BNA) (Aug. 9, 2013).

[132] *See* Hines, Jr. *supra* note 132, at 10 ("Despite this position, the U.S. does often agree, in an exchange of notes, to grant a tax sparing provision to countries with whom it negotiates tax treaties if it ever grants such a provision to another country in a subsequent tax treaty."). *See*, e.g., Brooks, *supra* note 130, at 520 ("If the United States reaches agreement on the provision of a tax sparing credit with any other country, the United States agrees to reopen negotiations with Bangladesh with a view to the conclusion of a protocol which would extend a tax sparing credit under the treaty."). Convention Between the Government of the U.S. and the Government of the People's Republic of Bangladesh for the Avoidance of Double Taxation and the Prevention of Fiscal Evasion with respect to Taxes on Income, U.S.- Bangl., Sept. 26, 2004, 2004 U.S.T. 207.

[133] Brooks, *supra* note 130, at 519–21 (citations omitted).

[134] *See generally* Paul R. McDaniel, *The U.S. Tax Treatment of Foreign Source Income Earned in Developing Countries: A Policy Analysis*, 35 Geo. Wash. Int'l. L. Rev. 265 (2003).

[135] CBO, OPTIONS, *supra* note 16, at 2.

Tax Incentives for Investment in Countries with Low Income or High Poverty Rates

The United States currently does not have a tax provision that encourages investment in countries with low incomes, high poverty rates, or high rates of economic inequality. A previous version of the Internal Revenue Code did allow for the exclusion of subpart F income of a CFC withdrawn from investment in lesser developed countries of the CFC.[136] This prior version of section 955 dealt with investment in emerging or developing economies by addressing "the amount of previously excluded subpart F income of a CFC withdrawn from investment in a less developed countr[y]."[137] Former section 955(c)(2), specifically noted that a less developed country corporation included those foreign corporations where "80 % or more of the gross income" consisted of gross income derived from hiring or leasing shipping vessels and aircraft registered in the developing country, and dividends and interest received from foreign corporations . . . and 10 % or more of the total combined voting power of all classes of stock which are owned by this corporation, and gain from sale or exchange of stock or obligation of foreign corporations which are such less developed country corporations, and 80 % or more of the assets are which on each day of the taxable year consists of (i) assets used, or held for use, for or in connection with the production of income described in subparagraph (A), and (ii) property described in section 956(b)(2).[138] This provision was repealed in the Tax Reduction Act of 1975.[139]

Tax Incentives and Special Regimes for Former Colonies, Territories, or Possessions

The Department of the Interior has jurisdiction over 13 U.S. territories (also known as possessions). Those territories with significant populations include: the U.S. Virgin Islands, Puerto Rico, the Commonwealth of the Northern Mariana Islands (Northern Marianas),[140] American Samoa, and Guam. With the exception of American Samoa, the residents of these territories are U.S. citizens.[141] American

---

[136] Revenue Act of 1962, Pub. L. No. 87–834, § 12(a), 76 Stat. 1013.

[137] Id.

[138] Id. at 76 Stat. 1015–1016.

[139] Pub. L. No. 94–12, § 602(b)(5), 89 Stat. 59.

[140] Puerto Rico and the Northern Marianas are commonwealths, meaning that there is a legal relationship with the U.S. set forth in a written mutual agreement. STAFF OF J. COMM. ON TAX'N, 112TH CONG.,FEDERAL TAX LAW AND ISSUES RELATED TO THE UNITED STATES TERRITORIES 1 (Comm. Print 2012), *available at* https://www.jct.gov/publications.html?func=startdown&id=4427 [hereinafter TAX ISSUES RELATED TO THE U.S. TERRITORIES].

[141] Id.

Samoa adopted its own constitution in 1967 and its residents are generally nationals, but not citizens, of the United States.[142] The United States does provide limited tax incentives and special tax regimes to its possessions, most notably, the five with significant populations. Generally, corporations formed in U.S. possessions are considered foreign corporations for U.S. tax purposes. As described in more detail in 1.1, above, foreign corporations are only taxed on income that has a sufficient nexus to the United States.

The tax rules for three of these territories, Guam, the Northern Mariana Islands, and the U.S. Virgin Islands, mirror the tax provisions of the U.S. Internal Revenue Code (Code).[143] For these three "mirror Code possessions," the Code is their internal tax law, with the name of the territory substituted for United States in the Code.[144] For example, the mirror provision for the Northern Marianas is found in section 601(a) of the Covenant to Establish a Commonwealth of the Northern Mariana Islands, and states that "the income tax laws in force in the United States will come into force in the Northern Mariana Islands as a local territorial income tax..."[145] American Samoa and Puerto Rico, on the other hand, are referred to as "non-mirror Code possessions" because these possessions apply their own internal tax laws.[146]

Although U.S. statutes apply to U.S. territories, in general, for tax purposes, these possessions are treated by the Code as foreign countries and corporations organized therein are foreign corporations.[147] As such, income derived from these territories is generally treated as foreign-source income.[148] However, corporations formed in Puerto Rico, the U.S. Virgin Islands, the Northern Mariana Islands, Guam, and American Samoa are accorded special treatment under the Code.[149] Section 881 generally imposes a tax of 30 % on the passive income received from sources within the United States by a foreign corporation.[150] Corporations organized in Guam, American Samoa, the Northern Mariana Islands, and the Virgin Islands are not subject to this withholding tax if less than 25 % of the stock is beneficially owned by foreign persons and "at least 65 % of the gross income...is shown to be effectively connected" income with a trade or business operating in a U.S. posses-

---

[142] *Id.* at 2.

[143] *Id.* However, it is generally only the income tax provisions that are mirrored. For example, 48 U.S.C. §1421i (d)(1) provides a non-exhaustive list of the mirrored Code sections in Guam. *Id.* at 8.

[144] *Id.* at 2. The mirror code provision for the U.S. Virgin Islands states that "the income-tax laws in the United States ... and those which may hereafter be enacted shall be held to be likewise in force in the Virgin Islands of the United States, except that the proceeds of such taxes shall be paid into the treasuries of said islands: [...]."48 U.S.C. § 1397 (2012).

[145] Covenant to Establish a Commonwealth of the Northern Mariana Islands in Political Union with the United States of America, sec. 601(a), Act of March 24, 1976, Pub. L. No. 94–241; 48 U.S.C. § 1801 (2012).

[146] Tax Issues Related to the U.S. Territories, *supra* note 141, at 2.

[147] *Id.* at 2, 7.

[148] *Id.* at 7.

[149] *Id.*

[150] I.R.C. § 881(a) (2014).

sion or the U.S. for the 3 year period preceding the close of the taxable year.[151] Dividends received from U.S. sources by corporations formed in Puerto Rico that meet these requirements are taxed at a reduced rate of 10 %.[152]

Puerto Rico

Although Puerto Rico is a U.S. territory, a corporation created in Puerto Rico is a foreign corporation under U.S. tax law.[153] Thus, income which is effectively connected with the conduct of a trade or business within the U.S. is subject to the regular corporate tax rates on a net basis.[154] Income of these foreign corporations from sources within the U.S. that is fixed, determinable, annual, or periodic income, is subject to flat rate tax of 30 % on the gross amount.[155] U.S source dividends paid to a corporation created or organized in Puerto Rico have a withholding tax rate decreased from 30 % to 10 % for parity with the generally applicable 10 % withholding tax of Puerto Rico on Puerto Rico-source dividends paid to U.S. corporations.[156] In 2009, President Barack Obama, in signing Executive Order 13517, expanded the "responsibilities of the President's Task Force on Puerto Rico's Status to [seek] recommendations on economic development."[157] The task force, with members from almost every Cabinet agency, convened in December of that year and later issued a report in March 2011.[158]

Previously, firms incorporated in the U.S. received tax benefits for the operations they conducted in Puerto Rico in order to "generate employment-creating investment" in Puerto Rico, as well as other U.S. possessions.[159] Since the 1921 Tax Act, the Code encouraged the development of the Puerto Rican economy through provisions that eventually evolved into section 936.[160] Initially, "qualified corporations deriving 80 % or more of their income from U.S. possessions were exempted from

---

[151] I.R.C. §§ 881(b)(1)(A)-(B) (2014). Furthermore, "no substantial part of the income of such corporation" may have been used to pay "obligations to persons who are not bona fide residents" of a U.S. possession or the United States. §881(b)(1)(C) (2014).

[152] I.R.C. § 881(b)(2) (2014).

[153] Tax Issues Related to the U.S. Territories, *supra* note 141, at 25.

[154] I.R.C. § 882(a)(1) (2014) (listing those activities that generate income that is not considered to be effectively connected with the United States).

[155] I.R.C. § 881(a) (2014).

[156] I.R.C. § 881(b)(2) (2014).

[157] Martin A. Sullivan, *The Treasury Bailout of Puerto Rico*, 72 Tax Notes Int'l 267, 277 (2014).

[158] *Id.*

[159] David L. Brumbaugh, Cong. Research Serv., RS20695, The Puerto Rican Economic Activity Tax Credit: Current Proposals and Scheduled Phaseout 1 (2000).

[160] Staff of J. Comm. On Tax'n, 99th Cong.,General Explanation of the Tax Reform Act of 1986 999 n. 2 (Comm. Print 1987), available at https://www.jct.gov/publications.html?func=startdown&id=3367 [hereinafter Tax Reform Act of 1986].

income tax on their foreign source income."[161] Congress acknowledged in 1976 that this "[f]ederal tax exemption had played an important role in Puerto Rican economic development."[162]

The 1976 Tax Reform Act added section 936 to the code,[163] converting the exemption system to a 100 % tax credit for income generated in Puerto Rico to U.S. corporations ("effectively exempt[ing] the corporation from U.S. tax on its possessions income.")[164] This was in essence tax sparing as the credit was granted even if foreign taxes were not paid, allowing the corporations to also benefit from tax incentives offered by the possessions themselves.[165] Although the Puerto Rico and possession tax credit applied to both passive and active income,[166] it was required that 80 % or more of the corporation's gross income from the preceding 3 year period be derived from sources within a possession.[167] Furthermore, 75 % of that income was required to be from the active conduct of a business within a possession.[168]

Treasury Department studies submitted to Congress in 1978, 1979, 1980 and 1983, challenged the cost effectiveness of these provisions, finding that the Federal tax expenditure per employee ranged from $3,000 to $35,000 per employee depending on the industry.[169] The Joint Committee on Taxation stated that the Puerto Rico and possession tax credit had yielded "little corresponding benefit to employment or investment in the possession."[170] In 1982, changes to section 936 were necessary to stop transfer pricing abuses with respect to intangible assets such as drug patents.[171]

The Small Business Job Protection Act of 1996[172] terminated the Puerto Rico and possession tax credit for the tax years beginning after December 31, 1995 because of the small number of companies that benefitted from the expensive tax expenditure.[173] Corporations that began operations in a possession in a tax year beginning on or after January 1, 1996, were not entitled to the Puerto Rico and possession tax

---

[161] *Id.* at 999.

[162] *Id.*

[163] Pub. L. No. 94–455, § 1051, 90 Stat. 1525.

[164] STAFF OF J. COMM. ON TAX'N, 109TH CONG.,AN OVERVIEW OF THE SPECIAL TAX RULES RELATED TO PUERTO RICO AND AN ANALYSIS OF THE TAX AND ECONOMIC POLICY IMPLICATIONS OF RECENT LEGISLATIVE OPTIONS 50 (Comm. Print 2006), *available at* https://www.jct.gov/publications.html?func=showdown&id=1496 [hereinafter TAX RULES RELATED TO PUERTO RICO].

[165] TAX REFORM ACT OF 1986, *supra* note 161, at 1000.

[166] I.R.C. § 936(a)(1) (2014).

[167] I.R.C. § 936(a)(2)(A) (2014).

[168] I.R.C. § 936(a)(2)(B) (2014).

[169] TAX RULES RELATED TO PUERTO RICO, *supra* note 165, at 51.

[170] TAX REFORM ACT OF 1986, *supra* note 161, at 1000.

[171] TAX RULES RELATED TO PUERTO RICO, *supra* note 165, at 52.

[172] Pub. L. No. 104–188, § 1601, 110 Stat. 1755.

[173] BRUMBAUGH, *supra* note 160, at 4.

credit.[174] Corporations operating in a possession before that date had to qualify as an "existing credit claimant" in order to claim the possessions tax credit for a transition period.[175] For these existing credit claimants, the credit fully expired for fiscal years beginning on and after January 1, 2006.[176] The phase-out provisions of all possessions except Puerto Rico were governed by section 936(j). Newly created section 30A specified that the corporation must have been an existing credit claimant with respect to Puerto Rico to qualify for the tax credit and provided appropriate phase-out rules.[177] There were no differences after 2002, however, between the provisions limiting the amount of the credit for the qualified corporations in the two sections.[178]

Once the federal tax incentives of section 936 were phased out, many corporations (including "most of the major pharmaceutical, instrument and electronics manufacturing companies in Puerto Rico") reorganized their operations into CFCs.[179] As described in more detail in 1.1, above, CFCs defer the payment of U.S. federal income taxes until that income is repatriated to its U.S. parent corporation.[180] CFCs are subject to transfer pricing rules for intangible income that differ from those that applied to the previous section 936 Corporations and are subject to a Puerto Rico withholding tax on the royalty payments that must be made "commensurate with income" to their U.S. affiliates.[181]

U.S. Virgin Islands

Similar to Puerto Rico, those corporations incorporated under the laws of the U.S. Virgin Islands are considered foreign corporations for U.S. tax purposes.[182] The U.S. Virgin Islands employs an income tax system that is very similar to that of the United States.[183] Because a corporation may be subject to tax in both the

---

[174] I.R.C. § 936(j)(1) (2014).

[175] A corporation is an "existing credit claimant" if (1) the corporation is engaged in the active conduct of a trade or business within the possession on October 13, 1995, and (2) the corporation has elected the benefits of the Puerto Rico and possession tax credit pursuant to an election which is in effect for its taxable year that includes October 13, 1995. I.R.C. § 936(j)(9)(A) (2014).

[176] I.R.C. §§ 30A(g), 936(j)(8)(A) (2014).

[177] I.R.C. § 30A(a)(2)(A) (2014).

[178] I.R.C. §§ 30A(d), 936(a)(4) (2014). The credit's phase-out rules were dependent on whether the existing claimant elected the economic activity limitation or an alternative percentage limitation. There was also an additional base-period cap that applied in either 1999 or 2002 depending on which limitation applied. BRUMBAUGH, *supra* note 160, at 4–5.

[179] Edgar Rios-Mendez & Jeanelle Alemar-Escabi, *Foreign Income: Business Operations in Puerto Rico*, 7320 TAX MGMT. (BNA) A-184 (2012).

[180] *Id.*

[181] *Id.*

[182] TAX ISSUES RELATED TO THE U.S. TERRITORIES, *supra* note 141, at 29.

[183] *Id.* at 28.

U.S. Virgin Islands and to the U.S., section 934 provides certain special tax rules. Under section 934, a foreign corporation is only subject to U.S. tax if it has U.S. source income or income effectively connected with the conduct of a trade or business in the United States.[184] U.S. Virgin Islands taxes a domestic corporation on its worldwide income, but the company is allowed a foreign tax credit against U.S. Virgin Islands tax for taxes imposed by the United States, foreign countries and other possessions.[185] A corporation that was organized in the U.S. is treated as a foreign corporation under the U.S. Virgin Islands' mirror Code.[186] Thus, these corporations are only subject to U.S. Virgin Islands tax if they have U.S. Virgin Islands source income or income effectively connected with the conduct of a trade or business in U.S. Virgin Islands.[187] Similarly, the United States taxes its domestic corporations on their worldwide income, but allows a foreign tax credit for taxes imposed by foreign jurisdictions, including U.S. Virgin Islands.[188]

Northern Mariana Islands

For Northern Mariana Islands tax purposes, domestic corporations are those organized in the Northern Marianas.[189] All corporations formed elsewhere are considered foreign corporations.[190] Northern Marianas corporations are subject to tax on their worldwide income and a foreign tax credit is allowed for income taxes paid to the United States.[191] Corporations in the Northern Marianas that meet certain income and ownership requirements[192] may be subject to a zero withholding tax rate on passive income from sources within the United States.[193] "Other U.S. source income will generally be taxed on a net basis at U.S. graduated rates."[194]

The full amount of corporate income tax liability is paid to the Northern Marianas government, but a certain percentage is returned to the taxpayer.[195] Corporations with a tax liability of $20,000 or less are entitled to a 90 % rebate, a tax liability of $100,000 or less receives a 70 % rebate, and tax liabilities over $100,000 receive a 50 % rebate.[196]

---

[184] *Id.* at 29.

[185] *Id.*

[186] *Id.*

[187] *Id.*

[188] Tax Issues Related to the U.S. Territories, *supra* note 141, at 29.

[189] *Business Operations in the Territories*, *supra* note 109, at A-163.

[190] *Id.*

[191] *Id.* at A-164.

[192] I.R.C. § 881(b).

[193] Tax Issues Related to the U.S. Territories, *supra* note 141, at 23.

[194] *Id.*

[195] *Business Operations in the Territories*, *supra* note 109, at A-164.

[196] *Id.*

Guam

A corporation organized in Guam is treated as a domestic corporation for Guamanian tax purposes and a foreign corporation for U.S. tax purposes.[197] Similar to other foreign corporations, a Guamanian corporation that has income effectively connected with a U.S. trade or business must pay U.S. tax on that income; however these corporations are generally entitled to a foreign tax credit for the taxes paid.[198] The Organic Act of Guam[199] applies the U.S. income tax laws as Guam internal tax law, with the name of the territory substituted for United States in the Code. Thus, income from foreign investment in Guam is taxed at the withholding rate of 30 %.[200] Tax treaties typically lower this withholding rate on income from foreign investment in the U.S. to rates ranging from 5 to 15 %. Guam was not considered part of the United States for treaty purposes, thus making the U.S. more attractive for foreign investors.[201] As a result, in 2002, Congress enacted the Guam Foreign Investment Equity Act,[202] which reduces withholding tax rates on income from foreign investments in Guam "by amending the Organic Act of Guam to authorize Guam to apply the tax rate that would apply 'were Guam treated as part of the United States for purposes of' the tax treaties."[203]

American Samoa

The United States taxes corporations in American Samoa only on income that has a sufficient nexus to the United States just like any other foreign corporation.[204] Generally, this would include a 30 % tax on the gross amount of its fixed, determinable, annual or periodic income from U.S. sources and a net basis tax at regular rates on income effectively connected with the conduct of a U.S. trade or business.[205] Corporations in American Samoa that meet certain income and ownership requirements[206] may be subject to a zero withholding tax rate on passive income from sources within the United States.[207] For American Samoa tax purposes, corporations

---

[197] TAX ISSUES RELATED TO THE U.S. TERRITORIES, *supra* note 141, at 20.

[198] *Id.* at 20–21.

[199] 48 U.S.C. § 1421 et seq.

[200] S. REP. No. 107–173, at *1-*2 (2002).

[201] *Id.* at *2.

[202] Pub. L. No. 107–212, §116 Stat. 1051 (2002).

[203] S. REP. No. 107–173, *supra* note 201, at *2; *see also* TAX ISSUES RELATED TO THE U.S. TERRITORIES, *supra* note 141, at 21.

[204] *Business Operations in the Territories*, *supra* note 109, at A-203.

[205] TAX ISSUES RELATED TO THE U.S. TERRITORIES, *supra* note 141, at 18.

[206] I.R.C. § 881(b) (2014).

[207] TAX ISSUES RELATED TO THE U.S. TERRITORIES, *supra* note 141, at 18.

organized in American Samoa are domestic corporations, while corporations formed elsewhere are foreign.[208] For American Samoa tax purposes, the taxable income of a corporation is calculated the same as for U.S. corporations under the U.S. Internal Revenue Code.[209] Foreign taxes paid by American Samoa corporate taxpayers are creditable towards their American Samoa income tax.[210]

Measures to Attract Economic Activity

In the past, the U.S. has undertaken various measures to encourage economic activity within its own jurisdiction. These incentives were struck down by panels established under the General Agreement on Tariffs and Trade ("GATT") or formed by the World Trade Organization ("WTO"). For example, legislation enacted in 1971 created the domestic international sales corporation ("DISC").[211] Its purpose was to "[e]xempt a proportion of U.S. exporters' profits by funneling export sales through a domestic subsidiary of the U.S. exporter."[212] After a GATT panel found that the DISC was an illegal subsidy, it was withdrawn and replaced with the foreign sales corporation ("FSC"), which lasted from 1984 to 2000.[213] During this time exporters were provided with a "[f]ederal income tax subsidy for operating through foreign sales corporations."[214] "In 2000, the European Union succeeded in having the FSC regime declared a prohibited export subsidy by the WTO."[215] The FSC was repealed and replaced by the extraterritorial income exclusion ("ETI").[216] In January of 2002, the WTO held that the ETI regime also constituted a "prohibited export subsidy under relevant trade agreements."[217]

The American Jobs Creation Act of 2004[218] repealed the ETI and replaced it with the section 199 deduction for domestic production activities.[219] "Congress under-

---

[208] *Business Operations in the Territories, supra* note 109, at A-201.

[209] *Id.*

[210] *Id.* Under § 901 *et seq.* as adopted by American Samoa.

[211] DOERNBERG, *supra* note 57, at 206; *See also* Marc Rosenberg, *How a Taxing Problem has Taken its Toll: A Common Person's Guide to an International Taxation Dispute*, 20 B.U. INT'L L.J. 1, 9–10 (2002) (discussing DISC).

[212] DOERNBERG, *supra* note 57, at 206.

[213] *Id.*

[214] *Id.*

[215] STAFF OF J. COMM. ON TAX'N, 108TH CONG.,GENERAL EXPLANATION OF TAX LEGISLATION ENACTED IN THE 108TH CONGRESS 166 (Comm. Print 2005), *available at* http://www.jct.gov/s-5-05.pdf. [hereinafter TAX LEGISLATION IN 108TH CONGRESS].

[216] DOERNBERG, *supra* note 57, at 206–7. *See generally* FSC Repeal and Extraterritorial Income Exclusion Act 2000, Pub. L. No. 106–519, § 942, 114 Stat. 2423, 2426.

[217] TAX LEGISLATION IN 108TH CONGRESS, *supra* note 216.

[218] Pub. L. No. 108–357, Title I § 101, 102, 118 Stat. 1418.

[219] This section provided a phase-in period. The applicable deduction was 3 % for taxable years beginning in 2005 or 2006 and 6 % for taxable years beginning in 2007, 2008, or 2009. I.R.C. § 199(a)(2) (2013).

stood that simply repealing the ETI regime, while bringing our tax laws into compliance with our obligations under the WTO, would diminish the prospects for recovery from the recent economic downturn by the manufacturing sector."[220] Section 199 rewards economic activity in the U.S. by allowing a 9 % deduction of the lesser of the income attributable to qualified domestic production activities or taxable income.[221] This provision was enacted to compensate for the loss of the ETI and to stimulate domestic manufacturers to create manufacturing jobs domestically.[222] Thus, the amount of the deduction is limited to "50 % of the W-2 wages of the taxpayer for the taxable year."[223]

Qualified production activities income ("QPAI") is defined as the taxpayer's domestic production gross receipts ("DPGR") reduced by the sum of the cost of goods sold that are allocable to such receipts as well as other expenses, losses, or deductions that are properly allocable to such receipts.[224] The items that qualify as DPGR are those gross receipts derived from various production activities such as the leasing, rental, licensing, sale or exchange of qualifying production property that was either manufactured, produced, grown, or extracted within the United States, including qualified films and electricity, natural gas, or potable water.[225] DPGR also includes gross receipts derived from the construction of real property performed in the United States by the taxpayer in the ordinary course of its trade or business.[226] Lastly, DPGR includes gross receipts from engineering or architectural services performed domestically by the taxpayer in the ordinary course of its trade or business for the construction of real property domestically.[227]

States themselves also provide their own tax incentives to attract economic activity. The use of tax incentives by the individual American states to attract investment has been the subject of much research.[228] A review of this research can provide a useful parallel for an analysis of the efficacy of the use of tax incentives by develop-

---

[220] TAX LEGISLATION IN 108TH CONGRESS, *supra* note 216, at 170.

[221] Section 199 allows "[a] deduction of an amount equal to 9 % of the lesser of – (A) the qualified production activities income [("QPAI")] of the taxpayer for the taxable year, or (B) taxable income (determined without regard to this section) for the taxable year. I.R.C. § 199(a)(1) (2014).

[222] TAX LEGISLATION IN 108TH CONGRESS, *supra* note 216, at 170; *see also* H.R. REP.NO. 108–755, at 314 (2004) (Conf. Rep.).

[223] I.R.C. § 199(b)(1) (2014).

[224] QPAI is defined as "[t]he amount equal to the excess (if any) of – (A) the taxpayer's domestic production gross receipts (DPGR) for such taxable year, over (B) the sum of – (i) the cost of goods sold that are allocable to such receipts, and (ii) other expenses, losses, or deductions (other than deductions allowed under this section), which are properly allocable to such receipts." I.R.C. § 199(c)(1) (2013).

[225] I.R.C. § 199(c)(4)(A)(i) (2014).

[226] I.R.C. § 199(c)(4)(A)(ii) (2014).

[227] I.R.C. § 199(c)(4)(A)(iii) (2014).

[228] *See*, e.g., Tracy Kaye, *The Gentle Art of Corporate Seduction: Tax Incentives in the United States and the European Union*, 57 U. KAN. L. REV. 93 (2008); *see also*, Tracy Kaye, *Corporate Blackmail: State Tax Incentives in the United States*, in STATE AID AND LAW (Alexander Rust & Claire Micheau eds., 2013).

ing countries. In *Investment Incentives and the Global Competition for Capital*, Professor Kenneth Thomas, documents how tax subsidies given to multinationals are increasing around the world.[229] He estimated total U.S. state and local incentives at $46.8 billion in 2005.[230] Because the United States does not have any strict controls or procedures over the granting of such incentives by the states,[231] bidding wars for incentives increase the size and number of incentives far beyond those encountered in the European Union.[232]

While competition to award subsidies to companies is indeed a global problem, the problem is much worse in the United States.[233] For 2005, Thomas estimated that American state and local subsidies to businesses were much larger than the location subsidies found in 15 EU Member States.[234] The United States also has markedly higher-aid intensity (the incentive amount as a percentage of the recipient's investment) and the locations granting these "investment incentives were substantially more prosperous than comparable EU regions."[235] As of 2011, almost every state offered some type of tax credit or tax incentive to persuade businesses to locate, maintain, or expand their operations within the state.[236] Although interstate competition to attract economic development has raised concerns regarding the smooth functioning of the national economy,[237] the proliferation of tax credits and incentives has continued relatively unabated despite the dire financial condition of many of the states.[238]

---

[229] KENNETH P. THOMAS, INVESTMENT INCENTIVES AND THE GLOBAL COMPETITION FOR CAPITAL 2–3 (2011). Because of the range of credits offered by U.S. states and municipalities as well as the lack of a universal data collection and recordation procedure, it is extremely difficult to achieve an accurate total of investment incentives offered throughout the United States. *Id.* at 102–106.

[230] Thomas, *supra* note 230, at 106–107. Further, he estimated for 2005 total state and local subsidies to be $64.8 billion and $69.8 billion if the benefits of accelerated depreciation are included in the total. *Id. See also* David Cay Johnston, *On the Dole, Corporate Style*, 59 ST. TAX NOTES 127 (2011) (citing Thomas, *supra* note 230).

[231] Thomas, *supra* note 230, at 96. State aid in the European Union is controlled through the adoption of overall regional aid guidelines. *Id.* at 96–97, 101.

[232] *Id.* at 97–102.

[233] *Id.* at 1. "Alabama ... in 2002 gave Hyundai about $117,000 per job on a present value basis ... ." *Id.*

[234] *Id.* at 176; *see also* Johnston, *supra* note 231, at 127.

[235] Thomas, *supra* note 230, at 98–99.

[236] Mark L. Nachbar, *Credits and Incentives: Alabama Through Hawaii*, 1450-2nd TAX MGMT., 1450.01-1450.02 (BNA) (2008); *see generally* Mark L. Nachbar et al., *Credits and Incentives*, Nos. 1450-2nd, 1460-2nd, 1470-2nd, and 1480-1st, TAX MGMT. (BNA) (2008).

[237] *See*, e.g., DAVID BRUNORI, THE FUTURE OF STATE TAXATION 6 (1998) [hereinafter BRUNORI, STATE TAXATION] (stating that "[c]ommentators generally agree that incentives violate the most basic principles of sound tax policy"); David Brunori, *"The Politics of State Taxation": Thou Shalt Not Use Tax Incentives*, ST. TAX TODAY 557 (2002) [hereinafter Brunori, *Thou Shalt Not Use Tax Incentives*] (stating tax incentives violate "the cardinal rule that tax systems should be designed so that they have a minimal impact on economic activity").

[238] *See* Brunori, *Thou Shalt Not Use Tax Incentives*, *supra* note 238, at 557 (describing States, corporations, and consultants as actively in pursuit of granting and obtaining tax breaks); *see also*

Tax Holiday

The United States provided a temporary tax holiday for American corporations to receive cash dividends from a controlled foreign corporation ("CFC")[239] and pay taxes at a reduced rate. Section 965 was enacted as part of the American Jobs Creation Act of 2004[240] and "[p]rovided for a one-time tax holiday on the repatriation of foreign earnings by U.S.-based multinational enterprises."[241] In general, foreign income earned by the subsidiary of a U.S. corporation is only taxed once it is repatriated.[242] Section 965 reduced the tax rate on this repatriated income from 35 % to an effective tax rate of 5.25 % by allowing corporations to deduct 85 % of their qualifying dividends from their taxable income[243] as long as the repatriations were invested in the United States as part of a domestic reinvestment plan.[244] This deduction could be claimed during 2005 or 2006.[245]

To qualify for this deduction, the dividends had to be extraordinary, that is they had to "[e]xceed the average dividend received from the corporation's CFCs over a base period defined as the 5 tax years ending prior to July 1, 2003."[246] Also, the amount of qualifying dividends was limited to the greater amount of: (1) $500 million; (2) the amount shown on the corporation's financial statement as the earnings permanently reinvested outside the United States; or (3) "35 % of the specific tax liability attributable to earnings permanently reinvested outside the United States."[247]

The main purpose of section 965 was to encourage corporations to repatriate their foreign earnings in excess of historical levels and invest in the United States in

---

BRUNORI, STATE TAXATION, *supra* note 238, at 6 (stating that tax incentives have increased "primarily because political leaders lack the will to reject them").

[239] A CFC is defined as "any foreign corporation if more than 50 % of (1) the total combined voting power of all classes of stock of such corporation entitled to vote, or (2) the total value of stock of such corporation, is owned … by United States shareholders on any day during the taxable year of such foreign corporation." I.R.C. § 957(a) (2014).

[240] Pub. L. No. 108–357, § 422, 118 Stat. 1418, 1514–19 (2004).

[241] Dhammika Dharmapala, C. Fritz Foley & Kristin J. Forbes, *Watch What I Do, Not What I Say*: *The Unintended Consequences of the Homeland Investment Act*, 66 J. FIN. 753, 782–3 (2011).

[242] STAFF OF PERMANENT SUBCOMM. ON INVESTIGATIONS OF THE S. COMM. ON HOMELAND SEC. AND GOVERNMENTAL AFFAIRS, 112TH CONG., MAJORITY REP. ON REPATRIATING OFFSHORE FUNDS: 2004 TAX WINDFALL FOR SELECT MULTINATIONALS 6–7 (Comm. Print 2011), *available at* http://tjn-usa.org/storage/documents/PSI.Repatriationreport.101011.pdf [hereinafter REPATRIATING OFFSHORE FUNDS].

[243] I.R.C. § 965(a)(1) (2014); *see also* REPATRIATING OFFSHORE FUNDS, *supra* note 243, at 6.

[244] I.R.C. § 965(a)(1); *see also* Melissa Redmiles, *The One-Time Received Dividend Deduction*, IRS, STATISTICS OF INCOME BULLETIN 102, 102 (2008), *available at* http://www.irs.gov/pub/irs-soi/08codivdeductbul.pdf.

[245] I.R.C. §§ 965(a)(1)-(2) (2014). ("[c]ould be claimed either in the last tax year that beg[an] before October 22, 2004, or the last year that beg[an] during the 1-year period beginning on October 22, 2004.").

[246] Redmiles, *supra* note 245, at 102.

[247] REPATRIATING OFFSHORE FUNDS, *supra* note 243, at 6–7. I.R.C. § 965(b)(1) (2014).

order to stimulate economic and job growth.[248] According to the IRS, only 843 corporations, out of a possible 9,700, opted to take the section 965 deduction.[249] However, these corporations, primarily from the pharmaceutical and medicine industry and the computer and electronic industry, repatriated $312 billion creating deductions of $265 billion.[250] Pfizer, Merck, Hewlett-Packard, Johnson & Johnson, and IBM repatriated one fourth of this total.[251]

Proponents of the legislation were concerned that failure to provide a lower repatriation tax rate would encourage corporations to invest their earnings overseas as opposed to in the United States.[252] However, empirical studies on the employment growth rate provided mixed results, indicating that the tax holiday did not create the desired result of an increase in domestic economic activity.[253] There is however, evidence that perhaps as much as 20 % of the funds were returned to shareholders through stock repurchase programs.[254] This may be because money is fungible and the law did not include a provision to track how the repatriated funds were used, and whether these funds were in fact invested with the desired purpose.[255]

Various proposals to reduce the tax rate on repatriated dividends from CFCs to their U.S. parents have been introduced in Congress.[256] The Administration's FY 2017 Budget Proposal would impose a minimum tax on the foreign earnings of U.S. corporations and their CFCs that is calculated on a country-by-country basis.[257] The Proposal also includes a 14-percent one-time tax on the previously untaxed earnings and profits of CFCs that were accumulated before January 1, 2017.[258] Although the prospect of another tax holiday for such dividends was considered, no legislation had passed Congress as of the summer of 2016. The Joint Committee on Taxation has estimated that although a second repatriation would raise revenue for the first 2

---

[248] S. Res.1637, 108th Cong., 150 CONG. REC. 2066 (2004) (enacted).

[249] Redmiles, *supra* note 245, at 103.

[250] *Id.*

[251] Rodney P. Mock & Andreas Simon, *Permanently Reinvested Earnings: Priceless*, 121 TAX NOTES 835, 835–48 (2008).

[252] S. Res. 1637, *supra* note 249.

[253] *See generally* Dharmapala et al., *supra* note 242; Thomas J. Brennan, *Where the Money Really Went: A New Understanding of the AJCA Tax Holiday* (Northwestern Uni. Sch. of Law, Law and Economics Series No. 13–35, drft. Aug. 19, 2013), *available at* http://ssrn.com/abstract=2312721; Floyd Norris, *Tax Break for Profits Went Awry*, N.Y. TIMES, Jun. 5, 2009, at B1, *available at* http://www.nytimes.com/2009/06/05/business/05norris.html.

[254] DONALD J. MARPLES & JANE G. GRAVELLE, CONG. RESEARCH SERV., R40178, TAX CUTS ON REPATRIATION EARNINGS As ECONOMIC STIMULUS: AN ECONOMIC ANALYSIS 8 (2011).

[255] REPATRIATING OFFSHORE FUNDS, *supra* note 243, at 7, 9.

[256] *See, e.g.*, H.R. 937, H.R. 1036, H.R. 1834, H.R. 2862, S. 727, and S. 1671, (House and Senate bills that were introduced in the 112th Congress). *See also* MARPLES & GRAVELLE, *supra* note 255, at 1.

[257] ADMINISTRATION'S FY 2017 REVENUE PROPOSALS, *supra* note 47, at 9–12.

[258] *Id.* at 13.

years, it would lose $96 billion over 10 years.[259] Furthermore, a CRS study notes that U.S. net exports could decline, as the demand for dollars resulting from the conversion of the foreign currencies, increases "the price of the dollar in world currency markets."[260]

Corporate Tax Rate Structure for Foreign and Domestic Corporations

The United States operates a partially integrated system of corporate and shareholder taxation in that a domestic corporation is taxed separately on its taxable income.[261] Shareholders who are individuals are also taxed on any dividend distributions from that corporation but at a preferential rate of tax.[262] A domestic corporation is one that is created or organized under the laws of the United States or one of the states.[263] Domestic corporations are considered residents of the United States and are taxed on their worldwide income, regardless of geographic origin.[264] The taxable income of a corporation is gross income less allowable deductions including a deduction for a portion of income attributable to certain manufacturing activities.[265] Corporations may not deduct dividends paid to shareholders.[266] The corporation must apply a graduated rate schedule to the computed taxable income.[267] However, the 15 % and 25 % rates are "phased out for corporations with taxable income between $100,000 and $335,000" so that a corporation with taxable income between $335,000 and $10,000,000 is effectively subject to a 34 % flat tax rate.[268] This latter tax rate is then "phased out for corporations with taxable income between $15,000,000 and $18,333,333" such that a corporation with taxable income equal to or greater than $18,333,333 is subject to a 35 % flat tax rate.[269] The maximum cor-

---

[259] *See* STAFF OF J. COMM. ON TAX'N, 113TH CONG., LETTER TO SENATOR ORRIN HATCH (Comm. Print 2014), *available at* http://www.hatch.senate.gov/public/_cache/files/1b24c4cf-6005-4a4e-bab7-3d9e3820c509/JCT%206-6-14.pdf.

[260] MARPLES & GRAVELLE, *supra* note 255, at 1.

[261] I.R.C. §11(a) (2013).

[262] I.R.C. §§ 61(a), 301(c)(1) (2013). As of January 1, 2013, the maximum rate on dividend income is 20 %. §1(h).

[263] I.R.C. § 7701(a)(4) (2013).

[264] CHRISTIANS, DONALDSON, & POSTLEWAITE, *supra* note 38, at 5.

[265] I.R.C. § 63 (West 2013). See question 10 for a fuller discussion of section 199.

[266] KAREN C. BURKE, FEDERAL INCOME TAXATION OF CORPORATIONS AND STOCKHOLDERS 1 (Thomson/West 2007).

[267] I.R.C. § 11(b) (2013).

[268] STAFF OF J. COMM. ON TAX'N, 113TH CONG., OVERVIEW OF THE FEDERAL TAX SYSTEM AS IN EFFECT FOR 2013 11 (Comm. Print 2013), *available at* https://www.jct.gov/publications.html?func=startdown&id=4498.

[269] *Id.*

porate tax rate since the Tax Reform Act of 1986 has been 35 %,[270] however, when state corporate taxes are considered, the tax rate can equal 39 %.[271]

Foreign corporations are subject to U.S. tax not on their worldwide income but only on income from sources within the United States or from any source if effectively connected to a U.S. business. This occurs if the income from any source "is connected with a U.S. branch of a foreign corporation" or if the income is of a certain type and "derived from sources within the United States" and earned by a foreign corporation.[272] According to section 881, U.S. source income received by a foreign corporation in the form of interest, dividends, salaries, wages, and similar items is subject to a flat tax of 30 %.[273] This rate may be subject to change if the United States and the foreign corporation's home country have so agreed in a bilateral income tax treaty.[274] There is no tax imposed on portfolio interest "received by a foreign corporation from sources within the U.S."[275]

Income of a foreign corporation is taxed like that of a resident corporation if the foreign corporation is engaged in a trade or business within the United States and the taxable income is effectively connected with the conduct of this trade or business.[276] Additionally, foreign corporations engaged in a trade or business within the U.S. are subject to branch profits tax so that foreign corporations operating through a U.S. branch and foreign corporations doing business through a U.S. subsidiary are given the same tax treatment.[277] Section 884 imposes a 30 % tax on branch profits, absent which a foreign corporation operating through a U.S. branch would only have to pay tax on effectively connected income.[278] The branch profits tax can be imposed on three different bases. First, a 30 % tax can be imposed on a foreign corporation's dividend equivalent amount, that is, the foreign corporation's current earnings and profits.[279] Second, a 30 % branch profits withholding tax can be

---

[270] KAREN C. BURKE, *supra* note 267 at 1; I.R.C. § 11(b)(1)(D) (2014).

[271] CBO, OPTIONS, *supra* note 16, at1.

[272] Jessica L. Katz, Charles T. Plambeck, & Diane M. Ring, *U.S. Income Taxation of Foreign Corporations*, 908-2nd TAX MGMT. (BNA) Detailed Analysis, at I. Overview (2008).

[273] A complete list of the types of gains, profits and incomes that are subject to tax are listed under section 881(a)(1). I.R.C. § 881(a) (2013).

[274] *See* e.g., United States, Model Income Tax Convention 2006, arts. 10, 11.

[275] I.R.C. § 881(c)(1) (2013). No tax is imposed on certain interest and dividends, namely interest on deposits that are not effectively connected with a trade or business within the United States, the "active foreign business percentage" of a dividend or interest "paid by an existing 80/20 company", income from a foreign central bank, or dividends paid by a foreign corporation that are treated as income from within the U.S. pursuant to section 861(a)(2)(B). I.R.C. §§ 871(i)(2), 881(d) (2013).

[276] I.R.C. U.S.C. § 882(a)(1) (2013). Treas. Reg. § 301.7701-5 (1967). Therefore, the foreign corporation is subject to the same graduated rates of section 11 on its taxable income effectively connected with the conduct of a U.S. trade or business. § 882(a)(1).

[277] CHRISTIANS, DONALDSON, & POSTLEWAITE, *supra* note 38, at 167; *see also* I.R.C. § 884 (2014).

[278] I.R.C. § 884(a) (2014); CHRISTIANS, DONALDSON, & POSTLEWAITE, *supra* note 38, at 167.

[279] I.R.C. § 884(a)-(b) (2014).

imposed on interest paid by a foreign corporation's U.S. trade or business.[280] Lastly, a branch profits tax can also be imposed on branch excess interest. Therefore, a foreign corporation is "liable for a 30 % tax if the amount of the interest deduction allowed to the foreign corporation under I.R.C. section 882 exceeds the amount of interest paid by that corporation's domestic trade or business."[281] These tax rates can be reduced if an income tax treaty exists between the U.S. and the foreign corporation's home country, and the foreign corporation is a "qualified resident of such foreign country."[282]

Bilateral or Multilateral Trade or Investment Agreements

The United States has signed multiple bilateral and multilateral trade and investment treaties with other countries. A complete list of the trade and investment frameworks signed is available on the United States Trade Representative ("USTR") website, and a list of the current bilateral investment treaties in force, and treaty text, is available on the Trade Compliance Center website.[283] According to the Trade Compliance Center, the U.S. has signed bilateral investment treaties with:

Country	Date of signature	Date entered into force
Albania	January 11, 1995	January 4, 1998
Argentina	November 14, 1991	October 20, 1994
Armenia	September 23, 1992	March 29, 1996
Azerbaijan	August 1, 1997	August 2, 2001
Bahrain	September 29, 1999	May 30, 2001
Bangladesh	March 12, 1986	July 25, 1989
Bolivia	April 17, 1998	June 6, 2001
Bulgaria	September 23, 1992	June 2, 1994
Cameroon	February 26, 1986	April 6, 1989
Democratic Republic of the Congo	August 3, 1984	July 28, 1989
Republic of the Congo	February 12, 1990	August 13, 1994
Croatia	July 13, 1996	June 20, 2001
Czech Republic	October 22, 1991	December 19, 1992
Ecuador	August 27, 1993	May 11, 1997
Egypt	March 11, 1986	June 27, 1992

(continued)

---

[280] Katz, Plambeck, & Ring, *supra* note 273, at I. Overview, D.

[281] *Id.*; CHRISTIANS, DONALDSON, & POSTLEWAITE, *supra* note 38, at 167.

[282] I.R.C. § 884(e) (2014).

[283] *See generally Trade Investment and Framework Agreements*, OFFICE OF THE UNITED STATES TRADE REPRESENTATIVE, http://www.ustr.gov/trade-agreements/trade-investment-framework-agreements (last visited July 14, 2014); *see also Bilateral Investment Treaties*, TRADE COMPLIANCE CENTER, http://tcc.export.gov/TradeAgreements/Bilateral_Investment_Treaties/index.asp_ (last visited July 14, 2014).

Country	Date of signature	Date entered into force
Estonia	April 19, 1994	February 16, 1997
Georgia	March 7, 1994	August 17, 1997
Grenada	May 2, 1986	March 3, 1989
Honduras	July 1, 1995	July 11, 2001
Jamaica	February 4, 1994	March 7, 1997
Jordan	July 2, 1997	June 12, 2003
Kazakhstan	May 19, 1992	January 12, 1994
Kyrgyzstan	January 19, 1993	January 12, 1994
Latvia	January 13, 1995	December 26, 1996
Lithuania	January 14, 1998	November 22, 2001
Moldova	April 21, 1993	November 25, 1994
Mongolia	October 4, 1994	January 1, 1997
Morocco	July 22, 1985	May 29, 1991
Mozambique	December 1, 1998	March 3, 2005
Panama	October 27, 1982	May 30, 1991
Poland	March 21, 1990	August 6, 1994
Romania	May 28, 1992	January 15, 1994
Rwanda	February 19, 2008	January 1, 2012
Senegal	December 6, 1983	October 25, 1990
Slovakia	October 22, 1991	December 19, 1992
Sri Lanka	September 20, 1991	May 1, 1993
Trinidad and Tobago	September 26, 1994	December 26, 1996
Tunisia	May 15, 1990	February 7, 1993
Turkey	December 3, 1985	May 18, 1990
Ukraine	March 4, 1994	November 16, 1996
Uruguay	November 4, 2005	November 1, 2006

Of these treaties, the treaties agreed with Lithuania and Mozambique do not include any taxation provisions.

The majority of the remaining treaties do, however, include an article that addresses taxation. However, this taxation article basically notes that any tax issues should be addressed through the bilateral tax treaties signed between the two countries, and that with respect to taxation the provisions of the bilateral treaty will only apply to expropriation (pursuant to the article of the treaty that handles expropriation), transfers (pursuant to the article of the treaty that handles transfers), or "[t]he observance and enforcement of terms of an investment agreement or authorization as referred to (particular articles of the treaty)."[284] Similar language is found in the other bilateral investment treaties, except for those concluded between the U.S. and Lithuania and the U.S. and Mozambique, as mentioned above.

---

[284] The Treaty Between the United States of America and the Republic of Armenia Concerning the Reciprocal Encouragement and Protection of Investment, U.S.- A.M., art. xii, Sept. 23, 1992, S. TREATY DOC. NO. 103–11.

Similarly, the U.S. has also signed multilateral investment treaties, including the North American Free Trade Agreement ("NAFTA") with Canada and Mexico, as well as the Dominican Republic-Central America United States Free Trade Agreement ("CAFTA-DR") with five Central American countries, Costa Rica, El Salvador, Guatemala, Honduras, and Nicaragua, and the Dominican Republic.[285] Further, the U.S. is currently engaged in negotiations to create the Transatlantic Trade and Investment Partnership ("T-TIP") with the European Union, and the Trans-Pacific Partnership ("TPP") with 11 countries, including Australia, Brunei Darussalam, Canada, Chile, Japan, Malaysia, Mexico, New Zealand, Peru, Singapore, and Vietnam.[286] These treaties gradually reduce and eventually eliminate the tariffs between the participating nations, but do not otherwise address taxation.[287]

Acknowledgment I would like to gratefully acknowledge the research assistance of Yasmine Fulena, David Marella, Stephanie Pisko and Courtney Abrahamson and the financial support provided by the Seton Hall University School of Law Dean's Research Fellowship program.

---

[285] *See generally Free Trade Agreements*, OFFICE OF THE UNITED STATES TRADE REPRESENTATIVE, http://www.ustr.gov/trade-agreements/free-trade-agreements (last visited July 14, 2014).

[286] *Id.*

[287] How did NFTA Affect Tariff Rates within North America?, NAFTANOW.org, http://www.naftanow.org/faq_en.asp#faq-8 (follow "Frequently Asked Questions Hyperlink"; then follow "How did NFTA Affect Tariff Rates within North America?" hyperlink) ("On January 1, 2008, the last remaining tariffs were removed within North America").

Chapter 20
In Pursuit of a Modern Tax System to Accommodate Foreign Investment. Case Study: Venezuela

Serviliano Abache Carvajal

Abstract Venezuela's tax regime has moved from territorial to one of worldwide taxation. However, dividends received from a foreign corporation (whether or not domiciled in Venezuela) are exempt from Venezuelan tax, unless the foreign corporation has a permanent establishment in Venezuela. Its controlled foreign corporation rules (International Fiscal Transparency Regime or IFTR) apply to entities resident in low-tax or tax haven countries. Income of these foreign subsidiaries is deemed to be actually distributed to the Venezuelan owner unless at least half of the subsidiary's income-producing assets produce active business income. The IFTR is one example of steps Venezuela has taken in order to conform its international tax regime to modern standards. Itself a developing country, Venezuela has acknowledged usefulness of tax incentives to attract foreign investment. With an eye toward enhancing its competitive position among countries in the region, Venezuela has participated in the Southern Common Market (MERCOSUR) and a number of other multilateral inter-governmental organizations to coordinate tax policy. Other features of Venezuela's legal regime may undermine its ability to promote enhanced investment. These include its status as a country that does not provide legal protection for physical and intellectual property rights.

Synopsis The Venezuelan international tax regime has moved from territorial (exempting foreign source income) to worldwide taxation. A Venezuelan resident separately states and pays tax on net income from Venezuelan activities (after deduction of related expenses) and net income from offshore activities (after deduction of related expenses).

Dividends received from a corporation incorporated or domiciled outside of Venezuela or from a corporation incorporated outside of Venezuela and domiciled in Venezuela are exempt from taxation, unless the foreign corporation has a permanent establishment in Venezuela. Venezuelan branches of foreign corporations

S. Abache Carvajal (✉)
Central University of Venezuela, Catholic University "Andrés Bello", Caracas, Venezuela
e-mail: sacabache@icloud.com

© Springer International Publishing Switzerland 2017
K.B. Brown (ed.), *Taxation and Development - A Comparative Study*,
Ius Comparatum - Global Studies in Comparative Law 21,
DOI 10.1007/978-3-319-42157-5_20

347

domiciled abroad but having a permanent establishment in Venezuela are subject to a type of branch profits tax, a 34 % tax on net income derived by the branch.

Venezuela's controlled foreign corporation (CFC) rules, known as the International Fiscal Transparency Regime (IFTR), apply to entities located in tax haven or low-tax jurisdictions. These rules are designed to strengthen the worldwide tax system by limiting the entity's ability to defer paying tax in Venezuela on income not subject to tax or subject to a lower-than-Venezuelan rate of tax or to defer payment of dividends to Venezuelan shareholders. Under this regime, the net income of the CFC is deemed to be distributed to the shareholders whether or not there is an actual distribution. These rules only apply if the taxpayer has the power to control distribution of profits or dividends. They also do not apply if 50 % of an entity's income-producing assets in the low-tax jurisdiction produce active business income. A so-called "black list" identifies low-tax jurisdictions, including many developing countries.

In general, Venezuela has taken steps to conform its international tax regime to most modern international taxation trends. In addition to adopting the IFTR regime described in the previous paragraph, Venezuela has updated its transfer pricing guidelines to conform to OECD criteria. It has also adopted thin capitalization rules to avoid shifting profits offshore in the form of deductible interest (generally not taxed to the recipient) rather than nondeductible distributions of earnings.

Venezuela is party to a number of double tax agreements (DTAs) that contain information exchange provisions which are broad enough to permit sharing of information on transactions in tax haven or tax competitive jurisdictions even if beyond the precise scope of the treaty.

Venezuela provides for special territorial tax regimes that allow customs free zones or, in some cases, preferential tax regimes to promote social and economic development in certain regions (free ports). A third program combining the benefits of the free zones or free ports is the free areas (*zonas libres*) tax regime that applies to cultural, scientific, technological, and tourist services activities in specified areas.

Itself a developing country, Venezuela has acknowledged the usefulness of tax incentives to attract foreign investment with an eye toward enhancing its competitive position among other countries in the region. This is demonstrated, in part, by its participation in multilateral organizations such as the Southern Common Market (MERCOSUR), the Latin American Integration Association (ALADI), and the Bolivarian Alternative of Latin America and the Caribbean (ALBA) which work to coordinate and harmonize, among other things, tax policy. The promise that these memberships held to situate Venezuela as one of the beneficiaries of policies, aimed to promote enhanced investment, has been undermined by other features of its regime. Unfortunately, Venezuela's status as a country that does not protect either physical or intellectual property rights does not make it an attractive foreign investment destination.

Venezuela nonetheless has implemented tax incentives designed to attract investment activity. These include a ten percent tax reduction for investments in industrial and agro-industrial construction, electricity, communications, and science and technology activities. In addition, there are credits of up to 80 % of amounts invested in tourist services-related, agricultural, livestock, and fishing, as well as environmental protection projects.

Venezuela is signatory to 26 bilateral investment treaties (BITs). In addition, it has signed 31 DTAs.

Venezuela taxes corporations at graduated rates of 15 %, 22 %, and 34 %. Companies that exploit hydrocarbons or engage in mining activity (and assign royalties and participations in this activity) are taxed at a rate of 50 %.

International Tax Regime in Venezuela

The foundation of the international tax *regime*[1] now in force in Venezuela is found –for the most part- in Article 1 of the Income Tax Law.[2]

The purpose of this chapter is to describe and comment on the Venezuelan international tax regime with its strengths and weaknesses and to provide an insight into how it works, the tendency, benefits and principal regulations. It describes the utility of the regime in developing Venezuelan law as it provides incentives to attract foreign investment. It observes whether these incentives create economic distortions and favor foreign investors directly and their countries of residence indirectly.[3]

Under present circumstances (given political, fiscal, regulatory, economic and other measures), it is not clear whether, notwithstanding investment incentives, the Venezuelan tax regime is favorable for the conduct or setting up of business[4] by foreign investors. These non-tax factors may affect the unfettered entry of companies, entrepreneurs, and individuals into Venezuelan markets.

Review will be made, on the one hand, of the aspects of the Venezuelan tax regime most relevant to international tax law and, on the other hand, of domestic regulations, policies and measures, tax as well as administrative, so that the reader may determine whether the regime provides incentives or non-incentives to attract foreign investment into Venezuela, which is itself a developing country.

---

[1] An explanation of the difference between tax *system* and tax *regime* seems appropriate here as it will prove useful later on in this report. A tax *system* is understood as the integrated and coordinated set of taxes (imposts, fees and special contributions) forming part of the laws and regulations and ruled by the constitutional principles of taxation, becoming a rational and reasonable whole. Meanwhile, a tax *regime* refers to a group of overimposed taxes that do not constitute an organized, logical and integrated set and do not abide by the constitutional principles of taxation as a fundamental piece of a country's tax order. In this respect, *vid.* ABACHE CARVAJAL, Serviliano and BURGOS-IRAZÁBAL, Ramón, «Parafiscalidad, sistema tributario y Libertad», in HERRERA ORELLANA, Luis Alfonso (Coord.), *Enfoques actuales sobre Derecho y Libertad en Venezuela*, Academy of Political and Social Sciences, Caracas, 2013, pp. 275–280.

[2] Official Gazette of the Republic of Venezuela No. 38.628, February 16, 2007.

[3] Cf. BAZÓ PISANI, Andrés E., «Incentivos fiscales y otras políticas tributarias ofrecidas por países en desarrollo. ¿Atraen inversión extranjera o desestabilizan la economía?», in DUPOUY M., Elvira and DE VALERA, Irene (Coord.), *Temas de actualidad tributaria. Homenaje a Jaime Parra Pérez*, Academy of Political and Social Sciences –Venezuelan Association of Tax Law, Caracas, 2009, p. 155.

[4] Cf. *Ibid.*, p. 153.

Worldwide and/or Territorial Taxation

In generally accepted international law, there are two bases for direct taxation. These are: (i) the territorial income-based system, with taxation based on the territorial source of income (following objective criteria), and (ii) the worldwide system of taxation in which worldwide income, regardless of source, is included in the tax base of those domiciled, resident in, or nationals of a country (following subjective criteria).[5] Many states have alternatively asserted a right to tax on both bases.[6]

This is precisely the case of Venezuela. Under its first Income Tax Law, which dates back to 1942,[7] Venezuela adopted the territorial income system, with some exceptions,[8] until 1999 when, following an integral reform of income tax legislation,[9] the Venezuelan regime additionally adopted, together with the territorial system, the worldwide income system in order to tax foreign-source revenues produced and obtained by residents or persons domiciled in Venezuela. Accordingly, the territorial approach gave way to worldwide taxation.

The regulation mentioned above is at present set forth in Article 1 of the 2007[10] Income Tax Law (ITL) along the following lines:

> «Article 1: Any annual, net and disposable income obtained in cash or in kind, shall be taxed pursuant to the provisions of this Law. Unless otherwise provided in this Law, every individual or corporation, whether a resident of or domiciled in the Bolivarian Republic of Venezuela, shall pay taxes on income from any origin, whether the cause or source of income is located inside or outside the country. (…)».[11]

Since 1999, the Venezuelan income tax covers three components: (i) the taxpayer net operating income from *territorial activities*, which is determined by deducting from territorial gross income the costs and expenses incurred in the country during the fiscal year, (ii) the *inflation adjustments* on taxpayer (non-monetary) assets and liabilities (holding gains), which will increase or reduce the net operating income mentioned in (i) above, and (iii) the taxpayer net operating income from

---

[5] Cf. EVANS MÁRQUEZ, Ronald, *Régimen jurídico de la doble tributación internacional*, McGraw-Hill, Caracas, 1999, p. 6.

[6] Cf. *Ibid.*, p. 8.

[7] Official Gazette of the Republic of Venezuela No. 20.851, July 17, 1942.

[8] On these exceptions, *vid.* CARMONA BORJAS, Juan Cristóbal, «Principios de la renta mundial y de la renta territorial», in DE VALERA, Irene (Organizer), *Comentarios a la Ley de Impuesto sobre la Renta*, Academy of Political and Social Sciences-Venezuelan Association of Tax Law, Caracas, 2000, pp. 23–29, and CARMONA BORJAS, Juan Cristóbal, «Factores de conexión en la legislación venezolana en materia de impuesto sobre la renta», in SOL GIL, Jesús (Coord.), *60 años de imposición a la renta en Venezuela. Evolución histórica y estudios de la legislación actual*, Venezuelan Association of Tax Law, Caracas, 2003, pp. 163–167.

[9] Official Gazette of the Republic of Venezuela No. 5.390, Extraordinary Issue, October 22, 1999.

[10] Official Gazette of the Republic of Venezuela No. 38.628, February 16, 2007.

[11] For a detailed study of territorial and worldwide income effective in Venezuela, *vid.* PAREDES, Carlos Enrique, *El principio de territorialidad y el sistema de renta mundial en la Ley de Impuesto sobre la Renta venezolana*, Andersen Legal, Caracas, 2002, 283 p.

extra-territorial activities, which is determined by subtracting from the extra-territorial gross income the costs and expenses incurred outside the country in obtaining that income during the relevant fiscal year. From the tax resulting from the above determination, any applicable *tax credits* will be deducted, including a credit for any *income tax paid abroad* by the taxpayer, provided it does not exceed the highest Venezuelan tax rate, which is thirty four percent (34 %).[12]

Domestic and Foreign Dividends

The dividend tax regime is regulated by Title IV, Chapter II, under «capital gains», and expounded in Articles 66 through 78 of the ITL. It sets forth, among other regulations, the meaning of a dividend, how it is taxed and withheld, and certain rules applicable to foreign dividends.

According to the sole paragraph of Article 67 of the ITL, a *dividend* is a portion of profits that corresponds to each share of stock in the profits of stock companies and other assimilated taxpayers,[13] such as those resulting from participation quotas in limited liability companies.

A *dividend tax* is, pursuant to Article 66 *eiusdem*, a proportional tax that has its origin in such net income of the paying company that is greater than or exceeds the taxed net fiscal income. For these purposes, it is necessary to understand the meaning of: (i) net income, and (ii) taxed net fiscal income. *Net income* is the result (profits) approved at the shareholders meeting on the basis of the financial results.[14] Meanwhile, *taxed net fiscal income* means the base to which corporate rates are applied.[15]

---

[12] Cf. ROCHE, Emilio J., «Transparencia fiscal internacional», in SOL GIL, Jesús (Coord.), *60 años de imposición a la renta en Venezuela. Evolución histórica y estudios de la legislación actual*, Venezuelan Association of Tax Law, Caracas, 2003, p. 670.

[13] According to the First Paragraph of Article 7 of the ITL, entities *assimilated* to stock companies means: limited liability companies, (ii) limited stock partnerships (*comandita simple por acciones*) (iii) civil associations, and (iv) irregular or de facto associations incorporated as stock companies, as limited liability companies, or as limited partnerships.

[14] For an analysis of the criteria regarding the accounting system that applies for declaring and paying dividends in Venezuela (*historical* accounting or *updated* accounting, i.e., *inflation*-adjusted), *vid*. ROCHE, Emilio J., «De la entrada en vigencia de la reforma de la Ley de Impuesto sobre la Renta de 2001 y del régimen sobre dividendos», *Impuesto sobre la Renta e ilícitos fiscales. VI Jornadas venezolanas de Derecho tributario*, Venezuelan Association of Tax Law, Caracas, 2002, pp. 159–179; and ROMERO-MUCI, Humberto, «Naturaleza jurídica de los principios de contabilidad de aceptación general en Venezuela y su incidencia en la determinación de la renta financiera para el cálculo del impuesto sobre la renta de dividendos (análisis de los artículos 67 y 91 de la Ley de Impuesto sobre la Renta)», *Impuesto sobre la Renta e ilícitos fiscales. VI Jornadas venezolanas de Derecho tributario*, Venezuelan Association of Tax Law, Caracas, 2002, pp. 181–251.

[15] Cf. ROCHE, Emilio J., «Parte general del Impuesto sobre la Renta. Relatoría Tema I», in KORODY TAGLIAFERRO, Juan Esteban (Coord.), *70 años del Impuesto sobre la Renta. Memorias de las XII Jornadas Venezolanas de Derecho Tributario*, volume II, Venezuelan Association of Tax Law, Caracas, 2013, p. 151.

Under the previously stated rules, the calculation of the shareholder dividend tax can be summarized as follows:

$$DNI = NI - (TNFI + EI + DRT)\ ^{16}$$

According to Article 73 of the Law, a dividend is subject to a thirty four percent (34 %) tax rate, which is withheld upon payment of the dividend.

Article 71 of the ITL introduces a very important distinction depending on whether a *domestic dividend* or *foreign dividend* regime is involved. In this respect, the first paragraph of Article 68 states that if dividends are received either (i) from enterprises incorporated and domiciled abroad or (ii) from enterprises incorporated abroad and domiciled in Venezuela, i.e., *foreign dividends*, such dividends will be treated as excluded from the net income for purposes of domestic calculations, unless the foreign corporation has a permanent establishment in Venezuela.

Lastly, under its Article 72, the ITL provides for a *presumptive regime* on foreign dividends in the case of (i) enterprises incorporated abroad and domiciled in Venezuela or (ii) enterprises incorporated and domiciled abroad and having a permanent establishment in Venezuela, pursuant to which they must pay thirty-four percent (34 %) on their net, neither exempt nor exonerated, income in excess of the taxed net income of the fiscal year, unless the branch demonstrates reinvestment in Venezuela for a least 5 years of the difference between the taxed net fiscal income and the net income.[17]

Tax Havens and Harmful Competition

Concept of Tax Havens in Venezuela

There are as many concepts or definitions of tax havens are there are tax havens, given that the semantics or terminology will depend on the criteria utilized.[18] Nevertheless, apart from the difficulty of defining a tax haven, low-tax jurisdiction, preferential tax system, or offshore jurisdiction,[19] because their status is determined by, among other things, political and legislative changes in the location, it is possible to identify common characteristics. These are (i) rates or aliquots that are either

---

[16] DNI: Dividend net income; NI: net income; TNI: taxed net fiscal income; EI: exempt or exonerated income; DRT: dividends received from third parties. In a similar sense, Cf., *Idem.*

[17] In this respect, *vid.* VECCHIO D., Carlos A., *El impuesto al dividendo presunto de las sucursales. Especial referencia a los tratados para evitar la doble tributación*, Venezuelan Financial Law Association, Caracas, 2004, 151 p.

[18] Cf. ROCHE, Emilio J., «Transparencia fiscal...», *cit.*, p. 666.

[19] Cf. DÍAZ IBARRA, Valmy J., «Las reglas de transparencia fiscal internacional en Venezuela. Consecuencias de la vinculación de contribuyentes venezolanos con sociedades en "paraísos fiscales"», in DUPOUY M., Elvira and DE VALERA, Irene (Coord.), *Temas de actualidad tributaria. Homenaje a Jaime Parra Pérez*, Academy of Political and Social Sciences-Venezuelan Association of Tax Law, Caracas, 2009, p. 341.

special, reduced or non-existent, (ii) commercial and bank secrecy, (iii) political and financial stability, (iv) absence of foreign exchange controls, (v) developed infrastructures, and (vi) self-promotion.[20]

The ITL does not define in Chapter II, Title VII, covering the International Fiscal Transparency Regime, what should be understood as *tax havens* or, as termed in the ITL, *low-tax jurisdictions*. Notwithstanding the foregoing, Ruling (*Providencia*) No. SNAT/2004/232[21] has established a method –a mixed and alternative one- for qualifying tax havens based on three criteria: (i) *preferential tax system* (maximum taxation of 20 % on income or capital), (ii) *black list* express inclusion (*blacklisted countries*), and (iii) *absence of double taxation agreement with an information exchange clause*. If any of these criteria exist, a jurisdiction will qualify as a low-tax jurisdiction or tax haven for Venezuelan purposes.[22]

The topic of tax havens and of jurisdictions with elements of *harmful tax competition*, the slight distinctions of which renders them often alike,[23] is especially relevant for the international fiscal transparency regime. The most relevant aspects are noted below in section "International Fiscal Transparency Regime (IFTR)."

International Fiscal Transparency Regime (IFTR)

Also known as *controlled foreign corporation*, or CFC, rules, this regime treats entities located in tax havens or low-tax jurisdictions as having no separate existence from their owners, or transparent. For this reason, an investor domiciled in Venezuela or non-domiciled in Venezuela but having a permanent establishment therein, must report the income, costs and expenses attributable to such an entity (whether or not the company and its members have, as they in fact do, different legal capacities),[24] even if dividends have neither been declared nor distributed.[25]

It is clear that the objectives of this regime are (i) to improve the application of the worldwide income system, given that tax is applied on such income obtained by the foreign entity that has not been subject to tax offshore or that has paid it at rates lower than the thirty-four percent (34 %) rate of Venezuelan law, and (ii) to avoid deferral of payment of income tax in Venezuela, thus discouraging deferral of declaration and payment of dividends by the foreign entity to the Venezuelan taxpayer.

---

[20] Cf. ROCHE, Emilio J., «Transparencia fiscal...», *cit.*, pp. 667–669.

[21] Official Gazette of the Republic of Venezuela No. 37.924, April 26, 2004.

[22] Cf. DÍAZ IBARRA, Valmy J., *op. cit.*, p. 358.

[23] While in *tax havens* the collection of income tax is not part of public finances and those places are promoted as an escape for residents of jurisdictions with high levels of taxation, *jurisdictions with harmful tax competition elements* are often characterized by collecting important sums of income tax and offering tax benefits for specific activities. Cf. *Ibid.*, pp. 341–342.

[24] Cf. FALCÓN Y TELLA, Ramón and PULIDO GUERRA, Elvira, *Derecho fiscal internacional*, Marcial Pons, Madrid, 2010, p. 243.

[25] Cf. ROCHE, Emilio J., «Transparencia fiscal...», *cit.*, p. 673.

Under this assumption, even if the investor does not receive any dividend payment, due to the fact that the entity is deemed transparent (as if it did not exist), the Venezuelan taxpayer must report its share of the income, costs and expenses, and Venezuelan tax will be applied to the extra-territorial income.[26]

Application Criteria

Article 100 of the ITL provides that taxpayers having investments made directly, indirectly, or through intermediaries, in branches, corporations, real or personal property, shares of stock, bank or investment accounts, and any manner of interest in entities with or without legal capacity, trusts, business associations, investments funds, as well as in any other similar legal body created or organized under foreign law and located in low-tax jurisdictions, are subject to the application of the IFTR regime.

The IFTR applies only if the taxpayer has the power to determine the time for distributing profits or dividends derived from low-tax jurisdiction, or when the taxpayer has control over dividend administration, either directly or indirectly or through an intermediary.

Article 102 of the Law provides that an investment is deemed situated in a tax haven or low-tax jurisdiction, as follows: (i) when the accounts or investments of any type are in institutions located in that jurisdiction, (ii) when a domicile or post office box is located in that jurisdiction, (ii) when the person has its actual or principal management or administration headquarters, or has a permanent establishment in that jurisdiction, (iv) when incorporated in that jurisdiction, (v) when there is a physical presence in that jurisdiction, or (vi) when there is conduct, regulation or consumption of any type of legal transaction under the laws and regulations of that jurisdiction.

The fiscal transparency rules do not apply if fifty percent (50 %) of the income-producing assets of the entity located in a low-tax jurisdiction are fixed assets that produce active business income, and also, if less than twenty percent (20 %) of the income obtained by the entity is from passive receipts (e.g. royalties, dividends, leases, etc.). In sum, whenever the entity conducts a business or industrial activity in the foreign jurisdiction, the international fiscal transparency rules will not activate.[27]

---

[26] Cf. *Idem.*

[27] *Ibid.*, pp. 674–675.

Blacklisted Countries

Under Article 2 of Ruling (*Providencia*) No. SNAT/2004/232, the following are low-tax jurisdictions expressly included in the black list: Anguilla, Antigua & Barbuda, Svalbard Archipelago, Aruba, Ascension, Belize, Bermuda, Brunei, Campione D'Italia, Commonwealth of Dominica, Commonwealth of the Bahamas, United Arab Emirates, State of Bahrain, State of Qatar, Independent State of Western Samoa, Commonwealth of Puerto Rico, Gibraltar, Grand Duchy of Luxembourg, Grenada, Greenland, Guam, Hong Kong, Cayman Islands, Christmas Island, Norfolk Island, Saint Pierre and Miquelon Island, Isle of Man, Qeshm Island, Cook Island, Cocos or Keeling Island, Channel Islands (Guernsey, Jersey, Aldemey, Great Sart, Herm, Little Sark, Brechou, Jethou and Lihou Islands), Falkland Islands, Pacific Islands, Solomon Islands, Turks & Caicos Islands, British Virgin Islands, United States Virgin Islands, Kiribati, Labuan, Macau, Malta, Montserrat, Niue, Palau, Pitcairn, French Polynesia, Principality of Andorra, Principality of Liechtenstein, Principality of Monaco, Kingdom of Swaziland, Hashemite Kingdom of Jordan, Dominican Republic, Gabonese Republic, Lebanese Republic, Republic of Albania, Republic of Angola, Republic of Cape Verde, Republic of Cyprus, Republic of Djibouti, Republic of Guyana, Republic of Honduras, Republic of Marshall Islands, Republic of Liberia, Republic of Mauritius, Republic of Nauru, Republic of Panama, Republic of Seychelles, Republic of Tunisia, Republic of Vanuatu, Republic of Yemen, Eastern Republic of Uruguay, Democratic Socialist Republic of Sri Lanka, American Samoa, Saint Vincent and the Grenadines, Saint Helena, Most Serene Republic of San Marino, Sultanate of Oman, Tokelau, Tristan da Cunha, Tuvalu, Canary Special Zone, and Ostrava Free Zone.

Adoption of International Taxation Criteria

As discussed in previous section entitled "International Tax Regime in Venezuela" above, in 1999, Venezuelan income tax legislation achieved an important change. By an integral reform of this fiscal sub-regime, it moved from an exclusively territorial system to a worldwide income system. This significant change was accompanied by the insertion of rules of international fiscal transparency and transfer pricing in the ITL, completing in 2007 the adjustment of the Venezuelan regime to the most modern international taxation trends, with the inclusion of undercapitalization or thin capitalization rules.[28] Below is a review of these changes and the adoption of international taxation criteria.

---

[28] Cf. DÍAZ IBARRA, Valmy J., *op. cit.*, pp. 352–353.

Taxation of Worldwide Income

Beyond any doubt, the adoption of the worldwide income system in 1999 by the Venezuelan ITL reflects an important change in the very idea of the country, typically regarded as a capital importer. Even though Venezuela is still characterized as an importing country, and even more at present given the multiple internal problems and official measures that discourage domestic production (noted below) the truth is that in an attempt to conform to worldwide economic globalization and commercial integration of countries, the Venezuelan tax regime has taken the significant step of revising the *principle of taxpaying capacity* set forth in Article 316 of the Constitution,[29] to capture the entire taxpayer income regardless of its source.[30]

This reform and adoption of the worldwide system means that since 1999 all foreign source income produced and obtained by residents or domiciled persons in Venezuela is taxed in accordance with the new regime.

International Fiscal Transparency

As previously stated, the purpose of international fiscal transparency, as embodied in the controlled foreign company regime, is to improve the worldwide income system. It involves taxing passive income (e.g., dividends, royalties, etc.) generated from foreign investments located in tax havens or low-tax jurisdictions by deeming it distributed to the Venezuelan taxpayer controlling such investment, whether or not the income is actually distributed.[31] In other words, for Venezuelan purposes, the foreign entity is deemed *transparent* –hence, the name of the regime- and for this reason the Venezuelan taxpayer controlling such entity must report and pay tax on income, as if it were his own, obtained in the tax haven. These rules constitute a presumptive lifting of the corporate veil (disregard of the legal entity).

Transfer Pricing

The system of transfer pricing was first introduced in Venezuelan income tax regulations with the 1999 reform, following the guidelines of the Brazilian legislation. With the legislative amendment of 2001, it was changed entirely by adopting the

---

[29] Official Gazette of the Republic of Venezuela No. 36.860, December 30, 1999, later reprinted with some corrections in the Official Gazette of the Republic of Venezuela No. 5.453, Extraordinary Issue, March 24, 2000. Its first amendment as well as the whole text of the Constitution was published in the Official Gazette of the Republic of Venezuela No. 5.908 Extraordinary Issue, February 19, 2009.

[30] EVANS MÁRQUEZ, Ronald, *Régimen jurídico... cit.*, p. 12.

[31] Cf. DÍAZ IBARRA, Valmy J., *op. cit.*, pp. 353–354.

criteria and directives of the Organization for Economic Cooperation and Development (OECD), such as applying the comparable price or comparable uncontrolled price (CUP) method. With the most recent reform of the ITL, in late 2007, the rules remain unchanged.

Transfer pricing rules are contained in Chapter III, Title VII, Article 111 through 170 of the Venezuelan ITL. Their purpose is none other than achieving the same financial results for transactions (supply of goods, provision of services) between *related parties* for tax purposes as for *non-related or independent parties*. All of it involves application of the *arm's length principle*,[32] i.e., allowing no transfers for prices –lower or higher than market value- in order to avoid shift of income to a country with the low taxation or shift of expenses to a country with high taxation.[33]

A *related party*, according to Article 116 of the ITL, is an enterprise that participates directly or indirectly in the management, control or capital of another enterprise or both enterprises when under the direct or indirect control, by the same persons in accordance with the sense of the OECD guidelines.[34]

These rules, as well as the ones discussed below, act as mechanisms against tax avoidance and to prevent the abuse of forms, with the ultimate purpose of reducing international tax avoidance or evasion.[35]

Thin Capitalization

Undercapitalization or thin capitalization rules were introduced for the first time in the ITL with the 2007 reform. These rules, or *antiavoidance clauses*, are intended to *avoid* (i) the transfer of the income tax base (*profit shifting*) from one jurisdiction to another, (ii) the concealing of dividend payments and, consequently, the non-payment of dividend tax in the country of origin, and (iii) the creation of a fictitious expense to reduce the tax base of the enterprise that repays interest on a loan.[36]

Pursuant to Venezuelan law, a *thinly capitalized enterprise* exists where debts to a related party exceed stockholders' equity. In these circumstances, the debt/equity

---

[32] Cf. ANDRADE, Betty, «La subcapitalización y los precios de transferencia en el régimen vene-zolano», *Jornadas Internacionales. Cuestiones actuales de Derecho tributario*, Foundation of Administrative Law Studies, Caracas, 2007, p. 218.

[33] Cf. FALCÓN Y TELLA, Ramón and PULIDO GUERRA, Elvira, *op. cit.*, p. 231.

[34] Cf. *Idem.*

[35] Cf. *Ibid.*, p. 223.

[36] Cf. FRAGA PITTALUGA, Luis, «Subcapitalización y reclasificación de los intereses no deduc-ibles», in KORODY TAGLIAFERRO, Juan Esteban (Coord.), *70 años del Impuesto sobre la Renta. Memorias de las XII Jornadas Venezolanas de Derecho Tributario*, volume II, Venezuelan Tax Law Association, Caracas, 2013, pp. 374–375.

ratio evidences excessive indebtedness of the borrowing enterprise under a financing (loan) transaction with a related party (lending enterprise).[37]

Article 118 of the ITL has the effect of limiting the deductibility of interest paid directly or indirectly to related parties. In order to determine whether the amount of debts exceeds the net equity of the taxpayer, the yearly average balance of the taxpayer debts to independent parties is subtracted from the yearly average balance of its net equity.[38]

Lastly, the Venezuelan rule provides that the portion of the amount of debts incurred by the taxpayer directly or indirectly with related parties that exceeds the average balance of net equity will be treated as net equity in any event. In this manner, contrary to what happens in similar legislation in other countries, the Venezuelan rule does not permit reclassification of non-deductible interest as dividends, but rather it treats such interest as net equity of the taxpayer.[39]

Double Tax and Information Exchange Agreements

The OECD Model Tax Treaty on income and capital provides in Article 26.1 for the *exchange of information* of tax relevance between contracting States, not only for the application of the agreement, but also when pertinent for managing any domestic tax issue, at any political territorial level, even if the tax is not expressly covered by the agreement, unless contrary to the agreement.[40] Article 26 is the primary basis for rules relating to exchange of information in Venezuela.[41]

---

[37] Cf. *Ibid.*, pp. 375–376.

[38] Cf. *Ibid.*, pp. 406–407.

[39] Cf. *Ibid.*, pp. 420–421. In the same sense, *vid.* CASTILLO CARVAJAL, Juan Carlos, «Relatoría general. Tema II. Temas especiales de la Ley de Impuesto sobre la Renta», in KORODY TAGLIAFERRO, Juan Esteban (Coord.), *70 años del Impuesto sobre la Renta. Memorias de las XII Jornadas Venezolanas de Derecho Tributario*, volume II, Venezuelan Association of Tax Law, Caracas, 2013, p. 57. Against, *vid.* ANDRADE, Betty, *op. cit.*, pp. 257–260.

[40] Cf. FALCÓN Y TELLA, Ramón and PULIDO GUERRA, Elvira, *op. cit.*, pp. 197–198.

[41] For a detailed study of Tax Administration cooperation, with special reference to the Venezuelan case, *vid.* CARMONA BORJAS, Juan Cristóbal, «Colaboración y asistencia mutua entre Administraciones tributarias», *Revista de Derecho Tributario*, No. 100, Venezuelan Association of Tax Law, Caracas, 2003, pp. 161–219.

Permitted Sources and Types of Information Exchange

In fact, the actual Double Taxation Agreeements (DTAs) ratified by Venezuela[42] constitute one of its sources for conducting *information exchange* with other States. As the DTAs that Venezuela has entered into follow, basically, the OECD Model, those exchange provisions, in line with Article 26.1 of the model, authorize competent authorities to exchange the information required in order to *apply* the various agreements made, but they are not restricted to the *scope of application* of the DTA and enable information requests on transactions in tax havens and in jurisdictions that have elements of harmful tax competition.

The information received by Venezuela and the States with which it has entered into such agreements is required to be kept secret, as must the information obtained on the basis of the local law of Venezuela and other States, and may be communicated only to authorities (including Courts and administrative agencies) competent for the management or collection of agreement-regulated taxes, the related declaration or execution processes, and the decision of any appeals filed against any submitted claims.

Information Exchange Restrictions Contained in the DTAs

Information exchanged under DTAs entered into by Venezuela can be used by the tax authorities only for *purposes of the agreement.* Any use outside of these limits would entail a violation of the limitations on use of information received pursuant to the agreement.

Importantly, Venezuelan DTAs adopt the typical three limits of the OECD Model, directing the contracting States not to (i) take any administrative actions contrary to their administrative practice or legislation or contrary to those of the other contracting State, (ii) provide information that cannot be obtained on the basis of their own legislation or in the exercise of their regular administrative practice or that of the other Contracting State, or (iii) provide information that discloses trade, industrial or professional secrets, trade procedures or information the transmission of which is contrary to public order.

Lastly, beyond the limits on information exchange between foreign and Venezuelan tax administrations established in the DTAs, no agreement can affect

---

[42] Article 122 of the Venezuelan Organic Tax Code (Official Gazette of the Republic of Venezuela No. 37.301, October 17, 2001), sets forth that: «The Tax Administration will have the faculties, powers and duties prescribed in the Tax Administration Act and other laws and regulations and it may especially: (…) 11. Enter into inter-institutional information exchange agreements with local and international agencies provided that the classified nature of such information is protected as set forth in Article 126 of this Code and ensuring that the information supplied will be used by tax competent authorities only». According to Article 126 *eiusdem*: «Any information and documentation obtained by any means by the Tax Administration will be classified and will be communicated only to the judicial or any other authority in the cases set forth by the laws. Any inappropriate use of classified information will bring about the application of the respective penalties».

the guarantees set out in the Constitution of Venezuela. For this reason, the *inviolability of home and correspondence* cannot be ignored by the agreements because these are fundamental individual and constitutional rights of the taxpayers.[43]

Special Territorial Tax Regimes

In general, customs territories are constituted by geographic spaces having special legislation that creates and delimits their special tax regime with extra-fiscal (tax benefit) purposes, regarding certain activities, customs controls, and customs duties. For tax purposes, it is possible to distinguish in Venezuela three types of customs territories: (i) *free zones*, (ii) *free ports*, and (iii) *free areas* (*zonas libres*).

Free Zone Tax Regime

Free zones are defined in Article 2 of the Venezuelan Free Zone Act[44] as «[T]he area of land physically delimited and subject to a special tax regime (…) where legal entities that for the purposes of this Act are authorized to engage in producing and marketing goods for export as well as in providing services related to international trade». The objective of the State is the *development of a specific activity* (industry, trade or service) in an economically depressed area that is artificially delimited in the Act, creating that zone.

The principles contained in the Free Zone Act are expounded in its Regulations,[45] which set forth the conditions and parameters for the creation, extension, reduction and termination of free zones.

There are three free zones in Venezuela, to wit: (i) *Zona Franca Industrial, Comercial y de Servicios ATUJA (ZOFRAT)*,[46] located in the San Francisco Municipality, city of Maracaibo, State of Zulia, under the authority and control of the Principal Customs of Maracaibo, (ii) *Zona Franca Industrial, Comercial y de Servicios de Paraguaná*,[47] located in the Paraguaná Peninsula, State of Falcón, under the authority and control of the Principal Customs of Las Piedras de Paraguaná, and (iii) *Zona Franca Industrial, Comercial y de Servicios de Cumaná*,[48] located in

---

[43] Cf. LEÓN ROJAS, Andrés Eloy, «La doble tributación internacional. Diferencia entre países desarrollados y en desarrollo», *IV Jornadas Venezolanas de Derecho Tributario*, Venezuelan Association of Tax Law, Caracas, 1998, p. 324.

[44] Official Gazette of the Republic of Venezuela No. 34.772, August 8, 1991.

[45] Decree No. 2.492 of 4 July 2003, Official Gazette of the Republic of Venezuela No. 37.734, July 17, 2003.

[46] Official Gazette of the Republic of Venezuela No. 36.096, November 29, 1996.

[47] Official Gazette of the Republic of Venezuela No. 5.145, Extraordinary Issue, April 30, 1997.

[48] Official Gazette of the Republic of Venezuela No. 36.249, July 16, 1997.

the Autonomous Sucre Municipality, City of Cumaná, State of Sucre, under the authority and control of the Principal Customs of Puerto Sucre.

Free Port Tax Regime

Free ports consist of a customs exemption regime boosting, via tax benefits and/or economic activity establishment benefits, the *economic development of a portion of territory* that in principle is economically depressed. As opposed to free zones, these areas are territorially delimited by the area of a specific political territorial entity and are created by special law.

Free ports in Venezuela are located in Santa Elena de Uairén[49] and in the State of Nueva Esparta.[50] The first free port consists of a preferential tax regime to encourage and promote the social and economic development of the region. This exempting regime covers the activities performed within the duly delimited territory of the free port. The goods entering under this free port regime are not subject to import duties, although they are subject to the fee for customs services (1 % *ad valorem*), nor are they subject to payment of domestic taxes, provided the goods are shipped for consumption at the free port.[51]

The second free port consists of a preferential (exempting) tax regime to encourage and favor the social and economic development of the State of Nueva Esparta. Goods entering under the free port regime are exempt from payment of import duties, Value Added Tax (VAT), taxes on cigarettes and manufactured tobacco, alcohol and alcoholic species, matches, and the like –unless domestic law determines otherwise- but are subject to payment of the fee for customs services (1 % *ad valorem*).[52]

---

[49] Created by Decree No. 3.112, of 16 December 1998, dictating the Regulations on the Free Port of Santa Elena de Uairén System, Official Gazette of the Republic of Venezuela No. 5.288, Extraordinary Issue, January 13, 1999.

[50] Created by the Free Port Act of the State of Nueva Esparta, of 3 August 2000, Official Gazette of the Republic of Venezuela No. 37.006, August 3, 2000.

[51] Consulted in:
http://www.seniat.gob.ve/portal/page/portal/MANEJADOR_CONTENIDO_SENIAT/04ADUANAS/4.4REGIMENES_TERRITOR/4.4.1PUERTOS_LIBRES/4.4.1.1SANTA_ELENA, February 15, 2014.

[52] Consulted in:
http://www.seniat.gob.ve/portal/page/portal/MANEJADOR_CONTENIDO_SENIAT/04ADUANAS/4.4REGIMENES_TERRITOR/4.4.1PUERTOS_LIBRES/4.4.1.2NUEVA_ESPARTA, February 15, 2014.

Free Areas (**Zonas Libres***) Tax Regime*

Lastly, *free areas* or *zonas libres* are a mixture of the two previously mentioned regimes, as they are intended for the *development of a portion of the territory by means of a specific activity*, usually in an economically depressed area that is also delimited by the area of a specific political territorial entity.

They comprise the Culture, Science and Technology Free Zone of the State of Mérida (*Zona Libre Cultural, Científica y Tecnológica* (ZOLCCYT))[53] and the Free Zone for Tourist Investment Development of Paraguaná Peninsula (*Zona Libre para el Fomento de la Inversión Turística de la Península de Paraguaná*).[54] The first is located in the State of Mérida in the territory of Libertador, Campo Elías, Sucre and Santos Marquina Municipalities, under the control of the Principal Ecologic Customs of Mérida. Its special preferential tax regime was established to promote the production, dissemination and distribution of the region's cultural, scientific and technological activities. Cultural, scientific and technological goods and services produced in the country, as well as goods and their parts coming from abroad and entering Venezuela with destination to the ZOLCCYT, are subject to the following preferential regime: (i) no customs duties, (ii) exemption from VAT and any other domestic tax directly or indirectly imposed on their import or sale, (iii) no customs service fees, and (iv) no tariff and para-tariff rates, except for those of a health-related nature.

The second zone (Free Zone for Tourist Investment Development of Paraguaná Peninsula) is located in Paraguaná Peninsula, in the area comprised by the territory of Carirubana, Falcón, and Los Taques Municipalities of the State of Falcón, under the control of Las Piedras-Paraguaná Principal Customs. Its regime covers the income obtained by tourist service providers on new infrastructure investments made by persons authorized to operate within the free zone. The exemption applies for a period of 10 years after verification that the investment has been made.

---

[53] Created by the Act on the Cultural, Scientific and Technology Free Zone of the State of Merida, of July 14, 1995, Official Gazette of the Republic of Venezuela No. 4.937, Extraordinary Issue, July 14, 1995; expounded by the Regulations on Cultural, Scientific and Technology Free Zone of the State of Merida, of September 9,1998, Official Gazette of the Republic of Venezuela No 36.611, December 19, 1998.

[54] Created by the Act on Creation and Regime of the Free Zone for Tourist Investment Development of Paraguaná Peninsula, State of Falcón, of August 6, 1998, Official Gazette of the Republic of Venezuela No. 36.517, August 14, 1998.

Tax Measures and Incentives to Attract Investment in Developing and Low-Income Countries

Tax incentives have always represented an important tool of fiscal policy,[55] especially in developing countries where they are used to compensate for other negative factors that may discourage foreign investment.[56] As early as the beginning of 2000, Venezuela was considering the necessity to carefully revise incentive policies to render them in line with postulates of economic reactivation and also to attain levels of competitiveness with other countries of the region.[57] But reality tells otherwise: Venezuela is now –and even more than before- far from competing with its neighboring countries, precisely due to the fiscal, regulatory, political and economic measures it has established that are unfavorable to foreign investment.

Presently, a number of fiscal measures are in force in Venezuela *formally* directed at attracting economic activities, investment, and capital.[58] These are both *domestic* (in national laws) as well as *international* (via treaties and agreements), such those established with the Southern Common Market (MERCOSUR),[59] the Latin American Integration Association (ALADI)[60] and the Bolivarian Alternative of Latin America and the Caribbean (ALBA), among others, of which Venezuelan is a member, which supports Latin American integration and harmonization.

Indeed, one of the main objectives of MERCOSUR, according to Article 1 of the Asunción Treaty is to achieve «[f]ree circulation of goods, services and production factors between the countries through, among other things, the elimination of customs duties and non-tariff restrictions to the circulation of merchandise, and any other equivalent measure», «[e]stablishment of a common external tariff (…)», and «[c]o-ordination of macroeconomic and sectorial policies between States Parties on: foreign trade, agriculture, industry, tax, monies, exchange and capitals, services,

---

[55] Cf. EVANS MÁRQUEZ, Ronald, «Los convenios para evitar la doble tributación internacional y otros aspectos internacionales de la política tributaria venezolana», in DE VALERA, Irene (Organizer), *Comentarios a la Ley de Impuesto sobre la Renta*, Academy of Political and Social Sciences-Venezuelan Association of Tax Law, Caracas, 2000, p. 58.

[56] Cf. BAZÓ PISANI, Andrés E., *op. cit.*, p. 172.

[57] Cf. EVANS MÁRQUEZ, Ronald, «Los convenios para evitar…» *cit.*, p. 59.

[58] On the matter, *vid.* PALACIOS MÁRQUEZ, Leonardo, «Medidas fiscales para el desarrollo económico», *Revista de Derecho Tributario*, N° 97, Venezuelan Association of Tax Law, Caracas, 2002, pp. 179–224, and SOL GIL, Jesús, «Medidas fiscales adoptadas en Venezuela para el desarrollo económico», *Revista de Derecho Tributario*, N° 97, Venezuelan Association of Tax Law, Caracas, 2002, pp. 225–248.

[59] For a study on the tax aspects of MERCOSUR and, in general, of Latin American integration, *vid.* VALDÉS COSTA, Ramón, «Aspectos fiscales de la integración con especial referencia a América Latina», *Revista de Derecho Tributario*, N° 58, Venezuelan Association of Tax Law, Caracas, 1993, pp. 7–18.

[60] On ALADI and tax harmonization in Latin America, *vid.* MONTERO TRAIBEL, José Pedro, «La armonización tributaria en los procesos de integración», *IV Jornadas Venezolanas de Derecho Tributario*, Venezuelan Association of Tax Law, Caracas, 1998, pp. 279–311.

customs, transportation and communications, and any others that may be agreed (…)». This demonstrates the relevance of the treaty to tax policy.

In this regard, in order to achieve the general objectives and postulates of MERCOSUR, it has been argued that the Venezuelan tax regime should be modified along the following lines: (i) progressive harmonization and elimination of para-fiscal contributions, (ii) flexibility of foreign currency control for countries of the block, (iii) revision of exporter VAT credit recovery system, (iv) implementation of income tax incentives, and (v) conclusion of DTAs with member countries of the block.[61]

However, apart from the existence and effectiveness of a series of tax measures and incentives prescribed in quite a number of treaties (discussed below under sections on "Income Tax Credits" and "Investment Protection, Taxation, Bilateral and Multilateral Exchange Treaties"), the Venezuelan Government has systematically adopted a series of guidelines that contribute little to the development and economic stability of the country, attract foreign investment or even maintain domestic investment. This chapter would fail in its mission if it were not to highlight this development.

On the one hand, there are the tax matters per se. In fact, the National Integrated Service of Customs and Tax Administration (*Servicio Nacional Integrado de Administración Aduanera y Tributaria*-SENIAT), the federal tax administration agency and highest competent authority in the area, has designed and implemented a number of measures within the framework of the highly-publicized –and questioned- «Zero Evasion Plan», which consists of imposing fines and penalties including temporary closing of enterprises for their purported failure to comply with formal obligations regarding indirect taxes.[62] In addition, there are a number of para-fiscal contributions that have been recently dictated, counting more than 30 to date, which have generated an important increase of taxes that do not integrate in a consistent and organized manner with tax laws and regulations. Together with imposition of taxes, this increases the accumulated tax pressure on taxpayers.[63] This does not make much sense when one also takes into account that historically Venezuela is a country that has depended on its *oil revenues*, rather than its tax revenues, which represent since 1950 on average more than ninety percent (90 %) of the *total revenues* of the country.[64]

---

[61] Cf. ATENCIO VALLADARES, Gilberto, «Cuestiones tributarias del Mercosur: aproximaciones desde el Derecho tributario venezolano», *Revista de Derecho Tributario*, No. 141, Venezuelan Association of Tax Law, Caracas, 2014, pp. 8–14.

[62] Cf. ABACHE CARVAJAL, Serviliano, «La responsabilidad patrimonial del Estado "Administrador, Juez y Legislador" tributario venezolano. Especial referencia al paradigmático caso del procedimiento de verificación» (National Report - Venezuela), *Memorias de las XXV Jornadas Latinoamericanas de Derecho Tributario*, volume II, Abeledo Perrot-Latin American Institute of Tax Law-Colombian Institute of Tax Law, Buenos Aires, 2010, pp. 349–350.

[63] Cf. ABACHE CARVAJAL, Serviliano and BURGOS-IRAZÁBAL, Ramón, «Parafiscalidad… » *cit.*, p. 256.

[64] Cf. ROSS, Maxim, *¿Capitalismo salvaje o Estado depredador?*, Editorial Alfa, Caracas, 2008, pp. 21–22.

On the other hand, combined with the fiscal measures, it has become internationally known[65] that since 2001 the Venezuelan government has not moved to secure property rights protected under Article 115 of the 1999 Constitution. According to the *International Property Rights Index 2012*, Venezuela occupied the last place in the world (130/130) in physical protection of property rights and was in next to last place (129/130) in respect of intellectual property rights. While in the *International Property Rights Index 2013*[66] Venezuela «improved» in both cases (123/130 in physical protection of property rights and 119/130 in respect of intellectual property rights), it provides the worst (130/130) legal and political environment, which assesses judicial independence (130/130) and Rule of Law (129/130) indices. Measures such as occupations, seizures, expropriations, price controls, etc., are taken into account for the above measures.

According to the Venezuelan Property Rights Watch Group, from 2007 to 2011, there have been 3,355 private property violations in Venezuela, distributed as follows: (i) 1,911 violations arising from «rescuing» lands fit for agriculture; (ii) 915 violations against the property of industries and businesses, and (iii) 529 encroachments or attempts of encroachment.

Instead of attracting economic activity, investment, and capital to Venezuela, these actions have had an internationally known negative effect internationally. A number of corporations and economic groups, unwilling to continue to tolerate these guidelines and policies of the State have departed from the jurisidiction.

Income Tax Credits

In the past, various forms of credits (reductions) against income tax liability were established as internal fiscal measures directed to attract economic activity, investment and capital. At present, two forms of credits are regulated, i.e.: (i) for *new investments* in (1) industrial, agro-industrial, construction, electricity, telecommunications, and science and technology activities, (2) tourist services, (3) agricultural, livestock, and fishing or fish farming activities, and (4) preservation, defense and improvement of the environment; and (ii) for *excess payments*.

---

[65] Cf. RONDÓN GARCÍA, Andrea, HERRERA ORELLANA, Luis Alfonso and ARIAS CASTILLO, Tomás A., «Case Study: Private Property Abolition in Venezuela», *International Property Rights Index. 2010 Report*, American for Tax Reform Foundation/Property Rights Alliance, Washington, 2010, pp. 55–57.

[66] Consulted in: http://www.internationalpropertyrightsindex.org/profile?location=Venezuela, February 16, 2014.

Reductions for New Investments

By virtue of Article 56 of the ITL a ten percent (10 %) tax reduction is granted on the amount of new investments, made in the 5 years following the effective date of that Law,[67] to owners of income arising out of *industrial and agro-industrial, construction, electricity, telecommunications, science and technology activities* and, in general, all industrial activities representing an investment in advanced or cutting-edge technology, in new fixed assets, other than land, and used to effectively increase production capacity, or to fund new enterprises, if not previously used in other enterprises.

At the same time, pursuant to the above provision the owners of income obtained from the provision of *tourist services* –enrolled in the National Touristic Register- are entitled to a seventy five percent (75 %) credit on the amount of new investments in building hotels, lodgings and inns, expanding, improving or refurnishing existing buildings or services, or providing any tourist service or training their employees.

In the case of *agricultural, livestock, fishing or fish farming*, the credit is eighty percent (80 %) on the value of new investments made in the area of influence of the production unit and intended for mutual benefit, both for the unit itself as well as for the community where it is established. A similar reduction is granted to *tourist activity and for community investments* when such investments are made by small and medium-sized industries of the sector.

A ten percent (10 %) credit, in addition to the above, is also established on the amount of investment in assets, programs and activities for the *preservation, defense and improvement of the environment*.

Lastly, credits for new investment in *fixed assets* must be made using *inflation adjusted figures* rather than historical cost.[68] All credits previously mentioned can be carried forward to the three (3) subsequent fiscal years.

Credits for Overpayment (Tax Credit)

The ITL also provides, in Article 58, that if, in the case of advanced payments or payments on account arising out of withholding tax, the taxpayer has paid more than the tax due for a given fiscal year, there is a right to credit in that amount on future tax returns in subsequent fiscal years in that the amount, without detriment to the right of refund.

---

[67] On the various possible interpretations of the 5 year term for using the credit, *vid.* ROCHE, Emilio J., «Parte general...», *cit.*, pp. 141–148.

[68] *Vid.* Ruling of the Supreme Court of Justice, Political-Administrative Chamber, case: *Goodyear de Venezuela C.A.*, March 4, 2008.

Investment Protection, Taxation, Bilateral and Multilateral Exchange Treaties

In addition to the DTAs, the Bilateral Treaties for the Protection of Investments (BITs) appear internationally as the minimum legal framework necessary to promote investments in countries and, consequently, are part of the external economic agenda of Venezuela. These basic instruments develop a State policy aimed at improving the legal conditions necessary for foreign investment,[69] in harmony with the goals described in "Tax Measures and Incentives to Attract Investment in Developing and Low-income Countries" above.

As it is well known, one of the factors that can adversely affect investment flow between countries is the phenomenon of double or multiple taxation of the same income or capital. This has generated an open and ever growing interest in countries to combat such pathology, as currently evidenced by the more than 2,000 agreements made and in force throughout the world.[70]

Countries with Which Venezuela Has Signed BITs

According to the Venezuelan National Council for Investment Promotion (CONAPRI): «[t]he main objective being sought by Venezuela with the signing of these Treaties is to encourage investment and increase the amount of flows of foreign capital towards its territory. In addition, favoring investment entails the promotion of the creation of jobs and technology development or transfer. This objective relies in the indisputable fact that a Bilateral Treaty with clear rules of mandatory execution, aimed at protecting the foreign investor, reduces the risks that may be encountered by the latter».[71]

Currently in Venezuela there are 26 BITs effective with: Germany,[72] Argentina,[73] Barbados,[74] Belarus,[75] Belgium-Luxembourg,[76] Brazil,[77] Canada,[78] Costa Rica,[79]

---

[69] Cf. EVANS MÁRQUEZ, Ronald, «Los convenios para evitar...» *cit.*, p. 61.

[70] Cf. *Idem*.

[71] Consulted in: http://www.conapri.org, February 15, 2014.

[72] Official Gazette of the Republic of Venezuela No. 36.383, January 28, 1998.

[73] Official Gazette of the Republic of Venezuela No. 35.578, November 1st, 1994.

[74] Official Gazette of the Republic of Venezuela No. 4.853, Extraordinary Issue, February 8, 1995.

[75] Official Gazette of the Republic of Venezuela No. 38.894, March 24, 2008.

[76] Official Gazette of the Republic of Venezuela No. 37.357, January 4, 2002.

[77] Official Gazette of the Republic of Venezuela No. 36.268, August 13, 1997.

[78] Official Gazette of the Republic of Venezuela No. 5.207, Extraordinary Issue, January 20, 1998.

[79] Official Gazette of the Republic of Venezuela No. 36.383, January 28, 1998.

Cuba,[80] Chile,[81] Denmark,[82] Ecuador,[83] Spain,[84] France,[85] Great Britain and Northern Ireland,[86] Iran,[87] Lithuania,[88] Paraguay,[89] Portugal,[90] Peru,[91] Czech Republic,[92] Russia,[93] Sweden,[94] Switzerland,[95] Uruguay,[96] and Vietnam.[97]

Similarly, Chapter VIII of the Group of Three Trade Liberalization Agreement, concerning investments, provides for an Investment Promotion and Protection Agreement[98] between Mexico, Colombia and Venezuela.[99]

---

[80] Official Gazette of the Republic of Venezuela No. 37.913, April 5, 2004.

[81] Official Gazette of the Republic of Venezuela No. 4.830, Extraordinary Issue, December 29, 1994.

[82] Official Gazette of the Republic of Venezuela No. 5.080, Extraordinary Issue, July 23, 1996.

[83] Official Gazette of the Republic of Venezuela No. 4.802, Extraordinary Issue, November 2, 1994.

[84] Official Gazette of the Republic of Venezuela No. 36.281, September 1st, 1997.

[85] Official Gazette of the Republic of Venezuela No. 37.896, March 11, 2004.

[86] Official Gazette of the Republic of Venezuela No. 36.010, July 30, 1996.

[87] Official Gazette of the Republic of Venezuela No. 38.389, March 2, 2006.

[88] Official Gazette of the Republic of Venezuela No. 5.089, Extraordinary Issue, July 23, 1996.

[89] Official Gazette of the Republic of Venezuela No. 36.301, September 29, 1997.

[90] Official Gazette of the Republic of Venezuela No. 4.846, Extraordinary Issue, January 26, 1995.

[91] Official Gazette of the Republic of Venezuela No. 36.266, August 11, 1997.

[92] Official Gazette of the Republic of Venezuela No. 36.002, July 17, 1996.

[93] Official Gazette of the Republic of Venezuela No. 39.191, June 2, 2009.

[94] Official Gazette of the Republic of Venezuela No. 5.192, Extraordinary Issue, December 18, 1997.

[95] Official Gazette of the Republic of Venezuela No. 4.801, Extraordinary Issue, November 1st, 1994.

[96] Official Gazette of the Republic of Venezuela No. 36.519, August 18, 1998.

[97] Official Gazette of the Republic of Venezuela No. 39.170, May 4, 2009.

[98] Official Gazette of the Republic of Venezuela No. 4.833, Extraordinary Issue, December 29, 1994.

[99] On January 25, 2012, Venezuela *denounced* the Convention on the Settlement of Investment Disputes between States and Nationals of Other States, to which it had been a party since 1993. Such denunciation had full legal effects 6 months after its notice pursuant to Article 71 of the Agreement and as result it is not longer possible for a foreign investor to bring to the International Center for Settlement of Investment Disputes (ICSID) the legal disputes arising in connection with its investment in Venezuela, unless the foreign investor has timely accepted an arbitration offer from Venezuela under some Treaty or convention made between the State of origin of that investor and Venezuela.

Countries with Which Venezuela Has Signed DTAs

Beginning in 1990, Venezuela was open to enter into DTAs with the principal countries of the world.[100] To this date, Venezuela has signed 31 Agreements[101] with the following countries[102]: Germany,[103] Austria,[104] Barbados,[105] Belarus,[106] Belgium,[107] Brazil,[108] Canada,[109] China,[110] Korea,[111] Cuba,[112] Denmark,[113] United Arab

---

[100] Cf. EVANS MÁRQUEZ, Ronald, «Los convenios para evitar...» *cit.*, p. 61.

[101] It is important to mention that the position of the Venezuelan government in DTA negotiations has been of wide openness to eliminate tax barriers with the contracting States, and that it is even considered that this position should have been more moderate given that the rates granted by Venezuela to those countries have been significantly below the average granted by other developing countries. This has a twofold reading: (i) Venezuela has lost in its collection of those items, which in turn reduces the tax revenues of the State, or (ii) Venezuela offers greater advantages than other countries of the region to foreign investors. Cf. *Ibid.*, pp. 65–66. Another important topic is that the OECD Model was not designed based on the reality of Latin American Countries. For this reason, its implementation by countries like Venezuela has generated no little inconvenience in practice. This explains why, among other reasons, the Latin American Institute of Tax Law (*Instituto Latinoamericano de Derecho Tributario*-ILADT) (www.iladt.org) has taken the excellent initiative and difficult task, by the team including professors Addy Mazz, Antonio Hugo Figueroa, Heleno Taveira Torres, Jacques Malherbe, Natalia Quiñones Cruz, and Pasquale Pistone, of preparing the *ILADT Model of Multilateral Convention on Double Taxation for Latin America*, which responds to the distinctive features, realities and needs of countries of the region. The Model can be viewed at http://www.iuet.org.uy/docs/Modelo_Multilateral_ILADT_FINAL.pdf, February 19, 2014. On the other hand, for an analysis of DTAs in Latin America based on the Andean Pact, *vid.* UCKMAR, Víctor, «Los tratados internacionales en materia tributaria», en UCKMAR, Víctor (Coord.), *Curso de Derecho tributario internacional*, volume I, Temis, Bogotá, 2003, pp. 104-110.

[102] Consulted in: http://www.seniat.gob.ve/portal/page/portal/PORTAL_SENIAT, February 15, 2014.

[103] Official Gazette of the Republic of Venezuela No. 36.266, August 11, 1997.

[104] Official Gazette of the Republic of Venezuela No. 38.598, January 5, 2007.

[105] Official Gazette of the Republic of Venezuela No. 5.507, Extraordinary Issue, December 13, 2000.

[106] Official Gazette of the Republic of Venezuela No. 39.095, January 9, 2009.

[107] Official Gazette of the Republic of Venezuela No. 5.269, Extraordinary Issue, October 22, 1998.

[108] Official Gazette of the Republic of Venezuela No. 38.344, December 27, 2005.

[109] Official Gazette of the Republic of Venezuela No. 37.927, April 29, 2004.

[110] Official Gazette of the Republic of Venezuela No. 38.089, December 17, 2004.

[111] Official Gazette of the Republic of Venezuela No. 38.598, January 5, 2007.

[112] Official Gazette of the Republic of Venezuela No. 38.086, December 14, 2004.

[113] Official Gazette of the Republic of Venezuela No. 37.219, June 14, 2001.

Emirates,[114] Spain,[115] United States,[116] France,[117] Indonesia,[118] Iran,[119] Italy,[120] Kuwait,[121] Malaysia,[122] Norway,[123] The Netherlands,[124] (denounced) Portugal,[125] Qatar,[126] United Kingdom,[127] Czech Republic,[128] Russia,[129] Sweden,[130] Switzerland,[131] Trinidad & Tobago,[132] and Vietnam.[133]

The countries with which Venezuela has signed both DTAs as well as BITs are: Germany, Barbados, Belarus, Belgium, Brazil, Canada, Denmark, Spain, The Netherlands, United Kingdom, Czech Republic, Sweden and Switzerland, thus increasing, at least theoretically, investment in Venezuela from those countries.

Countries with Which Venezuela Has Signed Bilateral or Multilateral Exchange Treaties

There are several hundreds of treaties signed by Venezuela with countries of Latin America and the Caribbean, Asia, Oceania, the Middle East, Europe, and Africa on subjects related –directly or indirectly- to bilateral or multilateral exchange. Therefore, instead of extensively listing such treaties, which cover fields such as

---

[114] Official Gazette of the Republic of Venezuela No. 39.685, May 31st, 2011.

[115] Official Gazette of the Republic of Venezuela No. 37.913, April 5, 2004.

[116] Official Gazette of the Republic of Venezuela No. 5.427, Extraordinary Issue, January 5, 2000.

[117] Official Gazette of the Republic of Venezuela No. 4.635, Extraordinary Issue, September 28, 1993.

[118] Official Gazette of the Republic of Venezuela No. 37.659, March 27, 2003.

[119] Official Gazette of the Republic of Venezuela No. 38.344, December 27, 2005.

[120] Official Gazette of the Republic of Venezuela No. 4.580, Extraordinary Issue, May 21, 1993.

[121] Official Gazette of the Republic of Venezuela No. 38.347, December 30, 2005.

[122] Official Gazette of the Republic of Venezuela No. 38.842, January 3, 2008.

[123] Official Gazette of the Republic of Venezuela No. 5.265, Extraordinary Issue, October 1st, 1998.

[124] Official Gazette of the Republic of Venezuela No. 5.180, Extraordinary Issue, November 4, 1997.

[125] Official Gazette of the Republic of Venezuela No. 5.180, Extraordinary Issue, November 4, 1997.

[126] Official Gazette of the Republic of Venezuela No. 38.796, October 25, 2007.

[127] Official Gazette of the Republic of Venezuela No. 5.218, Extraordinary Issue, March 6, 1998.

[128] Official Gazette of the Republic of Venezuela No. 5.180, Extraordinary Issue, November 4, 1997.

[129] Official Gazette of the Republic of Venezuela No. 5.822, Extraordinary Issue, September 25, 2006.

[130] Official Gazette of the Republic of Venezuela No. 5.274, Extraordinary Issue, November 12, 1998.

[131] Official Gazette of the Republic of Venezuela No. 5.192, Extraordinary Issue, December 18, 1997.

[132] Official Gazette of the Republic of Venezuela No. 5.180, Extraordinary Issue, November 4, 1997.

[133] Official Gazette of the Republic of Venezuela No. 39.183, May 21, 2009.

petrochemistry, mining, energy, electricity, trade, economics, among others, the reader is referred to the official source (http://www.asambleanacional.gov.ve/tabs/aprobatorias) that lists all signed and effective treaties, and expressly mentions the Approving Law promulgated by the National Assembly and in turn permits direct consultation and appreciation of the current trend of the government on those subjects.

Tax Rate Structures for Individuals and Corporations (*Compañías Anónimas*) (Domestic and Foreign)

The Venezuelan ITL establishes two large groups of taxpayers: (i) *individuals* and (ii) *corporations*, and their assimilated entities. From this classification the various rate or aliquot structures according to which those persons pay tax are determined in principle. There is a special rate list depending on the relevant income-producing activity.

Individuals

Individuals and similar taxpayers pay tax according to Article 8 of the ITL based on the rate and other tax types contemplated in Article 50 of the Law, except when the income is derived from the activities mentioned in Article 12 (operation of mines and assignment of such royalties and participations).

In this respect, Article 50 of the Law contemplates rate No. 1 for individuals, expressed in *tax units* (T.U.),[134] as follows:

RATE No. 1

1. For the fraction up to 1,000.00: 6.00 %.
2. For the fraction that exceeds 1,000.00 up to 1,500.00: 9.00 %.
3. For the fraction that exceeds 1,500.00 up to 2,000.00: 12.00 %.
4. For the fraction that exceeds 2,000.00 up to 2,500.00: 16.00 %.
5. For the fraction that exceeds 2,500.00 up to 3,000.00: 20.00 %.
6. For the fraction that exceeds 3,000.00 up to 4,000.00: 24.00 %.

---

[134] The tax unit (T.U.) is designed as an inflationary correction technique that utilizes a monetary module to restate automatically the nominal fixed values utilized by tax regulations (tax obligations, penalties, etc.). This unit is readjustable by the Tax Bureau, based on the previous year variation of the consumer price index (CPI) in the Metropolitan Area of Caracas, which must be published by the Central Bank of Venezuela at the beginning of each year. Cf. ROMERO-MUCI, Humberto, «Uso y abuso de la unidad tributaria», en SOL GIL, Jesús (Coord.), 60 años de imposición a la renta en Venezuela. Evolución histórica y estudios de la legislación actual, Venezuelan Association of Tax Law, Caracas, 2003, pp. 469–472.

7. For the fraction that exceeds 4,000.00 up to 6,000.00: 29.00 %.
8. For the fraction that exceeds 6,000.00: 34.00 %.

Non-resident individuals, i.e., individuals whose stay in the country is not longer than one hundred and eighty three (183) days in a calendar year, and who do not qualify as domiciled in Venezuela, will pay tax according to the thirty-four percent (34 %) aliquot.

Companies Engaged in General Business

Pursuant to Article 9 of the ITL companies (*compañía anónimas*) and similar tax-payers (whether domestic or foreign) who perform *general economic activities* (i.e., other than the exploitation of hydrocarbons and related activities) pay tax under the rate set forth in Article 52 *eiusdem*, also expressed in tax units (T.U.), as follows:

RATE No. 2

For the fraction up to 2,000.00: 15 %.
For the fraction that exceeds 2,000.00 up to 3,000.00: 22 %.
For the fraction that exceeds 3,000.00: 34 %.

Companies and Individuals Engaged in Special Hydrocarbon and Mine Exploitation Business

Those companies (*compañías anónimas*) and similar entities engaged in the exploitation of hydrocarbons and related activities and *individuals* who obtain income from the exploitation of mines and assignment of such royalties and participations, pay tax according to rate No. 3 set forth in Article 53 of the ITL:

RATE No. 3

(a) Proportional rate of sixty percent (60 %) for the income specified in Article 12 (individuals).
(b) Proportional rate of fifty percent (50 %) for income specified in Article 11 (corporations).

References

Abache Carvajal, Serviliano. 2010. «La responsabilidad patrimonial del Estado "Administrador, Juez y Legislador" tributario venezolano. Especial referencia al paradigmático caso del procedimiento de verificación» (National Report – Venezuela), *Memorias de las XXV Jornadas Latinoamericanas de Derecho Tributario*, volume II, Abeledo Perrot-Latin American Institute of Tax Law-Colombian Institute of Tax Law, Buenos Aires.

Abache Carvajal, Serviliano and Burgos-Irazábal, Ramón. 2013. «Parafiscalidad, sistema tributario y Libertad», in HERRERA ORELLANA, Luis Alfonso (Coord.), *Enfoques actuales sobre Derecho y Libertad en Venezuela*, Academy of Political and Social Sciences, Caracas.

Andrade, Betty. 2007. «La subcapitalización y los precios de transferencia en el régimen venezolano», *Jornadas Internacionales. Cuestiones actuales de Derecho tributario*, Foundation of Administrative Law Studies, Caracas.

Atencio Valladares, Gilberto. 2014. «Cuestiones tributarias del Mercosur: aproximaciones desde el Derecho tributario venezolano», *Revista de Derecho Tributario*, N° 141, Venezuelan Association of Tax Law, Caracas.

Bazó Pisani, Andrés E. 2009. «Incentivos fiscales y otras políticas tributarias ofrecidas por países en desarrollo. ¿Atraen inversión extranjera o desestabilizan la economía?», in DUPOUY M., Elvira y DE VALERA, Irene (Coord.), *Temas de actualidad tributaria. Homenaje a Jaime Parra Pérez*, Academy of Political and Social Sciences-Venezuelan Association of Tax Law, Caracas.

Carmona Borjas, Juan Cristóbal. 2000. «Principios de la renta mundial y de la renta territorial», in DE VALERA, Irene (Organizer), *Comentarios a la Ley de Impuesto sobre la Renta*, Academy of Political and Social Sciences-Venezuelan Association of Tax Law, Caracas.

Carmona Borjas, Juan Cristóbal. 2003a. «Colaboración y asistencia mutua entre Administraciones tributarias», *Revista de Derecho Tributario*, N° 100, Venezuelan Association of Tax Law, Caracas.

Carmona Borjas, Juan Cristóbal. 2003b. «Factores de conexión en la legislación venezolana en materia de impuesto sobre la renta», in SOL GIL, Jesús (Coord.), *60 años de imposición a la renta en Venezuela. Evolución histórica y estudios de la legislación actual*, Venezuelan Association of Tax Law, Caracas.

Castillo Carvajal, Juan Carlos. 2013. «Relatoría general. Tema II. Temas especiales de la Ley de Impuesto sobre la Renta», in KORODY TAGLIAFERRO, Juan Esteban (Coord.), *70 años del Impuesto sobre la Renta. Memorias de las XII Jornadas Venezolanas de Derecho Tributario*, volume II, Venezuelan Association of Tax Law, Caracas.

Díaz Ibarra, Valmy J. 2009. «Las reglas de transparencia fiscal internacional en Venezuela. Consecuencias de la vinculación de contribuyentes venezolanos con sociedades en "paraísos fiscales"», in DUPOUY M., Elvira and DE VALERA, Irene (Coord.), *Temas de actualidad tributaria. Homenaje a Jaime Parra Pérez*, Academy of Political and Social Sciences-Venezuelan Association of Tax Law, Caracas.

Falcón Y Tella, Ramón and Elvira Pulido Guerra. 2010. *Derecho fiscal internacional*, Marcial Pons, Madrid.

Fraga Pittaluga, Luis. 2013. «Subcapitalización y reclasificación de los intereses no deducibles», in Korody Tagliaferro, Juan Esteban (Coord.), *70 años del Impuesto sobre la Renta. Memorias de las XII Jornadas Venezolanas de Derecho Tributario*, volume II, Venezuelan Association of Tax Law, Caracas.

León Rojas, Andrés Eloy. 1998. «La doble tributación internacional. Diferencia entre países desarrollados y en desarrollo», *IV Jornadas Venezolanas de Derecho Tributario*, Venezuelan Association of Tax Law, Caracas.

Evans Márquez, Ronald. 1999. *Régimen jurídico de la doble tributación internacional*. Caracas: McGraw-Hill.

Evans Márquez, Ronald. 2000. «Los convenios para evitar la doble tributación internacional y otros aspectos internacionales de la política tributaria venezolana», in DE VALERA, Irene

(Organizer), *Comentarios a la Ley de Impuesto sobre la Renta*, Academy of Political and Social Sciences-Venezuelan Association of Tax Law, Caracas.

Montero Traibel, José Pedro. 1998. «La armonización tributaria en los procesos de integración», *IV Jornadas Venezolanas de Derecho Tributario*, Venezuelan Association of Tax Law, Caracas.

Palacios Márquez, Leonardo. 2002. «Medidas fiscales para el desarrollo económico», *Revista de Derecho Tributario*, N° 97, Venezuelan Association of Tax Law, Caracas.

Paredes, Carlos Enrique. 2002. *El principio de territorialidad y el sistema de renta mundial en la Ley de Impuesto sobre la Renta venezolana*, Andersen Legal, Caracas.

Roche, Emilio J. 2002. «De la entrada en vigencia de la reforma de la Ley de Impuesto sobre la Renta de 2001 y del régimen sobre dividendos», *Impuesto sobre la Renta e ilícitos fiscales. VI Jornadas venezolanas de Derecho tributario*, Venezuelan Association of Tax Law, Caracas.

Roche, Emilio J. 2003. «Transparencia fiscal internacional», in SOL GIL, Jesús (Coord.), *60 años de imposición a la renta en Venezuela. Evolución histórica y estudios de la legislación actual*, Venezuelan Association of Tax Law, Caracas.

Roche, Emilio J. 2013. «Parte general del Impuesto sobre la Renta. Relatoría Tema I», in Korody Tagliaferro, Juan Esteban (Coord.), *70 años del Impuesto sobre la Renta. Memorias de las XII Jornadas Venezolanas de Derecho Tributario*, volume II, Venezuelan Association of Tax Law, Caracas.

Romero-Muci, Humberto. 2002. «Naturaleza jurídica de los principios de contabilidad de aceptación general en Venezuela y su incidencia en la determinación de la renta financiera para el cálculo del impuesto sobre la renta de dividendos (análisis de los artículos 67 y 91 de la Ley de Impuesto sobre la Renta)», *Impuesto sobre la Renta e ilícitos fiscales. VI Jornadas venezolanas de Derecho tributario*, Venezuelan Association of Tax Law, Caracas.

Romero-Muci, Humberto. 2003. «Uso y abuso de la unidad tributaria», in SOL GIL, Jesús (Coord.), *60 años de imposición a la renta en Venezuela. Evolución histórica y estudios de la legislación actual*, Venezuelan Association of Tax Law, Caracas.

Rondón García, Andrea, Herrera Orellana, Luis Alfonso and Arias Castillo, Tomás A. 2010. «Case Study: Private Property Abolition in Venezuela», International Property Rights Index. 2010 Report, American for Tax Reform Foundation/Property Rights Alliance, Washington.

Ross, Maxim. 2008. *¿Capitalismo salvaje o Estado depredador?*, Editorial Alfa, Caracas.

Sol Gil, Jesús. 2002. «Medidas fiscales adoptadas en Venezuela para el desarrollo económico», *Revista de Derecho Tributario*, N° 97, Venezuelan Association of Tax Law, Caracas.

Uckmar, Víctor. 2003. Los tratados internacionales en materia tributaria», in UCKMAR, Víctor (Coord.), *Curso de Derecho tributario internacional*, volume I, Temis, Bogotá.

Valdés Costa, Ramón. 1993. Aspectos fiscales de la integración con especial referencia a América Latina», *Revista de Derecho Tributario*, N° 58, Venezuelan Association of Tax Law, Caracas.

Vecchio D., Carlos A. 2004. *El impuesto al dividendo presunto de las sucursales. Especial referencia a los tratados para evitar la doble tributación*, Venezuelan Association of Financial Law, Caracas, .

Websites Consulted

www.asambleanacional.gov.ve
www.conapri.org
www.iladt.org
www.internationalpropertyrightsindex.org/
www.iuet.org.uy
www.seniat.gob.ve

Questionnaire

Taxation and Development/La fiscalité et le Développement

This topic examines the ways in which a country uses its tax law to provide incentives for investment in developing, emerging, or low-income countries. Policy analysts debate whether it is appropriate for a country to use its tax system to encourage or discourage investment behavior or business activity. Some argue that tax laws should be neutral and should not encourage or discourage economic behavior. Others contend that a country's use of its tax laws to encourage investment behavior or to attract investment may be harmful to (or may unfairly compete with) other regimes. A country may arrange its tax system to encourage its multinational enterprises to go abroad to compete with other companies on the same footing. It may arrange its tax system to provide an incentive for its multinational enterprises to invest in specified regions in order to encourage business activity in developing or emerging economies, low-income countries, in areas of severe poverty and economic inequality, or in former colonies, former or current territories, possessions, or protectorates. It may also use its tax system in order to itself compete with other similarly situated countries for investment or business activity. This Report examines on a comparative basis whether, and the extent to which, countries support the use of tax laws to encourage economic activity in targeted regions, in specified countries or to attract investment within its own borders.

1. Please describe the international tax system of the country for which you are preparing the Report.

   (a) Does the country tax worldwide income of its residents or citizens and allow a credit or deduction for taxes paid to another country on foreign source income?

   (b) Does the country have a territorial regime in which it exempts from tax all or specified types of foreign source income?

© Springer International Publishing Switzerland 2017
K.B. Brown (ed.), *Taxation and Development - A Comparative Study*,
Ius Comparatum - Global Studies in Comparative Law 21,
DOI 10.1007/978-3-319-42157-5

(c) Does the country exempt from tax dividends paid to resident companies by wholly or partly owned foreign subsidiaries? Does the system recognize a participation exemption for dividends paid from one corporation to another (foreign or domestic)? Is the system a hybrid of the above?

2. Does the country have tax laws designed to discourage investment in tax haven jurisdictions? Are sanctions employed to enforce these laws? What are the criteria used to determine whether a country is a tax haven? Which countries are considered tax havens?

3. Does the country have tax laws designed to discourage investment in harmful tax regimes? How does it define a harmful tax regime? Is it a party to any agreements to sanction such regimes or does it impose penalties against such regimes (such as refusal to enter into a tax treaty, denial of tax benefits, etc.)?

4. Is the country a party to any regional/international agreements conventions or codes of conduct regarding countries deemed to unfairly compete for capital or to discriminate against or favor certain types of investment (such as prohibitions on state aid, etc.)?

5. Does the country participate in the OECD's Global Tax Forum? Has its tax regime been modified to conform to internationally accepted practices?

6. Is the country party to information exchange agreements? What types of information exchange are approved? What are the limitations on these agreements? Are these agreements concluded by treaty only? In these agreements, do any of the parties seek information relating to transactions in tax haven jurisdictions or in countries deemed to have a harmful tax regime?

7. What tax incentives, if any, does the country provide for investment in emerging or developing countries? Are these provided by statute or by treaty?

8. What tax incentives, if any, does the country provide for investment in countries with low incomes, high poverty rates or high rates of economic inequality?

9. Does the country provide tax incentives or special tax regimes for former colonies, territories, possessions, or protectorates?

10. Has the country taken measures to attract economic activity to its own jurisdiction? Are these measures in the form of reduced tax rates, credits, deductions, or enterprise zones? Has the country taken measures to make its tax regime friendlier to investment or multinational business? Do these measures involve specialized industries (e.g., film making, manufacturing, research and development, etc.) or specified types of income?

11. Has the country provided or does it expect to provide a tax amnesty or tax holiday for income from specific types of investments (e.g., for profits invested offshore)?

12. Describe the corporate tax rate structure for foreign and domestic corporations in the country for which the report is prepared.

13. Is the country prohibited from providing or forbidden to provide tax incentives for investment abroad or in developing countries either through internal law or regional or multilateral agreement (including prohibitions on state aid)?

14. Does the country enter into bilateral or multilateral trade or investment agreements? Do these agreements or treaties contain tax provisions or concessions? List the countries with which such agreements have been concluded.

CPSIA information can be obtained
at www.ICGtesting.com
Printed in the USA
LVHW050320220221
679585LV00004B/18